G

John Knight was initiated into a life of crime at the age of twelve by his older brother Ronnie, and never looked back, mixing robbery with running a number of successful businesses. He planned and executed the Security Express robbery, for which he served twelve years in prison.

Ronnie Knight was married to Barbara Windsor for twenty years, during which time he owned a number of West End clubs, as well as engaging in many less legal enterprises. He was sentenced to seven years for laundering money from the Security Express robbery.

Peter Wilton joined the Metropolitan Police in 1958 and the Flying Squad in 1980. He was promoted to Detective Superintendent during the course of his investigation into the Security Express robbery. He retired in 1989.

Pete Sawyer is an investigative journalist. His work has appeared in many national publications, including the *Mail on Sunday*, *Sunday Times*, *Observer* and *Punch* magazine. He is also a freelance television producer working on news and current affairs stories.

RONNIE KNIGHT, JOHN KNIGHT, PETER WILTON

WITH PETE SAWYER

GOTCHA!

THE UNTOLD STORY OF BRITAIN'S BIGGEST CASH ROBBERY

PAN BOOKS

First published 2002 by Sidgwick & Jackson

This edition published 2007 by Pan Books
an imprint of Pan Macmillan Ltd
Pan Macmillan, 20 New Wharf Road, London N1 9RR
Basingstoke and Oxford
Associated companies throughout the world
www.panmacmillan.com

ISBN 978-0-330- 45462-9

1 3 5 7 9 8 6 4 2

A CIP catalogue record for this book is available from
the British Library.

Typeset by SetSystems Ltd, Saffron Walden, Essex
Printed and bound in Great Britain by
Mackays of Chatham plc, Chatham, Kent

For the women in our lives

Contents

Co-author's Note

What you are about to read is the true account of an astonishing crime, which in turn sparked off an extraordinary investigation by Scotland Yard's elite Flying Squad.

It is the inside story of how the robbery was planned and how most of the robbers were tracked down and caught. For the gang it was an initial triumph, but in the end a combination of greed, disloyalty and painstaking detective-work was to prove to be their undoing.

Gotcha! is based largely on the verbal and written testimonies of John and Ronnie Knight, and retired Detective Superintendent Peter Wilton. John Knight planned the robbery, Ronnie Knight helped spirit away some of the proceeds, and Peter Wilton was in charge of the crack team of Flying Squad detectives – nicknamed the 'Dirty Dozen' – that brought them both to book.

Over the course of a year I had many lengthy interviews with the three men. Most, but not all, of what they told me I have been able to corroborate through Court documents and by talking to other witnesses.

I am particularly grateful to the following former members of the 'Dirty Dozen' who gave up their free time to talk to me about their own roles in the police investigation: Colin Burke, Bernie Butler, Charlie Collins, Cliff Craig, Malcolm Jeffery, Jim Keeling, Terry Mills, George Moncrieff and Simon Webber.

I would also like to thank Robert Smith for giving me the opportunity to write this unique book; publisher Gordon Wise for allowing me to realize its potential, and my editor, Ingrid Connell, for much wise counsel.

John and Ronnie Knight have told their side of the story as

well as they felt able: that is, without incriminating anyone else. I can state that they never discussed the roles of any of their associates with me, not even those who were subsequently convicted for taking part.

The story is far from ended. Twenty years after the robbery, the police investigation remains open. Two men are still wanted for questioning. One of them, Ronnie Everett, was extradited from Spain for other, unrelated drugs offences. However, because of the conditions attached to his extradition from Spain, he cannot be formally charged with the Security Express robbery. Another man still wanted for questioning, John Mason, remains in Spain, legally beyond the reach of the British Authorities.

Pete Sawyer
February 2003

PROLOGUE

Wednesday, 2 March 1983. A fresh spring day. Clouds scudded across the sky, bringing with them the occasional shower of light rain. A group of police officers from Scotland Yard's Drugs Squad were searching a large scrap yard in Dalston, a poor, inner-city district of East London.

The officers were looking for pills. It was a daunting task. The yard, which was sandwiched between railway viaducts, covered some three acres of ground. It was littered with stacks of steel pipes and girders, piles of scaffolding, and the wrecks of motor vehicles. Small fires were lit here and there, filling the air with an acrid stench.

The yard was a hive of activity. Radios played from the workshops and lock-up garages clad with corrugated iron that were huddled under the Victorian brick arches of the railway. Nearby there was a weighbridge for lorries, stores piled high with bales of scrap paper, and lean-to sheds full of unidentifiable pieces of heavy machinery.

The officers, led by Detective Inspector Ian Malone, gingerly picked their way between the oily puddles and rusted metal towards the yard's prefab two-storey offices.

The owner of the yard was a man named Jimmy Knight, who they knew to be a very wealthy man. He had made a fortune out of the scrap metal business and had put the money into a leisure complex in Stanmore, North London. The officers thought, wrongly as it later turned out, that Jimmy's scrap yard was being used to manufacture and hide drugs destined for the club scene.

They knew that Jimmy Knight had two younger brothers,

John and Ronnie. Two other brothers had died some years beforehand: one was murdered in a vicious Soho brawl, and the other was struck down by a tumour on the brain.

John was quiet and kept himself to himself, seemingly a respectable businessman. Among other things, he ran a garage in North London. Ronnie, by contrast, was a very public figure. He was married to actress Barbara Windsor, from the *Carry On* films, and owned a nightclub in the West End.

The officers strode into Jimmy Knight's large untidy office, where they found six chairs roughly arranged to form a semicircle around his desk. It was as if a meeting had been in progress and had been quickly broken up, possibly when the officers had been clocked at the yard gates. Plastic cups half full of warm tea littered the desk. To the officers' minds, whoever had been there had left in rather a hurry.

Jimmy had nothing to say, but the officers' suspicions were heightened when they found five smartly dressed men lurking in a room nearby, behind a locked door. The men, all in their forties, had an air of self-confidence about them that, to the experienced officers, spoke volumes. They'd seen it all before.

The five were highly evasive, reluctant to tell the police what they were doing, meeting at the yard like that. So the officers took down their details. One man turned out to be a wealthy North London property dealer called Terry Perkins. Another man, John Mason, ran a nearby launderette. He was there with his mate Ronnie Everett, the landlord of a pub in the Gray's Inn Road.

Another man tried to give the police a false name and address, but he was quickly recognized by one of the officers as Billy Hickson. His identity was confirmed after further questioning at a local police station. Hickson had done time for armed robbery.

The fifth man was Jimmy Knight's younger brother, John.

To the officers it was all very intriguing. They knew that the Knight family had some heavy connections, but they were surprised at the set of people they had found hiding in that room. All the men had form in one way or another.

During the thorough search of the yard a box was found

containing some specialist glassware, the kind one might use for the chemical synthesis of drugs – or so the officers thought. Jimmy Knight was charged but later acquitted. He told the magistrates that the glassware belonged to someone else in the yard. Jimmy said he knew nothing about it. 'How should I know what goes on? All I do is rent out the lock-ups. What the men do inside them is their own business.'

Despite the police's suspicions, the five men meeting at the yard that day had done nothing wrong. But still, the meeting was duly logged by the officers. The men's names were added to the Drugs Squad's intelligence database, purely for its own internal use.

And no more was thought of it.

1
CURTAIN ROAD

Back in 1983, Shoreditch, which lies just to the north of the City of London, was best known for its tumbledown warehouses, sweatshops, and boarded-up bombsites. The urban renewal schemes of the 1990s, which were to transform the district into a mix of chic New York-style loft apartments and glass-fronted offices, were but twinkles in the eyes of a few far-sighted property speculators.

Curtain Road runs right through the heart of Shoreditch, from north to south. The road was named after an Elizabethan playhouse, called the Curtain. In its day the Curtain was the place of great drama, drawing crowds of spectators from all over London. There, it is said, Shakespeare acted Henry V in person.

But the playhouse was not to everyone's tastes. In the summer of 1597, after a long-running campaign by the aldermen of the City, Queen Elizabeth's Privy Council ordered that the Curtain, along with London's first-ever permanent theatre, which was called simply, 'The Theatre', in nearby Finsbury Fields, be 'plucke down quite, the stage galleries and rooms that are made for people to stand in' because of 'very great disorders committed in the common playhouses, both by lewd matters . . . handled on the stages and by resort and confluence of bad people'. The owners resisted the order as best they could and the Curtain remained in use for a few more years. The Theatre however closed; its heavy oak timbers were used to construct the Globe theatre on the south bank of the Thames, well away from the restraining influence of the aldermen.

By the end of Queen Victoria's reign, Shoreditch had

become a poor and crowded urban district, full of artisans and tradesmen. Over the ensuing years, Curtain Road became renowned for its furniture trade. But the Second World War changed all that. The bombs of the Blitz took a heavy toll on this part of London, leaving behind great swathes of rubble and wasteland. And then, in the years after the war, the great docks closed, one by one. The economic lifeblood of the East End sapped away. Warehouses, once full of the goods of empire, became empty, derelict shells.

In the 1950s and 1960s clothes and leather sweatshops sprang up, often crewed by poor Bangladeshi and Pakistani women, whose husbands had been lured to Britain with the promise of a better life. They soon discovered that it really wasn't that simple. They found themselves on the breadline, working all hours God sent, living on squalid, high-rise housing estates in nearby Bethnal Green. With scant prospects and little education, you had to be determined and tough to survive. But that had always been the way of the East End. Its harshness was an ideal breeding ground for enterprise. And that, of course, included criminal enterprise.

Come Sunday morning, Curtain Road was chock-a-block with the light vans owned by the East End market traders and hawkers working the Petticoat Lane clothes and Brick Lane bric-a-brac markets, which sprawled along the nearby streets. Just before dawn, the traders would congregate in a small café around the corner from Curtain Road. There, at 5 a.m., you could get a mug of hot, strong, sweet tea and a fried-egg sandwich. The café was bright, warm, and welcoming. Its neat rows of yellow, Formica-topped tables were always clean. Arranged with military precision on each table top were a stamped metal ashtray, glass salt, pepper, and sugar pots, and three ominous-looking squeezy sauce bottles made of dimpled plastic, one red, one yellow, and the other brown. The men would cram themselves on to the dolls'-house-sized wooden benches, rolling their roll-ups and gossiping between mouthfuls of white bread.

To the north of Curtain Road lay Hoxton, a run-down district noted for its pickpockets and petty criminals. On

Sundays, con men and fly-by-night hawkers from Hoxton, their battered suitcases crammed full of fake goods, would mingle with the market traders in the streets of Shoreditch. There they would notch up their hapless victims, one by one, melting back into the crowds, home in time for the Sunday roast.

For most of the rest of the week Curtain Road was deserted: a ratrun for those in the know wishing to leave the City in a hurry. Occasionally, lone tourists looking for Petticoat Lane would lose their way and chance upon the road. But they would never stay long.

Curtain Road's main saving grace was that it was just a stone's throw away from the banks in the City of London, which is why Security Express and several other security firms had built their fortress-like warehouses and depots there.

Business was good for Security Express. Its large, angular, green and yellow vans were a familiar sight on Britain's high streets, as its uniformed guards with their strongboxes collected cash from high street shops and banks up and down the country.

Under a Conservative Government led by Margaret Thatcher, the economy was beginning to boom again. Britain had defeated Argentina, which had invaded the Falkland Islands Dependency in the South Atlantic the previous year. The country was riding on the crest of a wave. Fostered by Thatcher, and spurred on by the success in the Falklands, there was a resurgence of national pride which, for most of the 1970s, had been sapped away as Britain slowly relinquished control over its last remaining colonies. By April 1983 the nation was gearing up for a General Election, which Thatcher would win by a landslide.

The City of London was awash with cash, which meant good business for firms like Security Express. In April 1983 the firm posted pre-tax profits of £1.17 million on a turnover of some £35 million. The company, owned by a powerful security printer, the De La Rue group, employed more than 2,600 people in its depots and warehouses throughout the country.

But the Curtain Road depot was the jewel in the crown. The four-storey brick building had reputedly cost many millions of pounds to build and was considered to be state of the art. Its ground-floor windows were bricked up. On the first and second floors were offices, and one of these floors was used to make up wage packets that were then sent out by van to shops and businesses all over London. At the top of the building was a penthouse flat, used mainly by the company's top brass and people on training courses.

The vault was on the ground floor, although if you had asked the locals in the pub they might have told you that it was in the basement. To be truthful, no local was really sure, unless, that is, he happened to work at the depot. But the one thing they were sure about was that the vault contained fabulous wealth.

To one side and at the back of the building was a large asphalt compound, completely enclosed by a ten-foot-high brick wall. Two closed-circuit television cameras, perched high up on the tops of poles, cast their beady electric eyes over the compound, which usually had six or seven yellow and green security vans parked in it. Behind the compound rose the stark form of another top security depot, taller and perhaps a little grander. This depot was owned by Brinks-Mat.

At night Curtain Road was eerily silent, aside from the occasional piercing screech of steel wheel upon steel rail as clattering goods trains negotiated the tight curve into nearby Liverpool Street Station. The road's one and only pub emptied promptly at 10.30 p.m., its customers making their excuses and hurrying home to their waiting families.

A dimly lit cobbled alley, popular with local lovers, ran along the other side of the high wall. Beyond this alley, overlooking the yard, was a flat-roofed, two-storey office block, which had been built in the 1960s. The office block was owned by Security Express, but in 1983 it was empty and to let.

Around midnight, after cleaning up the pub, the landlord would take his dog for a walk. They would walk due north up towards the Security Express depot. Sometimes he would let the dog off its lead and it would scamper off down the alley that ran alongside the yard. The landlord would follow, whistling and cursing, stumbling in the dark on the uneven cobblestones.

On the other side of the high wall, sodium floodlights bathed the Security Express yard in eerie yellow light. The depot was manned at all times. It was said to be impenetrable, and even the locals, stalwarts for scepticism, dubbed it 'Fort Knox'. But the building was to prove the security industry's equivalent of the *Titanic*. Its greatest security flaw was laid bare by its occupants' penchant for an early morning cuppa.

2
THE RAID

It was 7 a.m. on 4 April 1983, Easter Monday. Greg Counsell drove through the wet streets of the City to the Security Express depot in Curtain Road. He parked his white Datsun outside the main entrance to the depot.

It was a bitterly cold day. He tapped impatiently on the glass double doors of the main entrance, his breath misting up the glass. A few moments later, he heard the soft click of the solenoids as the doors were unlocked by the young nightwatchman, David Howsam, sitting in the control room. Counsell pushed open the door and hurried inside into the warm lobby.

'Everything all right, David?' he asked.

'Yeah, fine, Greg. No problems.'

'Anyone up in the penthouse?' Counsell gestured towards the top floor of the depot.

'Nope.'

After a few words of polite conversation Howsam left and Counsell was on his own. He was the supervisor for the day. Thirty-seven years old, married and with a young baby, he had worked at Security Express for more than six years. Before that, he had worked for a Securicor subsidiary. He was an old hand.

Most businesses were closed for the bank holiday, so it was going to be quiet. Later on, a few vans were scheduled to make some runs to the Ideal Home Exhibition in West London and to a cash and carry, to pick up cash. Counsell was bracing himself for a long day, but neither he nor the other guards knew then just how long the day would turn out to be. It was going to be one of the longest days of their lives. Curtain Road was again about to become a stage for great drama.

Outside the depot, the road was full of the overspill from the surrounding streets as the Petticoat Lane market stall-holders found somewhere to park their small vans. There was a special market on Easter Bank Holiday Monday, so there were more vans parked in Curtain Road than on a normal weekday, but not as many as there would have been on a Sunday morning, the day of the regular market.

If anyone had been walking along Curtain Road, they might well have noticed that one van in particular was having more difficulty than most in finding somewhere to park. The van had done a complete circuit of the road twice. On its second pass, it had slipped into a spot that had just been vacated, next to a red telephone box. The telephone box happened to be almost directly opposite the Security Express depot gates. The driver switched off his engine, wound down his window, and waited.

An astute passer-by might have wondered why the driver had been so keen to park in that particular spot, when there were plenty of other free parking spaces further down the road. Perhaps he might also have noticed the van's curious colour scheme, which at first glance looked strangely similar to that of a Security Express van.

The van was conspicuous in other ways. It had a double axle at the rear, and was the type of van normally used for moving very heavy goods about. Your average market stall trader certainly wouldn't have used it – they prefer smaller, lighter, more manoeuvrable vehicles.

And then there was the red telephone box. Every now and then, the driver would cast a quick, impatient glance through the van window at the payphone inside the box. It was as if he were expecting a call. In 1983 mobile phones were very new, very rare, and very expensive. What's more, they were about the size and weight of house bricks.

But, at that time of the morning, the few passers-by in Curtain Road were far too busy minding their own business to care about the suspicious van with its shifty driver, parked near the entrance to the depot.

£££

Greg Counsell knew nothing of what was going on outside the depot in the road. He was busy getting on with his daily routine, which revolved around the cavernous vault on the ground floor.

Once inside the yard, Security Express vans with their valuable cargoes of cash and cheques could back right up to the depot building. The vans would reverse down a shallow concrete ramp into a meshed-off area, nicknamed by the guards 'the cage'.

At one end of 'the cage' were electrically operated gates, which sealed off the van from the yard while it was being loaded and unloaded. Securely enclosed, the driver–guards would slide trolleys out of the van, through reinforced steel shutters in the depot wall, and into a windowless secure room immediately outside the vault.

The room was lived in. Stacked lever arch files, crammed full of delivery notes, clung desperately to metal shelving. The walls were adorned with posters and calendars. In one corner was the desk used by the vault custodians. Lined up along one wall were empty trolleys, essentially steel-framed, open-topped boxes with wire-mesh sides. They had wheels on them similar to those found on a shopping trolley, but larger and more manoeuvrable. The concrete floor of the secure room was coated with the tracks of thousands of rubber skid marks from the wheels.

The vault itself was reached through a thick steel door. Inside, the contents of the trolleys were sorted, shifted, humped, and stacked into waist-high steel cages. The vault's bare white walls were broken only by a large electric fan, mounted on a steel bracket, which looked down on the rows of cages.

In one corner were seven safes, at first glance looking like left-luggage lockers; in another corner, a plain old wooden chair and a desk with some clipboards dangling over it on strings. Fixed to the wall above the desk were the large white notice-boards by which staff kept track of how much was in the vault – and who it belonged to.

There were thirty to forty cages in the vault, each one piled high with sealed packets of coin and banknotes, and linen bank bags full of used banknotes and cheques. At any one time the vault could hold up to £10 million in cash. A lift connected it directly to the upstairs offices where the wage packets were made up.

The ground floor of the depot also had a control room, called by the guards the 'reception' control room. On weekdays, during normal office hours, a female receptionist would sit there minding the phones, but not on a bank holiday or at weekends. At night it was the preserve of the nightwatchman.

A wide, wooden desk in the control room looked out through a large window on to the building's main entrance lobby. Most of the desk was taken up with two bulky PBX telephone switchboards, which routed calls throughout the building. To the left of the switchboards was an intercom set. Two ordinary telephones, not often used, sat nearby. There were buttons and controls to open the doors into the building. The rest of the desk was cluttered with bunches of keys, clipboards, and unwashed coffee mugs. Especially so on bank holidays and at weekends.

To get into the innards of the depot you had to walk by the window of the control room. If you were recognized you were 'buzzed in' through a security door ahead of you. The door led into a short corridor, termed by the guards an 'airlock'. Once in the airlock, you had to press a button to open an inner door. This would only open if the outer door was shut tight.

To the right of the wooden desk were mounted two large closed-circuit television monitors on a heavy metal stand. One gave a clear view of the yard and gates. The other was perpetually on the blink, its black-and-white image slowly cycling down the screen. It was usually turned off. The room was stuffy, although a portable electric fan perched on top of the monitors alleviated the worst of it.

Through a door, off to one side of the control room, was a small, grubby kitchenette lit by a single neon striplight, where the guards could make snacks and hot drinks. Two or three empty milk bottles were usually stacked along a narrow shelf at the back of the tiny sink unit. The draining board was far too narrow, so plates and bowls would be wedged precariously between the high taps to dry. The kettle, and a small oven, its hotplate covered in layers of grease, lived on the ledge to the right of the sink. Lurking underneath was the fridge. The airless and windowless loo, blighted by the bank holiday weekend, was through another door.

To operate all the door controls, alarms, and cameras, you really had to know what you were doing. You couldn't just walk into the control room, sit down, and start running the depot. The control room was all buttons, lights, and levers. Banks of winking yellow lights told the guards that the vaults and the perimeter of the building were unbroken and secure. There were red lights and buttons for the fire alarm. And then there were other controls, their functions unidentifiable to the casual observer. The regular guards didn't even know what some of the buttons did.

The depot had another control room by the electrically operated main entrance gates, through which the vans came into the yard. This control room was equally complex. It was generally used only during the daytime when vans were scheduled to deliver. It was known as the 'main' or the 'gate' control room. Staff entering and leaving the depot normally used the entrance alongside, which led directly into the yard.

The main control room was much like the reception control room, only a little more untidy. The guard would sit at a desk in the corner of the control room on a high swivel chair. A panel on the wall in front of him housed the red and green buttons needed to open and shut the gates. Arranged around him on the desk were telephones, intercoms, closed-circuit television monitors, and a console for panning the cameras. The room smelt of stale cigarettes and spilt coffee.

Other control boxes, levers, and switches were arrayed on either side of the desk. Hidden discreetly away underneath the desk was a large and mysterious silver foot pedal. Nearby was a sink unit, boiler, and, of course, the kettle. One wall of the room was partially covered with large, black, shiny metal boards. Slotted into the boards were thin metal strips, which gave details of the van delivery schedules – dates, locations, pick-up times, and crew names. The staff rota.

A small hatch in the wall of the room faced Curtain Road.

That was where the milkman left the milk bottles in the morning. The hatch was an important part of Counsell's daily routine, because his daily routine normally began with a cuppa. When he was the first person in, one of the first things he did was to go across to the main control room by the gate to fetch some fresh milk from the hatch.

To do that, he needed a rather large bunch of keys. It was a complex procedure. He would switch off the alarms, walk along a corridor, down some stairs, along another corridor, through the large basement locker room, up some stairs, and unlock a door at the top. Then he would walk through a crew room, where the van drivers got ready, and unlock a door leading out into the yard. He would walk down some steps and across the yard to the gate control room. Then he would unlock the outer door, go through, and unlock the inner door.

According to Counsell, that April morning's routine was no different from countless other mornings. He collected milk, sugar, and coffee from the main control room, locked the control-room doors, and walked the five yards back across the yard to the steps leading to the back door.

On the way, he walked past a wide steel gate, behind which were stowed some large industrial bins. The gate, which badly needed a coat of paint, was normally bolted shut. Behind the bins was another steel gate, rarely used, which led on to Curtain Road.

Once back in the reception control room, Counsell made himself a coffee in the grubby kitchenette next door. He was on his own. The vans leaving the depot were not due to start for a few hours, so he sat there, just biding his time.

It was much easier to deal with the van deliveries from the main control room by the gate. So, come mid-morning, Counsell prepared to get ready to switch control rooms. He unlocked the outer door leading into the yard and stepped out into the bright daylight. He stood there by the door for a second, wavering, staring at the long steel gate next to him. Perhaps something had caught his eye. Perhaps he had noticed that it was ever so slightly ajar.

Suddenly, from behind the gate, a group of darkly clothed

figures emerged. Before Counsell could react, he had been pushed up against the wall of the depot, with medical sticking plaster strapped over his eyes. It was the start of his worst nightmare.

'Keep your head to the fucking floor! Look down!'

Counsell felt something hard and cold pressed to the side of his face.

'Do what you're told and you won't get hurt.'

He was pushed back through the yard door into the depot.

'Is anyone else in the building?'

'No.'

'We saw a light on. Come on! Tell us. It'll be worse for you if you are telling lies.'

'No. I promise. There's no one else here.'

They led him down the stairs into the locker room.

'Where are you taking me?'

'We want to go upstairs.'

'It's the wrong way.'

'Lift up your blindfold and look on the floor.'

The men pushed Counsell along the corridor and tried to force him through a door leading into a storeroom.

'That's not the way either,' he told them. 'You have to go upstairs.'

At the bottom of the stairs they boxed him into a corner. His head was pulled back and cold metal was pressed under his chin.

'You know what this is?' one of the men said.

'Yes.'

'Do as you're told and you won't get hurt. And don't touch anything.'

He was taken into the control room and sat down on a wooden chair in front of the alarm boxes.

'You sure there's no one in the building?'

'Yes. Just me.'

The men tied Counsell's hands behind his back. One of them pushed a gun into his side. 'What are these boxes for?' he asked. They lifted the tape up over his eyes so that he could see a little. 'What about these keys?'

'Can I look up?' he asked. 'I don't want to see your faces or nothing.'

They released his hands. He stood up and pointed out one of the alarm boxes. 'That's for the whole building,' he said. 'I've switched that off already. The other one is for the vaults.'

'Tell us about that one.'

'I don't know anything about it.'

They sat him back down in his chair.

'How many vans are coming in today?'

'None. We've got some going out.'

'What's your name?'

'Greg.'

'Are you sure?' one of the robbers asked. 'I thought it was John.'

They manhandled him over to the wide wooden desk, which looked out on to the lobby, and sat him down in a swivel chair.

'Act normally,' they told him. 'Remember, don't be silly. Don't do anything silly and you'll be all right.'

They removed the plaster from his eyes and untied one of his hands.

'Which button do you press to let the staff in?'

Counsell moved to point to a small box in front of him.

'Don't touch it! Don't fucking touch it!' they shouted, thinking it was an alarm button.

Then two of the men swung underneath the wooden desk. Counsell felt the sharp prod of metal in his groin. 'Do as you're told or we'll blow yer fucking balls off.'

With Counsell sat white-faced at the desk, the men moved around the control room from console to console, button by button, asking Counsell to explain how each and every one worked. 'We know the answers,' they assured him. 'We just want to make sure you aren't lying.'

'There were two vans in yesterday. How many today?'

'I don't know. The sheet's in the other control room,' Counsell replied.

'So that's four drivers.' The men started talking among themselves, trying to work out how many guards were likely to show up that day. One of them turned back to Counsell. 'So who else is coming in?' he asked.

'I don't know, but the vault staff have to come in.'

'Two vault staff, the same as yesterday?'

Counsell nodded.

'Does one of them have a bad foot?'

'Yes. Jamie Alcock.'

'Has one of them got an Alsatian?'

'That's Tommy Thompson. He won't be in today.'

'Who's the chap smoking a pipe who drives a white car?'

'That's John, Tom's opposite number. He'll be in later.'

'So who's got the white dog?'

'Alan Grimes.'

'Does he work in the vaults?'

'Yes.'

'Is he working today?'

'I don't know.'

To Counsell, the men seemed remarkably well informed. Suddenly, loud bells rang out all over the building and thinking that the alarm had somehow been tripped, the men panicked. 'What's going on?' they shouted.

'It's the telephone,' Counsell told them.

'You'd better answer it properly. No funny business, mind. Tell whoever it is that you're with the managers and you can't talk at the moment.'

Counsell picked up the receiver. It was Susan, his wife. 'I can't talk right now,' he told her. 'I have some of the managers with me.'

'Fine,' she said. 'Don't forget to bring a loaf of bread home with you.'

'OK. Listen, I have to go.' He put the phone down.

'Who was it, then? Who was it?' asked one of the men.

'My wife.'

'What was that call all about. Come on, tell us. Don't mess us about.'

'My wife!' Counsell screamed at them. 'She wants a loaf of flaming bread!'

'OK, OK. It's cool, he's cool,' said one of the men, trying to calm things down.

'Act normally and be polite on the telephone,' said another of the robbers. 'Do what you're told and you won't get hurt.' It was by now a familiar refrain.

£££

At 11 a.m. the first guard arrived at the front entrance. His name was Keith Jordan. Aged forty-one, Jordan was a former lorry driver and had worked for Security Express for five years. He was Welsh and had travelled up by train from Newport in South Wales in his uniform that morning. He wasn't due to start work until 1.30, so, armed with a newspaper, he had decided that he would go and have a coffee with whoever was on duty at the depot.

He rang the doorbell and heard the click of the electronic lock as Counsell let him in. Jordan acknowledged him as he walked through the lobby. Counsell gave him the craziest, most insane smile he could muster, and let him into the airlock.

'Tell him not to bloody smile any more,' said the man standing by the door to the two men crouched underneath Counsell's desk.

'We've got people outside so don't you go smiling at people like that, or do anything silly, because the first one who gets it will be you,' they said, prodding him with their guns.

Inside the airlock, the oblivious Jordan pressed a button to open the second door. As he started to walk through, a man wearing a mask with a large, droopy nose confronted him. He pushed a sawn-off shotgun into Jordan's cheek. 'Don't struggle.'

Two more men appeared on either side of him, and the three of them bundled Jordan into the darkened control room. They put sticking plaster over his eyes, spun him round in a chair, and tied his hands. 'Kill the bastard! Shoot him!' one of the men shouted at him. They all spoke with strange Irish accents. 'Are you a vault custodian or a driver–guard?'

Jordan could see where the conversation was leading. So he lied. 'Driver–guard,' he said.

They picked him up and carried him down to the locker room, put a coat down on the tiled floor for him to sit on, tied his hands around a concrete post, and tied his feet together.

'Keep calm, don't struggle and you won't get hurt,' said one of the men. 'What's your name?'

'Taff.'

'Who else is working today?'

'Pat Lynch.'

'How is he coming in? By car?'

'I don't know.'

'Who else?'

'Steve Hayes.'

'Is he going to give us any trouble?'

'I don't think so.'

'Who else?'

'Dave Sawyer.'

'How is he coming in?'

'He's got his own car.'

'Is he going to give us any trouble?'

'No.'

'Who's the controller?'

'I think it is John Atkinson.'

'Is he the one with the dog?'

'No, that's Tommy Thompson.'

'What does he look like?'

'He's got a beard and glasses.'

'Is he going to give us any trouble?'

'I don't think so.'

'OK. Sit still and don't struggle,' they said. 'We'll keep that animal upstairs,' said one of the men, referring to the man who had threatened to shoot him. 'We won't let him come down here.'

'Someone will be in the room all the time,' said a man with a quiet voice.

He left the room. Ten minutes later, he was back. 'Taffy,' he said in his quiet voice. 'You lied.'

Jordan felt the pit of his stomach go.

'You're the custodian.'

'Yes . . . I am.'

'So why did you tell us you were the driver–guard?'

'I was confused,' he said. 'It was the first thing I could think of.'

The man seemed to accept that. 'Do you smoke?' he asked.

'Yes, roll-ups. They're in my pocket.'

The man took the tin out of Jordan's jacket pocket and rolled him a cigarette, putting it to Jordan's lips so that he could lick the adhesive. He handed him the roll-up and lit it for him. 'I'll get you a cup of tea later,' he said. 'There's always someone here, Taffy, so don't struggle.' And then he left.

Jordan could hear two people walking around him. In the background he heard the sound of steel lockers, in which the guards kept their clothing and helmets, being opened.

'You married?'

'Divorced.'

'What do you do socially?'

'I go out for a drink. I like dancing.'

'We'll put something through your letterbox for you.'

The man with the quiet voice returned. 'Where's the tea and sugar?' he asked.

'I don't know.'

'Do they put hot water in the urn outside?'

'Yes.'

He went away and returned a few minutes later. 'I've got some tea, Taff, but it's hot. Would you like another roll-up?'

'Yes.'

The man rolled another cigarette for him just as before. He lit it and let him take a few puffs, and then he held up the cup for him to drink. Jordan took just a few sips. The tea tasted funny. It crossed his mind that they might have put something in it.

£££

Half an hour later the next guard arrived, Pat Lynch, aged fifty-nine. He had worked for Security Express for around five years. Before that, he had been a milkman.

Lynch had first gone to the staff entrance by the main gate

of the depot, but found the gate control room unoccupied, its metal blinds still drawn. He assumed that he was early. 'The night man must still be here,' he thought to himself as he walked back up to the building's main entrance. He peered through the front door and was surprised to see Greg Counsell sitting all by himself in the control room. He knew that Counsell wasn't the usual night man but assumed that, being a bank holiday, there were staff shortages.

Counsell 'buzzed' him in as he had done with Jordan. Lynch was just about to go into the control room to ask what was going on when he, too, was pounced upon by the men lying in wait.

He felt something cold pressed against the back of his neck. He thought someone was larking about, turned, and started laughing when he saw the masked man dressed up in a Security Express helmet and jacket. Lynch half turned to walk away. 'Come on,' he said, 'stop fucking around!'

But it was no joke. 'Stand still!' growled the man. Lynch saw the sawn-off double-barrelled shotgun pointed at him. He looked questioningly towards Counsell sitting in the control room. Counsell shrugged his shoulders and pursed his lips. 'It's for real, Pat,' he said.

Lynch felt another gun barrel pressed into the small of his back. He put his hands up. 'All right, guv. I'll do as you say. I'll do anything you want. Just don't hurt me.'

'Tie him up,' said the first man.

'Put your hands behind your back!'

Lynch was marched off downstairs to the locker rooms. Halfway there, the men sat him down on the stairs. 'Give us your spectacles.'

'Carry on down. What's down here?'

'The locker room.'

'How many more of you are coming in this afternoon?'

'There's four of us.'

The robber pushed the gun barrel into his neck. 'Don't tell lies!'

'I'm not.'

'Who's in charge?'

'Keith Jordan. There's Steve Hayes and Dave Sawyer to come as well.'

'How about the bloke with the dog?'

'That'll be Mr Thompson. He's in control.'

They took him into the locker room and stuck brown parcel tape over his eyes.

'Lie down on the floor.'

'I can't.'

'Get down.'

He was firmly but gently lowered to the floor.

Shortly afterwards Lynch heard the sounds of two other guards being made to lie down on the floor. Then there was silence. All he could hear was the pacing up and down of one pair of footsteps. A few minutes later he felt a tap on his forehead.

'Your controller's a long time coming. Where's Thompson?'

'We usually come in and go straight back out,' Lynch replied. 'They're here when we get back to the depot.'

£££

It was approaching lunchtime. Upstairs in the control room one of the men had been showing off a black-barrelled automatic pistol to Counsell. He stood in the doorway clicking the bullets together.

The two men under Counsell's desk had been whispering to themselves all morning. Now Counsell heard some rustling sounds. 'Is this your apple?' one of the men asked.

'Yes.'

'Mind if I eat it?'

'No,' said Counsell. 'Do whatever you want.'

The man under the desk crunched away at the apple. There was silence, followed by more rustling.

'Can I have your cheese roll?' he asked.

'Yes. Of course you can.'

'I've got a liberty, haven't I?' the man said, chuckling. 'By the way, there's a thread loose on your coat button.'

Around 1 p.m. the radio in the control room crackled to life. It was John Atkinson, call sign 'Zulu 13', the senior operations controller. Atkinson, aged forty-seven, had worked for Security Express for fourteen years, having worked his way up from night patrol driver. He told Counsell that he would be at the depot in half an hour. Atkinson was not supposed to be on duty that day but on Good Friday he had swapped shifts with Tommy Thompson.

'Have you opened up the control room in the yard?' he asked.

'No. I'm still in the front reception.'

Atkinson was a little puzzled by that as he drove on towards the depot.

£££

Just after one o'clock, David Sawyer, also forty-seven, arrived at the front doors of the depot. Sawyer was a fully qualified specialist toolmaker. He had worked for an engineering company in Greenwich, but the company closed down just before Christmas 1981. There were only two other companies in the country that did his kind of engineering work. So, after a brief spell on the dole and a few months working as a garage forecourt attendant, he landed himself a job at Security Express. He had been there for just under a year.

On his way in to the depot, Sawyer had noticed that another Security Express yard in nearby Worship Street, where they would park the empty vans, was still locked up. Then, as he drove past the main entrance to the depot, he noticed that the blinds were down in the main control room. He knew he was early, so he thought little of it.

Sawyer walked through the lobby, the airlock, and then into the corridor, which was in complete darkness. Suddenly, he saw two people either side of him. Both put sawn-off shotguns to his ears. 'Don't do anything stupid,' the man on his left said, in what Sawyer thought was a southern Irish accent. The man was medium height and wearing a yellow helmet and a round plastic mask, the kind you might wear for a fancy-dress party.

A man walked towards him from the stairs. 'Don't do anything stupid and you'll be all right,' he said.

They lifted him up from behind and he was taken down the

stairs. He was led into the crew locker room with a gun pressed into his back.

As he went into the room he saw another man standing there, around six feet tall, of slight build, wearing a dark, full-length raincoat, a woollen balaclava, and a yellow helmet. There was a hole where his face should have been. It was like it had been covered with a stocking. He was carrying a long stick.

'Lie down.'

Sawyer's glasses were taken from him. He was lying at Pat Lynch's feet.

'Can you roll me a cigarette?' Lynch asked.

The robber obliged. 'Where's your baccy?'

'In my anorak pocket.'

He rolled Lynch a cigarette, letting him have two or three puffs on it before taking it away.

'Anybody else want a roll-up?' he asked.

'Yeah, me!' said another guard.

'I hope you're not giving them all my tobacco.' said Lynch.

'Don't worry,' said the man, 'I'll leave you half an ounce behind.'

£££

At 1.15, another guard arrived. Twenty-five-year-old Steve Hayes had walked down to the yard in Worship Street, where the empty vans were kept. He saw that it was all locked up, went to the main control room by the gates, and found that locked too. So he walked up to the main entrance, nodded an acknowledgement to Counsell, and walked through the airlock door. He pressed the button to go through the second door.

Just as he realized that the corridor was in darkness, he was grabbed from behind. A gun was pushed into his neck, forcing him to bend over. Another man in front of him bent over and pointed a sawn-off shotgun at him.

'This is an armed raid,' one of the men said. 'Don't be silly.'

The man behind him guided him forward and forced him to the stairs. Halfway down the stairs he was made to sit on the stairs. The two men stood above him on the stairs.

'What's your name?'

'Steve.'

One of the men moved round to his front. Hayes saw that he was wearing a clear rubber mask, which distorted all of his facial features. With both hands he showed him the sawn-off shotgun.

'This is an armed raid. Don't do anything silly and you won't get hurt.'

'All right.'

They pulled him to his feet. 'Just you go down the stairs and you'll be all right,' one of the men told him, speaking with an Irish accent.

Hayes was steered into the locker room and was pushed face down on to the floor, his hands tied behind his back and his feet tied together.

A third man came from the front and lifted Hayes's head up.

'Put your head on this.' He put a Security Express jacket under his head. Hayes heard the sound of some tape being pulled and then they put it over his eyes. They tapped him on the back.

'Just you lie still and you won't get hurt. We aren't going to hurt any of you.'

They left him alone. He could hear someone walking around, making sure everyone was tied up properly and comfortable.

'What's your starting time, what time do you finish, and what are you supposed to be doing this afternoon?' one of them asked him.

'I start at one thirty and finish about nine. That's all I know.'

£££

A minute's drive from the depot, Atkinson again radioed Counsell. 'I'm one minute away,' he said. 'My ETA is 13.30 hours. Which control room are you using now?'

'I'm still in the main building,' Counsell told him.

'Why's that?'

'I'm waiting for you to come in.'

By the time he had parked his car and walked up to the front doors Atkinson was riled. That was no answer. Counsell should have been in the gate control room by now.

He heard the click of the electronic front-door lock and strode into the entrance lobby. He looked into the control room. All the lights were off, but he could just about make out the dim silhouette of Counsell standing by his desk. Atkinson walked through the airlock, through the inner door, and into the main corridor. Unusually, the corridor lights were out, so he turned left to go into the control room to ask Counsell what was going on. But before he could, he was confronted by a short man, not much over five feet tall, wearing a yellow helmet.

To Atkinson the man appeared to have no face at all. There was just a black patch where his face should have been. Like Keith before him, at first he thought it was a practical joke. Then he saw the light glinting on the twin barrels of a shotgun, which was pointed directly at his throat.

'Get back! Get back!' the man said in a hoarse whisper.

Another man appeared at his side and pushed a gun barrel under Atkinson's ear. He sensed a third person standing behind him and felt another gun in his back.

All three men were giving him directions at once.

'Go forward!'

'Come back here!'

'Put your hands up!'

'Get your hands down!'

He was frogmarched over to the stairs leading down to the basement.

'Sit on the steps and put your head down!'

'Go on down the stairs!'

'I'll blow your head off if you move!'

He was marched on down the stairs.

'Open your mouth!'

The man behind him stuffed the smooth barrel of a handgun into it.

'I'll do as I'm told,' he choked, 'but for Chrissake can't just one of you give the orders?'

The man took the gun out of Atkinson's mouth. 'Look

straight in front of you.' The three men marched him into the locker room, one gun pressed behind his ear, another in his back.

'Can I have a pee?'

'No.'

'Yeah, let him.'

'Use the waste-paper bin.'

His glasses were removed and he was taken to the far end of the locker room. There he could make out other guards lying on the floor. A bandage was slapped over his eyes. 'Kneel down. Lie down with your hands behind your back.' His hands and feet were firmly tied. Someone put a coat under him, to make him feel more comfortable on the hard floor.

Another man arrived. 'Don't you move and don't try anything,' he said. 'There's two men here with you at all times.' He spoke in a disguised voice, as if he had something in his mouth.

'Why are you late?'

'No reason. I'm on time. It's one thirty.'

'No. You're late. The vans are supposed to be going out at one thirty.'

The man seemed to know the guards' routine better than Atkinson did.

'What runs are there this afternoon?' he asked. 'What about the cash and carry?'

'Which cash and carry?'

'Come on, don't fuck us about. You know which one. LAM.'

'I don't know about it. If there's any paper about, it's in the yard control room.'

'What time is this cash and carry collection?'

Atkinson couldn't reply. He didn't know.

The man raised his voice. 'You know what time it is.'

'It's any time now,' Atkinson stammered. 'They demand an early call. If they don't get a call they'll be calling us up.'

'What other calls have you got this afternoon?'

Atkinson paused to think. 'Edgware Road and the cash and carry. That's all.'

'Where's this cash and carry?'

'Haringey.'

After each bout of questions the man would go away to consult with one of the others. Atkinson had hesitated after each question, and the robber was getting more and more annoyed. This time, on his return, he poked his gun into Atkinson's knees, then his thigh and the small of his back.

'Don't you hesitate when I ask you questions,' he said brusquely. 'I can get very nasty indeed.'

Lynch, who was lying nearby, could sense that the man was losing his patience with Atkinson, so he blurted out the answer they were looking for. 'The dog track,' he said.

The robbers then spoke among themselves, deciding what excuse they could use. 'We can tell them we're running late,' they agreed.

One of them turned back to Atkinson.

'What time are the vault staff coming on duty?'

'Two thirty.'

'Which is the one with the dog?'

'Alan Grimes.'

'What's he look like?'

'He's a young fellow.'

Atkinson got the feeling that the robbers were checking his answers with information they already had.

There the guards lay, on the cold floor of the locker room. Sometimes they would ask permission to move their arms or legs. Someone would say, 'Yep,' or 'OK.'

Once, Atkinson tried to move his arms without permission. 'Lie still!' said the Irish-sounding voice.

'It's not worth losing a kneecap for,' said another, older-sounding man.

The ties they used on Atkinson were cutting off his circulation. He could feel his right arm going numb. But when it became too bad to be bearable, if asked, one of the men watching over them would come over and massage it for him.

£££

Up in the control room Counsell was, by now, having to fend off phone calls from irate customers wanting to know where their vans were. One call was from the cash and carry. 'It's running very late,' Counsell told the man.

A while later the man called back. By now he was getting agitated.

'The van has broken down,' Counsell told him. 'We're waiting for a mechanic.'

'Can't you run another van?'

'That's not possible, but we'll have a van out to you by seven o'clock,' said Counsell, and promised to call him back. 'I'll ring back if that is acceptable,' said the man sniffily.

'That's a good excuse,' said one of the men under the desk. 'Keep it up and you won't get hurt.'

'I'm tired,' Counsell told them. 'I hope you bloody hurry up.'

'So are we. It's been a long night,' said one. 'Yeah, fucking tired,' said the other.

'Is he all right? Is he behaving?' asked a man with a high-pitched voice, standing at the door.

'Yeah, Greg's all right,' chorused the men under the desk, 'It's cool. He's cool.' One of them touched Counsell's hand. 'Don't worry,' he said in a reassuring voice. 'It'll soon be over.'

Later on they made Counsell a cup of tea.

'When we tell you, close your eyes and look down on the desk,' they said. Counsell knew that it was the television monitors that they were worried about him seeing. Something was happening out in the yard.

The monitors were later switched off.

£££

At around 2.15 the first vault custodian arrived. Two different sets of keys and combinations were needed to get into the vault. Normally, the shift supervisor, the 'Number One' man, held one set. Another person on the shift, known as the 'Number Two' man, held the other set.

Alan Grimes, married, aged twenty-nine, was the 'Number Two' man that day.

He arrived at Curtain Road, parked his car outside the main entrance and walked towards the reception. He saw that there were no lights on, and so walked towards the main gates, but finding the blinds were still down in the main control room, he walked back up to reception.

Grimes spied Counsell through the window and waved. He walked through the lobby, through the airlock, to be met by three men, all hooded, one wearing a yellow crash helmet. All three held sawn-off shotguns at his head.

'Look down!'

One of the men put sticky plaster over his eyes. 'Where's your dog, where's your dog?' he shouted. He appeared to have an Irish accent.

'I haven't brought him today.'

'Is he in the car?'

'I haven't brought him.'

'What's your name?'

'Alan.'

'Everything will be all right. Just keep calm,' said a man with a softer voice. To Grimes, he sounded older than the others, perhaps in his forties.

They took him downstairs into the canteen and sat him down in a blue plastic chair. 'Where are your keys?' said the softer-voiced man.

'In my pocket. Should I get them out?'

One of the men felt around in his pockets.

'Get them out.'

Grimes handed them over.

'What's the combination?'

Grimes was so frightened that he said several different numbers. He was getting confused. 'I've got it written down in my wallet. Do you want me to get it?'

'Yes,' said the man with the Irish accent.

Grimes took his wallet out and handed it to the man with the soft voice.

'Is this the combination?'

'I can't see.'

They lifted the plaster from his left eye so that he could see a little. The number was handwritten on a white Security Express label.

'Yes.'

'How does the combination work?'

He told them the sequence.

'Now can you tell me again?'

He went through it again and got it muddled.

'Again?'

He got it wrong again, but they didn't seem to notice.

They replaced the plaster. The men were getting impatient. They were beginning to worry about the time. 'What happens when the vans don't go out?' asked the soft-spoken man. 'What do the customers do?'

'They just phone in and try to find out what the delay is,' Grimes told him.

'What's the other bloke with the keys like?'

'Jamie Alcock? He's a bit older. He was in the war, so he might get a bit funny with you.'

Two of the men left the canteen. One remained, holding a gun to Grimes's neck. A few minutes later, Grimes heard the sound of a scuffle on the stairs.

£££

It was 2.30. Jamie Alcock had arrived at the front entrance of the depot. He was sixty years old and had worked for Security Express for approaching twenty years. Before joining, he had been a bus driver based at Peckham Garage. He changed jobs because his wife hated the shift work. Over recent years he had been the victim of no less than four armed raids.

Alcock wasn't normally a vault keyholder. But, the day before, the 'Number One' man, Vic Vincent, had called him to tell him that, as he wasn't due in until Tuesday, he had left the 'Number One' keys and the 'Number One' combination in the reception area.

So, between them, Grimes and Alcock would open the vaults up that day. Thus, Alcock was the man the robbers had been waiting for.

Alcock walked into the lobby, looked across at Counsell, and saw that Counsell, normally a happy person, was looking pretty damn miserable. As he walked through the inner airlock door and into the dark corridor, he saw a man standing straight in front of him. He was about six feet tall. The man put a double-barrelled shotgun to Alcock's forehead.

'Be quiet and you won't get hurt.'

Another man to his right, a little shorter, put a pistol to Alcock's right temple. The two men walked him down the stairs. As he passed the open door of the canteen he saw Grimes in a chair, bending over.

They removed Alcock's glasses, put sticky plaster over his eyes, and led him into the storeroom.

'We want the vault keys,' said the big man. He spoke with a quiet voice. To Alcock it sounded like a Midlands accent.

'I don't have the keys.'

'Yes, you have the keys.'

'I haven't.'

'You have.'

'I haven't.'

'We'll search him,' said the man with the handgun, who spoke with an Irish accent.

They searched Alcock's pockets and took out his front-door keys, wallet, identity card, and his driving licence, which had his home address on it.

'If we don't get the keys we have nothing to lose,' said the man with the English accent, 'but as for you . . .' His tone of voice turned threatening. 'If you have to go on an ID parade you'll recognize no one. We know where you live.'

£££

Next door in the canteen, Grimes was still being held with a gun pointed at his neck. The two other men returned to the room. 'Jamie didn't have the keys,' they said.

'They must have been left in reception by the previous shift then,' said Grimes.

One of the men went upstairs to the control room to check this out.

By now Counsell was of little further use to the robbers,

and had been taken from the reception desk to a partitioned-off area where the alarm boxes were situated. He had been made to sit down and face the wall.

Now, he was confronted by the man from downstairs. 'Where are the fucking keys?' he said.

'What keys?'

'They've said you've got them up here.'

'I don't know what keys you are talking about,' said Counsell. 'I've only got the keys to the yard.'

The man started placing bunches of keys in front of him. 'Are these them?'

'No.'

The men rummaged around the control room, looking for keys. They found the bunch of keys Counsell had used to open the door to the yard. 'Are these them?'

'Yes.'

The man took the set of keys downstairs to show Grimes in the canteen. He fumbled as he tried to remove the plaster from Grimes's left eye. It took him several attempts.

'They're the wrong ones.'

The man replaced the plaster and, enraged, ran back upstairs to Counsell. He pushed a gun into Counsell's back. 'You're telling lies!' he shouted. 'You're fucking us about. These aren't the keys.'

'They are the only ones I know about.'

The men were rapidly losing their patience. Time was running out for them. They were worried that sooner or later the customers would stop believing Counsell's excuses about the late vans and call the police.

Meanwhile, in the storeroom next door to the canteen, Alcock was going through his own private hell. As he was later to recount to police, it involved a can of petrol and a box of matches.

'Here, smell this,' said the man with the handgun. 'I'm going to pour it all over you and set you on fire if you don't give us the keys.'

'The keys are in the building.'

'You liar, you fucking cunt! Bastard!'

The man poured the petrol over Alcock's left trouser leg. Then he rattled the box of matches at him. Alcock could feel it soaking into his skin. He was petrified.

'All right, they're in the cubbyhole in a brown envelope,' he said.

'Where?'

'In the control room.'

Few, faced with the prospect of turning into a human torch, would have held out.

One of the men went upstairs to find the brown envelope. The other took Alcock to the locker room to be tied up with the rest of his colleagues.

In the control room the men searched the cubbyholes, quickly found the brown envelope and ripped it open. Inside they found the set of Number One keys and a white Security Express label with the Number One combination code written on it by hand. 'We've found the keys!' they shouted. Triumphantly they carried them back downstairs to the canteen to show Grimes. 'Are these the keys?' they asked, lifting the plaster from his eye.

'Yes.'

They replaced the plaster. 'Right. Come with us,' one man said. 'We want you to switch off the alarms and open up.'

Grimes was taken up to the control room. The plaster was removed from his eyes again and he found himself standing behind Counsell and in front of the alarm boxes.

'Switch off the alarms,' ordered one of the men. 'Don't do anything silly. Tell me what you are doing before you do it. Greg has told us that the house alarm is already switched off.'

Grimes could see that the men were getting very jumpy. So he warned them about what would happen so that they wouldn't panic. 'When I push the button it may sound like the alarm is going off, but it isn't,' he said. He switched the alarms off.

Blindfolded again, Grimes was marched out of the room by some of the men. Meanwhile, Counsell was made to get to his feet.

'You've done all right,' one of the men told him. 'You've saved your mates' lives by not being silly.'

Counsell was taken down to the locker room to join his colleagues.

£££

Grimes stood at the door of the vault airlock. The men stood behind him and removed the plaster from his left eye. He went to undo the Number One lock.

'Stop! Stop!' shouted one of the men. 'You're supposed to undo Number Two lock first.'

'It doesn't make any difference once the alarms are off,' Grimes told them.

He continued unlocking the door and stepped into the vault airlock. Four or five men piled in behind him. 'Lock the door behind us,' said the man with the Irish accent. 'Now unlock the second door.'

The men stood in silence in front of a grille made of vertical steel bars. Behind the grille was a short passage that led up to the steel safe door of the vault. Grimes opened a gate in the grille and they walked through.

'Is there just one vault door?' asked one of the men as he put the plaster back over Grimes's eye.

'Yes.'

They walked Grimes up to the door and removed the plaster from his eye.

'Don't turn round.'

Grimes held the two labels with the combination numbers written on them in the palm of his hand. The labels were sopping wet with sweat. Each label had four sets of two figures written on it. He spun the two combination dials in turn, turned the heavy wheel, and pulled opened the thick steel door. Immediately behind the vault door was another grille.

'Is there a panic button in the vault?

'No.'

'Are you sure? We've been told there is.'

'No, there isn't.'

Grimes was walked up to the grille.

'How do you open the grille?'

Without saying a word, Grimes unlocked it.

'Where's the light switch?'

'Top right-hand corner.'

Grimes made a move to show them the light switch but the man pulled him back.

'No you don't!' he said. 'Look at the ground!'

There was a hum as the starters fired and the fluorescent lights flickered to life, bathing the vault in a greenish hue. For a second, the gang stood there in silence, gazing in awe at the rows of trolleys piled high with wrapped coins and linen bags.

'C'mon lads. Start loading. Get the bags. Leave the coins.'

'How do we get into the yard?' they asked Grimes.

Grimes gestured. 'Through the end tub.' They walked him over to it.

'Is it alarmed?'

'No, it just pulls open.'

'How do I undo the shutter into the yard?'

'It's the button on the wall over there.'

One of the men pressed the button. 'It's not working.'

'Yes it is. It's offset.'

They sat Grimes down at a desk, tied a pair of tights around his eyes, and put a bag over his head.

'Don't you move. Someone is watching you.'

Grimes heard the sounds of the trolleys going in and out of the vault for some ten minutes.

'How do you undo the safes at the back in the vault?'

'They're on time locks. I don't know if the locks are on. You'll have to push the button and turn the key to find out.'

'Go in and show me.'

They led him back into the vault, with the bag over his head, to the seven safes. They took the bag off and lowered the tights from his eyes so that he could open the safes for them. By now, the time locks on the safes had been automatically switched off because men were due to be working in the vault that day.

Covering his head again, the robbers led Grimes out of the vault and sat him down. He could hear them hurtling past him with the trolleys. And then they stopped. After that, he could hear them throwing heavy bags to each other, calling each other

'Paddy' as they did so. 'Paddy, don't go out in the yard without your helmet on,' said one of the robbers.

'Pass me that iron bar,' said one of the men, speaking in an Irish accent.

Grimes braced himself, knowing his task was done and expecting the worst. Instead, there was a crash nearby as something was broken open.

The ransacking of the vault had taken around twenty minutes. When they had finished, two of the men led Grimes back out of the vault to lock the two airlock doors. 'Look at the ground,' they said, as they removed the bag from his head.

'You're a good boy,' said the older man, patting him on the head. 'Everything will be all right.'

'Don't worry,' he added. 'We'll let you have something in the post but it won't be for a little while yet. It'll be a long time, but don't worry.'

They took him down to the locker room and tied him up.

£££

The guards tied up in the locker room listened despondently to the sound of the trolleys trundling about in the vault above them, their wheels rolling overhead at high speeds. The robbers had managed to breach the vault, with all its elaborate security.

'Not long now. Ten minutes,' said the man watching over them.

They heard Grimes being brought down to the locker room and tied up. He didn't have to say a word. The other guards knew exactly how he felt.

Lynch pleaded to go to the toilet. 'Turn on your side and go,' he was told.

Finally the pacing up and down stopped. The trolleys could no longer be heard above them.

'It's all gone now,' said the man guarding them.

'Can I please go to the toilet, mate? I'm bursting,' asked Lynch, again. He desperately needed a pee. He had been pleading for hours. Finally, they let him, moving a couple of the guards out of the way.

'You'll have to piss on the floor,' said the man. 'Here, use this waste bin.'

Then the robber with the heavily disguised voice came back. He made what amounted to a leaving speech. 'We're going now. Don't you move! And don't try to rush us as we leave. We've got a man upstairs. He's gonna be there for twenty minutes just watching out for you. He's got a shooter and he's as fucking mad as they come.' The man's shoes scuffed on the concrete floor as he turned to go. 'And don't pick anyone out,' he added. 'I've got all your names and addresses.'

The footsteps receded.

'Someone will be here for three more minutes,' said a voice from out of the darkness.

The guards waited for a few minutes. Then one of the guards changed position. 'Keep still. We're still here,' a voice snarled back at him.

All went quiet. For the next few minutes, the guards remained silent, not daring to move, wondering whether the robbers were still somewhere on the premises.

'Can I have permission to move my hands?' asked Atkinson.

No reply.

'Is it all right if I sit up now, mate?' asked Hayes.

Still no reply.

'I think they've gone,' said Hayes to Atkinson.

'Yes. I think we're alone now,' he replied.

'Right lads, we're on our own!' Sighs of relief swept through the locker room as the guards started to move. Hayes sat up and easily got his hands free. Atkinson, too, quickly worked his hands free. They set about untying the others.

All of them had been bound with the same type of silk stocking. Six were tied up on the floor. Counsell and Grimes had been given the dubious honour of being tied to chairs.

As he was promised, Lynch found his tobacco pouch on the stairs, neatly placed inside his upturned helmet. But Alcock never recovered the keys to his front door. Fearful of the threat made by the robbers, Security Express later paid for him to change his locks.

The pay phone in the locker room had been sabotaged, its mouthpiece and earpiece deftly removed. Other phones in the immediate vicinity had also been wrecked. The guards had to go up to another control room, the top control room, to find a phone still working. Between them Counsell and Jordan raised the alarm.

And then all hell broke loose.

£££

It was just after 3.30 p.m. The curious-looking green and yellow van with the double rear axle sped northwards through the quiet streets of Shoreditch. Two cars followed closely behind. The van stopped twice on the way, dropping off two passengers. The men collected their cars, parked at the side of the road, and made their own way to a pre-arranged secret rendezvous.

3

WILTON OF THE FLYING SQUAD

From the outside it seemed like a perfectly ordinary building, a nondescript office or perhaps a local council depot. It was only the security vans turning through the electric gates into the yard that gave away what it was really used for.

From the front door it was just a few short steps up into the foyer. There, you had a glass window through which the controller could see who was coming in and out. Once you were inside there were gates, buttons, rooms, lockers, and all sorts of twists and turns as you went down stairs towards the vaults.

The question Detective Chief Inspector Peter Wilton found himself asking as he walked around the building was, 'Would any team of robbers go into a building not knowing something about what was inside?' Peter thought not. All his years of experience in the job told him that.

Stockily built, with tousled dark hair, brown eyes, and a determined jawline, Peter was based at one of the Flying Squad's satellite offices in Walthamstow, East London, just a few miles from Curtain Road. Gregarious, a keen sportsman, yet extremely dedicated to his work, he was a popular figure at the station.

There had been only a skeleton staff on duty that day when the call had come through from Scotland Yard. Being a bank holiday, most businesses were closed, so there was little for the Flying Squad officers to do. Some sat around playing cards, whiling away the time until they could head home to their wives and children. Others were cleaning their cars in the station yard.

The call from Scotland Yard was taken by one Detective Sergeant Paddle. At first he thought it was a wind-up, and anyway, for the Flying Squad to accept an investigation the crime had to fall within certain categories. The men had to be armed and the cash had to be either in transit or from a bank, building society, or post office. Besides, it was a bank holiday, and Paddle was going to play hard to get.

'There's been a robbery on the vaults at Security Express.'

'Oh yes?' replied Paddle, in his strong West Country accent. 'Sounds like a burglary to me.'

'Well, they were heavily armed and they tried to pour petrol over one of the guards to make him surrender the keys.'

'Oh, sounds bloody serious, that.'

'Oh yes, and another thing. The value of cash stolen could be approaching eight million.'

Paddle paused in thought. 'Best we get down there then, hadn't we?' he said.

And so started one of the most protracted and intense investigations in the history of the Flying Squad, the Metropolitan Police's crack team of detectives.

One would have imagined squad cars racing to the scene but that was not how it was. The officers made their way to Curtain Road in whatever vehicles they could muster. Some were allowed to drive their own cars while they were on duty, so one officer, Detective Constable Simon Webber, who was to play an important role in the enquiry, poodled along there in his big old Volvo estate, call sign 888.

Several officers, Peter one of them, had their bank holiday spoilt because they were called back into the office. Peter had been at a family reunion 200 miles away in Somerset. At 4.30 p.m. the office had called him at his parents' home and told him to get back to London as fast as he could make it. He arrived at Curtain Road at around seven o'clock in the evening.

The scene he met was one of utter chaos. The young whippets in uniform from nearby City Road station were already there. There were scene-of-crime officers crawling all over the place on their hands and knees, searching for clues. There were police photographers snapping away at everything in sight. And then there were the team managers, such as Peter, who were supposed to organize it all. It was a daunting task.

And camped outside in the gathering darkness behind the police lines were the press in their hordes, braying for something to print – anything – for tomorrow's first editions.

Peter briefly interviewed most of the staff that had been tied up. Some were badly shaken, others not so. He talked to Greg Counsell, who, to Peter, seemed strangely calm, considering that he had endured several hours of sitting in his office with a shotgun pointed at his crotch. He talked to the guards who had come into the offices, only to be confronted by masked raiders pointing firearms at them, blindfolded, and tied up in the locker room.

He knew, right from the outset, that there were going to be no clues at the scene of the crime that would help the investigation. This had been a highly professional job, skilfully planned and executed with great precision. Fingerprints were out of the question. Identification was out of the question: none of the guards saw any faces.

But one thing was becoming clear to Peter as he walked around that depot. Throughout the evening, the estimate for the amount of cash stolen was rising and rising, which would make it the biggest cash robbery ever in the United Kingdom. The press loved that headline.

Peter worked through the night and on into the following evening, gathering what little evidence was to hand. It was the longest continuous working shift he had ever done – something like twenty-eight hours. For Peter the case was to be the highlight of a career stretching over thirty years. It was to tax his mind for the next seven years. He would never have imagined when he had started out on the uniformed beat all those years ago that he would ever get to be involved in such a lengthy, complex and high-profile enquiry.

£££

That evening, Flying Squad officers set about taking detailed statements from the eight guards who had been held hostage. All were pretty shaken up by their ordeal. The officers pieced together what had happened to them as best they could.

It quickly became apparent that the robbers had a well-worked-out strategy in place. For the gang it had been a game of patience as they waited for the drivers and then the vault custodians to report for duty. Peter could well imagine the scene . . . the quiet control room . . . just the faint ticking sound of the electric clock on the wall, and the harsh buzzing of the electric solenoids as the guards came through the security doors, one by one, to be met by a masked man brandishing what looked like a shotgun. As they trooped in, the guards were blindfolded, gagged with insulating tape, and taken downstairs by one of the robbers, to the locker room.

The robbers were edgy yet friendly. For most of the day they showed a surprising amount of respect towards the guards. Each of the men asked the guards their first names and had called them by their first names. Seemingly, they had bent over backwards to be as compassionate towards the guards as they dared. The officers heard how they had made them tea, rolled them cigarettes, and placed clothes under them to make them more comfortable on the hard locker-room floor. One had even walked around the locker room massaging the guards' limbs and wrists when their bindings had cut off their circulation.

But there could be no doubt that the robbers had turned vicious towards the end, when they realized that James Alcock did not have the other half of the keys and combination needed to open the vault. By then, the gang must have been getting desperate. They knew they were running out of time. The customers awaiting the van pick-ups would eventually have become suspicious of Counsell's endless excuses and raised the alarm.

Jamie Alcock had thus borne the brunt of the robbers' wrath, claiming that one robber had gone as far as pouring petrol over his knee. The forensics on his trouser leg had proved inconclusive, but another guard, Atkinson, had smelt petrol in the locker room, as had a policeman at the scene. Grimes, too, had told the officers he had been threatened with being doused with petrol and set on fire. But his recollection of the exact nature of the threat was rather less clear.

The guards' recollection of the robbers themselves was confused. They ascribed a plethora of heights, sizes, builds, and masks to the men. Some had spoken in strange Irish accents that, on occasion, had been dropped when the robbers thought the guards were out of hearing. One of the robbers had called another 'Ron', but the others used no names, although they did on one occasion refer to themselves as 'Paddy One', 'Paddy Two', 'Paddy Three', and so on.

The officers learnt from the guards that the security set-up at the depot left much to be desired. David Howsam, the twenty-year-old nightwatchman who had let Greg Counsell into the building that morning, told them about the problems he encountered in checking the yard at night. 'The closed-circuit television screen in the control room in the building only covers about a quarter of the yard and I have no access to the remainder,' he said. 'I think if I tried to go into the yard the alarms would go off and I have no way of resetting them. I cannot go out of the front doors as they are airlocked and I have no way of operating them from the outside.'

But the most serious security breach was in the morning, when just one guard was on duty, and would leave the main building unattended to go to the gate control room. To get from one control room to the other, the guard had to walk across the yard. By so doing, the integrity of the building was breached. That was the weak point on which the gang had homed in. But how had they known about it?

There was little else that the guards could tell. One of them had noticed on his way to work three men hanging around outside the depot. They turned their backs to him, pretending to ask directions. One of them was carrying a green plastic bag in his hand.

Apart from the guards, there was only one other witness to the robbery of any note. Noel McCabe was a printer working in a factory close to the Security Express depot. At around 3.30 p.m. he had left the factory to fetch some cans of drink. He cycled north along Curtain Road and, as he approached the depot, he saw the back end of a navy-blue Ford Cortina that had just come out of the yard gates. McCabe could make out two men in the front of the vehicle and one in the rear.

He heard the noise of the gates closing behind the car. And

then he saw someone running towards the car and frantically trying to squeeze through the narrowing gap between the gate and the wall.

The man didn't quite make it and was pinned to the wall by the electric gate, so the driver of the car got out to help free him. But by the time the driver had reached him, the man had already freed himself. The driver got back in, his colleague got into the back, and the car sped off northwards. McCabe remembered it all very clearly because he thought it was hilarious – a scene worthy of an Ealing comedy.

There was little in the way of house-to-house enquiries to be done, as the area was mainly industrial. Enquiries in the street proved fruitless as well. Curtain Road was right on the edge of the City; on a bank holiday weekend, there was nobody in sight. Absolutely nobody. During the day nothing untoward was noticed. And anyway, most of the action occurred indoors.

Index numbers from witnesses – car registration plates – were coming in, but nothing of particular use. Peter thought it likely that the robbers had transport similar to the Security Express wagons. And if any vehicles were seen driving away people would have assumed that they were connected with the company.

The scene-of-crime people had found some scuff marks on the wall of the yard, by the cobbled alley, where someone or some people might have climbed over. There was a cigarette butt, which had been found in the loo. And that was it. As Peter had suspected, there were no fingerprints, no nothing.

£££

The large barn was dimly lit, quiet, with just the sound of the wind whistling through the open eaves. A solitary light bulb swung on a cord over a long, makeshift trestle table constructed from bales of hay and some wooden boards.

At the far end of the barn were stacked more bales, the remnants of the winter's feed. Bags of horse pellets were piled against one wall. There was a small but useful collection of farming tools, including a pair of garden shears, hanging on some long nails haphazardly knocked into the rough walls. The uneven concrete floor was strewn with loose patches of hay and straw. In the centre stood the fake green and yellow Security Express van, its side and rear doors flung wide open. A number of men were milling around it.

John Knight had rented the spacious barn from a friend of the family some four weeks before the raid. It had two large, wooden, slatted gates, wide enough and high enough to easily drive a van inside. There was a small, wicker side door. The barn backed on to a paved yard, which was well hidden from the road.

It wasn't too far from the City, just the other side of the small Essex town of Waltham Abbey. But it was far enough out of town to avoid the immediate attention of the police. It was easy to get to, straight up the A10, through Dalston, past his brother's scrap-yard, and then on through Stoke Newington, Tottenham, Edmonton, and Enfield. The barn was around fifteen miles from Curtain Road. With no traffic it took forty minutes. John had timed the run himself.

'Why do you want it?' the friend had asked John. 'Don't you have lock-ups in London?'

'Just for a bit of extra storage,' John said in an offhand kind of way.

From John's reply, the friend knew better than to ask any further questions. He was just thankful to have a bit of extra cash for his barn, which stood empty and unused for most of the year. John offered him £100 a week for it. A few days later he towed a horsebox up to the barn and left it there.

Safely inside the barn, away from prying eyes, the men quietly unloaded the hefty sacks from the van. They had changed into new clothes and had piled their old clothes and masks in a heap on the floor.

Under John's watchful eye they started to sort through the sacks of money, which had been placed in a straight line on the floor of the barn. They used a pair of garden shears to snip through the security seals of the green cotton bank bags. 'A bit of gardening,' they joked. They still couldn't believe their luck. The firm stuffed the packets of notes into rough, hessian sacks.

They worked away quietly, methodically, without much of

a sound. The banknotes were roughly counted. They started slitting open the brown-paper packets full of notes but it was taking too long and they had to call it a day. They decided to count it properly elsewhere.

They were parched. There was a tap outside in the yard but the men had no cup, so they would take turns to stick their heads underneath the running water.

Plastic and brown-paper wrappings, the green cotton bags used by the banks, and anything that could not be banked, such as cheques, were immediately discarded and stuffed into several large sacks. These were loaded into the back of the horsebox.

Anything that might have been identifiable, for instance clothing, was loaded into the horsebox. So, too, were the ladders used for scaling the wall, along with leftover tape and rope used for tying up the guards. The guns were also disposed of. The fake one was dismantled and later cut up on a guillotine, and the real one was given to an underworld contact to be 'recycled'.

The plan was for the horsebox, complete with a resident horse, to be taken by one of the gang members up to the north of England. The horse would be sold and the concealed sacks of rubbish burnt. The horsebox was supposed to be burnt too, but John thought that its more likely fate was a good scrub and a paint job. The Transit van was too hot to be moved, so they left it in the barn. A week later someone turned up to take it away, to be cut up for scrap.

By the time they had finished cleaning up the barn it was eight o'clock in the evening. It had been a long and eventful day. John sat on an upturned wooden crate smoking a cigar. The others, faces still glowing with excitement, sat around on some bales of straw. But there was no great celebration. The men were exhausted and just wanted to go home. They had to get their alibis straight, ready for the almost inevitable questioning.

They filled a sack full of the one-pound notes. They were regarded as a bit of a burden as they were bulky and hard to get rid of, so the men discussed what to do with them. John eventually decided to pass them on to a trusted associate in Essex. The associate paid 60 pence for every pound note, making 40 pence profit for himself. The sack contained £100,000.

From the barn, around half the cash was taken away by two of the gang members. They never told John where they took it and he never asked. Those two were on their own from then on and they looked after their own interests. The split was partly done as a kind of insurance policy, in case half of the cash was lost. There was an understanding that the two halves would be 'equalized' at a later date. Expenses still had to be paid out. The men trusted each other implicitly.

John's half – just over £2.5 million in cash – was taken away to a lock-up garage in nearby Waltham Abbey. From there, John planned to move it to a house where it could be counted up properly and further divided.

'Take it easy,' John said as they all waved goodbye to each other. 'Now don't go and do anything silly. Don't flash your money around. Go and carry on doing whatever it is that you're doing. Carry on running your businesses. Live your life as normal.'

For some of them at least, John's wise words would fall on deaf ears.

4

CITY ROAD

On Tuesday 5 April, the morning after the robbery, Frank Cater, the commander of the Flying Squad, called a briefing at City Road police station for everyone assigned to the enquiry. There were so many officers present that it had to be held in a room normally used for briefing officers monitoring football crowds.

The raid had dominated the front pages of the morning's newspapers. *The Times*, under the headline 'Gun gang take £5m in biggest cash raid' claimed that the raid was the largest theft of money in British history. The newspaper – with an irony that would become only too evident as time went on – quoted Great Train Robber 'Buster' Edwards as saying that the gang's worst fear would be betrayal by criminal associates – supergrasses – anxious for the £500,000 reward put up by Security Express, and 'greedy minders' of the haul would remain a constant threat. 'There are not many firms big enough to have pulled off something like this and people know who is working and who is not . . . It's a problem knowing what to do with all that money and where to keep it.'

No one in the briefing room doubted that. The country – and the Government – had been horrified by the way that the robbers had kept the guards hostage at gunpoint. There was a political incentive to throw resources at this one. It was going to be a major enquiry.

Already, the press had embroidered the story with colourful detail. The previous evening, reporters had spotted five empty red-wine bottles and three or four empty glasses in the entrance lobby of the depot, leading to speculation that the robbers, fully aware that they would be in the depot for some eight hours, had taken in their own refreshments – it appeared to be bring-a-bottle. Another story doing the rounds was that one of the robbers had wandered around looking for the keys to the vault – only to find them in his own back pocket. Part of the team's work that day was to sort out the speculation from the reality and piece together exactly what had happened in those eight hours. It was no easy task.

The briefing room was chock full of U-shaped desks. Commander Cater, a small, wiry man with a somewhat abrupt manner, stood in front of a whiteboard, rag in one hand, marker in the other. At the start, a buzz of excitement swept through the room, but that soon gave way to a sense of bafflement as the officers discussed the leads they had gleaned from the guards the night before. The guards had presented them with a confusing mosaic of descriptions and events. With no forensic evidence and only one other witness of note, there was little to go on.

Thus, the Met's crack team of detectives was at a loss.

'Let's get out and rattle some cages,' suggested one officer, Detective Constable Jim Keeling. He thought that if they pulled in the right people, they might just hit lucky. It was bottom-of-the-barrel stuff, but it illustrated their conundrum.

For the next few months at least, the enquiry was to be based at City Road police station, which was in fact located in a quiet street just off City Road, called Shepherdess Walk. The station was only half a mile from Curtain Road and, because the robbery had occurred within its local area, it had been obliged to give the Flying Squad office space. Next door to the station was a large, traditional pub called the Eagle. That was where the boys hung out after work.

City Road was a fairly new police station but Peter knew it well and it brought back quite a few memories. It was where he had started his CID career as an aide, way back in 1964.

£££

The funny thing was, Peter almost never made it into the police force. Yet here he was, working with the best detectives the Met had to offer, the crème de la crème.

When the day came for him to leave Yeovil Grammar School in Somerset in 1956, aged just sixteen years and a bit, Peter had decided that he should go into accountancy. He started as a clerk with a small local firm called Hunts. But although he tried extremely hard, he found the office work dull. 'Wearing a collar and tie every day is just not for me,' he told his disappointed parents. After a few months in the accountancy firm, he suddenly decided that he wanted to be a policeman. He applied to join the Somerset Constabulary, because it was near his parents.

Eventually he got an interview and, to his surprise, got through to the final stage. He passed all the medical and fitness tests with flying colours. He got right up to the interview with the Chief Constable, who was then a Mr Steel. But during the interview, Steel candidly told Peter that he had not been accepted. He still remembers the conversation, clear as a bell, the words ringing in his ears.

'Well, Mr Wilton. You have passed all our tests but I am afraid we are going to have to let you go.'

Peter was dumbfounded. 'Any particular reason, sir?' he blurted out.

'It's your height. You see, we are concerned that you are a little on the short side, and we don't think you are likely to grow much more.'

It was immensely disappointing. At the time Peter was about five feet seven inches tall. And five feet nine was the minimum entrance requirement for Somerset. Despondently, he went home to tell his parents. His father wasn't surprised. A former army officer, he never really believed his son had a chance. But the knock-back simply made Peter all the more single-minded.

Undeterred, he decided to try the Metropolitan Police. The minimum height for a Met officer was only five feet eight inches in those days. 'I'm almost there,' he thought, 'so why not give it a try?'

In 1956 it was quite an adventure for a seventeen-year-old to travel up to London. He took the train, arrived at Paddington and made his way to Beak Street police station in the West End for the interviews and tests. He had to stay overnight. The first person he met was a proud young Scotsman, Alasdair Cameron Ferguson McLeod.

The interviews and tests went well and, to his father's astonishment and his mother's great joy, the Met accepted him into the senior cadets. He was able to join soon after his eighteenth birthday. So, in 1958, he found himself at Hendon Police Training School in North London. It was a strange, new, institutional world, full of long corridors and bare classrooms. He had left many of the things he had cherished behind in Somerset. But, soon after he arrived at Hendon, he couldn't help but grin as he heard a familiar voice bellowing down the hallway. 'Alasdair Cameron Ferguson McLeod.' The two of them were to become the closest of friends over the next few years.

The rough and tumble of the thirteen-week training course really brought Peter out, although there were many instances when he was picked on because of his size. On several occasions one of his old school chums, 'Nobby' Clark, who had joined up at the same time, had to come to Peter's rescue.

At the end of the course, Peter volunteered to box as a supporting bout in a competition. The main contest was between two heavyweights. One of them, Ron Chapman, won a tremendous fight with a tall, ginger-haired chap and it brought the place down. That night Peter fought another senior cadet, a young Scotsman called Jock McLean, who later became famous as the chief bodyguard for Prince Charles. McLean taught Charles to ski and stayed with the Prince for many years before his retirement. Needless to say, McLean gave Peter a good thumping that night.

At the end of the evening, the cadets passed out on parade. Peter arrived home in the West Country at five o'clock in the morning, on what was then known as the 'milk train'. He was battered and bruised, but a lot bigger and stronger than when he had left thirteen weeks before. It had been a big experience for him. His family, particularly his father, were amazed.

He waited for his papers to arrive and was eventually posted to Islington police station as a senior cadet. He thoroughly enjoyed being taken out by the established police constables. Nobby Clark was posted close to him and they would often travel back to Somerset together, sharing the driving and the cost of the vehicle hire. It was during one of those weekend breaks back home that Peter met up again with his childhood sweetheart, Valerie. She had lived just around the corner from him. They had been the best of friends – almost inseparable. And now, slim, with curly dark blonde hair and grey-blue eyes, Valerie had become a most desirable woman.

On 27 April 1959 Peter was made up as a police constable and was posted back to Islington, where he had already made lots of friends. His friend Ron Chapman was made up as a police constable on the same day, and they stayed in constant touch over the years. In fact, Chapman was the supervising officer at the Flying Squad the day the Security Express robbery went off.

Peter was now PC 295G in Islington, and the five years he had in uniform were a wonderful experience. He thoroughly enjoyed every minute of it and came to regard it as the best years of his life – the carefree schooldays he never had.

Although Peter worked hard, he played hard too, playing as much sport – especially rugby – as he possibly could. In those days everyone was encouraged by the duty sergeants to play lots of sport, all the way through the ranks, right up to senior level. The idea was that it encouraged camaraderie and improved their knowledge of the world. It made them all better people, and Peter never doubted that.

It was while at Islington that he got together with Valerie permanently. She came up to London to live with him, and in 1961 they got married.

During his time in uniform he was more inclined to go for crime arrests than motorists. So he applied to join the CID and the infamous G Division aid squad, which, in those days, was like a mini-Flying Squad. It had some of the best young policemen just out of their uniform and into plain clothes, all at the beginning of their careers. It was his first experience of plain-clothes work, targeting mainly small-time crooks and market racketeers. It involved little of the mundane paperwork that was to become a feature of the later, more serious investigations.

Some of his colleagues turned out to be some of the best detectives the Met ever had: men like Bob Robinson, Bill Laver, George Ness, Bill Peters, and Geoff Parratt, who was nicknamed 'Poirot' because of his success in the Murder Squad.

That was the first time Peter encountered Jock Forbes, the senior police officer in charge at City Road, another Scotsman. Peter would have jumped over the hill for him. He was a wonderful chap.

It was while Peter was at City Road that four of Forbes's team were awarded the George Medal. They were chasing a famous crook called Walter 'Angel Face' Probyn from Hoxton, who had escaped from prison. At the briefing, just before everyone went out on the operation, Forbes said that they had so many people that if anyone wanted to go home they were welcome to. Valerie was expecting their first child at any moment, so Peter decided he should really go home to be with her.

Later that day the young trainee detectives chased Probyn, who was armed, over the rooftops of Stepney. They disabled his getaway car with the aid of a broom handle and eventually captured him, but not without a fight. Peter may have got a medal. Or he may have got shot at. One of the four officers who did get the medal was Peter's old friend Alasdair Cameron Ferguson McLeod.

After a couple of years Peter was made a detective constable. One of the criteria for being a CID officer was that you had to pass the Civil Service exam. Peter was lucky because he had already passed it, and so leapfrogged over some very good potential detectives.

In 1966 he officially joined the CID. He went through all the usual courses and was transferred to the Regional Crime Squad at Hornsey, where he was made a detective sergeant. His progress was steady, his career not flamboyant, but he was quite satisfied. It was his subsequent posting to Kings Cross as an acting detective inspector that really opened his eyes to what criminals were all about. At police stations like Hornsey and Edmonton crime was rife, but it wasn't in the same league as the Central District. It was a wake-up call.

After two years at Kings Cross Peter was made detective inspector. He was transferred to Barkingside in J District for eighteen months, and then, in 1976, to the Detective Training School. For the next two years he taught young, budding CID officers the tricks of the trade. It was good fun, and he managed to become proficient at some of the subjects he taught. But he wasn't really cut out to be an instructor, so he was posted to Tottenham police station, where his old mate Geoff Parratt was now chief inspector.

It was while at Tottenham that Peter had his career breakthrough. He found out through an informer some information on a team of robbers in Tottenham, which he then passed on to C8 – the Central Robbery Squad, as the Flying Squad was then known.

The man Peter dealt with at the Flying Squad was Detective Chief Inspector Tony Lundy, who had pioneered sometimes-controversial techniques of utilizing informers to fight serious crime. Lundy had a unique set of informants.

Not everyone agreed with Lundy's ways of working. He played his cards close to his chest, and his success instilled a lot of jealousy among his colleagues. Many felt that he overstepped the mark, giving informers de facto immunity to carry out serious crimes in return for 'intelligence' on their fellows – usually their gangland rivals. Nevertheless, through Lundy, Peter gained some recognition. In 1980 he was promoted to chief inspector and transferred to the Flying Squad. And thus his ultimate goal – to be a Flying Squad detective – had been achieved.

In those days, coverage of London was split between two teams at New Scotland Yard in Westminster, where the Flying Squad commander was based, and teams based in four satellite offices at Walthamstow, West Drayton, Finchley and Rotherhithe police stations.

Peter was posted to Walthamstow, where the Flying Squad occupied the top floor of the station. The office had been set up in the early 1970s and there had been several chief inspectors before Peter, each of whom had left their own mark. Peter took over in 1980 and built up his own team of officers, many of whom were involved in the Security Express enquiry.

There was Detective Inspector Reed McGeorge, a dour Scotsman with a ruddy face. Painstakingly thorough, he was a mine of information. He was also a terrier. He never let go. He would worry away at leads until they had been well and truly worked loose. Reed was to play a leading part in the enquiry. In fact, aside from a brief spell in uniform working for Islington CID, he stayed on the case for an astonishing sixteen years. When, in 1999, he was told that the enquiry was closing, he handed in his papers and retired.

Another officer, Detective Sergeant George Moncrieff, also played a key role. George was very cautious and very reliable. He would often investigate a lead completely on his own initiative, without so much as a word to the rest of the team. He was never afraid to speak his mind. 'Someone should be doing this,' he would say, stubbing his cigarette out on the carpet.

To the amusement of the squad, wherever George stood, he would invariably be surrounded by a circle of cigarette butts.

Good with figures, George acted as the enquiry purser, handling expenses claims and payments. But he was mainly in charge of exhibits, items that would later be presented to the courts as part of the case for the prosecution. The exhibits had to be checked, bagged, and, if necessary, sent off for forensic examination. George's deputy, a detective constable by the name of Malcolm Jeffery, did much of the legwork. Slightly younger than the others, good-looking, with bright blue eyes, Malcolm had a cheeky, razor-sharp wit that kept them all on their toes.

There was one woman officer, Detective Constable Julia 'Jules' Pearce, who also stayed with the enquiry for many years. She was not the glamorous type, but was very dependable and down-to-earth. She had to handle everything to do with females, whether witnesses or suspects. But she was a crafty ferret when it came to tracking down information. She, too, had a keen, sparring sense of humour – important in a team largely composed of men. She could drink with the lads and she gave back as good as she got.

The enquiry had been given almost a complete floor of City

Road police station, including the use of the station's 'silver' control room, normally used for major incidents. All told, there were now some seventy officers involved. It was a melting pot of detectives from all over London. Five squads helped out with the enquiry, three from Walthamstow plus two from the Yard.

Peter knew quite a few of the men from the Yard by sight through the police rugby circuit, which in those days was very active. One of them, Detective Sergeant Cam Burnell, was a particularly close friend. Cam was a massive man and just about unstoppable on the pitch. He took his rugby very seriously indeed. He was obsessed with losing weight and, sadly, some years later, he was to die of a heart attack after a particularly arduous training session. It was one of those deaths that made absolutely no sense to Peter. It was a cruel hand of cards to be dealt.

£££

The first few days of the enquiry were taken up with obtaining statements from other Security Express staff involved. The make-up of money, the keys, what members of the staff had keys, and the combinations that must have been in existence to open the safe and vaults – all these details had to be logged and verified.

The timing of the raid was perfect. Security Express vans had collected vast amounts of cash from the *Daily Mail* Ideal Home Exhibition, bringing it back to the vaults to store. Because nothing could be banked over the long-weekend period, the vault contained far more cash than usual.

They went back to some of the guards who had already been interviewed in the hope of prising more leads out of them. Jamie Alcock, who had been threatened with petrol, was sure that he had previously come across the man who had threatened him. He told the police that early one morning, in February 1979, he had been delivering cash to a cleaning factory in Stepney Green. There was just him and the driver – no guard. They had around £30,000 in cash on the van and were supposed to deliver £2,400 to the factory offices. However, six men had beaten up the caretaker, taken control of the factory, and lain in wait for the van. Most of the men wore balaclavas and were armed with double-barrelled shotguns, but one man in particular stood out from the others. He wore a postman's uniform, postman's hat, and a silly plastic party mask with oversize glasses and a long, pointy nose. The disguise was completed with a handgun and a particularly nasty attitude.

The gang had waited several hours for the delivery van to show up. When Alcock and his driver arrived at the factory with the cash the gang forced them both to lie down on the floor. They took the £2,400 but they were really after the contents of the van. They marched Alcock at gunpoint to the van, but he tricked them and set off the alarms. The gang made their getaway, firing three shots through the van windscreen at him. Alcock thought that the man in the plastic party mask was the one who had threatened him in the Curtain Road depot.

One thing was for sure. From what the guards had said, there was clear evidence of inside information. It was as if the robbers had knowledge of the shifts but not of the unofficial swaps and changes. That would explain why they were expecting Tommy Thompson to be the controller rather than John Atkinson. The two men had swapped shifts only a few days before the robbery, and some days after the official rota had been published. Knowledge of a slightly out-of-date rota would also explain why, when the robbers asked Greg Counsell his name, they had expected him to say 'John'.

They also knew about the hastily arranged collection from LAM, the cash and carry in Haringey. That had surprised Atkinson, because it was not a routine collection and had only been arranged the previous week. The details on the LAM pick-up had been written on a special sheet in the yard control room that Atkinson himself had not seen. The gang also appeared to know that a regular collection from another cash and carry had been cancelled for the day.

But the robbers knew more than just the staff rota and the times of pick-ups. They also knew something of the system, the way the depot operated. Grimes had said that when the robbers had got to the vault airlock doors he had moved to open the top lock first. But the men had stopped him. They told him that he was supposed to open Number Two first. Both the top and bottom locks were unmarked keyholes. There was no way of telling which was which. Yet the robbers knew that the top lock was called 'Number One' and the bottom lock was 'Number Two'. Grimes told the police he would not have expected anybody but the vault staff and the management to know that.

The robbers also knew another security measure. Before Grimes could attempt to open the second airlock door leading to the vault, he had to lock the first airlock door. The second door would not have opened if he hadn't, and the robbers were clearly aware of that.

The robbers also kept asking him about a panic button in the vault itself. He kept telling them that there wasn't one. However, since the robbery, he had found out that there *was* a panic button, and that it was located underneath the light switch in the vault. So that might have explained why the robbers had pulled him back from the vault as he went to switch on the lights.

Indeed, the robbers had left most of the guards with a distinct impression that they had a mole within Security Express. The robbers had also been the beneficiaries of some luck. Victor Vincent, the previous day's 'Number One' man, had set the time delays on six of the vault safes to fourteen hours because he knew that the vault staff would be in on the Bank Holiday Monday. If there had been no vault staff coming in, he would have set the time delay for the Tuesday morning, thus denying the robbers any chance of access to those safes.

As they conducted the interviews with the guards it became clear to the officers that there was an inadequate level of security at the premises. On a Saturday or Sunday if the weather was nice, some of the guards, Greg Counsell included, would bring their cars into the yard and wash them down. One of the video cameras overlooking the yard wasn't working properly and it was a standing joke among the guards.

Yet despite all this, within a matter of days Security Express would get a payout from its insurers for the cash stolen in the robbery. The irony was not lost on one officer, who had been arguing for weeks and weeks with his insurance company over a £300 payout for a failed freezer.

£££

Peter's overriding first impression of the enquiry was that there was little or no direction, just sixty or seventy officers looking for something to fall from heaven. It was a battle among themselves as to where the robbers had come from. The various theories involved just about every big robbery team in London. There were also suggestions of a connection with the notorious 'Quality Street gang' in Manchester, which was thought to dabble in everything from armed robbery to gunrunning for the IRA.

The officers from East London were by far the greater in number, so most of the resources went into looking for teams from north of the river. But the officers from south of the river were convinced that the crime was committed by people in their patch, so the team concentrated on several targets from that area too.

Day after day Peter would sit in his office, back to the door, until late in the evening, sifting through files. The officers had to pass his office to get to the main operations room, and all of them felt frustrated by the lack of any obvious progress. So one evening a detective constable by the name of Rex Sargent, perhaps a little more outspoken than the other officers, poked his head around the door. 'Guv'nor, you shouldn't be in there, looking at them files all day,' he said, speaking in his broad West Country accent. 'We should be out there knocking on people's doors.'

Well, it wasn't quite as easy as that.

City Road station was a very busy station. At times it was chaotic, and allied to that, there were the usual rivalries and gripes between officers. The squad would liaise closely with officers from C11, the Met's criminal intelligence branch. Liaison officers from C11 were attached to every Metropolitan Police division and were authorized to go to New Scotland Yard and access the Met's highly sensitive criminal intelligence files.

Just a few days after the robbery Peter was working on some of these confidential dockets from C11, which detailed telephone intercepts between potential Security Express robbery suspects. He had worked on the dockets until late in the evening and had left them on his desk.

The following morning Peter discovered that one of the dockets had walked, which caused him a huge amount of embarrassment and concern. The culprit turned out to be a young detective who later said that he wanted to teach Peter a lesson for leaving files out unlocked overnight. The detective had long held a gripe over a bottle of whisky 'fine' meted out by Peter, a traditional Flying Squad 'punishment' for minor disciplinary offences such as being late for an appointment or meeting.

There was an internal enquiry into the docket incident that Peter could have done without. It rumbled on for months and created a lot of extra paperwork for him. Peter was never entirely sure whether there was more to the incident than just gripe. It wasn't unheard of for policemen to sell information to underworld contacts, although in this case there was no evidence that that had happened. Even so, the young detective quickly found himself back in uniform.

Convinced that the Security Express affair was an 'inside job', Peter ploughed through records of vans that had been robbed either in transit or on delivery. The Squad compiled lists of guards associated with the robberies. And then, just over a week after the Curtain Road raid, it made its first arrest, a Security Express driver by the name of Rooston.

Rooston was accused of passing inside information to a team of robbers. He was interviewed over two days – until 4 a.m. on the second day. Peter took part in the interrogations. As a result of the interviews the Squad got enough to charge Rooston with setting up the robbery of a couple of bags of cash from a Security Express van. It was a substantial sum of money.

That Friday Rooston appeared in court, represented by an Indian solicitor called Ralph Haeems. It was the first time Peter had come across Haeems, but certainly wasn't going to be the last.

After a lengthy trial, Rooston was acquitted at the Old Bailey. It was a disappointment, but the information had led to another coup. When vetting Rooston for the job, Security Express had done the obvious thing. It had checked out Rooston's own family connections, but it hadn't thought to check out those of his wife. The Flying Squad found that his wife was related to a notorious South London criminal family called the McEvoys.

The squad carried out a lot of surveillance work on the McEvoy family, and some five weeks into the enquiry had some success in recovering a fantastic arsenal of weapon from a warehouse in South London. But it was no closer to solving the Security Express robbery.

As the weeks rolled by, the Flying Squad commander, Frank Cater, was becoming increasingly frustrated. Cater was a former East End detective who had built his reputation on triumphantly successful investigations into organized crime. As a chief inspector, he had cut his teeth on the enquiry into the Kray twins some fifteen years earlier. At the time he had been deputy to Leonard 'Nipper' Read, the legendary Scotland Yard detective who brought the Krays to justice.

Cater went to City Road almost every day to conduct the Security Express enquiry, and he was desperate for a result on this one. His reputation was at stake and there was a lot of pressure from above to pull something out of the hat. As with all these things, there was a great deal of internal Yard politics involved. Careers were on the line.

One morning there had been a leak to the press from one of the officers, and Cater did his nut. 'From now on there will be no more secret briefings to journalists,' he stormed at the morning briefing session. But the very next day he was spotted by some of the officers in the Eagle, having lunch with a *Daily Mirror* journalist.

'Up and down the City Road, in and out the Eagle,' sang the lads, teasingly.

Cater got his exclusive.

5

THREE WISE MONKEYS

It had been touch and go. When John Knight thought back on the raid, many things had very nearly gone wrong. But in the end it had all worked out just fine. Now, he was getting used to the idea of being a seriously wealthy man.

Just two days after the raid, two members of the firm had gone and booked a holiday in Spain, but John was a little wiser than that. Personally, he thought they were reckless. He knew that he had to remain discreet and was too wily to be ostentatious with his new-found wealth. The police would be looking for that.

He also knew that the underworld was full of people who would not hesitate to squeal for the right reward – and in the right circumstances. That, after all, was the only way serious crime was solved – or so he thought. John always chose his friends very carefully indeed.

He kept himself to himself, working on his secluded house near the picturesque village of Wheathampstead in Hertfordshire. The house, called High Trees, overlooked a golf course and was tucked away at the end of a long, gravel track. It was surrounded by three acres of garden, and John had the option to buy more.

He had bought High Trees some eight years before. For what John had in mind it was perfect. It afforded him plenty of privacy. It was in the sort of area where people were naturally discreet. There was a businessman next door, a doctor further along the track, and a lord up at the far end by the main road. The rest of his neighbours were all retired people. It was a low-profile, wealthy man's house. Out of sight, out of mind.

John had spent a fortune on the house, making it look nice, adding little luxuries here and there. In the long dining room he installed an elegantly carved white marble fireplace. He lined its walls with antique furniture, paintings, and gold-framed photographs of himself and his striking wife, Diane. He had plans to redecorate a few of the other rooms in the same manner. In fact, the place was looking grander and grander by the day.

John was a perfectionist. He wanted all the trimmings of wealth. And he spent a lot of time making the leafy grounds look the part. He built a summer house, tennis court, installed a swimming pool, and, of course, grew his own vegetables.

He always did love his gardening, but that summer he had a very special reason for attending to the young tomato plants in his greenhouse. Some months earlier he had shovelled all of the soil out of the greenhouse until he had scraped along its concrete foundation. He had got hold of a large steel box and lined it with a strong plastic bag so that no moisture could get in. Inside this plastic seal, John had carefully packed thousands of pounds' worth of notes.

There, throughout the summer months, the box had stayed, buried underneath the pungent green tomatoes. Every now and then, John would carefully lift out the tomato plants in their fertilizer bags and take some of the cash out of the box. As he brushed the damp soil off the rusted lid, he recalled the click of the vault door as it opened; how the vault had lit up; and how they had all stood there gawking at the trolleys loaded with cash and coin. It was only a few months ago, but it seemed like a lifetime.

John's firm had disbanded and all had gone their separate ways. They talked occasionally by phone, but were generally wary of meeting one another face to face. They knew that the police were going to spend a lot of time solving this particular crime, and could well be watching their every move.

John never flashed his money around and was careful not to give the impression of suddenly coming into new wealth. He had a good cover. He was, after all, a legitimate businessman, running a hotel in Dover, a busy repair garage in

Southgate, North London, and a large, highly profitable pub in Dalston.

He was a pillar of the local community, a Freemason no less. On the first Monday or Tuesday of most months John would go off to the secretive lodge meeting in the City, dressed to the nines, carrying his apron in a discreet black-leather pouch. His lodge, No. 7331, Fairchild Lodge, was not old, but it was wealthy. It was well known for its charitable work, and had paid for a ward at the Royal Masonic Hospital. It had been founded in 1954 by a Church of England clergyman, the Reverend Davies.

It was through the good Reverend that John's elder brother Jimmy was first introduced to freemasonry. Then Jimmy, ten years John's senior, would invite John along to the lodge's ladies' nights, which were open to anyone. One evening, while John was in the gents' toilets, someone suggested that he join. 'Why not?' he thought to himself. He was proposed by a man from Essex. Jimmy, of course, seconded him. Although John didn't know it at the time, by sheer coincidence his proposer happened to be a friend of Peter Wilton's. John passed his interview held at Grand Lodge, became an Entered Apprentice, and slowly worked his way up through the three degrees to become a Master Mason.

John's brother Ronnie, a couple of years older than him, was scornful and would have nothing to do with it. He thought freemasonry was all a bit absurd, what with all those silly aprons and what have you. But John and Jimmy saw it differently. They loved the sense of order, the rituals and ceremony of the lodge meetings, and the social connections that the after-meeting dinners brought with them. With the social connections came business connections. John, in particular, loved the lodge interiors, with their ornate fixtures, their black-and-white chequered tiled floors and finely decorated blue ceilings sprinkled with painted gold stars. He always appreciated fine craftwork.

Over the years John had progressed through the ranks of the lodge. That year, 1983, he was Junior Warden. If events hadn't taken their course, he would have been Worshipful

Master of the Lodge in 1985, just as his brother Jimmy had been in 1956.

At first Ronnie didn't know John was going to lodge meetings, although he knew that John and his wife Di would often go to the lodge's ladies' nights. One Saturday evening, he stopped by Jimmy's restaurant in Stanmore for a social chat. 'He's at a meeting,' one of the members of staff told him. 'John's with him and all.'

Later, Ronnie asked John where he had been. 'You were at a meeting? What meeting's that?'

'It was a Masonic meeting.'

'You what?' said Ronnie.

'I'm in it, Ronnie! I'm in the Masonic game.'

'What's the secret sign then?' said Ronnie. 'Holding your tie? Come on, show us!'

'I can't tell ya.'

'C'mon, Johnny. I'm your brother!'

'I can't tell you. Anyway, if you knew a sign they would know you was a cheater. If you go back to the Ancient Egyptians with King Solomon, and you pretended to be one, you know what they used to do with you? They'd take you round the back of a big rock and stone you to death!'

John was only half joking.

£££

A pillar of the community John may have appeared, but the truth was somewhat different. He had never really been straight.

While he was a young tearaway, roaming the streets of his native Hoxton, he used to see the old-time villains suited and booted, always immaculately dressed. He would gaze at them with awe. He admired them because they all stood their ground. They just didn't care who they crossed – and they took the consequences like real men. To him, they always seemed to look better than ordinary people. 'That's how I want to look when I grow up,' he would say to himself. He knew full well that they hadn't got where they were by earning an honest crust.

John was a little too young to remember the terraced house where the Knight family lived, back in the 1930s, but Ronnie and Jimmy could remember it well. It was poky and damp, its ceilings riven by cracks, its brickwork crumbling. It had two rooms downstairs, two upstairs, and an outside toilet. Their mother, Nellie, made the best she could of it for her ever-burgeoning family.

The house stood in Downham Road, in De Beauvoir Town, a district then principally noted for its appalling slums, raw poverty, and soaring crime rates. A wooden-stake fence ran along one side of Downham Road. Behind the fence, small factories and workshops surrounded an old canal basin, which was partly derelict. Tucked away in a cobbled yard at the end of a mews was a sawmill called Jinkinson's.

There were huge heaps of sawdust and plenty of rats, and Ronnie and Billy, being older that John, used to go and play there for hours on end. The family had a little white terrier called Girl-Girl. She would go ratting in the sawdust, trailing sawdust everywhere she went, and the boys would come back from the yard covered from head-to-foot. John, then only three years old, was a little too young to join in the sawdust antics.

Oldest brother Jimmy had fallen in love with Maisey, one of the Jinkinson girls, and ended up marrying her, so the Knights had become part of the family. Jimmy asked them to give their father Jim a job at the sawmill, driving the lorries. They did.

'Come get in the motor! I'll take you for a ride,' Jim would say to young Ronnie and Johnny. They would climb up into one of the lorries and drive to the sawmill and collect sawdust, which would then be delivered to pie-and-mash firms, butchers, and pubs all over London, to be strewn on the floor. Afterwards, Jinkinson's would come back and collect it for burning in the incinerators of a local furniture manufacturer. So Jinkinson's was getting paid to deliver it and to take it away again afterwards. Later on in life, John always thought that was rather clever.

Jim worked all the hours under the sun. Most days he would come home around seven o'clock, but on Sundays he would get home at three, to find the whole family waiting patiently for him to cut the joint. No one was allowed to touch the meat until after he had arrived.

Just before the war broke out, the local council condemned the Knights' cramped home in Downham Road. The area was earmarked for slum clearance and replacement with blocks of high-rise flats, then the latest ugly fashion. The family was offered a brand-new flat a mile away in Arcola Street, Dalston. The brothers could well remember the tears in Nellie's eyes as she bade farewell to the tiny house in Downham Road – and the joy on her face when she saw their new home, flat 113, Hindle House. The block of flats was far from finished, with bare concrete floors covered in duckboards, and building materials piled outside. But it was like a palace to them. Sadly, the dog had to go. Council rules. It broke their collective hearts.

In 1939 the phoney war came, followed by the real war. Their father joined the ARP. He would go and drag the bodies out of the rubble after the bombs had fallen.

The balcony of their flat was three floors up and overlooked their school, which happened to be right next door to Simpsons, who were making uniforms for the army. The whole area was blasted during the Blitz and the school often got bombed. There was so much debris and glass about that it was unsafe, and the boys were moved on to temporary schools. John went to about four different schools, and as a result his education suffered. Ronnie, a little older, suffered less.

From the balcony of the flat the boys could hear the German doodlebugs droning over their heads on their way to targets in the City. They would listen for the engine cut-out, to be followed ten or fifteen seconds later by a crump as the bomb detonated on the ground.

Eventually, the boys were moved out of London altogether to families in Welwyn Garden City in Hertfordshire. Billy and Jimmy, being rather older, were kept together. John and Ronnie were moved to a big farm in the country. The house was filled with people from London. There was no school but they could work on the farm. To them it was like a holiday, something they had never experienced before, but pretty soon they grew to hate the place. John would call up home saying, 'Pick us up, Mum, we don't like it here.'

The Knights were rascals even when they were very young. John and Ronnie hated greens. The old lady used to bring them up to their room by the plateful. Ronnie would wait until she left before chucking them out of the window. The ploy worked well, until one day she found strings of congealed spinach dangling from the trees and bushes in the garden. After that, she didn't really want Ronnie and John there any more. So they were moved on.

Years later, John would take his mother over that way to show her how much it had changed. All the big farms that they knew as kids were broken up, parcelled into new housing estates, not a field in sight.

Ronnie was moved out and went to stay with a couple and their daughter in Carshalton in Surrey. The family was nice but very strict, particularly when it came to bath-time, which Ronnie hated with a vengeance. The couple would fill a tin bath with water in the middle of the room and Ronnie had to get in. He was always embarrassed because the daughter was there.

Before the war ended, the Knights were reunited in their flat in Arcola Street. Soon after, however, Ronnie ended up in hospital with a serious leg infection, so serious it took him three years to recover. The doctors said he had picked up a horse germ while playing in the fields.

While he was being treated, there were two more additions to the family: Patsy, followed by David. There was a bedroom for the four boys, and their baby sister was given her own room.

Meanwhile, John, Ronnie, and Billy were busy building on their reputations as local scallywags. At Arcola Street the family got the blame for everything. Every time they walked in with shopping, the curtains would flicker to see what they had.

Jimmy was the one the younger brothers all wanted to take after. By then he was in his twenties and quite a successful businessman. Ronnie would nick his suits to go to school in. Jimmy was always around, and if anything went really wrong he would come over and sort it out. His younger brothers rarely called for his help. They were determined to show him that they could look after themselves.

John and Ronnie were not only brothers – they were the best of friends. They stuck together because they knew they could trust one another. They were also partners in crime. John's big advantage was that he was smaller than Ronnie, and his wiry frame could easily squeeze through windows and skylights.

So John, with Ronnie's encouragement, started thieving.

John's first 'job' came when he was about twelve. Ronnie asked him if he wanted to climb through a fanlight into a café and open the door, so that he could rifle the till. John got in all right, but couldn't open the door. Then he heard the owner coming down the stairs. So he grabbed the till and climbed back out of the fanlight with it. The two of them made off with three or four pounds – a lot of money then.

Jim was as strict as he could be, but he soon realized that he couldn't handle his errant sons. For one thing, they all got so much bigger than him. He was strong as an ox – he could give them a clump and an argument – but there wasn't much he could do to straighten them out. As the lads grew older, he didn't want to know their business, and he didn't ask any questions. He'd come and bail them out if they were in trouble, and would give them a belt in front of the Law. 'That ain't nothing. You wait until you get home!' he would say. But it was largely for show.

Their poor, long-suffering mother despaired of them all. She was horrified at the way her sons had turned out. Only their baby sister Patsy was as good as gold. She went on to marry an Indian man who had made millions out of the Indian restaurant trade. She would have nothing to do with any of her brothers.

Throughout their teens the Knight brothers were always in trouble with the Law, but John's first serious brush came when, aged around fifteen, he stole an Austin motor car. John had discovered that he could put a hairclip into the side of the door, wiggle it about a bit, and then spring it open. John had a friend with him at the time but the friend wouldn't get in. He kept walking by the side of the car as John drove it slowly down the road. John drove the car around for a few hours but was eventually spotted on account of his erratic driving. He pulled into a cul-de-sac, jumped out, and hid behind a wall, but he was soon found. Meanwhile, he had left the engine running – off the car chugged, smashing into some dustbins at the end of the road.

John was arrested and up before the magistrates in no time. To teach him a lesson they put him into a remand home but, far from putting John back on the straight and narrow, the home simply taught him new tricks. It was the East End equivalent of a Swiss finishing school. John was put on probation for a year, but pretty soon he was back to his old ways.

Because he was always arguing and fighting at school, John's PE master had suggested that he join a boxing club. 'You can fight as much as you want there,' he said. So John did. He and a mate called Roy started going to a club once a week over the other side of Stoke Newington. John never forgot his first fight there. A big fellow called Derek asked him if he wanted to get into the ring with him. It was a set-up. Derek started getting rough with the young novice, so John retaliated in the only way he knew. Big Derek threw his gloves off and climbed out of the ring. 'I'm finished mate,' he said.

'Cor, John, you fucking done him,' said Roy on the way home, laughing. 'He must have thought you was a mug.'

Soon afterwards, John and Roy joined another club, the Repton Club, which was open three or four times a week. Ronnie would often turn up with two young boxers he had met at the Royal Ballroom in Tottenham, who were then beginning to make a name for themselves on the amateur circuit – their names were Ronnie and Reggie Kray. Upstairs, in one corner of the gym, the twins could be found training, doing press-ups and sit-ups, and punching the bags like there was no tomorrow. No one else was up there. Fanatic in their ambition, they were training for a big fight at York Hall.

Although Ronnie tagged along with the Krays, he wasn't really interested in boxing. His forte was always football. In fact, he could have joined the junior squad at Tottenham – but he'd rather have gone down the pub.

Sometimes, after John's training sessions, John and Ronnie would go downstairs and play a game of pool with the Krays. Later, Ronnie would go out with them as they made their social calls. It was the beginning of a strong family friendship – a special relationship – between the Knights and the Krays. That friendship was to prove important.

The Knights got into all sorts of scraps with local gangs, but they usually won out. They had a special trick up their sleeve: they would go for the ringleader. They would watch who did most of the talking, and then John would single him out for a whack. More often than not the leader would make a run for it, and the rest of the gang usually followed, hard on his heels. Through this mixture of cunning and barefisted bravado, John, Ronnie, David and Billy had earned the respect of the circles they moved in. Respect counted for everything in the old ways of the East End. It was your passport and your life-insurance policy all rolled into one.

But the Krays were something else. They played by different rules and knew no limits when it came to terrorizing their opponents. They had set new standards in intimidation. By 1951 the bloodletting between rival teenage gangs in Hackney had achieved national notoriety. A young man had been slashed with a knife and whipped with a motorbike chain, and left lying in a pool of blood in a dark alley. The sixteen-year-old, from a good home, later died in hospital, but there were two witnesses who identified the culprits as the Krays. They were arrested and sent for trial at the Old Bailey, but it never came to court. The witnesses had been threatened, and both refused to testify. The case against the Krays was dismissed through lack of evidence.

It illustrated the level of violence and sophistication any opponents of the Krays had to contend with – and counter – in order to survive. To be included within their circle of friends was therefore a distinct honour.

In late 1952, when the Kray twins were on the run from the army, having absconded from the Royal Fusiliers, it was only natural that they should come knocking on the door of the Knight family. To the Krays, the Knights were like the three wise monkeys: 'See nothing. Hear nothing. Say nothing.' The Krays liked that.

Nellie let them stay for three weeks. She cooked for them and made them cups of tea. The twins would sit either side of the fireplace in their straight-backed chairs, their silhouettes occasionally passing fleetingly across the drawn curtains. They loved Mrs Knight like their own mother, Violet, and would talk to her for hours on end.

They were just biding their time, waiting to be slung out of the army. They had already spent a month in Colchester Prison for desertion and had no intention of ever going back. They were glad of the sanctuary.

In the evenings, when John came home from his work as a scaffolder, they would still be sitting there in the dark, with the curtains drawn.

'Hello, John,' they would say, almost in unison.

'Hello, Ron. Hello, Reggie.'

'Nice day?'

'Yeah, not bad.'

The twins would exchange a few words before getting ready to go out, when all was dark and quiet – they wouldn't go out in daylight in case they were spotted. John would have a wash, get changed, have his dinner, and leave them to it. Later in the evening his brother Ronnie would turn up in his car, which happened to be an old taxicab. The Krays would dive in the back and Ronnie would take them on their rounds: visiting people; fixing things here and there; doing silent deals. Wherever they wanted to go, Ronnie took them.

One thing about the Krays was that they never forgot favours done for them. That was the old code of honour of the East End. They always remembered the Knight family for their straightforward hospitality in what was one of their darkest and most difficult hours. And they were especially fond of Nellie.

But respect was about as far as it went. The Knights never became directly involved with the Krays' business. There was one occasion when Ronnie was asked to help sort out a local gang in North London. He joined in because they were mates, certainly not because he considered himself part of the Krays' entourage of hangers-on.

Instead, the Knight brothers pursued a life of clandestine crime, operating in the shadows of legitimate businesses. John became a magician. He could make lorry-loads of goods disappear overnight. The goods would be sold on to 'fences' and disposed of through shops and markets in Hackney and the East End.

The vanishing trick could involve anything: electrical goods; metal sheeting; you name it, and John could get it. From that came a natural progression into stealing lorries. John got to know his transport well, and that was to become invaluable later on. As time went on he became cleverer and cleverer. The more he did, the more he learned how not to get caught. So, by the time he reached adulthood, John was a very accomplished thief. But he didn't want to be just any old thief. He had ambitions.

Some of the people who ran the fencing operation became the most powerful people around. One of them started money-lending in the clubs and casinos. He would sit at the side, at a reserved table, a holdall full of cash at hand. When the regulars ran out of money he would lend it to them, but he would add on the interest up front. So £300 would turn into £400, to be paid back within the week. He always made sure he was paid back and had no qualms about getting heavy.

From there it was a small step to 'sorting out' protection rackets for local shops and businesses. He would help the shopkeeper by sending his thugs in to deal with the small-time gangs running the rackets. The shopkeeper would be thrilled. 'What can I do for you?' he would say, expecting to have to stump up more protection money. 'Don't worry about it,' came the nonchalant reply.

But nothing is ever for free. Sooner or later there would be payback time. The man would come along with some nicked goods, maybe a couple of fridges or some stereos. He would ask the shopkeeper to buy them at slightly less than wholesale price and put them in the shop, among the legitimate stock.

The punters wouldn't know any different. But that way the fence would get a much higher price for the stolen goods than through a hurried sale in a pub or on a market stall. 'Just a small favour,' he would say. The shopkeeper, of course, would have little choice but to go along with the scam. He knew full well what would happen if he didn't.

John never went down the protection route. Instead, he stuck to the thieving end of the business. He liked to control the world he moved in. Besides it was the culture he had been brought up with. During the war, crime had flourished in the confusion created by endless blackouts and bombings. It was a thieves' paradise. The shortages and rationing created a hungry black market that lingered until the early 1950s. The demand for stolen commodities was insatiable. John sought to satisfy that need. The way of thinking became almost second nature to him. If he saw a vehicle or building with a prize in it he would be thinking about how he could break in. Questions would run through his head. What were the best times? Was it better in the dark or in the daytime? Could people see him? Were there any blind spots? Could you load up a lorry? Did you need a car? If it's a big load, you need a van. So you go and steal a van, load it up, and dump the van later.

These were the skills that no one could teach. John quickly learnt that well-worked-out transport was key to any successful robbery. Instead of stealing cars, a group of them would put some money together to buy a car. It would be used as a 'change-over' after the van or lorry had been stolen. The police had got a lot better at stopping stolen vehicles, so everyone decided to buy a car. A forged tax document was usually put on the windscreen to stop it getting stopped by police. They were very strict on tax in those days.

At the time there were loads of fiddles going with lead, copper, and glass. You could just climb over a yard wall and take a few sacks. People who had jobs in warehouses and yards often had a fiddle going on the side, but they needed someone to sell to. A better way was for them to give the nod to John, and he would steal it on their behalf in return for a cut.

Soon it was lorry-loads of gear – fashion goods, metal

sheeting, electrical – whatever would sell. Radiograms especially would fetch a lot of money. Sometimes John would get together with some of his mates to plan a job: John, Ken, Ted, and Leslie. They would line up the buyers through recommendations, and were told what they would like to buy. It was 'theft to order', and the beginnings of John's own firm. If John needed an extra man to make the firm up he would naturally go to someone who was close to him. That person was invariably his brother Ronnie.

They called it the 'jump-up' routine. They would scour the streets for unattended lorries and vans full of booty. When they found them they would look under the tarpaulin see what was there, then break the cab window, open the door, get in, start it up with a bunch of skeleton keys, and drive it away. Sometimes they did it while the lorries were unloading. Sometimes they waited until the lorries had been parked for the evening outside a bed and breakfast.

The Krays themselves had dabbled in it for a brief time, trying unsuccessfully to break into lorries parked up for the night on some derelict bombsites along the Commercial Road. They quickly decided it wasn't for them. It was small beer. They left the Knights to it and moved on.

£££

By the time of the Coronation in 1953, Jim Knight senior had stopped working for Jinkinson's and had started driving for a local firm of scaffolders. Through that, he got Ronnie a job as a scaffolder.

Ronnie had been seeing June, a girl from the flat downstairs, who he had known since school. He moved into her flat, and when she announced she was pregnant was happy to marry her. They had a daughter, Lorraine.

Ronnie started working for Billy at the yard. Billy was busy selling anything he could lay his hands on – old rags, paper, metal, and wood. His philosophy was simple: everything had a price, and as long as he sold it for a lot more than it cost him, anything was saleable. Ronnie was assigned the task of collecting old, good-quality woolly jumpers from local kids. In return he would give out jam jars with a goldfish or two in them and party balloons. It was rag-and-bone-man work and he hated it, but he now had a young family to support and needed the money.

A few years later, while June was expecting their second child, Ronnie was jailed for fifteen months for receiving stolen goods. But by then his marriage to June was on the rocks and he had started seeing Barbara Windsor, then a rising star of West End musicals.

Ronnie served his time in Brixton and Wandsworth Prisons, and was released in October 1960. Waiting for him at the prison gates were Barbara and his brother John. Both had arrived separately and without the other's knowledge – John in his car and Barbara in a cab. Barbara was certain that John was waiting to take Ronnie back to June, but it was not to be the case. Ronnie went over and had a word with him before getting in the cab with Barbara. It signified the end of his marriage to June, who now had a son, Gary.

Barbara soon became part of Ronnie's extended family – for better or worse. Early one August morning the following year, after a night out at the theatre, they were woken up by the Robbery Squad banging on the front door. The flat was turned over and Ronnie was arrested and charged with the armed robbery of £8,000 from a power station in Lots Road, Chelsea. Jimmy, as always, came to the rescue. He found Ronnie a lawyer, and in January 1962 he was acquitted, largely thanks to a brilliant young female barrister.

John, meanwhile, had put together a fledgling criminal enterprise. Between themselves, the firm had hired a couple of yards and lock-ups in false or 'moody' names where stolen vans and lorries could be hidden until their cargo of goods were sold. The rental of the yards and lock-ups was deliberately made as complex as possible so that the real owner could always deny that he had anything to do with the stolen goods. The stolen transport was 'recycled' and sold on through a chain of second-hand dealers stretching across the country, so that it too couldn't be traced.

But not everything went smoothly. Around 1961 John's firm

stole a lorry-load of electrical goods – wooden radiograms and the like – valued at £100,000. The load was worth around £25,000 on the black market – in those days a small fortune. As usual, the firm already had a buyer lined up. The stolen lorry was parked outside the man's premises in Holloway. Suddenly, the buyer got cold feet. He phoned John up. 'I can't shift the goods,' he said. 'Can you come and take the lorry away?'

So, when it was nice and dark, John went over to Holloway to pick up the lorry and drive it to a commercial lorry park in Seven Sisters Road. Little did he know that he was followed to the lorry park by police, led by an inspector called Durrell. At Seven Sisters John managed to park the lorry in a good spot, then one of the coppers came over to talk to him.

'Can we have a word with you?' he asked.

'Why? I ain't done nothing wrong.'

John could see that he was about to be arrested. The copper knew him by name, and knew what he was hiding. So John chinned him and was on his way. He ran up the ramp and over the railway line, narrowly missing being hit by a train. He jumped over the fence and cut through a back garden. Spying an old couple having their tea in their kitchen, he tapped loudly on the window.

'Excuse me,' he said, as they opened the back door. 'Someone's after me. Can I come through?' Before they could even answer, he had shot down the hall and through the front door. He tore off down the street and jumped on a bus at Stamford Hill.

The police were looking for John for months. In those days they didn't have a go at your wife or family. They would always just ask a few polite questions: 'Where is your son? Hasn't he come home yet?' These days, they'd nick the whole family and pull them all in until they had an answer.

John later found out that his potential buyer had been caught and couldn't sell the load, so he had grassed John's firm to the police, thus setting John up to save himself. John could well imagine the scene. 'Come on. Start telling us some names or we're gonna nick ya.' The man had a wife and young daughter, so John couldn't blame him.

Worse was to come. Six months later, a job involving a lorry-load of stolen nickel went badly wrong. Nickel was expensive and the load was worth around £180,000. On the black market they would have got maybe £50,000 for it.

The stolen nickel was stowed in 500-gallon drums on a big lorry. John's firm had rented a yard in Stepney under an alias, and the drums had to be offloaded from the side of the lorry and into a small warehouse in the yard. Opposite the warehouse was a block of flats and a bank.

John knew they had to be very careful hanging about the yard – once you had unloaded something like that you had to keep away for a while. But in this instance, his strategy backfired. Some nosy parker in the flats opposite noticed there was no activity in the yard. She thought it was odd and started wondering what kind of business would rent a yard and then leave it alone for days and days. One day she saw a different face there, so that made her more suspicious still. She soon decided that the yard wasn't being used for business at all and rang the police.

The police climbed over the fence, saw the stolen nickel, and very likely said to themselves, 'All right, don't touch it, let's wait for the gang to come and collect it.' They watched and waited for someone to appear.

Sure enough, they did. John's firm soon found a buyer and went down to the yard to collect the nickel. As soon as they started loading up the drums, they were surrounded by the policemen. John made a run for it. He climbed through a window, ran down an alley, and into a pub on the corner of the street. At the rear of the pub there was a gents' outside toilet and John ducked in there to hide, but someone saw him go in.

The officers piled in after him. 'You're the one we want,' they said, cornering him by the urinals. They got his arms behind his back and took him back to the inspector, waiting in his Jaguar by the yard.

'I'm going to hand you over to one of my men,' said the inspector. The biggest policeman there took John back into the yard, and while the rest of them looked the other way, gave John a clump on the chin. It was tit for tat. There was nothing

John could say about it. They had got their own back, and if he had complained to their guv'nor they would have said they were only defending themselves. Anyway, in those days, you took your punishment like a man. It was all part and parcel of being a professional criminal.

John got eighteen months for the electrical goods and three years for the nickel – four and a half years altogether – to be served concurrently. He was put up by the police as the guv'nor. The rest of his firm got eighteen months. He learnt a few things from that little episode. One was that policemen could be very vindictive indeed. 'There's nothing else you can do with them, they are policemen, they'll get you again,' he told Ronnie afterwards. 'They can slap you around the earhole, but if you hit them back they don't like it. You can't turn round and tell the judge, "He hit me first," can you?'

In 1963, while John was inside, the Great Train Robbery took place. It was the talk of the landing, not just because of the stiff sentences eventually handed down, but because everyone wanted to get lucky. John was envious. 'I want to do something like that,' he said to himself.

John's spell inside wasn't so much a punishment as further education. He met a lot of the old-school villains there, learnt new tricks, and made new contacts in the criminal underworld. It also made him resolute. John vowed not to get caught in future.

In March 1964 Ronnie married Barbara, the woman he was by now crazy about, at Tottenham Registry Office. The wedding day was a disaster: it rained cats and dogs, and the reception amounted to a couple of drinks in the nearest pub. The honeymoon had to be postponed because Barbara was due to make her debut on the set the following day for *Carry on Spying.* A few weeks later, when the couple did eventually set out on their honeymoon to Madeira, that, too, was nothing short of a disaster – a delayed plane, a ferry from hell, and a 'bridal suite' not much bigger than the creaky double bed. For the majority of the next ten days it rained. Still, they loved each other.

Ronnie soon jacked in Billy's job and briefly went into the

scaffolding business with his own yard in Harvey Street, in De Beauvoir Town, just the other side of the canal from Jinkinson's sawmill where he used to play all those years ago. The legitimate front was lending it out, but the real money was in nicking it. But scrap and scaffolding weren't really Ronnie's scene. For one thing, it didn't suit his image. He tried his hand unsuccessfully at singing. And then, when the chance came to go into the club business with an old mate, Micky Regan, he jumped at it. Together they bought a run-down club in Charing Cross Road called the Artistes and Repertoire Club. The owner was badly in debt and was prepared to sell at a snip.

They did the place up and Ronnie fronted it. He brought in live music sessions in the afternoons. Pretty soon, the A&R Club, as it was renamed, was the haunt of many a rising sixties star. It became a melting pot, with rock musicians rubbing shoulders with actors from the *Carry On* films, big-time villains, and off-duty members of the Old Bill.

Ronnie's move into the club scene changed his life. There was to be no more humping scaffolding poles around, no more hands covered in thick engine oil. The West End suited him to a tee. He had always been the more gregarious, partying sort, while John had always hung back, happy to do things in his own quiet, unassuming way. John had never been that keen on the West End. Besides, John had to get up early in the morning to run his businesses, and he missed his early-morning training sessions.

John had got parole for the last nine months of his sentence and was given a job working for the local council. After that had ended, he was on his own. Things had changed dramatically. Everyone he knew from his old firm had grown up, got married, got on with their lives, and settled down with their own businesses.

Soon after his release, the first of a series of family tragedies struck. Some years before, his older brother, Billy, had gone into the motor trade and had bought a breakers yard just off Rectory Road in Stoke Newington. Called Heatherly Street Breakers, the yard backed on to the railway line. It was just around the corner from Blonde Carol's flat, where Reggie Kray famously did away with Jack 'The Hat' McVitie. Legend has it that they rolled up McVitie's body in a carpet and put it by the side of the railway line close to Billy's yard first. The body was never found. Freddie Foreman, a close friend of Ronnie's from south of the river, helped dispose of it.

Like John and Ronnie, Billy too had had his fair share of fights. One time he was out drinking with the two brothers and some of their mates, among them an old 'face' called Buller Ward, who came out of Haggerston, just down the road from Dalston. Ward was a boxer.

After a couple of hours boozing something was said. It was corrected, but Buller seemed to want to argue. Billy got outside the door, Buller chinned him and he tumbled down the iron staircase just like in a film. There were barrels down there in the yard and the two were crashing about among them, arguing for well over an hour. Billy got badly mashed in the head. No one won but everyone agreed that it was a good fight.

Although Billy's business was prospering, Billy himself was showing signs that all was not well and was beginning to act completely out of character. Billy was always a hard worker, up at six, ready at seven thirty, and open for business at eight, but suddenly he couldn't get up in the mornings. Mary, his devoted wife, was frightened. So one day she got John and Ronnie to drive over and take a look at him.

Billy himself was worried. He told them he couldn't drive properly any more. They thought he was having them on, until he asked John to put his Vauxhall Cresta away in the garage for him. He couldn't get it in without scraping the sides. John saw the gouge marks in the paint for himself, and then he knew that Billy was showing signs of a serious complaint.

Billy knew he was going to die. He asked John to take over his yard for him and give his wife a decent wage. John gladly agreed and, for a few years, used to take Mary's wages round every Friday afternoon. The whole family rallied round. David, the youngest brother, worked at the yard for a while too, along with Billy Hickson, a long-time family friend.

They found out later that it was a tumour on the brain. The doctors did what they could but in those days that wasn't much.

It was all very primitive compared with today. John remembered seeing Billy with his hair shaved off, ghost-white, his face drawn and hollow. Within three years Billy was dead. John and Ronnie often wondered whether it was the fight with Buller among the beer barrels that had triggered off Billy's illness.

In 1969, the council came along and put a compulsory purchase order on Billy's yard. They wanted to build flats for a new generation of immigrants.

After the compulsory purchase order, David went on to set up his own scaffolding business with Billy Hickson. They called themselves HK Scaffolding and moved to Jimmy's yard in Ridley Road. By now David had settled down, was married, and had a young child.

Jimmy had bought his scrap yard, which ran from one end of Ridley Road to the other, on a ninety-nine-year lease. The place was huge. He had sheds galore, smelters for lead, a weighbridge for lorries, and his very own railway siding. He had a car park going at one end, too. He was never the book-reading sort. Year in, year out, he worked every day in that yard. There he was, come rain or shine, in overalls, filthy dirty, mucking in with everything. He would man the crane and the forklift himself to load the railway wagons with scrap metal to send down to the Ford works at Dagenham.

Jimmy was very self-contained. His wife Maisey would help him out in the yard but he didn't need anyone else to work for him. He worked long hours because that was how he had been brought up. But he didn't really have to.

He was different from John and Ronnie in other ways. He didn't yearn for the material trappings of power. He wasn't worried about status symbols and, in the old days, he'd drive anything. He'd go and have a drink or a meal in an old lorry if necessary. He would park the lorry without a care in the world, and without any thought as to what other people might think.

John, meanwhile, went on the lookout for another yard, and eventually took over a repair garage in Southgate called Mills & Miller. He renamed it M&M Bodyworks. He thought M&M had a nice Masonic ring to it (MM stands for Master

Mason), but whether that helped him bring in business, who is to say? It probably did.

John was now running a legitimate business, but still he couldn't resist the urge to duck and dive. 'I'll charge you £300 if it goes through the books, and £200 if you pay me cash,' he would say to his prospective customers. They nearly always paid in cash.

In May 1970, a second tragedy struck the Knight family. David was murdered.

The episode was to have far-reaching consequences. For one thing, it confirmed to the Knights what they had long suspected – that the police were out to get them, whatever the cost.

It had started when John had a falling out with a local 'face' out of Hoxton called Jimmy Isaacs. Words were exchanged, then blows when John gave Isaacs a 'clump'. One evening David was sitting in a pub in the Angel, Islington, having a quiet drink with Billy, when Isaacs came up to him looking for an argument. 'Your brother Johnny took a liberty with me the other day,' he said.

David just smiled. 'If John's done you any wrong then you go and sort it out with him. It's nothing to do with me.'

But Isaacs wasn't looking for an answer to his question. He moved to hit David but Billy hit him first. That was the signal for four others to join in. They hit David with ashtrays and bottles – whatever came to hand. David was in a bloody mess by the time they had finished.

His wife was in tears. Ronnie started to make a few enquiries and soon found out what had happened. 'Look, we've got to sort this out now,' he said to John, 'before it all gets out of hand.' Together they went to Isaacs's favourite haunt, the Latin Quarter Club, in Soho, with David and Billy Hickson in tow.

Isaacs wasn't there, but Billy Stanton, who ran the club, came up to Ronnie to shake his hand. Stanton had been there the night David got hurt. Before Ronnie could respond, Hickson flew off the handle. Ronnie pushed him up against the wall. 'What you doin', you prat?' he said. But by then it was too late. Everyone was up on their feet.

The barman of the club was a man named Alfredo Zomparelli,

nicknamed 'Italian Tony'. He too had taken part in the earlier attack on David. Now he dived towards the kitchen and came back brandishing a large knife. As David tried to get past, Zomparelli stabbed him twice in the back, the long blade piercing his body. The second lunge of the knife went straight into David's heart.

John had gone downstairs to the toilet and missed the start of hostilities. He came up the stairs to find David staggering towards him along the corridor, obviously hurt, and Zomparelli wielding a knife. He grabbed a stool to defend himself. Then David slumped to the floor. John and Ronnie could see David was badly injured. Ronnie made his way over to him, knelt down, and cradled David's head in his arms. David couldn't speak. Blood was pouring out of his chest. He was dying.

Pretty soon the police had arrived. David was taken by ambulance to hospital, accompanied by Ronnie and John, escorted by police officers. The doctors worked for over an hour to save David's life but to no avail. Ronnie left the hospital in a rage. He vowed to find Zomparelli and kill him.

Before Ronnie could find him, Zomparelli had fled London. He had dumped his bloodstained clothes in a locker in Leicester Square, boarded the ferry to France at Dover, and was on his way back to Italy. Three weeks later, however, he turned himself in at Heathrow Airport, and in November 1970 he was put on trial for murder. He pleaded guilty to manslaughter, saying that he had acted in self-defence. He got four years for manslaughter – but was out after two and a half.

Meanwhile, Ronnie, John, and Billy Hickson were charged with affray. Hickson got a twelve-month suspended sentence but the jury couldn't make up its mind over John and Ronnie. The judge ordered a retrial; the prosecution offered no further evidence, so they were both acquitted. 'Be careful in future,' the judge told them. They were seething at the perceived injustice of it all. Later Isaacs got another clump from Ronnie for starting it all.

After his release from prison in 1974, Zomparelli started a travel agency in Frith Street, Soho. He could often be found playing pinball in an amusement arcade around the corner in

Old Compton Street. In September that year he was shot dead – a bullet to the head and three to the chest while working the flippers. At his inquest in March 1975, the verdict was 'unlawful killing by a person or persons unknown'.

The shooting bore all the hallmarks of a contract killing. The press went wild with speculation, claiming that the Italian Mafia was involved, and that Zomparelli was involved with all manner of rackets, ranging from drugs and prostitution to amusement arcades and imported second-hand cars. But the theory that the police homed in on was that it was a revenge killing, and Ronnie Knight was their chief suspect. He was taken in for questioning and he told them that, yes, he wanted Zomparelli dead, but someone had beaten him to it. The police had nothing on Ronnie other than motive, so he was released. And that was the end of the matter, or so Ronnie thought.

David's murder took a heavy toll on the family. Their mother never got over it and ever after there was a sadness in her eyes. Their father had died not long after David's death. It was a sudden and incomprehensible death. As his children recall, he had caught himself on a rosebush and a thorn had got stuck in the back of his neck. Pretty soon a bump started coming up. He went to hospital and they said it was a virulent form of cancer. There was little they could do but watch in horror as the cancer spread.

The day before he died, he called them all together. 'I'm popping off,' he said. 'Keep your chins up, look after yourselves, and behave.' One by one, he solemnly shook their hands. 'Take it easy, boys,' he said. 'I'm finished.' When he died he left £700 in an old coat to look after Mum. 'If anything happens to me just feed it to your mother when she needs it,' he told them.

£££

Things were never the same after the spate of deaths in the family. The way that the police had handled the Zomparelli episode made both John and Ronnie very bitter. Nevertheless, the three Knight brothers were doing well in their respective, but very different, businesses.

John and Ronnie had started spending a lot of time abroad.

Between them, they had bought a villa in Spain. They called it El Limonar because they had planted lemon trees in the grounds.

Jimmy, who had made a fortune through his yard at Ridley Road, had bought a large mansion in Stanmore from the Page family, of aeronautical fame, friends of Scott of the Antarctic. He decided to turn it first into a restaurant and function room, and later into a nightclub called the Limes. The function rooms soon became popular for local bar mitzvahs, and at weekends the nightclub was a roaring success. The place could hold 3,000 people. There was nothing like it for miles around.

Life for the three brothers was rosy when, in January 1980, Ronnie was again arrested on suspicion of the murder of Zomparelli. It came completely out of the blue, in the form of a dawn raid on his flat in Hendon Hall Court that he shared with Barbara.

John, too, was arrested over the murder, and was accused of supplying a brand-new shooter to Ronnie so that he could have Zomparelli shot. The police took all six of John's family's passports. John told them to write down the day when he was supposed to have given the gun to Ronnie.

They did. Then they opened all the passports. John was away on that date with the whole family. 'There's five witnesses there, including my wife,' he said. 'What are you going to do about that?'

The incident officer looked at him with a scowl as he slid the passports across the counter. 'There's your passports back,' he said. 'You'd better go.'

'No,' said John. 'I want to know where my brother is.'

'Your brother is being charged with murder.'

'I want to see him. Where is he?'

'West End Central.'

'I'm going round there.'

Outside the station, John's friend Terry Perkins was waiting in a car for him. The two of them immediately drove to West End Central, but when they arrived all the doors to the station had been locked. John went up to the main vehicle gate and rang and rang the bell until, finally, an officer came out to see him.

'What d'you want?'

'My brother's in there. I want to see him.'

'If you don't fuck off I'll nick you,' came the curt reply.

Later that night John rang up the station and was told that Ronnie had indeed been charged with murder and was on his way to Brixton Prison. Alleged murderers on remand were routinely incarcerated in the prison hospital wing in Brixton. They were considered far too dangerous to be allowed to mix with ordinary prisoners.

After two weeks on remand in Brixton, Ronnie was released on £250,000 bail, organized by Barbara.

'There were some right nutters in that hospital wing,' Ronnie told John afterwards. In the mornings, one of them would go to the washroom sinks with a long tube of shaving soap. When he had finished shaving with it he would stick it up his bum. 'He was a big bloke, mad as a hatter,' said Ronnie. The screws wouldn't let any other prisoner near him, particularly when he was shaving.

At West End Central police station, Ronnie had been interrogated for hours. He had been shown a photograph of a clean-shaven man called George Bradshaw. He told the police he didn't recognize him. It was only later that he was told that George Bradshaw was the alias of a gangland killer he knew as 'Maxie' Piggott. He regularly turned up at Ronnie's club in Soho with another man called Alfie Gerard and his son Nicky – only then, Maxie had a great big drooping moustache.

Bradshaw, alias Piggott, had just been sentenced to life for the murder of Zomparelli, but he had turned supergrass and had told on more than a hundred criminals in the hope of getting his sentence reduced. He claimed that Ronnie had set him up with a shooter and put up a grand for the murder, and that Nicky Gerard had pulled the trigger.

Ronnie told the police that, while Zomparelli was away doing time for manslaughter, his woman had shacked up with Bradshaw. When he got out, she went back to Zomparelli, so Bradshaw, consumed with jealousy, shot Zomparelli. The police didn't believe a word of it. During the summer, Ronnie had his bail rescinded and found himself back in prison, with a trial date set for November that year.

During the trial the prosecution produced another witness, a man called Gerald Knight, who claimed that he had overheard Ronnie and Bradshaw plotting the murder in the A&R Club. Ronnie knew Gerald well. He had ripped Ronnie off over a property deal by handing over a dud cheque for £7,000. Luckily for him, Barbara was able to find the cheque and prove it, so the prosecution's witness was discredited. 'I can't talk no more. Get me out of court,' he said.

The case was on the verge of collapse, but the judge insisted that Gerald's evidence be kept in, even though he had lied. In the end, the judge let it go to the jury. Ronnie was cleared, largely thanks to Barbara. But he was sure that, ever since that date, the police had it in for him.

John had sat through the entire case. He knew that the jury would find Ronnie not guilty. He could see the look on their faces. They were wondering why on earth this man was here, standing before them. To John's mind, it was yet further confirmation that the police were out to break the Knight family at all costs.

£££

Looking back over the years, John could see that he had come a long way from that ramshackle house in Hoxton. Now, he was in his forties, married to Diane, his second wife, whom he had known since childhood. He had four children around him, and wealth far beyond his dreams. He had made it. With the dust from the robbery settled, John was looking forward to leading the life of a country squire. He could devote his time to his family, his beautiful house, and, perhaps, invest some of the robbery money in some more Spanish property.

The profits of crime would be ploughed into legitimate businesses. John had done it many times before. Now his main concern was to get that cash out of the ground and over to the relative safety of Spain. To do that, he decided to enlist the help of his oldest, most trustworthy, friend, his brother Ronnie.

6

ARBOUR SQUARE

The caller seemed genuine enough, a man, perhaps middle-aged. What you might call a Concerned Citizen.

'I just wanted to tell you about something I saw,' he told the duty officer. 'It struck me as a bit odd.'

'Go on.'

'I'm not sure if I'm doing the right thing by telling you this . . .'

'It's all right. This is all strictly confidential. We don't need to know your name or anything.'

'Well, it's like this, you see,' said the caller. 'I was walking down the high street with my wife when I saw one of them Security Express vans drive by, really fast like. In fact, so fast it nearly knocked me and the wife over.'

The officer tried to stifle a sigh. He knew what was coming next.

'Could it have been the robbers?' asked the caller, in all earnestness.

'Security Express has lots of vans, all over the country, sir,' the officer politely told the caller. 'It was probably a genuine van, perhaps driving a little too fast.'

'Oh. Yes, well, I thought it might have been the robbers. You never know, do you?' said the caller. 'I just wanted to be helpful, so that you can catch those awful people. Have you caught them yet?'

'No, but thanks for your call anyway,' said the officer.

He replaced the handset, put down his pencil, and stared at his pad. He was amazed at just how many similar calls he had received from people who had merely spotted a Security Express van. Then there were the calls from those claiming to have personally seen the robbers, who would usually turn out to be bored housewives suspicious of their neighbours' antics in the garden shed. In addition, they had received hundreds of well-meaning calls from mediums offering to use their psychic powers to find the robbers. He only wished it was that simple.

Most of the calls would turn out to be red herrings. Some sounded completely batty – one caller had even claimed that the money was stashed in a well-known East End pub called the Axe. Many calls were from lonely old-age pensioners who wanted to have a natter about how bad crime was in this day and age. Nevertheless, all the callers had to be carefully listened to, just in case there was a grain of information there that would move the enquiry along.

It needed all the help it could get. Admittedly it was early days, but the team was flailing around in the dark, without even a match to see the way forward. As swiftly as they had arrived, the robbers had melted back into the underworld without leaving so much as a trace. Sometimes the mediums' offers were sorely tempting.

All the information coming in from the general public was logged, together with information from informers, contacts, other police units, and from sheer door-to-door legwork. Everything had to be laboriously written out by hand on index cards. For different types of information there were different-sized cards: motor vehicles would be recorded on small cards; people on larger cards; events and incidents on larger cards still. All the cards were given numbers so that they could be cross-referenced with other cards. To maintain the system was an enormous task. Several officers devoted large parts of their working day to it.

In addition, the office would keep a book with phone messages in it from the several officers taking calls from the general public. The pad was in triplicate. One copy went to the message recipient, one to the office managers, and one to the bosses. Every message was either 'actioned' or marked 'no action'. If it was 'actioned' it would be assigned an 'action number'. The thin piece of paper would be secured on a pad with two metal spikes at the top. When the pad was full of messages it would be sealed with a brass clip and filed away.

As the 'action' progressed and was dealt with, the officer assigned to it wrote it up, detailing exactly what was done and when. The actions themselves would, of course, generate yet more index cards. In those days the Flying Squad had no computers. Officers worked intuitively, relying on their own initiative and on well-organized files to reveal the leads and connections that were needed.

It was all rather laborious and cumbersome compared with today. But that was the way things had been done for the best part of a century. In 1984 the powerful minicomputers needed to run a relational database were expensive and occupied a room. 'HOLMES', the Met's computerized enquiry system, which now logs all incidents and allows detailed database searches, was barely out of its planning stage.

With no computers, a large and complex enquiry needed an efficient and disciplined office manager to keep on top of it all. Thankfully, the Dirty Dozen had one, in the shape of Detective Sergeant Bernie Butler. Bernie was thorough, precise, and exceptionally well organized, and thus handy with the paperwork. He was also very bright and easy-going.

Assisting him was Detective Constable Jim Keeling. Apart from helping Bernie run the office efficiently, Jim handled everything relating to the courts, particularly witnesses.

Jim called himself 'the head of intelligence' in a typically self-deprecating manner, and he kept them all sane with a never-ending stream of humorous incidents and comments, which became collectively known as 'Keelingisms'. He came out with so many that the Squad kept a book of them, which sadly has been mislaid over the years.

From the very start of the enquiry, Jim had them in fits of laughter. 'Guv'nor,' he said during one particularly gruesome briefing, 'let's go and get a hundred warrants for all the villains in London and I think we'll crack it.' Commander Cater couldn't tell if Jim was being serious or joking. But then nobody could ever tell with Jim.

A typical Keelingism was the time Jim paid a social visit to an officer by the name of Bob Sayers, a forbidding fellow with a big black beard. Jim was in the kitchen, staring out of the window.

'Is that your greenhouse then, Bob?' he asked.

'No,' Bob replied, completely straight-faced.

'Is it not?'

'No. What it is, you see, is that my neighbour is a mad-keen gardener and he wanted more space to grow his vegetables. So he asked if he could put his greenhouse in my garden. I said, of course you can!'

'Why, that's the most neighbourly gesture I have ever heard of,' said Jim.

Nobody remembers quite how it came about, but it was during the enquiry that another incident involving Jim became the stuff of station lore. He had found a teenager hiding in the loft of a house he was searching. The boy, who happened to be black, was there, as the cliché goes, with no good reason, so Jim took him down to the station for further questioning.

He was booking him in when he noticed a small silver ampoule on a chain around his neck. 'What's that?' he asked suspiciously. He snatched it from around the teenager's neck and proceeded to unscrew the top. The teenager watched with mounting horror as Jim unceremoniously tipped the contents, a fine, greyish powder, on to the table. 'Drugs!' exclaimed Jim.

The teenager burst into tears. 'It's my mother's ashes,' he sobbed.

Jim nearly died of embarrassment. 'I'm so sorry, lad,' he said. He scraped up the ashes strewn on the desk as reverently as he could, and tipped them back into the silver ampoule. 'You can go now,' he said.

Then there was the time when Jim told everyone about his fight with a hole-in-the-wall cash machine. He had gone shopping with his wife down Ilford High Street when suddenly he decided that he wanted to buy a lawnmower. So he went to withdraw some cash from the bank.

Jim explained at great length what happened next. 'I goes to the Midland Bank, I'm in a great big queue and then it's my turn. I get my card out and I put it in, and all of a sudden this thing goes shloonk. It all cuts off and won't open up.

'I had to go and use my credit card to buy the lawnmower,' he said indignantly. 'Two days later I got a right 'orrible letter from the bank manager, asking me to refrain from using my library ticket in the cash machine.'

One of Jim's biggest idiosyncrasies was his obsession with the Fats Domino song 'Blueberry Hill'. The obsession lasted for some months, but with Jim the song always took the form of a one-liner: 'I've found my thrill . . . on Blueberry Hill . . . On Blueberry Hill,' and so on. And on, and on, and on. And on.

Very soon the rest of the office cottoned on to Jim's little ditty. And everywhere Jim went, the one-liner would start up, beginning as a gentle background hum. Whenever Jim walked into the pub, it wasn't so much 'Hello Jim', as 'I've found my thrill . . .'

As the enquiry dragged on the office couldn't be manned all the time, so sometimes Jim used to leave messages on the answering machine so that people could know the results of some lead or other, or the times when they had to be somewhere in the morning. One morning Jim had to leave a message for someone coming in later that day. Jim's message came out quite clearly but in the background one could just make out the rest of the crew humming 'On Blueberry Hill'.

Jim may have given the appearance of office clown, but few doubted his detective skills. He was a good, old-fashioned copper at heart. Underneath that quirky sense of humour, he was deadly serious. Although he could take a joke, he would always make sure that the answering-machine tape was wiped clean, ready for the next message.

£££

By now it was May 1983. The enquiry had been moved from its temporary home in City Road police station to Arbour Square, a small station right in the heart of the East End. Shortly after the move, many of the officers who had been assigned from the Central Squads to help out with the enquiry in its early days were moved back to New Scotland Yard. They said goodbye in typical style with a lavish Chinese meal and a party.

With so many officers on the case, all of them working in different rooms, things had grown a bit fragmented. Small cliques had developed. With the departure of the Central Squads the atmosphere was quieter and less fraught. But still the pressure was on to solve the largest cash robbery in British history. The actual loss in cash and cheques was still in dispute. Security Express's loss adjusters said the total loss, including cheques, amounted to £6,464,768.52. However, one of Peter's officers, Detective Sergeant Geoff Cameron, made up his own schedule, based on what the thirty-six vault customers had told him. He made the total loss to be £6,375,205.91.

Whatever the precise figure, Commander Cater was becoming more and more restless. He was getting a lot of stick from the press. The investigation had had some success. One person had been arrested for handling £1 notes from the robbery, and they had recovered the McEvoys' cache of weapons in South London. But no one had been arrested for the Security Express robbery itself. Cater needed results – and fast.

The pressure from above prompted him to come down one day to Arbour Square to wave a stick at them all. He gathered a few of the team together around a desk and showed them a signature on a driver's licence, which, he was convinced, was meaningful to the enquiry.

'Can't you see it?' he said, exasperated.

The men gathered around him honestly couldn't. They just looked at him blank-faced, while he ranted and raved about the significance of the signature. Afterwards they all trooped off down to the pub, while Cater stayed behind with Peter. 'They are all zombies, aren't they?' he said.

'The boys are on the case and they know what they are talking about,' Peter replied.

They walked together across the road to the pub to join the others. There, Simon, who was a keen parachutist, was recruiting some volunteers for a charity jump. With the aid of a stepladder borrowed from behind the bar, he was demonstrating to the great amusement of everyone the art of the forward roll. It was essential training for would-be parachutists. He jumped off the stepladder just as Cater came through the door of the bar and directly into his flight path. Simon landed squarely on Cater, knocking him down to the floor.

Cater never did have much of a sense of humour.

After that Simon got some T-shirts made up with 'The Flying Zombies' emblazoned on the front.

The Peacock, the pub across the road from the station, did well out of its association with Peter's squad. In fact, it did so well that the landlord was able to build an extension and a second bar. The new bar became the squad's second office and was known for some reason as the 'Wilton Bar'.

The Portuguese man behind the bar was from Goa. He was fascinated with Peter's work. 'I'd love to do what you do,' he would often say to Peter. He showed so much enthusiasm that eventually Peter said, 'Why don't you join up?' He did, and he made a first-class detective.

Apart from their shared love of detective-work, Peter had one other thing in common with the man behind the bar, which sparked many a lively conversation. Peter, too, had spent his childhood in India, although in a different part and under very different circumstances.

£££

Peter was born in 1940 at a British Army base in India called Deolali, not far from Bombay. Deolali was also home to an army sanatorium where sick soldiers would be sent to recover while awaiting transfer back to England. The wait could be interminably dull and was enough to push even the sanest people over the edge. From that came the expression to 'go doolally', meaning to go mad.

Peter's father was an army officer and had been posted to India in 1939, at the outbreak of the Second World War. Peter was the second child to come along, closely followed by Victor and Anne. His eldest sister, Edith, had been born in England just before they had left.

He never had particularly fond memories of India. Life seemed to be one big round of jabs and vaccinations, which sometimes resulted in several weeks of wearing his arm in a sling. The family was moved from place to place: he hardly stayed in one place for longer than six months, and was constantly changing schools – sometimes he had to be taken on as a boarder because there were no English schools close enough to home. It was always a new environment, and often very lonely. And he wasn't getting the kind of attention he would have received at a school in England. As a result, his schooling suffered somewhat.

Then there were the animals: the constant sounds of insects, snakes, and lizards rustling around on the verandas outside the tin-roofed classrooms, in the grass, and in the trees and bushes. Once he went to school and had to suffer no lunch, because it had been snatched from his hands by some kind of eagle zooming in from above the trees. It taught him a valuable lesson: to be on his guard at all times. Especially during playtime.

Peter was still only very young, but in 1947 he realized that life in India was changing. He sensed the mounting anxieties of his parents as India threw off the yoke of empire. His father was by then a captain, but from what Peter can remember he spent most of his days in the officers' mess. He was invariably brought home at night in a staff car by the troops from his regiment.

In 1947 India gained independence. The British Army was out. The long journey by train to Bombay, and the agonizing two- or three-week wait for a boat to take them back to England, was a frightening time for his parents. When finally the magnificent *Empress of Scotland* arrived in port it was a relief for everyone. The luxury liner with its three large funnels and open promenade deck had been requisitioned for troop duties at the start of the war. She had originally been called the *Empress of Japan*, but after Pearl Harbor she had been renamed on Churchill's explicit orders.

Peter lost all his marbles on that boat coming back from India. Who would ever have believed you would lose your marbles on deck because the liner was swaying from side to side? Of course, most of the marbles rolled overboard.

They arrived in Liverpool, and Peter never forgot the long

journey for the family down to the West Country, where his parents came from. The family stayed at an uncle's pub in Chard in Somerset for several months, while his father waited for his papers to come through. The four young children all promptly contracted chicken pox. They had no natural immunity and suffered really badly.

The war had ended some three years previously, but the country was still in a state of turmoil. The destruction and ruination caused by the air raids was everywhere to be seen, and many basic foods were still rationed. People were sombrely and wearily rebuilding their lives. It was a very different place from the England that his parents had left in 1939.

The family moved to Yeovil, a thriving market town set in the beautiful Somerset countryside. The town boasted a fine fourteenth-century stone church with a large, square tower, a bustling marketplace, and a lively football club. Its somewhat run-down historic centre owed its fortunes to the medieval cloth-making industry that had, however, gone into rapid decline in the eighteenth century.

The town had managed to avoid the levels of destruction wreaked on some of its neighbours in the infamous German 'Baedeker' raids, which had been inspired by a series of tourist guidebooks on historic English towns. In the aftermath of the war the military and aviation industries now played an important part in the town's economy, which serviced nearby RAF, naval and army bases. Nevertheless, the pace of life in the town remained slow and leisurely. Just like India.

Peter's father stayed for a short time in the army as a driving instructor at nearby Houndstone Camp, but then he was made redundant. He had been in the army for eighteen years and, like many others, found it very difficult to make the transition to Civvie Street. There was no help given to those leaving the army to enable them to adjust to life in the outside world, but that didn't stop the second half of Peter's family coming along: Sue, Chris, and the youngest of all, Kevin.

All seven children were schooled in Yeovil, and it was while at primary school that he met his childhood sweetheart Valerie. They soon became friends, and courted throughout their teens.

Peter was the oldest boy in the family and went to Yeovil Grammar School, soon to be followed by Victor and Christopher. At school, Peter was a late developer; he was always the smallest in his class and being a 'W' he sat at the back of the class as well. Needless to say, his grammar-school days weren't particularly fulfilling, but he did reasonably well. He only wished he had grown as quickly as some of his fellow classmates.

His childhood could not have been further removed from that of John and Ronnie Knight.

7

BROTHER TO BROTHER

According to Ronnie Knight, his first involvement with the Security Express robbery was when his brother John turned up at the penthouse flat he shared with Barbara Windsor in Hendon Hall Court, with a brown-leather holdall stuffed full of cash.

Ronnie knew all about the raid from the radio reports, and when the robbery went off he had a sneaking suspicion that his brother might have had a hand in it. But he wasn't sure. For some weeks he'd been phoning John's house to find that he was never in, with no explanation offered. 'Where was he, then?' he thought to himself. 'Why doesn't he want to speak to me?' He was beginning to take it personally.

Then one evening, a few days after the robbery, John called him up out of the blue. He sounded urgent. 'You on your own, Ronnie?'

'Yeah.'

'Babs away?'

'Yeah.'

'I've got to come over and see you. When are you going to be in?'

'I don't go out till eleven usually. But give us a ring before you come.' Ronnie paused. 'What's it about, Johnny?'

'I'll tell you when I see you.'

Hendon Hall Court was a fine old apartment complex that had seen better times. Once it had its own outdoor swimming pool, roof garden, bar and gym, and during the 1960s the attached hotel used to host the England football team whenever they played at Wembley. Now, with its ageing but somewhat wealthy residents, it was quietly respectable. It afforded Ronnie some sanctuary from the eyes of the press.

He usually had the penthouse to himself as Barbara was often away for months at a time, performing in pantomimes or plays. Their marriage had gone through some very rough times lately and had almost ended. The previous year Barbara had accused him – yet again – of having an affair with Sue Haylock who, for many years, worked as a barmaid at his A&R Club in Soho.

He knew Barbara had been suspicious for a long time. He had rented a house in Edgware, close to Sue's flat, so he could be a little more discreet, but Barbara had caught him red-handed coming out of Sue's front door. Even his brother Jimmy had told him off for that indiscretion. 'You are a silly bugger, Ronnie, you really are,' he said. 'After all Barbara's gone and done for you.' Back at their pad, Barbara had chucked all his suits and socks out of the window and hadn't let him home for a week.

Anyway, they had managed to patch things up, after a fashion. Ronnie had taken her over to Spain for some rest at the villa. And then, earlier that year, they had bought the penthouse at Hendon Hall Court together. It was a brave attempt to rekindle the marriage – it was in that very apartment block that he and Barbara started married life, all those years ago, in 1964.

His brother Jimmy was probably right. He usually was. But the truth was, Ronnie couldn't get Sue out of his mind. He was still seeing her, whenever he could chance it. It was a bad case of the heart ruling the head.

£££

Once inside the penthouse flat, with the door closed and safely locked, John pulled open his leather holdall to reveal the rows of neatly packed banknotes. Ronnie grinned.

John plumped himself down on the sofa. 'We knew there would be a good prize, Ronnie,' he said. 'Two or three million, maybe. But not six million!'

John sat on that sofa for hours telling Ronnie all about the raid, over endless cups of tea, plates of biscuits, and sandwiches. He felt he had to go through everything, just in case something happened. Ronnie had a right to know. Chances were that, if it came to a tumble, Ronnie would get a pull too. The police had it in for the Knights. They both knew that.

The story that he had to tell made it all sound like plain sailing, but the truth was that the raid had taken careful planning, and plenty of it. John never really knew whether something was going to work or not. But he did know that if he planned it well, and if he was careful, he stood a good chance of getting away with it. He was a thorough man, the sort of person not given to making rushed decisions, but this really was the biggest gamble of his life.

In the end, everyone on the job had netted around £400,000 each. That was enough to buy each of them a large house in the country, with plenty of land. But there had been expenses. Lots of them. Two small-time garage-men who had helped with the logistics had been paid around £30,000 each. In addition, the transport had had to be bought, hidden away weeks in advance of the raid, and then disposed of afterwards. Trustworthy drivers had to be found and hired – they were paid some £100,000 apiece. Guns had to be sourced. It had all required a lot of organization.

John knew that in the underworld the rule was, the bigger the job, the more it would cost you in 'expenses', which bore no relation to the actual cost of the service required. The threat was that, should the money not be enough, you might not be able to count on continued loyalty. This was a big job. So it all added up to a lot of dough.

He told Ronnie the idea for the raid had come to him while he was on his way to look in on M&M Bodyworks, his repair shop in Southgate. On his way he would often stop off and have breakfast at a Wimpy Bar in the area. Early one Monday morning in January 1982, he was sitting in his favourite seat by the window, eating his eggs and bacon, when he noticed a Security Express armoured van pull up outside a bank opposite.

The two guards got out and hung around talking, smoking cigarettes, waiting for the bank to open. They were early. It was perhaps 7.30 a.m.

John had a business meeting to go to later that morning. After checking that everything was all right at the garage, he made a mental note to go to the meeting via the Wimpy Bar. At 9.00 a.m., just before the bank opened its doors for business, John was there, sitting in the window, observing. He noticed that the guards were unloading hefty bags of coins. There would have been no time to load the van in the morning and get to the bank in time for opening. So John realized that it was unlikely that the van had been loaded up with coins, or 'silver', that morning. It had to have been loaded up the previous evening. And as it was Monday, the chances were that the van had been loaded up on the Friday. If that was the case, then the van had been sitting somewhere, over the weekend, fully loaded with silver.

John decided to find out where the main Security Express depot was. That was simple enough. At the time, the firm was advertising for drivers and guards in the *Evening Standard*, so he rang the offices and asked them where he should send his CV. '54 Curtain Road, London EC1,' they told him.

That Friday evening, armed with an *A–Z* street atlas, John drove over to Shoreditch and had a close look at the depot. It was a bitterly cold, foggy winter's night. There was snow on the ground, a rare thing for London. The dimly lit cobblestone alley running alongside the depot looked like something straight out of Jack the Ripper's times.

John needed a vantage point, somewhere where he could watch the goings-on in the yard without being spotted. A modern, two-storey office block overlooking the yard, empty and to let, was perfect. The offices were owned by Security Express. The irony tickled him.

Late one night John scaled a wall and climbed on to a low, lean-to roof at one end of the office block. From there he climbed through a tiny window into what must have once been the gents' toilets. He put his foot straight into a washbowl full of dark-green slime.

Inside, the building was stripped bare, no electricity, no water, no furniture, and no blinds on the windows. John found his way downstairs to the door that opened on to the alley, unscrewed the metal plate covering the lock mechanism, and removed the lock, securing the door from the inside. He put the lock into his duffel-coat pocket and, the next day, took it to a locksmith who made a new key for it, no questions asked. A few nights later, John replaced the lock. He was in.

£££

Night after night, John would creep down the narrow alley and duck into the doorway of the empty office building. He would unlock the door with the copied key, climb the dark stairwell to the first floor, and, leaning against the wall to avoid the yellow glare of the lights, observe the comings and goings in the yard.

Slowly he pieced together the routines of the depot guards. He noted every detail – the guards' changeover times, where the vans were parked, and where the cameras were pointed. He loved the watching. It was an exciting time, observing those guards go about their business, unaware that they were being observed.

John kept up the surveillance for months on end, returning home in the early hours of the morning. Di knew better than to ask where he was going or who he was seeing. She knew it was probably work.

Next, John had to put together a firm to carry out the raid. Here was such an opening that he had to make doubly sure that they didn't try to run off and carry out the raid on their own. He had to trust them implicitly. The firm he chose was made up of people he had known and worked closely with for years. Ronnie, too, knew them well. Some were long-term family friends.

Everyone had a key and they took turns to go into the building to observe the depot and work out its weak points. Routines were established. On Wednesdays, they would see the trolleys come up from the vaults so that the girls on the third floor could make up the wage packets. The vehicles coming in and out of the yard also followed a pattern. A blue van would regularly go in to collect shredded paper.

But it was the laxness of the guards that really amazed John.

On Saturday evenings, regular as clockwork, a man with a big case would walk down the road to the pound where Security Express parked its empty lorries. Once there, he would change all the locks on the vans and the drivers would be issued with new keys for the following week.

On Sundays the guards could be seen washing their cars down in the yard, the back door to the depot propped wide open. One of the guards would regularly let his large dog run about the yard. It would bound up to the parked vans by the wall, and piss against the tyres.

John's original intention had been to go for the silver in the vans. He had spent Easter Bank Holiday 1982 watching the depot and he knew that the vans sat in the yard all weekend, loaded with silver. Perhaps this was the opportunity he was waiting for.

He hatched a plan to cut a circular hole in the vans parked by the wall, unload the silver, and hump it over the wall and into the empty office building. From there they could carry it up the stairs, ready to be loaded on to a waiting van at the back of the building. The hole in the van had to be large enough for a man to climb through. And it had to be cut by hand, as an electric drill would have made too much noise. It was an engineering problem. So John asked an engineer. The man came up with an ingenious solution – again, no questions asked.

'The only way you can do it is to make your own cutter up,' he said.

His idea was to drill a large hole in the side of the van with a hand drill and then insert a long bolt into the hole, with an end that would spring out once it was inside the van, thus locking the bolt into position. Then they could screw a long steel arm on to the top of the bolt. At one end of the arm was a hardened-steel cutting blade. As the arm was tightened on to the bolt, the blade would plough into the metal – or that was the theory, anyway. The drill hole would have been made close to the brick wall so that they would be screened from the cameras by the bulk of the van.

John got someone to make up the contraption for them. Over the next few months they tested it out in someone's lock-up garage, on various types of metal plate to see how well it would cut and how long it would take. They guessed the thickness of the armoured plate on the Security Express vans. The contraption worked, but in the end, ingenious though it was, it was never used. By early 1983, after many evenings of heated argument among members of the firm, John had decided to go for the main building. The vault.

'There was so many plans to get in that building, Ronnie,' said John. 'We thought about getting on the roof and going into the apartment and coming down the stairs. Or using a ladder on the fire escape to get on the roof. It was an apex roof and you could walk around the sides and then lower yourself into the apartment.

'The other one was the man with the big case, who used to go and change all the locks on a Saturday morning. We were going to follow him inside. In the end we went in the back door.'

The firm had noticed that every weekday morning, one of the guards would walk across the yard to collect something from the hatch in the side of the building. A pint of milk. That was the weakness that John spotted. 'Security Express lost £6 million over a pint of flaming milk. No kidding!'

'Come on, Johnny. You must have had a little inside help,' said Ronnie, as he got up to go into the kitchen to make some more sandwiches.

'We got a lot of information from retired guards, and we got a lot of information by just following the guards about.'

Ronnie looked at him disbelievingly.

'Yeah, well, we did have a little bird singing,' John laughed.

To deal with all the guards in the depot, they needed more manpower. That meant that they had to bring in another firm to help out. Again, John turned to friends of the family, people that Ronnie knew well. The deal was simple: half the proceeds to them and the other half to John's own firm.

John knew the greater reward justified the smaller cut.

They also needed to know more about the guards, so the firm hired a twelve-seater minibus. Posing as American tourists, replete with baseball caps, they would park in Curtain Road and count the people going in and out of the warehouse. Sometimes they followed the guards home, gathering information about their personal lives that could later be used to put the frighteners on them.

The cameras, too, were a problem. Standing in the darkened upstairs room of the office block, as far away from the windows as possible, they had many whispered conversations over what to do about them. Late one night, one of them climbed up on to the wall and tried to rock the post, which turned out to be a fourteen-foot piece of scaffolding tubing. To their surprise it moved. So one idea was to use a sea-fishing rod, equipped with a strong line and large steel hook, to pull the cameras over a few inches to one side, thereby creating a blind spot in the yard.

The fishing-rod device was tested on another building, but in fact wasn't needed. They had heard that the yard already had its blind spot. To prove it, one night, two of them slipped over the wall and ran right up to the top of the building's fire escape, and then ran all the way back down again. There was no reaction from anyone in the building.

From that, they worked out that they could easily get to the area of the yard where six large dustbins were stored. There they could remain unnoticed, lying in wait for the guard who came out to collect the milk in the morning. And Bob's your uncle. They would be in the building.

To pull it off, the right transport was vital. It had to look similar to the Security Express vans, and it also had to withstand the weight of several tons of cash. Eventually they decided on a transit van with a double axle at the rear. John had arranged for another van as a changeover, but in the end they hadn't used it. The red van had been parked a few streets away from the depot. A getaway car was parked nearby, in case the van didn't start.

There were six people and two drivers on the job, eight in all.

'The guard had been in there all night,' John told Ronnie. 'We had to be in the empty building by midnight. Curtain Road is a very quiet place. So everyone had their own key to let themselves in.'

John had delivered everything they needed the night before: two ladders (one for each side of the wall); sticky tape; pickaxe handles; silk-stocking masks; and ropes to tie the guards up with. He told Ronnie that they also took in one double-barrelled shotgun; one fake shotgun, made up from a piece of copper tubing; and a replica handgun. The real shotgun wasn't loaded. But they had the cartridges in their pockets.

'We all got together there in that building while the night-watchman was on. We decided to go over the wall at three-thirty. We got over the wall, around the blind spot, into the dustbin incinerator part, and while we waited there a long time, it was getting near the time of the night guard changing with the other guard.

'The one who was on all night just came out and checked something in the office next to where we were waiting. I think he was looking for the milk but it wasn't delivered yet. Then he ran back inside. We heard him change over, start his car up, and go home. He very likely said, "I ain't got your milk, it wasn't there," because the new guard came to that back door. He saw the iron gate ajar, and he paused a bit. "Must be kids," he said. And then we got him.

'They're not supposed to do that, Ronnie. That's why he got the biggest bollocking going because they thought he was in it. He fucking wasn't. He was just an ordinary worker who was captured by thieves. I heard they reckon he owned up and let us in, but he had nothing to do with this robbery. He just happened to be on.

'We had to release him so he could work things out and not look conspicuous. And then after we done the business he told us how to operate the gate control room. You had to go to the other office to do that but once you press the button the gate doesn't stop until it gets to the other end.

'We made a mistake with some of the inside information, though,' he said. 'We didn't turn a light on. We didn't open some blinds. The guv'nor who had come in couldn't make it out why the blinds weren't open. He nearly blew the whistle on us.

'The rota we had wasn't completely accurate either. The guard with the dog never came,' he added.

They had decided that if anyone pressed the alarm, the only way out was the front door, but with their hands up. There was no other way out. The police would have easily sealed off the alley running down the side of the yard. With a good 'brief' they thought they probably would have been all right, as long as no one inside got hurt. They would have been done for breaking and entering with intent to commit robbery. They could have said they were just after the silver in the vans in the yard, and someone would have taken the hit for the real shotgun and maybe got a five. But as the day progressed, the stakes got higher. They could have been done for taking the hostages, a serious offence attracting quite a hefty sentence. So the tension racked up a bit.

'There were a few lighter moments, though,' said John. 'One of the guards wanted to have a piss. The message came up and I went downstairs to see what was going on. "I'm dying for a pee," he said. "Can I?" "Yeah", I said. "Stand him up, but don't undo him – he might press a button." He stood there and he said, "I can't get it out." "Wee in your trousers," I told him. "Oh mother, I can't do that!" he said. I looked around at the others. "Who's going to get it out for him, then?" I said. Anyway, one of the firm managed to get it out for him and he pissed all over the floor. He had gloves on but he's never lived it down since.'

Ronnie laughed. 'Who was that then?'

'You can probably guess,' John replied. 'You know what I said to the guard then, Ronnie? I said, "You know what you're doing now?" He looked at me, really serious. "Yes." "If your guv'nor could see you he'd fucking sack you!"'

They both guffawed at that.

'We couldn't do anything until after a certain time because of the time lock,' said John. 'The door clicked, it all lit up and we stood there gawking. There were trolleys and trolleys, green bags from pick-ups. It was chock-a, chock-a-block – proper money with the amounts on: £10,000 from Boots; another £13,000 from Argos. It was a lovely sight, Ronnie.'

'I'll bet it was.'

But, despite the success, there was one thing that John had very nearly slipped up on. He needed somewhere nice and quiet to take the robbery proceeds to, to sort it out. So a few days before the raid he had asked a woman in Stanmore, a close friend of the family, if he could borrow her lock-up garage and her spare room for an evening. She wasn't told why – for all she knew it could have been a van-load of stolen dresses. She agreed, and arranged to go out until midnight and leave them to it.

'I was going to go into the lock-up and take it up, seven at night, through her back door and count it. Then I got a message through Terry that she didn't want to do it,' he told Ronnie.

'Terry had met her on the road, shopping. She told him straight, "By the way, can you tell John that he can't use my place?" I went round to her and pleaded with her again. I offered her cash, but she said she couldn't do it.'

'So what did you do?' asked Ronnie.

'I used my business partner's place.'

A frown momentarily crossed John's face. He tapped the top of the leather holdall lying on the coffee table. 'I've got to get this money over to Spain, Ronnie.'

'Yeah, leave it to me,' Ronnie replied. 'I've got a way of getting it over. We don't have to carry it over ourselves no more. None of that stuffing it in our pockets.' He laughed.

John never cared to ask Ronnie how he was going to get the cash over there. But he knew that it would be there, waiting for him, the next time he went to Marbella.

8

OP17

'The people you want are meeting in the Albion.'

'Go on.'

'I can't say no more, not now. But listen, I'll call you again. I promise.'

There was a click as the line went dead. The anonymous caller had hung up, and Peter was left staring thoughtfully at the receiver. The Albion? He knew the place. It was a rough old pub in Dalston, in East London, a favourite haunt of the local villains.

Luckily for Peter, a few days later the informant phoned back. He was given a code name, and whenever he phoned he was asked to identify himself. Over the course of the next few weeks he told them all about the Albion public house, which, he said, two or three men responsible for the Security Express robbery were frequenting, in the company of the owner of a garage that was just around the corner. The garage man's name was 'John', Peter was told.

All summer, Peter ran surveillance operations on teams they thought might have been involved in the robbery. In essence, they were conducting the Flying Squad equivalent of a fishing expedition, but it was based on credible information.

By May 1983 Peter decided it was worthwhile putting the information to the test. It was time to set up another surveillance operation. He called two of his men, Detective Constables Charlie Collins and Terry Mills, into his office. Both regularly worked together. A big man, Charlie was Irish, with the gift of the gab. He could blend into a local pub scene without sticking out. He was naturally friendly, interested in people, and well able to quickly strike up conversation with complete strangers. But although he gave the appearance of being easy-going and laid-back, at the same time he had a knack of following conversations on the other side of the room.

Terry, meanwhile, had an eye for detail, a meticulous, almost photographic memory. Not much would escape him. He loved his racing, whether it was the dogs or the gee-gees. That always helped to get people talking, especially in the area in which they were going to operate.

In short, they were perfect for the job.

'There's been a tip-off,' Peter said. He told them all about the anonymous caller and his intriguing piece of information.

Later that day, Charlie and Terry changed into old jeans and T-shirts and drove up to take a look at the Albion, which stood on the corner of a run-down residential street called Albion Drive. The pub was surprisingly grand-looking. It had a whitewashed-stone exterior and an imposing stucco entrance porch supported by two pillars on either side. The name of the pub was emblazoned on the front of the porch in large gold letters on a regal red background.

Black cast-iron railings separated the pub's forecourt from the pavement. Behind the railings sat four long, wooden tables and benches – suntraps that served to make the pub immensely popular in the summer months. A cast-iron pole with an old-fashioned, swinging pub sign completed the picture.

Just around the corner, in Malvern Road, perhaps less than a minute's walk from the entrance to the pub, was the garage workshop run by 'John'. It was called Alpine Motors and had clearly seen better days. Its potential customers were greeted with peeling paint and discarded tyres.

The two officers had to work out a way of watching the pub and the garage without being noticed. Malvern Road was quiet and narrow, lined with large Victorian houses. A parked van, the Flying Squad's usual ploy, would have stuck out like a sore thumb – the locals were pretty clued-up to the ways of the police and word would have quickly got round. So Charlie and Terry decided to try to find a suitable building that could be used. As luck would have it, they found the perfect spot.

Peter laughed as the two officers gleefully reported their find and discussed how best to carry out the op. 'It'll be home from home,' he told them.

A barrister had just bought the crumbling house they had spotted. With little hesitation he offered it up to be used for the surveillance. At least, he thought, it would stop the place being commandeered by squatters.

The house was in total disrepair. The floorboards were non-existent in places, and the roof was leaking badly. There was no electricity. In fact, it was little more than a shell. But for what the Flying Squad had in mind it was perfect. From the upstairs windows you could not only see the Albion pub across the street, but also the entrance to the run-down garage just around the corner in Malvern Road.

The observation officially commenced on 1 June 1983, at 12.30 p.m. precisely. It was code-named OP17. There were so many other things going on that nobody thought much of it at the time, but OP17 was to have far-reaching consequences.

Charlie and Terry spent many a day up in that bare shell of a building, 'the shithole' as Charlie affectionately termed it. They would arrive early in the morning clutching their sandwiches and flasks, and leave late at night. They dressed as builders would, wearing paint-splattered jeans and thick, open-necked shirts, an old sports bag slung over their shoulders. If they left during daylight hours they would carry a workman's toolbox with them, or maybe a piece of splintering two-by-four timber. And if anyone got a little too nosy they would bang a few rusty old nails in, and hump things around a little.

They had draped a piece of old net and some ragged curtains across one of the upstairs bedroom windows, which looked down on Albion Drive. Behind this half-drawn rag they set up their camera equipment. They would sit there for hours on end, taking photographs of anyone entering the Albion pub or visiting Alpine Motors, simultaneously logging the precise time and date in their police notebooks. That way one corroborated the other. They had to be painstakingly accurate in case any of the information had to be presented in court. Every few weeks, to relieve the monotony, they would be replaced by other officers from the enquiry.

That summer was exceptionally hot. Day after day the sun shone down from a clear, blue sky. Charlie and Terry would be sitting up in that room gasping. They watched with envy as 'Dumpy', as they nicknamed him, would leave the garage to sink a cool lunchtime pint of lager in the Albion. It was torture watching him drink it.

Meanwhile, back at Arbour Square, Peter turned his attention to other leads. One in particular was proving to be particularly intriguing. It had been triggered by a phone call to the Flying Squad's chief superintendent at Scotland Yard, Don Brown. The call came from an ex-pat who was working in a hotel in Saudi Arabia. He had read about the Security Express robbery in the papers and wanted to tell the police about somebody who had approached him with detailed floor plans for a Security Express depot. He told them that the plans apparently included diagrams of the vaults.

Peter had no idea which branch of Security Express the man was talking about, but it caught his eye because of his growing conviction that there had to be an inside man, a mole, deep within Security Express. He therefore decided to follow it up.

But there was something slightly odd about this informant. Peter came to regard him as a bit of a Walter Mitty character. Every time Peter phoned Saudi Arabia to talk to him, he would make an excuse. 'I can't talk to you, it's a religious festival,' he would say, or 'I can't talk to you now, call back later.' It was clearly his place of work that they were phoning and everyone, including his Saudi managers, was getting upset and frustrated.

The ex-pat came from Matlock in Derbyshire but wasn't due home for some months. Peter wanted to fly out to Saudi Arabia to meet the man. In late August he and a couple of officers had their jabs ready for the off. But before they could get a chance to go, another lead was to preoccupy the enquiry. It had been generated by the ongoing OP17 surveillance operation – and augmented by the Squad's own network of underworld contacts.

£££

Every now and then, Charlie and Terry would meet up with Peter or Reed McGeorge to go through the photographs they had taken of the comings and goings at Albion Drive.

The owner of the garage, Alpine Motors, was a scruffily-dressed man with a pot-belly. His was hardly the busiest garage in the world. He would arrive mid-morning and would often finish around three. It had been easy enough for the Squad to identify his name from official records. It was John Horsley.

According to the paperwork, Horsley had a business partner, Stan Atwell, but he was rarely to be seen at the garage. The two men Horsley was regularly meeting were a little harder to identify. Nothing obvious connected them to him. Both were smartly dressed. More often than not they would arrive in a two-tone blue Ford Granada with a very distinctive number plate. One of the men would go straight into the garage, as if he knew Horsley well. The other would hang back, before being invited in. The two smartly dressed men would stay and talk to Horsley for a few minutes, then leave the garage together.

Most evenings, all three men would get pissed in the Albion. There was clearly no shortage of cash. But even hardened drinkers have to go to bed sometime. So, when they were able to, Terry and Charlie would slip out of their wreck of a house and attempt to follow the men back to their homes. By 'housing' them like this they would be able to work out who they were, from official government records.

They quickly identified one of the smartly dressed men as Billy Hickson, a convicted robber and a well-known figure in the London underworld. The Met had a fat file on him already. But Peter needed more than that. He needed to know who Hickson's associates were. He knew that the Prison Service would have detailed intelligence files on Hickson. Everything about his personal life would have been logged, from the names of the people he wrote to, to the identities of those he sat with in the prison mess.

Jim Keeling was given the task of calling up the Home Office to get a copy of these records. 'This is Detective Constable Jim Keeling of the Flying Squad,' he said, in the most officious tone he could muster. 'I'm calling in reference to a William John Hickson. I wondered if you would be so kind as to let us . . . erm . . .' Then, to the amusement of the whole office, he dropped his mock formal tone. ' . . .'ave a butcher's at yer files.'

The other man in the Albion, the one usually driving the blue Ford Granada, was more of a mystery and would remain so for some months. He cut a suave, debonair figure in his tailored suits. In fact, he was so smartly dressed that, for a while, they thought he might have been an ex-copper.

To help identify the mystery man, Charlie and Terry were pointed in the direction of Fred Halligan, the owner of a pool-table manufacturing company who knew many underworld figures. They showed him some surveillance photographs of the man standing outside the Albion with Billy Hickson. Although Halligan didn't recognize Hickson, he did identify the other man as someone he knew as 'Billy'. Halligan was asked to keep his eye out for the men in the photos.

Meanwhile, the files obtained by Jim Keeling from the Home Office revealed that Billy Hickson had long-standing ties with the Knight family going back at least to the 1960s. Some time in the late 1960s Hickson had gone into partnership with David Knight running a car-breaker's yard in Stoke Newington. After the council compulsorily purchased their premises they went on to set up a scaffolding company, called HK Scaffolding, but they fell out and the business folded. When David was stabbed to death in a club, HK Scaffolding apparently died with him. In 1970 Hickson bought a couple of garages. His brother George ran them, but George apparently bled the businesses dry and, in 1974, was made a bankrupt.

In 1976, while serving a prison sentence for armed robbery, Hickson found out that his wife was having various affairs with his associates, including Billy Adams, another figure well known to the Flying Squad. Hickson reputedly told his prison mates that it was a 'blessing in disguise'. Shortly after his release from

Maidstone Prison he got a divorce and moved in with another woman, called Maureen.

Hickson was not a man to be messed with lightly. Peter had to make sure that he had enough on him to make it stick, because if he didn't the chances were that other potential witnesses in the investigation would be threatened.

Peter had one other piece of information, which leant weight to the theory that Hickson was somehow involved with the Security Express robbery. One day, a few weeks after the robbery, he had got talking to a retired Flying Squad commander who then worked for a tobacco company. Naturally enough, they chatted about the robbery. The retired commander had his own tangle of informers in the underworld. He told Peter that one of his contacts had warned him some weeks before the robbery that the Knight family and their associates were busy planning their biggest job ever. At the time nobody had taken it seriously.

Over the summer months Peter had made direct contact with the informer, who said that he had been up to one of the robbers' homes. Peter spent many a day with him driving around the suburbs of North London trying to find the exact place, but every time they got to the Cambridge Roundabout, the informant seemed to get completely lost. Eventually they identified the house, which turned out to be occupied by one Janet Hickson. In early September they made some enquiries to check out her family background and found out that she had been married to Billy Hickson, seen and identified on the OP17 operation, and that she was now living with Billy Adams, another underworld figure.

From the informant's information, Peter compiled a circular clock-face chart of likely suspects. At 12 o'clock was Ronnie Knight. They had connected the Knight family with Billy Hickson years ago. They knew that Hickson's estranged wife Janet's maiden name was Bear, and that she was the sister of Terry Bear; they also knew that Terry Bear's associate was Billy Adams. As Janet Hickson, née Bear, was now living with Adams, it was all a very tight circle, or so Peter thought. The Flying Squad had thus decided to concentrate on Adams and

Bear, but only Adams could be located, then living in Edmonton. However, the association between them all was strong enough for Peter to request the specialist surveillance services of C11, the Met's criminal intelligence division. And in mid-October, things came dramatically to a head.

£££

From his hidden vantage point high up above the busy, rain-sodden street, Peter was watching a man wearing a light windcheater sauntering along the pavement below. The man walked with a brisk, purposeful stride, past a small car parked alongside the kerb. Through the car's dirty windscreen Peter could make out the indistinct shapes of several men.

The car began to move off. Windcheater man paused. He stood looking into a shop window, surreptitiously observing the car in its reflection, until it slipped out of his sight. Then he briskly turned round. 'Taxi!' he yelled.

He gestured towards a black London cab parked across the street. The cab edged towards him and he quickly climbed in, exchanging a few words with the driver as he did so.

Peter followed the black cab as it weaved its way through the slow-moving, lunchtime traffic towards the Tower of London, and then northwards into the City. Just before it disappeared from view, he could see that the cab had tucked itself in behind the small car. Both disappeared from sight. Peter looked at his watch. He had been doing this for weeks now, watching and waiting. Observing.

The man in the windcheater was one of the best surveillance officers the Met had. His name was John Fordham, who was later to die in the line of duty. The cab driver was another top surveillance officer, Roy Chivers. He, too, was to die in tragic circumstances.

John Fordham was a legend. He had joined the CID in 1974 from the Auckland City Police. Over the ensuing years he received four commendations but had consistently refused promotion because he wanted, as he put it, to 'stay at the sharp end'. He volunteered for special C11 duties in 1981, and trained with the SAS and RUC in special 'survival' surveillance techniques.

It was now a full six months since the Security Express robbery. With nothing clear to go on, the enquiry had spent months chasing a plethora of leads. Some had petered out. Others had netted crooks, but not the right ones. Some were still being worked on. This particular lead, prompted partially by OP17 and partially by Peter's 'clock face', was based around Billy Adams's network of associates.

Since late summer, Fordham and Chivers had spent many weeks following Adams and his fellow conspirators around. Peter knew that they were up to something. If only he could catch them at it. Then he would have the chance of getting some interviews with them, and from that would doubtless come more information that might just lead him to the Security Express robbers.

Peter suspected that the men in the small car below him were planning to hijack and rob a post office remittance van as it came out of the main post office sorting depot in Whitechapel. Among the men were several well-known East End figures. The robbers had been studying the movements of the post office vans as they drove in and out of the sorting office for weeks. They had been noting the timings and following the vans. But they didn't realize that they, too, were being watched.

It had been a very delicate and intense job, using surveillance cameras, informants, and crack undercover surveillance backup from C11 – men like Fordham and Chivers. The Squad had set up surveillance posts near the sorting office, above shops, in parked vans, and, in Peter's case, on the roof of a brewery, which dominated the whole area. To get there he and his fellow officers had to wend their way up through a maze of corridors and back stairs so as not to alert anyone in the main brewery offices.

They had watched the robbers week after week, morning after morning, noting how they observed the post office, waiting for vans to come out. Bearing in mind how delicate the enquiry was, and knowing the calibre of his adversaries, Peter knew he had to be very careful.

Early one morning the police surveillance team managed to follow the gang all the way down to Whitechapel again. But it nearly went very badly wrong.

One officer was in an observation point close to the focus of the gang's attention, the sorting office. Suddenly, for no apparent reason, he came out of his observation point and walked around the narrow streets of the East End wearing the brightest red pullover Peter had ever seen. What's more, it had the Flying Squad's distinctive motif on it. Peter was mortified.

Some hours later, the squad had a debriefing session back at the station. Peter had got hold of the biggest baseball bat he could lay his hands on. 'It is unbelievable!' He brought the bat down squarely on the table, nearly splitting it in half. 'What the hell did you think you were doing?' he snarled at the hapless officer.

The officer, lip quivering, had nothing to say. There was nothing he could say, really. There was no excuse for it.

'Never ever again!' bellowed Peter. 'This matter is far too delicate to take risks like this. You could have blown the whole enquiry.' And with that he stormed out of the room. His men sat there in stunned silence.

Peter never did fully understand why the officer had broken his cover like that. But it was an open secret that in the evenings he was moonlighting, working as a private investigator. He probably had to make an urgent call or something to one of his clients. In those days taking on private work was frowned upon by the force because it caused a conflict of loyalties, which is exactly what appeared to have happened in this case. But some officers had to do it to make ends meet.

The officer later recovered some face with the force. One day he was on a double-decker bus when, by chance, he sat down next to a well-known escapee, and promptly arrested him on the spot.

The police surveillance operation on Whitechapel Road continued without further mishap. It became apparent that the gang was waiting for one post office van in particular. Finally, one Thursday morning in late October, it all kicked off. The officers were all in their various observation posts, and those officers in cars were put into strategic positions so that, if they had to go in, they would all be in a position to effect an arrest.

The Squad had a fake post office van, which was following

the original van the robbers were trying to hit, which itself was being followed by the robbers. Another van filled with half a dozen big Robbery Squad detectives was standing close by.

When the robbers decided to attack, the van pulled up alongside them and the detectives from the Robbery Squad surrounded the little car with the robbers in it. The detectives, all armed with baseball bats, promptly smashed the glass in the windows of the robbers' car. 'It was like an assertion of authority,' Peter would say to his troops. 'It's like in reverse when villains go in to rob a place they shout at everybody, produce weapons, make it look as though they were in charge. The same has to apply when the Flying Squad makes its arrests. You have to tell them who the guv'nor is.'

'Lie down, sit down, and keep your hands in!'

£££

It was a dramatic picture, seeing those big men lying on the pavement just about to be handcuffed. Billy Adams was captured, a very rewarding sight after months of painstaking work. But Peter had no time to gloat on it. He had discovered that his mysterious informer from Saudi Arabia, was planning a holiday on the Greek island of Rhodes. The enquiry decided that that was the best place to make contact with him. Peter and Chief Superintendent Brown had been nominated to go out there, find him, and interview him. They were due to leave the very next day.

When officers travelled abroad, the Yard worked out the temperature difference and issued them with an appropriate suit. Being a hot climate, they were issued with lightweight suits. And because of Brown's rank, they went Club Class on the aeroplane. It was all rather enjoyable. Bearing in mind they still hadn't got very far, this was quite a lead that they had to follow up.

First, they had to go to Athens to establish a rapport with the Greek police. They stayed in a charming hotel, but Athens was noisy, dirty, and muggy, and the two men were glad to escape to the relative tranquillity of Rhodes.

A young detective called George was assigned to liaise with

them. There weren't that many police officers on the island. His office was little more than a room with a telephone and an old manual typewriter in it.

George took them to Lindos, an ancient village nestling on the cliffs beneath a craggy acropolis. It was, to Peter, the most wonderful place he'd seen, something straight out of a picture postcard. Whitewashed houses and winding alleys tumbled down the hillside towards a dazzling, turquoise sea. Above the village, on a rocky promontory, stood an ancient temple dedicated to Athena. For Peter, the trip was a real eye-opener. Until then, he had never been further than Leicester with the Met. Now this really was something out of this world.

George's job was to establish exactly where their man was staying. He was a good detective, but still it took a couple of days. So while they waited they explored the village of Lindos, sunbathed on the sandy beach, and took a trip up to the acropolis on hired donkeys. Eventually, contact was made. Sometime in the early afternoon of the second day George told them that the person they wanted to see was in a restaurant at the furthest end of the bay. He was staying in some apartments attached to the restaurant.

Detective Chief Super Brown always insisted that when they were working they had to have their working clothes on, in other words lightweight suits, collar, and tie. So the two officers strolled down to the beach in their suits, and made contact with their informant, who was lounging in his swimming trunks.

He was really a very odd merchant. He wouldn't look at them directly, and talked out of the side of his mouth, so that no one could notice. He clearly didn't want to talk to them there on the beach and kept wandering off towards some jagged rocks. The policemen followed him as best they could, gingerly picking their way over rock pools, in their shiny black shoes and standard-issue lightweight grey suits.

They managed to fix up a meeting with him in a few hours' time at a local restaurant that overlooked the beach. Surprisingly, he showed up, and the three of them sat outside the restaurant at a table under one of the beach sunshades made of rushes – they suited and booted, he still in his swimming trunks, the three of them surrounded by scantily clad women in their bikinis.

They talked for hours, trying to get their man to come out with something just a little bit more concrete. They talked so long that, by six o'clock in the evening, darkness had fallen like a blanket over the three of them sitting there. They were the only people left on the whole of the beach. If anyone had seen them, they must have had a chuckle to themselves.

They never did get a name from him, but they got the gist of the plan.

They spent a few more days with George touring the island of Rhodes and had a great time. Peter even won some money at the casino. George took them to a traditional Greek wedding and they were made very welcome. On his return Peter kept in contact with George, who became a firm friend of the Flying Squad. He came to see them the following year and they showed him around London, arranging a trip on the river for him with the Thames River Police.

Peter had returned from Rhodes in an upbeat mood. While he had been away, the Squad had interviewed the robbers caught in Operation Nab. But, going through the statements, Peter soon realized that there was no way that he could connect Billy Adams with the Security Express robbers. Terry Bear wasn't even in the country at the time – he was believed to be in Spain. It had been a red herring. It was back to square one.

They decided to concentrate on the man from Saudi Arabia and his intriguing story of Security Express plans for sale. They eventually identified the ex-employee of Security Express who was supplying the plans as a man named Gallagher. Peter took a day trip to Security Express's Reading branch to talk to the man's supervisor. The supervisor was helpful but he made it quite clear that the man could not have had access to plans for the Curtain Road depot. Despite that, they decided to continue with this line of enquiry.

Somewhere along the way they had retrieved a plan Gallagher had allegedly drawn, showing the outline of the building, the vaults, and the rooms of a Security Express branch. They then discovered that the man in question was now living in Lanzarote, and that he was working as a residential caretaker of several blocks of holiday flats. Careful consideration was given to going out there to make enquiries. Once more permission to go was granted, something that probably wouldn't happen in these more austere times.

Meanwhile, another lead showed up, again through an informant, and this time to do with the notorious Quality Street gang in Manchester. Peter and some of the other officers spent three days there in late November, working with Greater Manchester Police, but drew a blank. When Peter got back to London he found that all the officers involved had put the drinks on his room's tab. It took their accountant a week to sort it all out.

They did have some cause to celebrate. They had, after all, just secured their first conviction. At Newington Causeway a garage proprietor from Essex called John Brodie was given an eighteen-month suspended sentence for handling £3,000-worth of pound notes stolen from Security Express. Brodie had been apprehended in May largely because of a fluke conversation on an Essex golf course. One day, over a round of golf, Bernie Butler had got talking to a businessman who tipped him off about Brodie and the notes.

Throughout his interviews with the police, Brodie had been unable to say where the notes had come from originally, and could not describe the man – or men – who had given them to him. Thus, he proved incapable of helping the police any further with their enquiries. Nevertheless, his conviction was a much-needed morale booster.

£££

The officers had long thought the supervisor on the day of the robbery, Greg Counsell, a strange character. He always seemed to be holding something back. Some witnesses to trauma just open the floodgates – they can't stop talking about what they've been through. But not Counsell. He spent a lot longer captured than anyone else, yet he had very little to say about it. What he did have to say had to be drawn out of him. At the time, though wrongly as it turned out, it had made the officers highly suspicious of him.

Counsell, for his part, grew tired of their incessant lines of questioning. He became increasingly uncooperative, to the point where, in exasperation, they more or less accused him – wrongly, as Peter later admitted – of being the 'inside man'. Not surprisingly, after that, he became openly hostile to the police. The war escalated, and on 6 December the Flying Squad turned his house over in Catford, South-east London. They found an unlicensed firearm – an old army revolver – and he was arrested and charged. They tried to use that to bring some pressure on him, to make him cooperate with them, but it just made him worse.

Meanwhile, the police did some digging and ran some checks on Counsell's financial status. They discovered that, a few months after the robbery, he had bought some property near the Welsh town of Merthyr Tydfil. He'd bought it with cash. Security guards weren't that well paid, they muttered to themselves.

Still harbouring thoughts that Counsell might well have been the 'inside man', Peter decided it was time to pay the property a visit. He decided to send some officers down to Wales to sneak a peek. Jim Keeling was assigned the task of phoning the local police station to get their cooperation for a visit. He had been given the name of an officer there that they needed to speak to, and had carefully written it down on a piece of paper. It wasn't a hard assignment, but Jim, in his own inimitable way, made it harder.

'Merthyr Tydfil Police. Can I help you?'

'Hello,' said Jim. 'Is, er . . .'

He scrabbled desperately around his desk for the piece of paper.

'Is, er . . . um . . .'

'Yes?'

'Is . . . er . . . Is Mr Tydfil there, please?'

'Are you taking the mickey?'

'No, really I'm not. I'm calling from the Flying Squad . . .'

That was quite enough for the station sergeant at the other end. He put the phone down.

Eventually they made amends with the Merthyr Tydfil police, and three officers, Simon Webber, the driver Alfie Howell, and Steve Farley, got down to Wales without further mishap to take a look at and search Counsell's property.

If they were expecting to find a luxury mansion, complete with iron gates, tucked away on a Welsh hillside, they were in for a shock. Counsell's property was a small terraced cottage, two-up, two-down. It probably didn't cost that much, certainly less than £20,000. Houses in Wales, then in the grip of economic depression, were a fraction of the price of the equivalent in London.

They called in to the station to report their findings, but decided that they wanted to have the night off with some of their Welsh colleagues. Simon called up Reed McGeorge, back at the office, who was in charge. 'Sir, the weather here is terrible. We're snowed in and there's freezing fog on the road. Is it all right if we come back tomorrow?'

'That bad, eh?' said Reed, scathingly. 'OK, well, fine. Can I have a quick word with Alfie?'

'Certainly, sir.'

'Here, Alfie, what's the weather like there?'

'Lovely, sir, clear as a bell.'

In the long-standing tradition of the Met, the fib would cost Simon a bottle of whisky when they got back to the office.

That night they all went out on the town with some of the local officers and had a skinful in a local pub. A good night had by all. Alfie fell asleep on his bed fully dressed.

At two in the morning Simon was woken up by a tremendous crash coming from Alfie's room, followed by the splintering of wood. He rushed next door to see what had happened. Alfie was sitting upright in the bed looking very sheepish. Next to him were the remains of the cupboard. It had been reduced to matchsticks.

'It's me braces,' he said. Alfie had got tangled up in them and thought he was being attacked.

Back at the station, the story amused them all. But really,

the trip was a disappointment. Counsell's Welsh cottage wasn't worth that much. He'd probably bought it with the proceeds from an article about the robbery he had sold to the *Sun*. There and then Peter decided that, if there was an 'inside man', Counsell wasn't it.

Although technically guilty of the offence of owning an unlicensed firearm, Counsell was let off by the court and given an absolute discharge. The revolver was destroyed. The whole incident didn't exactly improve his attitude to the police and by the time the robbers were brought to trial he was assumed to be a hostile witness. He was never called to the stand.

Simon had brought back a bottle of Welsh whisky to pay his fine for fibbing. For a long time it remained on a shelf in place of honour at Teddy Pine's bar where they all drank. Reed, being Scottish, didn't rate Welsh whisky.

£££

For the trip to Tenerife in early December Peter joined forces with a detective inspector called Peter Ireland, who had made some contacts with the police in Tenerife over a drugs matter. The plan was that they would go there together, helping each other with their separate enquiries.

Again, the two officers were issued with lightweight suits, which they obtained from a shop affiliated to the Metropolitan Police close to Piccadilly Circus. In those days the officers had to go down to the shop to be measured. The suit was handed to the officers on a wooden hanger stamped with the words 'Metropolitan Police'. The shop had had special hangers made up, so that when it billed the force for the suit there was no question that it had gone to the police.

The stark volcanic islands were a sight to behold, rising sheer out of the green Atlantic. First, the officers had to go to the island of La Palma to make contact with the local police force. Following that, it was a short hop over to the island of Tenerife. They stayed in the Bougainville Hotel, a large hotel between Playa de las Americas and the former fishing village of Los Cristianos, and they had to while away the time around the swimming pool.

The local police were very helpful. They completed the drugs investigation and then hopped over to the island of Lanzerote to carry out the second part of the visit. They had to trace Gallagher. And then all they had to do was to find out exactly when and where he would be returning to the UK. Once they knew that, they could make plans to arrest him as he came into the country.

They had quite a few days to make their enquiries. The two of them frequented the local hostelries and hotels, and eventually tracked down Gallagher. He was living in an apartment attached to the flats that he was looking after.

The two officers pretended that they were looking for apartments to buy and sell. It was a good cover story. It would be natural enough to approach the caretaker of the apartments to ask him which ones might possibly be for sale. That would get him talking. So that's what they did.

Gallagher was decidedly down at heel. He was open and friendly, and not the remotest bit suspicious. He told them all about the apartments, which ones were likely to be sold, and who was likely to sell them. The two officers slipped in a few personal questions to make him feel at ease. And eventually they popped the question: 'So, um, when are you going back to the UK?'

Gallagher more or less told them the exact date, the flight, and who he was flying with. He was due back in the UK just before Christmas 1983.

Armed with that knowledge, the men had completed their mission. All the time they were there, before they met him, they felt this could be the man they were looking for. The Mr Big. They walked around the Lanzarote beaches carrying the biggest lens you had ever seen on a camera, taking photographs of anyone they thought could remotely be a villain in the hope of identifying them later.

Once back in England, there was just enough time for Peter to arrange a reception committee. A few days later, a large posse of around twenty plain-clothes detectives descended on Gatwick Airport. Everything was allowed for. They expected Gallagher to make a run for it, so the airport authorities had to be fully informed.

Peter really hoped that this would be the inside man they were looking for and lead them on to better things. But the planes came in and went out. The detectives, getting more uncomfortable by the hour, sat around fidgeting, wondering why they were there. Peter, too, was getting restless. 'Maybe the next flight,' he would say to them. But by mid-afternoon it was quite obvious to all concerned that their man from Lanzarote certainly wasn't coming into Gatwick that day. After the last possible flight had arrived they disbanded, hugely disappointed.

Why didn't he turn up? It puzzled Peter greatly as he drove home that evening. He mulled it over and over in his mind. Why had this man, who had told him all this information, not stuck to his schedule? He had told the two detectives that his flight was already booked. What could possibly have made him change his plans?

Peter had a nagging suspicion that he was somehow to blame. And then he remembered. 'Bloody coat hanger,' he thought to himself. He had left it in one of the wardrobes of the apartment they had stayed in. And writ large on the wooden hanger were the words 'Metropolitan Police'.

The apartment cleaner must have found the hangers. If Gallagher had anything to do with the running of the apartments and blocks of flats then whoever was responsible for cleaning them would have contacted him. That one coat hanger had probably blown the operation, or so Peter thought.

The next day Peter got on with the job of finding out where he had gone. Someone in the office was tasked with going through all the passenger lists to find out when the man was coming home. They made extensive enquiries with the airlines, and the passenger lists were also searched at the other end, from Tenerife. Eventually, as luck would have it, they discovered that the man was due to arrive in Exeter, Devon – Peter's part of the world.

Triumphantly, he called a briefing to tell the team when and where the man was due to arrive. And then, his face turning red with embarrassment, he slipped in the small matter of the 'stray' coat hanger. The team sat in silence and stared at him in disbelief. It wasn't often that the boss slipped up like that.

George Moncrieff, Jim Keeling, and Simon Webber were dispatched down to Exeter in the fastest car the Flying Squad could muster. The team went there the day before Gallagher was due to arrive, so that they could complete their enquiries in Exeter, rather than having to go back another day. This time the man did turn up and he was promptly arrested at his home address.

While they were there, there was one particularly difficult prisoner in the cells. He was plainly disturbed, and had been shouting all kinds of obscenities at everyone and no one in particular.

A duty lawyer, young, fresh from law school, and full of himself, had come to see him.

'You'd better let two of us come in with you,' the duty sergeant said. 'This one's real trouble.'

The lawyer thought he knew better. 'I'll be fine,' he said.

He was let into the cell and locked in. Meanwhile, unbeknown to all concerned, the cell occupant had concealed a large turd in his hand. He produced it with a flourish and rubbed it into the lawyer's face just as he was about to introduce himself.

The lawyer screamed, and hammered on the cell door to be let out. The officers were perhaps a little slow in unlocking the door. He came out of the cell shaking with rage, scarcely able to walk, covered in excrement, but was greeted with little sympathy.

'I told you he was trouble,' said the straight-faced sergeant.

After the lawyer had cleaned up and gone home, the officers all had a jolly good laugh about it. To them it somehow seemed, well . . . symbolic. There never was much love lost between the police and the legal profession. Especially defence lawyers.

The men were still chuckling when Peter arrived later that evening. He had stopped off in Yeovil, Somerset, to pay his mother a visit on the way down.

They stayed in Exeter that night and celebrated their capture with some of the local officers in a lovely restaurant. During the meal, Jim, ever mindful of the Met's tough rules on subsistence payments, jokingly asked the waitress if she would put down their drinks as 'extra potatoes'. By the end of the evening the 'extra potatoes' had come to several hundred pounds.

Everyone felt a little the worse for wear the next day as they set off with their suspect on the long journey back to London. In truth, the celebrations turned out to be a little premature. After a day of questioning it became clear that Gallagher was not the 'insider' they were hoping for. However, the former employee did admit to making a plan and trying to sell it to someone. He was charged and dealt with by the courts and sentenced to at least three years' imprisonment. The other person, the Walter Mitty character who had tipped them off and been such a pain to deal with, had a very strong connection with the plan, but he was never formally charged. It was decided there was insufficient evidence.

However, it turned out that the plan for sale was of a Security Express depot near Watford. It had nothing to do with Curtain Road. So, after all that, Peter was back where he started. But he felt in his bones that this was the kind of thing the robbers must have done to get the kind of precise details of Curtain Road that were needed to successfully pull off the raid. They must have had a mole: someone like Gallagher, prepared to compromise Security Express in return for a packet of notes.

Meanwhile, it was back to the drawing board for the Dirty Dozen.

£££

The OP17 surveillance operation had dragged on throughout the autumn months and well into winter. By that time it was freezing in the ramshackle house in Albion Drive that served as Charlie and Terry's home from home. But as the weeks dragged on into months, slowly but surely, patterns of meeting were emerging. Names were being linked. Connections established.

Throughout the operation an official photographer from C7, the Met's technical support unit, would sometimes join them in the house. 'Ah! The gas man is here!' Charlie would exclaim to Terry. 'About bloody time too!' Terry would reply.

The 'gas man', dressed in overalls, would arrive carrying a heavy canvas holdall, full of 'tools'. 'Why is it that whenever I work with you two guys I always get really shit jobs?' he muttered as he climbed up the rickety wooden staircase to the bedroom. By then Charlie and Terry knew by heart which steps were safe to tread on and which ones they had to avoid.

The men became experts on the local neighbourhood: who visited who and when; the affairs; local rivalries. It was never really boring. As Charlie remarked afterwards to Peter, 'Human nature is fascinating. As long as you are watching humans, there's always something to keep you occupied.'

However, one big mystery remained. They had still not been able to identify the smartly dressed driver of the two-tone blue Granada car. It was by now imperative that they uncover his identity. On 5 September Charlie and Terry finally succeeded in following the car and its mystery driver to a home address in Enfield. The driver was thus 'housed' and identified from records as Terry Perkins, but they had almost nothing on him. There was no Home Office file for him. They could only find out that he was into property. Lots of it.

They traced the car and discovered that it was registered to a large, rambling garage in Southgate, M&M Bodyworks, which they found was run by a man named Alan Opiola. They established that Perkins regularly visited the garage.

This was a huge leap forward. By November, Charlie and Terry had got to John Knight. They discovered that Knight had been a previous owner of the car, and the way they found out was through a piece of good, solid, old-fashioned leg work.

Terry recalled that some five years before, when he was based at Edmonton, he used to go into a nurses' bar near the North Middlesex Hospital for a drink with one of his mates. There, he remembered meeting a bus driver called Opiola. It was such an unusual name that they had to be related, and in fact the man later turned out to be Alan Opiola's brother. It was quite a coincidence.

Charlie and Terry went to see Alan Gibbs, Terry's old collator of records at Edmonton police station. Gibbs was a copper very much of the old school. He kept flawless files going back years listing people of interest in the area, together with their car number plates. As luck would have it, the distinctive number plate of the car was in Gibbs's files. They found that John Knight was top of the list of the former keyholders for the car. Opiola had bought the car on Knight's behalf.

One day Terry took his own car, an old Renault 9, into M&M Bodyworks for an MoT test. The testing area was at the front of the garage, and the service area was right at the back. There was a dip in the middle of the garage, which made it very difficult to see from a distance what other cars were in there being serviced. While he was there, Terry clocked another blue Ford Granada on the ramp but this was a different registration number from the one they had seen before. This one was registered to a certain John Knight at High Trees, Wheathampstead.

It was an extraordinary stroke of luck. John Knight's home address wasn't a well-known fact. At the time it certainly wasn't to be found in the files of any of the police intelligence bureaux.

'Knight certainly likes his blue Ford Granadas,' Charlie mused. Now was it because he hated change and liked what he drove? Or was there another reason? Perhaps he liked confusing potential witnesses.

Some weeks later, Terry went up in a helicopter with a police photographer to obtain aerial photographs of the house. It was a hair-raising experience because they ended up flying into a thunderstorm.

For a while, Charlie and Terry were pulled off their surveillance work to deal with an IRA bomb that had gone off at Harrods just before Christmas. Young, inexperienced officers had made a pig's ear of taking the initial statements from bomb witnesses, so experienced officers from all over the Met were brought in to re-do the statements. But by then the two officers had been on to the golf course in front of High Trees dressed in tracksuits for 'strict training sessions'. They had even 'hunted for golf balls' in a patch of scrub that backed onto Knight's house. Once, they hid deep in the bushes for three or four hours, just watching the comings and goings at the house. One morning while they were watching, a car came out of Knight's driveway. It was the Granada that Terry had seen on the ramp at M&M Bodyworks.

In between working on other enquiry leads, Charlie and Terry followed Hickson, Perkins, and Knight around for weeks. From this they established who were friends with who. A network of associates was beginning to be pieced together. But was it the right one? Did these men carry out the Security Express robbery?

Peter was still not entirely convinced.

£££

In November 1983 another robbery took place that, to the Flying Squad, appeared to be a copycat of the Security Express robbery. The armed raid on the Brinks-Mat warehouse near Heathrow Airport had netted the robbers three tons of gold bars – at the time worth an estimated £26 million. Again, it appeared to involve the use of inside information and, once again, the guards were threatened with petrol.

The practical result was that many officers on the enquiry were transferred to the new investigation. Peter also lost the use of John Fordham, reassigned to surveillance duties on the Brinks-Mat investigation, in what proved to be a tragic turn of fate.

The Flying Squad suspected that the proceeds of the raid had been laundered by Kenneth Noye who, ironically enough, happened to be one of its own informants. One January evening Fordham was undercover in the wooded grounds of Hollywood Cottage, Noye's house near West Kingsdown in Kent, with a colleague, Neil 'Smurf' Murphy. Police officers were waiting at the gates of the house armed with a search warrant. Fordham and Murphy's task was to keep a clandestine watch to see if Noye and his associate tried to dispose of any evidence or made an attempt to escape.

A high wall capped with barbed wire surrounded the mock-Tudor house, which was set in twenty acres of woodland. Three Rottweiler dogs roamed loose in the grounds. The dogs had been assessed by police dog handlers through a hidden video camera. They had decided that a few tasty yeast tablets would probably sort them out. How wrong they were.

'Dogs hostile,' Murphy radioed, 'Dogs hostile.' He was forced to climb back over the high wall. Fordham, however, stayed where he was. Suddenly he was surprised by one of the dogs. The other two soon joined in the commotion.

'Someone out, halfway down drive, calling dogs,' he radioed.

Noye, armed with a kitchen knife, possibly with an associate, had come out of the house to see what all the fuss was about. When he saw the intruder in his garden he repeatedly stabbed the undercover officer to death. Fordham was unarmed.

Smurf, by that stage over the wall, could do little but radio for help as his colleague bled to death on the lawn. He never got over that, and afterwards he suffered terrific trauma. He had witnessed his colleague being murdered and he just went off the rails. He never ever forgave himself, but in truth, there was little he could have done. He never really was fit to work in a police force again. Eventually he retired from the force on ill-health grounds.

Noye and his wife were arrested immediately after the killing. 'He shouldn't have been on my property,' Noye told the arresting officers. 'I hope he dies.' Noye's associate, Brian Reader, was picked up along the road. All were charged with Fordham's murder.

In 1986 Noye was convicted of handling stolen bullion from the Brinks-Mat robbery, and jailed for fourteen years. However, to the deep disappointment of Fordham's colleagues, Noye was acquitted of murder.

Noye's wife's defence team had obtained a pathologist's report that concluded that the injuries sustained by Fordham were consistent with those of a man being held down by one man while another wielded the knife. Fordham had been stabbed ten times. There were no defensive wounds to the hands or arms, and some of the stab wounds were in his back. However, inexplicably, the prosecution dropped the case against

Noye's wife so the pathologist's report was never revealed to the jury.

Noye claimed that he had acted alone and in self-defence. His defence exhibited a photograph of a man in a balaclava helmet and fatigues and suggested that any reasonable householder would have done the same. The jury accepted that Noye had 'stabbed and stabbed in blind panic' and he was acquitted.*

Roy Chivers, who worked alongside Fordham on the Whitechapel Road surveillance, died in equally tragic circumstances. He had retired from the force and was on holiday with his wife in Kenya. Just as they were leaving their hotel together, Roy was attacked by a gang of street robbers. They demanded his valuables and his camera, but Roy put up a fight. So they stabbed him to death and then ran off. It was an incongruous end to an illustrious career.

* In April 2000 Noye was convicted for a road-rage killing and sentenced to life imprisonment.

9

BREAKTHROUGH

Friday, 20 January 1984, was going to be a very long day for the Flying Squad. As Peter drove through the darkness towards Arbour Square police station, he pondered over the day's work ahead.

A strange coincidence had come to light. A car, thought to have been used by the Brinks-Mat robbers, had been found abandoned close to the Albion pub and John Horsley's garage. It had rekindled interest in OP17, the masterful surveillance operation carried out by Charlie Collins and Terry Mills the previous year.

The Flying Squad decided that the car find gave them a perfect excuse to haul Horsley in for questioning. At the same time they planned to search his house in Waltham Abbey, the Albion public house, his repair garage round the corner, and a scaffolding yard run by his business partner Stan Atwell. Also on the list of places to search was Jimmy Knight's scrap yard in nearby Ridley Road.

The thirty or so officers involved had to be at Arbour Square for 5.30 a.m. The briefing started at 6 a.m. sharp. There was an air of excitement in the office as they got themselves organized. Altogether there were seven premises to be searched and five arrests to be made. By 7 a.m. all the teams were in position and in radio contact, ready to move in.

George Moncrieff was in charge of the raid on Horsley's modest house in Waltham Abbey. Horsley wasn't there, just his wife Gwen and daughter Tracy. The signs of new money had been plastered, quite literally, all over the house. Horsley had started to redecorated and new double glazing had been put in.

The officers searched the house and turned up a pile of documents and letters. Mrs Horsley was arrested and taken back to the station for further questioning.

Simon Webber and Jim Keeling went to Alpine Motors in Malvern Road where they found Horsley with his son Gary. They searched the garage and found nothing much of great interest – except for seven drums of stolen paint thinners that had been hidden away at the back. Both father and son were arrested and brought down to the station for questioning.

The other raids and arrests that morning produced little of immediate interest. Jimmy Knight was nowhere to be found at his scrap yard. The landlord of the Albion public house was arrested and brought in for questioning because Peter had a suspicion that he was somehow involved with the men. But in the end that proved not to be the case. He just ran a good pub, and rogues happen to appreciate a well-pulled pint.

Back at the station George and Peter sifted through the paperwork recovered from Horsley's house. It confirmed what they had suspected. Letters and bank statements clearly showed that, within the space of just a few months, Horsley had gone from teetering on the verge of bankruptcy to living the life of the proverbial Riley. All manner of debts had been paid off in rapid succession.

Gwen Horsley knew very little, but confirmed that her husband's fortunes had dramatically changed for the better. She didn't know why, and never asked any questions about it, but was glad that, for once, they did not have to worry about a knock on the door from the bailiffs.

Officially, Horsley had been arrested and brought in by the team of detectives investigating the Brinks-Mat robbery to help with their enquiries. At the beginning of their interview Horsley was shaking. But when he realized it was Brinks-Mat that the detectives were interested in he got all his confidence back.

Horsley, of course, knew nothing about the parked car by the Albion. 'That's all we want to speak to you about,' the officers said, as they closed up their notebooks and got ready to leave. Horsley gave a sigh of relief and made as if to get out of his chair.

'Hold on. Where do you think you are going?' said George, who until that moment had been sitting quietly in the corner with Simon, who was busy taking notes.

Horsley visibly wilted. 'They were talking nonsense,' he said, half laughing. 'I don't know anything about the gold job.'

George cut straight to the chase: 'The first thing I want to do is sort out your current financial position. Has there been any drastic change in your finances in the last year?'

'No, not really.'

'Come on, John, that's not the case at all, is it? In January last year you were in financial trouble.'

'Well, I had a few debts, yeah.'

'And yet by July you were able to open a building society account with a cash deposit of six thousand pounds.'

'That's savings.'

'Where from?'

'I do cash jobs on Saturdays and Sundays. I've just saved it over the years.'

'So where was this money prior to opening the account?'

'Indoors.'

'Just lying about?' George looked at him incredulously. 'It's not just six thousand is it, John? From correspondence found at your house it's obvious that you were in debt to the tune of two grand or so. Already that's eight grand to account for.'

'I've told you where that come from.'

'John, you must be aware that your wife has been spoken to. Apart from the eight grand, you have bought two cars, one for your wife and one for yourself. This was at the same time as the six thousand appeared. You then had a holiday in Greece and you've had double glazing and other work done on your house.'

'Business has been really good in the last year.'

'When last year?'

'All the time.'

'But you were unable to pay off debts in January and February. That only leaves three or four months for all this money to accumulate. On a rough estimate this all amounts to thirteen or fourteen thousand pounds.'

'I've told you, it's from the business.'

George sighed. 'John, I've watched your garage for substantial periods of time. There's no way, on the amount of business you do, that you could take out anything like that amount of money.'

Horsley was defensive as George leafed through the paperwork recovered from his house, which charted the sudden rise in his family's fortune.

'You see, John, all this happens in the space of a couple of months, June and July last year, when on 14 March you had to appear at the County Court over a debt of £891 to a finance company.'

George gestured towards the untidy pile of letters and bank statements lying on the table.

'It's all here in black and white, John. We know where the money came from. You know where it came from. Shall we stop messing about and have the truth?'

'Look, all I did was a favour for someone. I just let them use my garage.' Horsley's voice was strained.

'Your business premises?

'No, the one at home.'

'Are you positive?'

'Yes. It was at home.' Horsley shot a questioning look at George. 'Who's grassed me up?'

'What was the garage used for?'

'You must know. I didn't think it would ever come to this.'

'Who used your garage?'

'You've got to be fucking joking.' Horsley let out a nervous laugh. 'I can't tell you that. I'd be a dead man.'

'All right. We'll come back to that question.' George paused to look over his notes. It was high time for Peter to take over. 'Listen. I intend to get the officer in charge to come and see you,' he said. 'But you'll be seen again shortly, OK?'

'Yes, but I can't tell you any more.'

Horsley refused to sign Simon's notes of the meeting and was taken back to a detention room.

It was lunchtime. George and Simon both went off to find Peter to brief him on the interview.

There was a chink of light showing now, but Horsley was plainly scared. The three officers sat round a table in the back room of a local pub discussing ways of getting him to talk. They all agreed that the best way was to get Horsley to tell his side of the story first, without implicating anyone else. That way he wouldn't be so worried about retaliation. Then they could maybe throw the book at him, pointing out that he could well be tried as a robber, before offering him a lifeline in the form of turning Queen's evidence. It was a dirty tactic but then again they had not nicknamed themselves the Dirty Dozen for nothing. The drums of stolen paint thinners that they had found in his garage could also perhaps be used to bring pressure to bear on him.

Around half past two the three of them went back to the detention room. Horsley looked up as they trooped into the room. It was going to be a tough, three-cornered interrogation.

'John, this is the senior officer I told you about,' said George. 'I've explained your fears to him, but first of all I want you to tell Mr Wilton what you have already admitted to us, without implicating anyone else.'

'I don't mind doing that but I'm not very good at explaining things,' Horsley said. 'Perhaps you could ask me questions?'

'Whatever you find easiest, John,' said Peter. 'What part did you play in the Security Express robbery?'

'I didn't know it was going to be as big as that.' The three policemen looked across at each other sceptically. Horsley continued: 'On my two kids' lives, I never knew it was that one.'

'You knew that, by the people you were dealing with, it was going to be a robbery, didn't you, John?' said Simon.

'All right, fair enough, I'm not saying I didn't know that, but not the fucking Security Express job.'

Peter calmed him down. 'All right, John, all right, John. I'm not suggesting that they would have told you the exact type of premises. But what I'm saying is that you weren't dealing with people that go shoplifting. You were dealing with people who were professional criminals, in fact, professional robbers. Isn't that right?'

'I only dealt with one man, whose name I can't give.'

'Why can't you?'

'Are you fucking joking? He'd get me done.'

'Yes, John, yes, because he's an evil man,' said Peter patiently. 'A robber.'

'Yeah, I take your point. The man I was talking to was a robber. I knew that, but not that it was going to be a job like that.'

'But an armed robbery?'

'Yes.'

'Anyway, let's get back to what this man asked you to do and what you subsequently did,' said Simon.

'I rented my garage to someone to store some gear.'

'When you say "gear" you mean cash from the Security Express robbery?' asked Peter.

'Before the robbery I never knew what they would be putting in there.'

'It could have been guns for all you knew,' said Simon. 'Guns perhaps which had been used or were going to be used for the robbery.'

Horsley looked rattled. 'I don't know why you talk about guns – it was the money,' he retorted. 'If it was just a few guns they wouldn't have needed a garage.'

'Carry on,' said Peter.

'He asked me for all of the keys to the garage and I gave him them.'

'How many and when?' asked Simon.

'Um. Two keys.' Horsley thought for a moment. 'I'm not very good on dates. It's a long time ago.'

'Yes, it is, but it's not a period of time, the time around the robbery on 4 April, that you are likely to forget,' said Peter.

'No. I shat myself when I knew it was the £7 million job. The person approached me about a week before the job.'

'And how long was the money in the garage?'

'They had the keys for two weeks but I don't know exactly how long the stuff was in the garage.'

'You never went in the garage?' said Simon, raising his eyebrows.

'No.'

'What was your share?' asked Peter.

'Fifteen grand.'

'Are you telling me you never once looked in that garage?' Simon said.

'No, I couldn't. I didn't have a key.'

'You must have asked the man who approached you about the job,' said Peter.

Horsley laughed derisively at him. 'You don't ask him questions like that.'

'No conversations after the job about it? You're the one who must be joking.'

'All right. He said it was the greatest thing that had ever happened and that it went as sweet as a nut.'

'When was this?' said Simon. 'You haven't said this before.'

'When I got the money he told me that.'

'How much and when did you get paid?'

'He paid me in three lots, five grand each time.'

'When and where?'

'He came round to my house. I've told you I'm not good on dates, but the first lot was a long time after the job. About a month after.'

'And the rest?'

'Two weeks after that, and again two weeks after that.'

Until then George had been quietly listening to his colleagues' lines of questioning. 'Was anyone else at home?' he asked.

'I'm telling you straight. None of my family know anything about this,' Horsley said.

Peter sighed. 'Listen, John, why not give the name?'

Horsley gestured towards George and Simon. 'I've told them and I'm telling you there's no way I can do that. I'd rather be sent up the Swannee than think that anything will happen to my wife.'

'Your family must have noticed an upturn in your lifestyle. They must have, John,' said Peter.

'No, they never knew about that. Listen, can I see my wife before I comment any further?'

George shook his head. 'John, she's still in custody. We have to be certain that you do not say anything to her which would compromise this delicate enquiry.'

'I'll be straight with you. I've told you so much. There's more that I could say. I've got to know that I'm doing the right thing. I won't say anything to her to fuck you. You can be in here if you want.'

'That would be the case anyway, John,' Simon said.

George looked over towards Peter.

'Well, sir?'

Peter nodded.

'Right, John, I'm going to let you see your wife,' said George. 'We'll go down and bring her up. But remember, if you start to say things that will compromise this enquiry the visit ends.'

'Thanks.'

Simon took Horsley back down to the cells while Peter and George fetched Gwen. Twenty minutes later he was brought back to the interview room to talk to her.

For Horsley, what then followed was an agonizing conversation. He told his wife about being implicated in the robbery. He said he knew he had a big decision to make as to what, if anything, he told the police. But, frankly, it was all beyond Gwen. She told him that she didn't really know what was happening. He would have to make his own mind up. After some twenty minutes of this, she was taken back to her cell. At a quarter past four, Peter returned to the interrogation room.

'Nothing of interest has been said by Mr Horsley, sir.'

'Sorry for the delay, Simon. Quite a bit happening.' Peter was smiling broadly.

'Right, John. It's obvious from what you said to your wife that you are seriously thinking about telling us the full facts as you know them.'

'I've got to, but I can't bring myself to commit myself, as you call it.'

George said, 'What do you mean by that?'

'I'm not saying anything. If I tell you what you want to know, will it get back to them?'

'Listen, John, whether you like it or not, as you see, everything is being recorded by the sergeant over there.' He nodded towards Simon.

'We can't force you to sign the notes even though we're obliged to give you the opportunity to do so.'

'That's all I'm worried about, signing things,' said Horsley.

'You can tell us, John, the name of the man who took the keys from you.'

'If you know that much about me you must know who that is.'

'Yes, John, probably we do,' George said. 'But we want it from you.'

'Billy Hickson,' Horsley blurted out. 'I've known him years. You know him.'

'Yes, John. It's to him that you gave the keys to your garage.'

'Yes. Listen. You know where he drinks?'

'The Albion.'

'I thought so.'

Peter took out a surveillance photograph of Horsley and Hickson standing outside the Albion. 'What do you think of that?' he asked.

'You know everything, don't you?'

'Not everything, John,' Simon said. 'You can confirm and in some respects knock down what we think we might know.'

'Have you any other photographs?'

'Lots,' Peter replied.

'I can give you another two names and a description.'

'Of what?' said Simon.

'Of who done Security Express.'

'Well, John, let's have them,' said Peter.

'I don't know if I'm doing the right thing . . . one's a good mate of Billy's. I only know his first name – Terry.'

'John, is this the Terry you're talking about?' said Simon. He took out another photograph, this time of Hickson and Perkins together.

'Fuck me,' said Horsley. 'Yeah, that's him.'

'The other man?' asked Simon.

'I didn't know who he was at the time but his name is John. His brother is married to Barbara Windsor. You must know them.'

'And the third?'

'The other man I can only describe. He's fifty years plus, an inch or so taller than me, and he wears glasses.'

'What sort of build is he?'

'He's average. A bit of a beer belly. I only saw him once. He looked a real scruffy sod.'

'How do you know they were on it?'

'I know, believe me, I know.'

'We need to know *how* you know.'

'I don't know why I'm telling you all this. I must be mad, telling you all this, but I'm torn between . . . I don't know what . . .'

'But you *are* telling us, John. Why do you think you are doing that?'

'I'm between the devil and the deep blue sea.'

'Perhaps, John, perhaps.' Peter gave him a wry smile. 'You're telling me names but nothing as to their parts in this.'

'Give me time. It's a big decision. If you were in my shoes how do you think you would feel or do?'

The implications of what he was doing dawned on him and Horsley grew nervous. 'You realize I'm not saying anything or writing anything down?'

'John, you can see him writing everything down.'

'I see that, but as far as I'm concerned that's it.'

George looked at him questioningly. 'What do you mean, that's it?'

'Until I write down myself or sign things you write, as far as I'm concerned everything's wide open.'

George sighed, 'John, try to understand this. You have admitted in some detail the part you have played in this serious matter, but apart from that, we will prove that in a period of time shortly after the robbery your financial position suddenly changes from that of debt to a position of some affluence.'

'You don't understand what I'm saying. I'm not saying I'll try and change what I've said. As to what I've done I'm up the creek.' Horsley put his head in his hands. 'I'm fucked. I've done what I've done. I'm finished, but I can't . . . you understand, if I go against the people I've mentioned, my family's finished. You know that as well as I do.'

'John, you keep saying you won't write anything down or sign anything. If you wish to make a written statement, you can.'

'Let me think about that. I suppose I can make a statement just about what I've done. I don't have to put other names down.'

'You can do. It's your statement. Is that what you want to do?'

'Not yet. Let me think about it.'

'All right. Let's leave it at that for the time being. I have to give you the opportunity to read and sign the notes you have seen Detective Sergeant Moncrieff write.'

'I told you. I just can't sign anything yet.'

'John, I'll read them to you. Everything you have said is there.'

'That's what I'm afraid of. You just don't seem to understand.'

At 4.30 Horsley was taken back to his cell. There he sat, a tormented man, deep in thought. A couple of hours later he asked to see an officer. 'I want to make that statement,' he said.

They had been expecting it. Simon and George took him back to the interview room on the third floor. The tale he told was one of a man badly in debt, tempted by the lure of easy money. 'It got to the stage where I just wasn't making enough money to live on,' he told them. 'At the end of March I was offered a good drink for the use of my garage. Because I've got a partner and I work there, I offered the use of my private garage at home. The man who approached me had a look at it and said it was all right. I gave him all the keys I had.

'I knew from the off that it had to be bent gear, but I didn't want to know,' he said. 'Roughly a fortnight after I handed over the keys I was given them back. I wasn't given anything apart from promises until about a month later, then I was given a carrier bag with five grand in all different notes in it. I was promised more money for later on. They kept their word.'

And that was all he was prepared to say.

'Listen,' he said to the two officers. 'I've told you my part and I'm going to have to pay for that, but like I've said all along, I can't give names. I just can't help you.'

£££

Later that evening Peter sat in his office, surrounded by piles of files, surveillance reports, and statements. He had read through Horsley's statement again and again. It wasn't going to crack the case, but it was a good start. Peter knew in his bones that there was more to come. He wondered how he could put a little more pressure on him to spill the beans. The next forty-eight hours were going to be crucial. He felt he had learnt enough to pull in both Billy Hickson and Terry Perkins for questioning.

Before he went home, he leafed through the Prison Service files on Hickson that had been obtained by Jim Keeling.

Hickson was a smart East End villain with an eye for the birds. He was no stranger to the Law, forty years old and with form as long as your arm. And he was seemingly cocky with it, too. By comparison, Terry Perkins's file was painfully thin. He had one offence for drunk driving, but apart from that he was clean as a whistle.

It wasn't going to be easy.

£££

The next day, Saturday, early in the morning, three officers went round to the flat where Hickson was staying. It was on a poor estate, full of narrow walkways and dingy brick stairwells, less than half a mile from Curtain Road.

The door was opened by Hickson's newly wed wife Maureen. 'We have a warrant to search this address,' said one of the officers. Without saying a word she let them in.

'Where's Billy boy?'

'In bed.'

The three officers clumped into the bedroom where Hickson was lying in bed, sleeping.

'We're police officers and I'm arresting you for armed robbery.'

It was a rude awakening. They waited while Hickson got dressed and then the officers turned over the flat from top to bottom. While they were searching the living room Hickson turned to Maureen. 'Remember what Ralph said. Don't say nothing.'

He was overheard by one of the officers.

'About what?'

Hickson just laughed.

'Is that Ralph Haeems?' said another.

'Yeah, he's my brief. His home number is on the wall in the kitchen,' he said pointedly, more for Maureen's ears than anyone else's.

They went downstairs to search his car, and then he was taken down to the station, where he was booked.

A little later that morning, Peter sat across the table from Hickson. Bernie Butler sat nearby, pen and notebook in hand. Hickson lounged back in his chair, brimming with confidence.

'We're investigating the Security Express robbery that took place on 4 April last year,' Peter said.

Hickson feigned surprise. 'Cor blimey, guv, that's a bit heavy.'

'Well, there you are, Billy. We've got a nice bit on you. What you've got to say now will show us what part you played in it.'

'You must be joking, guv.'

'We've got a lot of evidence against you,' Peter continued. 'We've got people in custody who we've spoken to and they've told us all about you. We've done a lot of work on this job and we've kept an eye on you, Billy. We know where you've been.'

'I'll be quite honest with you, guv. This frightens me. I don't know what you've seen or been told, guv. I don't know what to say.'

Peter leaned forward across the desk. 'Look, Billy, you've come into a lot of money, haven't you?'

Hickson sat there in silence while Peter continued, 'You've

just got married again, had a nice honeymoon, spent a lot of money on that and your new home. What's your new wife going to think about all this, Billy? She's sitting at home wondering what she's let herself in for.'

'She don't know nothing, guv.'

'Well, how does she account for your sudden wealth? She's got to be spoken to about all this, hasn't she? All those nice presents. All that furniture.' He paused. 'Tell us what you did in the robbery. How many others were there with you?'

'How can I tell you who they were? If you've done your homework right you know what I can say. You shouldn't ask me questions like that.'

Peter changed tack. 'Tell us, Billy, do you know the Albion?'

Hickson nodded.

'Do you know who owns it?'

'Yes, we go back a long way.'

'How often do you go there, Billy?'

'A bit. Why?'

'You used the pub a lot last year, didn't you?'

Hickson shrugged. 'If you say so.'

'Who did you meet?'

'You tell me.'

'Think about this before you answer.'

'Well, Derek and other people. You must know that.'

'Who? John and Stan?'

'John and Stan who?'

'The garage people. The people who have the little place at the back of the pub.'

'You tell me.'

'Well, it's quite simple. Do you know John Horsley and Stan Atwell?'

'You said you knew all about me.'

'We saw you visit their garage virtually every day of the week last summer.'

'I don't want to say anything.'

'But, Billy, you suddenly don't want to talk about these people because you've got something to hide. What about Terry?'

'Terry who? You told me you knew all about me. If that's true, why ask me so much?'

Peter smiled. 'Now wait, Billy. You're evading questions about the very people we know are involved with you in the robbery.'

Hickson scratched his head in deliberation. 'No, listen,' he said. 'I've just had a thought. When was this robbery?'

'It was 4 April 1983.'

'I've got you there!' he announced triumphantly. 'You lot were watching me!'

'What do you mean?' asked Peter curiously.

'A friend of mine, a stallholder, told me you were watching me and taking pictures. You must have them.'

'Where were we taking pictures from?'

'Above Lipton's.'

'What, in Whitecross Street?' asked Bernie.

'Yes,' said Hickson, beaming at the two officers. 'You were watching the alley!'

Peter hesitated for a moment. 'No, wait a minute,' he said. 'That was a bank holiday. There wouldn't be a market and I doubt if any of our people would be watching you on that date.'

'Well, that's what I was told.' Hickson looked across at the two officers sitting opposite him and laughed. 'This is ridiculous. I thought I had been nicked about a fight.'

'What fight was that?'

'My brother-in-law.'

'What, your new brother-in-law?'

'Yes. But I don't want to talk about it.' Hickson fixed his gaze on Peter. 'Look, guv, you've told me where I drink and the names of a couple of people I drink with. Show me what else you know and then I'll decide.'

'You've blanked us on the garage owners and Terry,' said Peter. 'Let me tell you that we know you put the money from Security Express into a garage at Waltham Abbey.'

Hickson shook his head. 'You've made a big mistake. I wasn't on the robbery.'

'Well, at the moment I've just put to you about a garage in Waltham Abbey.'

'I've got to think about this.'

'It's quite simple, Billy. You got Horsley to let you use his garage before the robbery. You had both the keys.'

'So he's said something?'

'I didn't say that.'

Hickson rolled his eyes. 'I knew it,' he sighed. 'So what's in using a garage? How does that involve me in a robbery?'

'Because we know the money was put in there.'

For a rare moment, Hickson was lost for words.

Peter pulled out some papers from his folder. 'What about this trip to Jersey?'

'What's so wrong with going to Jersey?'

'You went with Terry Perkins and a couple of others.'

'So what?'

'How well do you know Perkins?'

Hickson shrugged his shoulders.

'We've seen you together a few times at the Albion last year.'

'You seem to know it all.'

'We also know that Perkins was involved in the robbery.'

'I told you. I'm not involved.'

'Well, we've seen all three of you, Perkins, Horsley, and yourself, around Horsley's garage in the summer.'

'Look, you're making a big mistake.'

'Billy! What are you doing now, work-wise?'

Hickson sat there in silence.

'Your flat is full of new furniture. You've just got married. Honeymooned in Paris. Had a holiday abroad before that. Bought a new car. Spent a lot of money on your reception.' Peter gave him a quizzical look. 'How can you afford all that?'

'I don't have to tell you about my money.'

'Just explain how you can afford it. You didn't appear to be working last year. How can you live so well? You're always in the pub.'

'I don't have to answer these questions.'

'Billy, listen to this. Other people have been arrested this morning and are being spoken to, you know,' said Peter. 'We've done a lot of work on this and you were involved in that robbery.'

'Look, guv'nor. I don't want to be rude. I appreciate you have a job to do, but this has all come as a bit of a shock.'

'Well, Billy, you just have a think about it.'

Peter asked him to sign the notes of the interview but Hickson refused. 'No thank you, guv'nor, I've had enough now,' he said.

'It's up to you. Well, we'll end the interview here and come and see you later,' said Peter. 'Interview terminated 11.50 a.m.'

Hickson was taken back to the cells.

£££

Meanwhile, John Horsley had had a sleepless night. Throughout Saturday morning he had been restless, pacing up and down his cell, as if deep in thought. In the afternoon he asked the duty sergeant if he could see George. So George went down to the cells to see him.

'I've been thinking all night about what Mr Wilton told me last night,' Horsley said. 'I've told you more than I should have,' he continued. 'I think I'm entitled to some help.'

'There can be no promises,' George replied. 'You have admitted your part in a serious armed robbery. You are going to be charged. If you do fully cooperate with us it's a matter for the courts to decide if you are entitled to a more lenient sentence.'

'Listen. What I'm talking about is giving evidence for you, then a bit more. I can tell you about the people concerned.'

George smiled. 'I think we had better get Mr Wilton over here.'

Horsley was taken up to the interview room while George got hold of Peter.

Some twenty minutes later, Peter entered the room.

'Sir, John tells me that he is considering giving evidence for the prosecution,' said George.

'Is that right, John?' Peter asked.

'That's in my mind,' said Horsley. 'I want to know where I stand.'

Rules were rules. They told him that he would have to be charged, regardless. 'When that has been done you can speak to us further,' said Peter, as they took him to the charge room.

That afternoon, Horsley told them where some of the Security Express money had been kept. It was, he said, at his father-in-law's flat in Waltham Abbey, Essex. George Carter didn't have a clue about the secret compartment in his own home that Horsley had constructed. So Gwen Horsley went there first to take her father out of the flat. Carter was seventy-six, and the sight of a dozen or so officers descending on the place might well have been too much for him.

Gwen returned at around 5 p.m. and handed George the key to the flat. An hour later, George, Peter, and John Horsley took a Squad car to the flat, arriving at seven. There, they were joined by Simon, Malcolm Jeffery, a scene-of-crime officer, and a photographer.

'There!' Horsley said, pointing towards a cupboard jammed full of coats just to the left of the entrance to the tiny flat. An officer climbed into the cupboard and fumbled around with a screwdriver. He removed two side panels to reveal a hidden space just about large enough for a man to stand upright in.

Inside this false compartment, the officers found three canvas bags and three box files. The bags and files were stuffed full of cash, all neatly bundled up. Each bundle contained roughly £2,500 in notes. A note had been wrapped around each bundle and secured with a rubber band. The notes had a musty smell of damp earth, as if they had been buried somewhere. On the top panel of the compartment the officers could make out figures, which had been scrawled in pencil. Clearly someone, probably Horsley himself, had kept a tally of how much money was there.

On the opposite side of the hallway, in another cupboard, they were shown a blue suitcase, presumably used to carry the banknotes. That was taken away for forensic examination.

The team got back to Leman Street police station at 9 p.m., and immediately started to trace where the canvas bags might have come from.

Frank Cater was over the moon when he heard the news. 'Finally, a result,' he said.

Cater wanted to put off counting the cash until the morning, but Peter was having none of that. He wanted the case to be absolutely watertight and he wasn't going to give the defence any opportunity to claim that there had been more cash in the hideout than there actually was, and hence cast a slur on his officers. So that night Peter called in police constables from stations all over London. They turned up and filed into a large room specially set up with row upon row of small, wooden desks. It looked like an examination hall. Under the watchful eyes of Malcolm, the uniformed police men and women, all wearing latex gloves, counted the notes by hand. They would not finish until the early hours of the morning. Once counted, the notes were again photographed alongside the bag or box in which they had been found.

£££

Just after midnight, Horsley made his second statement under caution to Simon and George. It began: 'The first thing I want to say about the statement the other evening is that I held back quite a lot, both about other people and about my involvement, and I've now decided to give the full story.'

It emerged that he had known Billy Hickson for seven or eight years. They had met in the Albion pub, just around the corner from his garage. Since then, Hickson had become a regular customer of Alpine Motors.

One day, in late March 1983, Horsley was working in the garage when Hickson turned up with a man he knew as Terry Perkins. Hickson did all the talking. 'Have you got a lock-up?' he asked.

'I've got one at my house.'

'What are your neighbours like?'

'They mind their own business. Why?'

'I want to use it to store something in.' Hickson glanced

across at Perkins, who nodded his silent agreement. 'We'll go and have a look at it,' said Hickson. 'If it's OK there'll be a nice drink in it for you.' Later on that day Hickson told him the garage was 'all right'.

On the Friday before the Easter Bank Holiday weekend, Hickson dropped by to see Horsley at the garage. 'The job is on for Bank Holiday Monday,' he said. 'Get your family out of the way. Meet me on Monday at six in the evening outside the Fortune of War pub on the Southend Road.'

Horsley's wife went off to see some friends on the Monday. His children were out for the day. He drove across country to the Fortune of War, and as he pulled up in the car park, he saw that Hickson was already there, waiting for him. He got into Horsley's car. 'It's too early,' Hickson said.

They drove back to Horsley's house, had a cup of tea, and watched a bit of television. A couple of hours later, Hickson said that it was time to go. While Horsley drove, Hickson directed him towards the East End. They drove down Kingsland Road, towards the City, past Shoreditch Church and then turned left opposite Great Eastern Street.

'Pull up here, John,' Hickson said. 'If we don't arrive by ten we won't be coming.' He got out and walked across the road and back towards Great Eastern Street.

Horsley drove back home and waited for Hickson to turn up at his house. While he waited, he watched the ten o'clock news. He saw the pictures of the Security Express depot crawling with police and reporters, and it frightened the life out of him. 'That must be it,' he thought to himself.

At ten thirty, there was a soft tap on his kitchen window. It was Hickson. Horsley let him in. Hickson was in a rush. 'Can I borrow your motor?' he said.

'Sure,' said Horsley, handing him the keys.

'I'll be back in half an hour.' And with that, Hickson was out of the door again.

Horsley watched out of his window and waited for Hickson to return. He saw the car pull up outside and he went out to meet him. While Hickson went indoors, to avoid the neighbours' stares, Horsley unloaded three large, heavy sacks out of the boot and into the garage. Hickson went off in the car again and, around twenty minutes later, returned with another four sacks. Again, he disappeared indoors while Horsley unloaded them. As he was moving the last sack, a Panda car drove by.

'We'll leave the rest,' Hickson said. He drove off in the car again.

After some twenty minutes he returned. This time there was another car with him, a yellowish Granada, driven by an older man and behind that, a third car. Three people were in that one, one of them being Terry Perkins.

Hickson got out. Horsley, Hickson, and the older-looking bloke unloaded three or four sacks out of the yellow Granada and into the garage. Perkins had disappeared indoors.

'We had to come back,' Hickson told him. 'The other place was full up.'

After the garage was closed they all drove off, except for Hickson. By now it was getting on for midnight. Hickson asked Horsley for a lift to Sewardstone Road. 'You'll get your drink for the work John,' he said, 'but you'll have to wait a while.'

Horsley dropped him off and went to pick up his wife and they drove home. After she went indoors, he had a look under the seats. There, he found a £500 bundle of notes. He stuffed it in his pocket.

Later he thought better of it. He told Hickson about it and said he'd put it back with the others.

'Take a few days off work,' Hickson said. 'Keep an eye on your garage.'

So Horsley told his partner Stan Atwell that he was ill. While he was off 'sick', he couldn't resist having a peek at all the sacks in the garage. They took up about a quarter of the space. There was some loose change and cheques strewn on the floor, where a sack had toppled over. He stuck the change in his jumper and carried it indoors and counted it up. It came to three grand. He burnt the cheques.

After a few days, Hickson got hold of him and said he wanted to come around. He spent the afternoon in the house. He got 'upset' because the others hadn't turned up when they were supposed to. Finally, about five o'clock, Perkins arrived. He was moaning about someone else. Shortly afterwards, a well-dressed fellow came in. Horsley shook hands with him but was never introduced.

Perkins had turned up in a white Bedford van. They backed it up to the garage doors, and while Perkins and Hickson loaded the van the well-dressed man disappeared; Horsley stayed by front of the van with the bonnet up, pretending to look at the engine. It was loaded within minutes and Perkins drove it away. Hickson followed in his car.

They never told Horsley where they were taking the money to next.

A month later Hickson came around to see Horsley and gave him a carrier bag with thirty grand in fifty-pound notes. Horsley put the money in the bottom of his wardrobe underneath his old working clothes. He knew that some six or seven million had been stolen, but he was well pleased with his share.

Later, Hickson told him not to spend the fifties. 'You can only get large amounts of fifties by ordering them,' he said. Soon afterwards, he came around and handed Horsley £20,000 in tenners, which he changed for the fifties.

Sometime later Hickson came to see Horsley. 'Do you know of a safe place where I can stash some money?' he asked.

'There's my loft.'

'Hmm.'

'The only other place I can think of is my father-in-law's flat,' Horsley told him. 'I could put a false panel in a cupboard.' Hickson agreed.

Horsley made the false compartment and then Billy brought two suitcases around. He counted the money on the pool table. Horsley later found out that Billy had stored £400,000 there.

Hickson never went to the flat after that. Whenever he wanted money, he would pop by the garage and tell Horsley. Horsley would then go and get the money from the false compartment and give it to him.

Around Christmas 1983 Hickson got married to Maureen, the girl he had been living with. The wedding reception was held in a pub in Dalston called the Fox, and there Horsley met the well-dressed man again, the one he had shaken hands with just after the robbery.

'Who's that bloke?' he asked Perkins.

'That's John Knight,' Perkins said. 'His brother's married to Barbara Windsor.'

After Christmas, Hickson asked him to tot up how much money he had left at the flat. He did, and it came to £290,000. It was then that Horsley realized that Hickson hadn't a clue about exactly how much cash he had. He had been too busy enjoying himself to notice. So Horsley helped himself to five grand.

Horsley finished dictating his statement at 1.15 a.m.. It was a result, and not a moment too soon. 'As you know, I've spent nearly all the money I got from this business,' he told the two officers sitting in the interview room with him. 'I'm prepared to help you all I can to identify the fourth man.'

Peter had dropped into the interview room every now and then to see how the statement was going. Personally, he thought Horsley was a 'led' character. He wasn't a strong man. The robbers had to use 'little' people and they were clearly the weak links in the chain. But it was also clear that Horsley was no fool. Peter chuckled to himself as he read through the bit about Horsley helping himself to Hickson's money. 'There's no honour among thieves,' he thought to himself.

£££

Peter was in a smug mood when the next day, Sunday morning, he interviewed Hickson for the second time. 'Well, Billy, how do you feel today? We want to talk to you again about the robbery and show you what we know.' He paused and glanced at Billy. 'Is there anything you want to say before I start?'

Hickson's face feigned exasperation. 'I can't work this out. I told you yesterday I wasn't involved in it.'

'Well, Billy, we know a little bit more about you and where you were on 4 April last year. All this about you being watched is rubbish. You were down the Southend Road in the evening –

after you had been down at Security Express committing the robbery.'

Hickson shook his head.

'We can prove that you have been spending lots of money since the robbery. Your wedding. Reception. Honeymoon. New furniture. Holiday. Cars.'

Hickson sat there listening, without saying a word.

'Have you ever been to John Horsley's garage near his house?' Peter asked.

'No.'

Peter let out a sigh. 'Billy. You took the money up there and put it in the garage!'

'You're wrong.'

'Have you ever been to Horsley's house?'

'I'm not saying nothing.'

'Well, Billy, we know you have. You went there after meeting Horsley out in Essex. You arranged to meet him after the robbery, didn't you?'

'I wasn't on the robbery.'

'We're not kidding, Billy.' Peter reached for his folder. He took out a surveillance photograph of Hickson and Perkins standing outside the Albion and slid it across the table.

'Who's that in the photograph, Billy?' Peter said mockingly.

Hickson stared sullenly at the photo.

'Billy! It's you and Terry outside the Albion in the summer!' Peter took out some more photos. 'We've got other photographs of the three of you.' He laid the photos out on the table for Hickson to see. 'That's you two and Horsley meeting after the robbery.'

'So what?' said Hickson.

'It confirms what I'm saying. You and Terry Perkins got Horsley to let you use his garage.'

'So we did. How does that put us in the robbery?'

'Because it was within a few hours of the robbery and you had organized the garage before it.'

'Look, I wasn't on the robbery.'

'Now listen to this then, Billy. Have you ever been to a flat near Horsley's house, 17 Edward Court, on the same estate?'

The colour began to drain from Hickson's face. 'I'm not going to answer that.'

'I thought you wouldn't want to now, because this is going to be a big shock to you, Billy,' said Peter. He took out a sheet of paper from his folder and waved it at Hickson. 'Your nest egg has gone.'

Hickson stared at him in disbelief.

'We've got it and I can prove it. Look. Look at this.' Peter tapped the sheet of paper. 'Billy, we've got £288,000 plus. It's only some of your share because we know you've spent a few bob. You might even have some more stashed away somewhere.'

But by this stage the words were lost on Hickson. Tears were welling up in his eyes as he stared out of the window of the interview room. He slowly shook his head, murmuring to himself, 'What's that stupid idiot done?'

Peter was on a roll. 'We've done our homework. Perkins has spent thousands of pounds he can't account for. So has Horsley. And so have you. The money is obviously from Security Express and the three of you plus others are all involved,' he continued. 'Now, it's not only for fixing the garage because if you've spent so much and we've recovered this amount you must have been on the job itself. That's a fair share. Horsley obviously only got a small drink because we can show he had £30,000. Yours is £400,000 at least.'

'So you've found some money in the old man's place,' Hickson said snidely.

'Who said it was an old man's place? We only said the address.'

'So I've been there. So what? You can't prove it's my money.'

'Your whole answer about the day of the robbery, the garage at Horsley's home, the flat where we found the money, have all been evasive.' Peter tapped the piece of paper lying on the table. 'You were on the robbery and that's your share, and so was Perkins.' He paused to watch Hickson's face. 'So was John Knight.'

Hickson stared poker-faced at Peter.

'Did Knight go to your wedding last year?'

'I don't have to answer that, do I?'

'You don't, because they are part of the team that did this robbery with you and we can show that you've been living like a king. We can show how much money you've spent. I would like to know what you spent £55,000 on. Was it a villa?'

'I ain't got no villa.'

Peter showed him a photograph of a villa, which they had found among his possessions. 'What's this then?'

Hickson shrugged.

'What about the holiday you had with Perkins in Portugal? We could probably show that on the back of the board.'

'What board?'

'The false panel where your money was hidden shows how much money you were taking out. What about the £5,000 for your honeymoon?'

'You've made a mistake. I can't believe all this.'

'Billy, we've even got the board to show you if you want. It's you who have spent all this and we can prove it. We know everything. We even know where you bought the canvas bags the money was in. We know you hired a white van. I'll prove it that you bought the bags in NW1. The people there will probably remember you.'

'All right, guv, I might have done a few things with the garage. But you've got to believe me. I wasn't on the robbery.'

'Well, it's up to you then. Tell us the full extent of your involvement and we'll listen.'

'I can't say any more. I think I should have a word with my solicitor.'

'You've never asked me for a solicitor in these two interviews,' Peter said. 'I explained to the station officer why you couldn't have one at this stage and I've explained to Mr Haeems. Tell me, when was the last time you saw Mr Haeems?'

'Last week. About me brother-in-law's fight I told you about.'

'Well, Mr Haeems will be allowed to see you. We still have a lot more money to recover. And more people to arrest. I think there is ample evidence that you, Perkins, and Horsley were involved in the robbery and you will be charged later on. Do you wish to say anything?'

'I want to speak to my solicitor.'

As he was leaving the room Hickson turned to Peter: 'Look, guv'nor, can we talk off the record?'

'What do you want to say?'

'Can we do a deal?'

Peter shook his head. 'I can't do any deals with you, Billy.'

'How about if I were to give you some names?'

'If you want to talk we'll get it down in writing, but I can't do any deals with you. I think you are one of the ringleaders in this job.' Peter folded his arms and looked him straight in the eye. 'Now, what do you want to say?'

Hickson shook his head in exasperation. Bernie and Malcolm took him back down to the station cells.

It was just after midday. Hickson was a broken man. He had lost his share of the loot – the one thing that might have made a long stretch inside more palatable. On top of that, his open offer to become a 'supergrass', and thus shorten any potential prison sentence, had been flatly refused.

Hickson was charged with robbery at 7 p.m. Terry Perkins, who was being held over at Bethnal Green police station, was charged soon afterwards. Perkins had been arrested at the same time as Hickson. When the Flying Squad searched his house in Enfield they had found £10,000 in cash on the premises, £5,000 in new notes and £5,000 in old. The way the notes had been folded had struck the officers as quite distinctive. It was like a signature.

During his interview, he had put down all of his sudden, new-found wealth to shrewd property dealings and a little tax evasion. At first he had been guarded about his dealings with Horsley, but eventually admitted going to Horsley's house. Then OP17, once again, had come galloping to the rescue. Perkins was shown a surveillance photograph of himself getting into a car with Horsley and Hickson. A few other pertinent details of his movements the previous summer were recounted for his benefit. He then admitted that he was an 'arranger' for the robbery, but not, he said, one of the actual robbers. He told them that on the day of the robbery he had visited his cousin to collect some rent. His cousin later refuted this.

On Saturday, WDC Julia Pearce arrested Perkins's wife Jacqueline and brought her in for questioning. At the house, Julie had found a hole in the floor under a wardrobe, which had very likely been used for storing cash.

During her interview, Mrs Perkins was surprisingly forthright. She had told them that the day of the robbery was Terry Perkins's thirty-fifth birthday. She had remembered it well because Terry had left early without even waiting for the usual birthday greetings from his children. Because of his attitude she had an inkling that he had been somehow involved with the robbery, but when he started giving her large amounts of money later on in the year she became convinced.

Because of legal rules on husbands and wives giving evidence against each other, Peter knew they wouldn't be able to use much of Mrs Perkins's evidence in court, but the birthday irony tickled them all nonetheless.

On the Sunday, Mrs Perkins made a statement that effectively put her in the frame for handling stolen robbery money. After that, they decided to try to demolish Terry Perkins's defence – that his sudden wealth had come from property. They planned to establish exactly how much property Perkins had, and where. It was a slow, painstaking, tedious process that would take them many months and create a mountain of paperwork, admirably handled by Jim Keeling.

One day, Jim was sitting at the typewriter with a fag hanging out of his mouth. Bernie Butler was sitting nearby. 'What's Terry Perkins's wife's name?' Jim suddenly piped.

'Mrs Perkins,' said Bernie.

Jim thought about that for a moment. 'No, you prat! That's his mum.'

£££

Overall, Peter was pleased with the weekend's work. He thought that the case was in the bag. But within a few hours he was to be dealt a serious blow, courtesy, albeit unwittingly, of his own boss and the press.

10

LOYALTY

John Knight spent much of 1983 putting his house, or rather houses, in order. By now it wasn't only High Trees, it was also a Spanish villa and a luxury apartment on the Costa del Sol.

He had to thank his brother Ronnie for making it easier for him. You couldn't just turn up at Luton Airport with £100,000 in your pocket. It was bad enough with £3,000 in your pocket. But luckily for John, Ronnie had transferred a large chunk of the money over for him, saving him the hassle.

Back home, John's businesses were flourishing. The Fox, the pub he owned in Dalston, was raking in the takings. His garage too, M&M Bodyworks in Southgate, was going from strength to strength.

Ironically enough, when John and his brothers were growing up in Dalston in the forties and fifties, the Fox was the one pub that they never went into. They knew that the Law would drink in there. But times change. Places change. When the tenancy came up in 1979, John could see that the place had a lot of potential. But he had 'form', and he knew that the brewery would never let him have the tenancy. So he got Clifford Saxe, a long-standing friend of the Knight family, to front it for him.

The deal was straightforward enough. John loaned him £9,000 cash to invest in the tenancy, furniture, and fittings, and Saxe ran the place. In return he paid John a weekly wage and shared some of the profits from the takings. The rest was his, to do with as he liked. At any time Saxe could buy it from him, for £16,000.

Saxe was a bit older than John, more his brother Jimmy's age group. Years ago, Saxe had worked as a scaffolder with

Ronnie. To John he was not only a trusted business friend – he also acted as a go-between. In effect, Saxe was John's eyes and ears on the ground in Dalston. He was a fixer. If John ever needed anyone to find out something for him, or go and ask someone to do something, he would ask Saxe to do it.

Somewhat abruptly, in October 1983, Saxe told John that he wanted to sell up the pub. He wanted to retire to Spain where, earlier in the year, he had splashed out on a couple of villas. So that's what they did, splitting the proceeds of the sale between them.

John could never say exactly why Saxe decided to quit. Perhaps he was a little weary from a life of hard drinking. Or perhaps he had a premonition of what was about to unfold. Either way, Cliff and his wife Vera remained close family friends of the Knights.

Alan Opiola, John's 35-year-old foreman at M&M Bodyworks in Southgate, was a recommended and trusted man, highly skilled at his job. Over the years, he and John had become good friends. Short, portly, with thin, receding blond hair, Alan was married to a buxom, dark-haired woman called Linda. Together they had a young daughter, Jeni. The family lived with Alan's Polish mother in a large, detached, suburban house in Enfield.

John had really helped Alan get his act together. When he first met Alan and Linda in 1973 they lived in a shambles of a place. There was rain dropping in on their heads when they went to the loo. To get them out of their dismal flat, he helped them out with cash to buy Di's bungalow in Tottenham, which they later sold in 1979 for a handsome profit. John did a deal with Alan over the garage so that, on paper at least, Alan owned and ran it.

The Opiolas were good company. The four of them, John and Di, Alan and Linda, would often get together for an evening meal or a drink. Linda was a couple of years younger than Alan but John always thought that she was the more streetwise of the pair. She was astute and had a good eye for business. Alan was good with his hands, but didn't always think things out carefully enough.

Nevertheless, they used to have a good laugh together. After Alan had sold the bungalow, John remembered going round one day to his new house in Enfield with a friend. Alan was busy building a shed in the garden and was mixing up some concrete for the floor.

'While you're doing out the concrete base you can put a nice hiding place there,' said John.

'Really?'

'Really! Cover it over, grow plants on it, but it's a lovely hiding place to put money in, any surplus gear – or a load of diamonds!'

Sitting in Alan's kitchen, John had chortled about it afterwards. 'You should always have a good hiding place,' he told Alan. But he didn't think for one moment that Alan would build it.

Thanks to Alan and Cliff, John's business interests ran by themselves. He left them to it. He could count himself lucky that he had good people around him, people he could trust. In his world, loyalty was priceless.

£££

By the time New Year came, John could breathe a sigh of relief that 1983 had passed off largely without any trouble. He could afford to relax a little. There was, however, one incident that had niggled John greatly. It had remained at the back of his mind, like a warning shot.

A few weeks after the robbery he had decided that he wanted a snooker table at High Trees, to put in a games room that he had built on top of the garage. Terry Perkins had told him about a man in Tottenham who made pool and gaming tables. His name was Fred Halligan.

One day in May 1983, John went over to Halligan's workshops to have a look at his tables. He saw one Halligan had in stock already made up, which had just come out of a pub. John bought it for £250 cash, but Halligan told him it would be a week before he could deliver it.

The following week it just so happened that, while Halligan

was installing the table at High Trees, Terry came over to visit John.

'I think I'll get one of them,' he said to Halligan, admiring the new table.

'Well, come down to the firm and I'll show you a couple.'

So, some days later, Terry turned up with John at the man's workshop to look at the tables.

'Here! I've seen your photo,' Halligan said to Terry.

Terry looked at him with surprise. 'My photo?'

'Walthamstow police station! They've got your photo up.'

'What's it up there for?'

'There's loads of photos up there. There's you and another man.'

'Christ!'

Halligan told them how, the previous week, he had been called to Walthamstow police station to have a look at a pool table that needed repairing. He was in the back office, looking at the wall, when he saw some photographs of Terry Perkins with someone else. Although he recognized Perkins, he didn't know who the other man was.

'You'd better go and get hold of Billy Hickson so that this man can have a look at him,' said John to Terry.

The next day John got Hickson and Perkins to walk to the yard where Halligan made the pool tables.

Halligan took one look at Billy. 'Yeah, your photo's up there and all!'

'Any one else's photo there?' John asked.

'No, only you two.'

That evening John, Terry, and Billy got together to have a chat about it. They were plainly worried.

'They must have been following Billy over that business with the pills in Jimmy's scrap yard,' said John. 'The coppers were knocking around the Albion trying to catch him with the pills.'

'Now we know that our cards have been marked. We might be watched. We've got to start being a bit more cautious,' said Terry.

But they weren't. Terry and Billy carried on going to the Albion pub. They were jumping planes to go to Jersey to salt money away, without passports, just for a day and a night. Terry would tell John that he was going to his uncle's, because he knew that John didn't like him hanging out with Billy. But John knew it was a lie.

£££

The weekend of 21 January 1984 was supposed to be no different from any other. Nothing out of the ordinary was planned. John read in the morning papers about John Horsley's arrest the day before, but he wasn't unduly concerned. He didn't really know Horsley and was sure that Horsley wouldn't remember him. After all, they had met only fleetingly in the darkness.

Regardless, John thought he was well covered. He had done as much as he could to distance himself from Curtain Road. Some months earlier, he had gone so far as to take a spin deep into the Hertfordshire countryside, find a secluded field, and throw away the copied key to the office building that had served so well as his vantage point. He had done a thorough job getting rid of evidence.

The arrests of Billy Hickson and Terry Perkins that Saturday morning gave him more cause for concern. When he heard about it on the radio he immediately made sure that he had missed nothing incriminating indoors. He cleared out his safe, checking that it contained only old passports and keys and logbooks from the garage.

After that, he took the precaution of stopping by the garage to have a word with some of the staff there. He wanted to warn them not to say anything about Terry. He always said that Terry would get into a lot of trouble if he hung around with Billy. So now that it had finally happened, he wasn't at all surprised. But both Terry and Billy were old hands when it came to dealing with the police. John knew he could count on them to keep their traps shut. They were honourable men. That's why he chose them.

His wife Di had spent the whole week at Henlow Grange, a

secluded health farm in Bedfordshire, relaxing and working out in the gym. By Saturday afternoon she was ready to go home.

Henlow Grange was where all the stars hung out. It was popular with footballers and film stars alike. Barbara Windsor had often gone there. She had told the Knights about it and, over the years, the retreat had become a firm family favourite.

That afternoon John arrived in his sports car to pick up Di and take her back to High Trees. But before leaving, he stayed a few hours, working out in the gym. Then, in the evening, they both left for home. John drove. They chatted on the way back, stopping off at a pub to get something to eat. They were in no hurry to get back.

After the meal they called High Trees and spoke to one of the children to say that they would be home in about an hour.

'Everything all right?'

There was a slight hesitation. 'Yes. Everything's fine. See you soon.'

It was shortly after midnight by the time they got to Wheathampstead. They were both tired and looking forward to climbing into bed. They wound their way along the narrow road that ran through the sleeping village, up the hill, and alongside the golf course. There, from the side of the road, you could clearly see High Trees through the shrubs. John cast a sideways glance in the direction of the house as he drove by and saw that every light in the house was on. In fact, it was lit up like a flaming Christmas tree. 'Strange,' he thought. 'The kids should all be in bed asleep. Why would they leave all the lights blazing like that?'

'There's something wrong there,' he said to Di, secretly fearing the worst.

He turned into the gravelled track that led up to the driveway of the house. The track ran past several other houses, all set back with their own drives. High Trees was right at the end of the track. As he spun along the gravel he saw in his rear window a car pull out of a drive behind him. He was boxed in. It was then that he knew for certain that something was wrong.

At the end of the track he rounded the corner and drove through the gates into the drive, which snaked up to the front door of the house. There were two unmarked cars already parked on the drive. The unmarked car behind him blocked his retreat.

He stopped short of the house and turned quickly to Di.

'Take this money just in case,' he said. He handed her £700 that he had in his wallet.

'What's going on?' she asked.

'Nothing. Don't worry.' He gave her a reassuring pat. 'Stay here.'

He got out of the car and strolled across the drive towards the front door of the house, but he was intercepted before he could get there. A man stepped out of the shadows by the porch.

'John Knight?'

'Yes.'

The man produced a warrant card. 'We're from the Flying Squad,' he said, searching John's face for a reaction. John was too wily for that. He gave nothing away.

'I'm arresting you for robbing Security Express. You do not have to say anything, but everything you say will be taken down and may be used in evidence against you. Do you object if we search your premises?'

'Do you have a warrant?'

The man flashed a piece of paper in front of his nose.

'Well, go ahead then. Search.'

They went into the hall and through into the brightly lit kitchen. John's four children, all in their teens, were sitting around the long kitchen table. They had been playing cards under the watchful eyes of a couple of officers. Tired, they looked up, relieved to see their parents at last. The police had been there for hours. They had been told not to say anything when John and Di had phoned earlier that evening.

'I'm sorry, kids,' said John shrugging his shoulders. 'You'd better go to bed now.'

'Yes,' said one of the officers. 'You can go and have a sleep now your dad's home.'

John heard the dog scratching and whining behind a door

leading to the lounge. 'My lovely new wallpaper,' he thought, and moved to open the door to let the dog out.

'Why go there in a hurry?' asked one of the officers, looking suspiciously at John.

'Just looking,' John replied.

The police proceeded to search the house from top to bottom. They looked in every nook and cranny, while John, Di, and the kids looked on in silence.

They searched Di's handbag and found the £700 that John had given her. That was confiscated by one of the officers. They also found a piece of paper on which John had scribbled the names and numbers of some building society accounts.

Stowed under the stairs they found fourteen paintings, which John had bought from some students and which were due to be taken out to Spain to be hung in the villa. The police confiscated them all, stating that they had been bought with the proceeds of crime.

While searching the bedroom, one officer found the briefcase that John used to take with him to Masonic meetings. Inside was a black leather pouch containing John's Masonic apron. The officer removed the pouch, opened it, and unravelled the finely embroidered apron.

'Is this yours?'

John nodded.

The officer looked up at John questioningly. 'Are you on the square?'

'Yes.'

The officer shook his head. Slowly, without saying another word, he folded up the apron and put it back into its pouch. He put the briefcase into a plastic bag for forensic examination, and left the room. John never saw him again.

At around two o'clock in the morning John and Di were driven down to Shepherdess Walk police station for questioning. A replacement shift of officers turned up at the house to carry on the search through to dawn. They left nothing unturned.

At the station, Di was put in the cell next door to John.

They let him look through the tiny cell window at her. She shrugged her shoulders at him, as if to say, 'I don't know anything.' Throughout the early hours of the morning he could make out her voice through the wall of the cell, but at breakfast time they told him that they had taken her away to another prison. He thought that had been done to upset him deliberately, to try to make him go supergrass. In fact, she had been taken back to High Trees so that they could continue the search of the house in broad daylight.

At High Trees, Di could see the envy in the officers' eyes as they gazed with awe at their palatial home. One of the officers clearly had a bee in his bonnet about it. He wanted to take a hammer and smash open John's beautiful marble fireplace in the lounge. That, to Di's mind, was sheer vindictiveness. There was no need for that. In the end, all the police found were a couple of Midland Bank wrappers, easily explained away, and a tin of John's containing letters.

Later that day she was taken to another police station to be questioned by a woman police officer. It was an intimidating experience. They would put her into a cell and then five minutes later they would open it up again.

'I'm going to take you upstairs, Mrs Knight,' they would say. 'Tell us what we want to know and then you can go.'

'I've got nothing to tell you,' she would reply.

So they would take her downstairs again. She could see the officers standing outside the cell door, silently observing her. They did it for hours. It made her scared. In fact, the stress of it all made her ill. It gave her a stomach upset. 'Don't flush the toilet,' she was told. It was ridiculous. 'What kind of evidence could possibly come out of my bottom?' she thought.

The other game they played was with cigarettes. 'Want a cigarette?' they would ask, poking their head around the door of her cell. They would hand one over then lock her up for the night, knowing she didn't have any matches. As a finishing touch they would put a box of matches in the window on the outside of the cell door. It was like a punishment.

Later that day she was released without charge, and that Sunday evening, when she got back to High Trees, John's brother Jimmy came around to see if she was all right. She was thankful for Jimmy, ever the rock, always ready to help his family in times of need.

When Di had some time alone to reflect on the weekend's dramatic events, it struck her that she must have been watched while she was at the health farm. She remembered how the manager had seemed strangely nervous in her presence. She remembered the over-friendly young women constantly circling her and engaging her in meaningless banter. 'Essex girls,' she had thought at the time. She recalled how one of them had called her while she was in her room that Saturday morning saying, 'Oh, you're still here then?' At the time she thought nothing of it, but now it all seemed so ominous. 'Perhaps, all along, the Dirty Dozen had been watching our every move,' she thought.

John, too, was sure that he had been observed when he stopped by the garage that Saturday morning. He remembered the strange cars parked in Chelmsford Road, just outside the garage, their wing mirrors angled towards the garage entrance, their occupants motionless.

£££

That Sunday morning, Ronnie Knight heard through the grapevine about the overnight arrest of his brother Johnny, and the arrests of Perkins and Hickson the morning before. He quickly arranged to leave the country. His suitcase was already packed as he had been planning to go anyway.

It dawned on him that, as he had helped to spirit his brother's money away to Spain, he could be a prime target for a knock on the door from the Old Bill. 'They always pull me anyway, regardless,' he thought to himself. By then he had sent over approaching £100,000, via Barbara Windsor's accountants, Fox Associates, although no one at the firm knew that the money had come from the robbery.

The way Ronnie had been treated over the Zomperelli murder a couple of years earlier was still sharply etched on his mind. He was convinced that, whatever he was charged with, he wouldn't get a fair trial. The police would make sure that he went down this time. He wasn't going to go back into prison, not even on remand. He'd been there and hated every minute of it.

By now, Ronnie's marriage to Barbara Windsor was on the rocks – again – and this time he knew it was probably beyond repair. Barbara had sold their penthouse flat in Hendon and had bought herself a town house in Swiss Cottage. She was never home. She had thrown herself completely into her work and he knew she was seeing other men. They now led completely separate lives.

Ronnie, however, was in love. Sue had become the new woman in his life. Now Ronnie felt that he wanted to make something more of the relationship. He wanted a new start.

He didn't have time to hesitate. He couldn't get on a flight to Malaga so he took the first one available to Barcelona. From the airport he got a cab all the way to the villa, where he waited apprehensively for Sue to arrive the following morning.

11
SUITCASES

On Monday 23 January, Alan Opiola drove in to work at M&M Bodyworks as usual. On the way in he picked up his secretary, Ethel Williams. Ethel had been around for a long time and she was always one for a bit of gossip. Today she was going to have a field day.

'Terry's been arrested,' she said breathlessly, as they drove through the traffic towards the garage. 'And Billy Hickson too, and another man from Hackney. They've all been charged with the Security Express robbery.' She paused, as if waiting for a reaction from Alan. 'If Terry has been arrested then John Knight is bound to be involved,' she added.

By the time they reached the garage in Chelmsford Road, the police were already there. Alan's brother Dick, who also worked at the garage, was waiting outside in the yard to fill him in on what had happened that morning.

After the police had left, Dick had a quiet word with Alan. 'John came in on Saturday morning,' he said. 'He looked worried. He told us that, if anyone should ask about Terry Perkins, don't tell them about the house he owns at the end of the road there.'

Alan could understand why John would have said that. He knew that Perkins was into property. And lots of it.

Later that morning, Di Knight rang Alan at the garage. She confirmed what everyone at the garage already knew, that John had been arrested over the weekend. Alan went home and told his wife Linda and then decided to drive over and see Di at High Trees. He felt she needed some moral support.

He arrived at High Trees at around midday and stayed with

Di for most of the afternoon. She was in a state. 'The only reason they've got John is because he is a friend of Terry Perkins,' she wailed, between floods of tears. 'And Terry got picked up because he's always drinking with that Billy Hickson. John always warned him not to drink with Billy. I told the police that Terry was a friend of John's brother and that they hardly saw one another,' she added.

Around mid-afternoon Alan went back to the garage, but he was in no mood for work. That evening Di phoned Linda and told her that John had been charged. He and Linda both drove over to High Trees to see her, and when they arrived they found her frantically making phone calls, trying to arrange bail. John's brother Jimmy later rang and said he would make the bail arrangements. He came over to see if she was all right but didn't stay long.

Di told them all about the rough time she had been given at the police station that day. She told them that on Sunday evening, John's brother Jimmy had turned up at the house with a carrier bag holding £10,000 to cover her living expenses. She had taken out £500 to pay the builders, but, just a few hours later, the police had turned up at the house demanding the cash. It was a mystery to her how they had known about it.

Alan stayed for a couple of hours and then left, but Linda stayed the night with Di at the house. Together, they sat in the kitchen until late at night, talking over what had happened, drinking endless cups of tea.

Di was worried. 'We've got money in Spain. I think we've got to do something about it. Thank God the place we have out there is almost paid for.'

£££

The following morning, Tuesday, John was due to appear before the magistrates to be formally remanded into custody. Alan had arranged to go along with Di, so Linda drove Di back to their house, where Alan picked her up. They parked near Jimmy's scrap yard in Ridley Road and then took a cab to the Magistrates' Court.

Neither of them had a chance to speak to John in court.

Di's brother Albie was also in the court, and after the hearing the three of them, together with Tony Beaumont, John's solicitor from Lesser & Co., went across the road to a pub.

Tony spent most of his time talking to Di, but at one point he turned to Alan. 'John wants to see you,' he said.

After the pub meal, Alan went back to the garage. Meanwhile, Linda drove Di and Albie back to High Trees. Nobody said a word on the journey. All were deep in thought, their minds occupied with different worries and fears. Di and Albie then went over to Jimmy's, returning around 6 p.m. That evening they sat around eating fish and chips and watching mindless television. Later, John's daughter drove Albie home.

Linda stayed overnight at High Trees, and while she was there she spotted four suitcases in a cupboard under the stairs. The sight of the suitcases unnerved her greatly. One was brown and looked strangely familiar and she wondered if it could have been one that Alan had given John. Suddenly it dawned on her that her and Alan's fate was inextricably tied to that of John and Di.

£££

The next morning, Wednesday, Linda went back home to Southgate. Alan had gone in to work as usual. Di went over to see John in prison, but later on in the day she turned up at the garage with Albie. With them came an air of necessity, as if they had something important to say, a favour to ask.

'Come on, Alan,' said Albie. 'Let's take a walk up the road and have a little chat.'

Albie waited until he was out of earshot of the other workers at the garage. 'We've been to see John,' he said. 'John wants you to say that when he owned the garage and you worked for him, you were giving him £1,000 a week.'

'£1,000 a week?' said Alan. He gave Albie an incredulous look. 'How can I explain that?'

'Takings from cash repair jobs,' Albie replied. 'John wants you to say that it was not going through the secretary's books.' He paused for a moment and looked Alan straight in the eye. 'John has to cover £400,000.'

Alan walked slowly back up to the garage, head down, lost in thought.

'I want to go see John in prison,' he said to Di, who was waiting back at the garage.

'OK. I'll sort it out for you,' she said. 'Jimmy's going up there tomorrow. Maybe he'll want to take you with him.'

When Alan got home that evening, Linda told him that Jimmy had already been on the phone. Alan had to be at the Limes by 8 a.m.

£££

The next day, Thursday, 26 January, Alan was up well before dawn. He went to the garage to check the books to see when Ethel had started working there. Then he went on to Jimmy's house. Together they drove to Wormwood Scrubs.

'I can't cover John for £400,000,' he told Jimmy in the car. 'John has only had the firm for two and a half years.'

Jimmy nodded in agreement.

At Wormwood Scrubs they both went in to see John.

'Well?'

'There's no way I can cover you for £400,000,' said Alan. 'You've only had the garage for two and a half years.'

'I thought I'd had it for five or six years,' said John.

'No. I've been down to the garage and checked it. I've only worked for you for two and a half years. The most I can cover you for is £200,000.'

John looked visibly upset.

'Don't forget that hotel you owned. You had that for five or six years,' said Alan, trying to be helpful.

'Oh, yes. I forgot that. Yes. What about Alan Martin?' John looked at Jimmy.

'Don't worry about Martin. If he's anywhere in the world I'll get him, even if I have to give him a few quid,' said Jimmy.

'Everyone is keeping quiet,' said John. 'Nobody is saying anything. They've found some money at Billy's place. He's going to say that he got the money from drugs. He knows he's going down.'

Alan turned his head away while John had a whispered

conversation with Jimmy. Alan overheard snatches of it. 'They've got the two keys,' John hissed at him.

'You've got nothing to worry about,' Jimmy replied. 'At the end of the day all you will have to do is to pay a bit of tax.'

Alan drove Jimmy home from the prison, and on the way they chatted. 'I'll get hold of Alan Martin. He's no trouble,' said Jimmy. 'All John will have to do is pay some tax but there's no problem. He's better off out here than in there. At least out here he can earn a pound note.'

After Alan had dropped Jimmy off at the Limes, he went over to see Di at High Trees. Over a sandwich, he told her all about the prison visit. 'John's worried about some keys,' he said. 'What are they?'

'The keys are for a bank safe-deposit box in Spain.'

'Oh. I see.' Alan finished his sandwich and then went back to work.

£££

By the time the weekend came, Alan was beginning to get worried. Linda had told him all about the suitcases she had spied at High Trees. Earlier in the week he had gone up into his loft with a torch to make sure that he had left nothing incriminating up there, but on Sunday he checked it again to make doubly sure. This time he rigged up an electric light on a long lead and had a thorough look around. He found a bank paying-in slip from Barclays, but nothing else. He heaved a sigh of relief. He showed it to Linda downstairs and burnt it in an ashtray on the kitchen table.

'That was lucky,' he told her, as they watched the wisps of smoke curl up towards the ceiling.

On Tuesday the following week, Alan and Linda went back over to High Trees to see how Di was getting on. While they were there, Di dropped a bombshell.

'They've found out that the police have found a suitcase with money in it. It had a fingerprint on it,' she told them. 'It was a brand-new suitcase.'

Alan and Linda looked at each other in utter horror. 'But . . . I bought the suitcases for John,' Alan stammered. 'Mine and Linda's fingerprints will be all over them. They took our personal suitcases as well. One from my mother's room! It was made in Poland.'

'Don't worry,' said Di. 'They've all been told to burn the new suitcases.'

'But what about the personal ones?' asked Alan, far from reassured.

Di stood up and went over to a cupboard. She rummaged around and pulled out a small brown suitcase. 'Is that yours?' she asked.

Linda looked it over. 'No,' she said.

'Thank God for that,' said Di, laughing. 'I thought I'd have to burn that one as well.'

Alan and Linda, their faces white as sheets, didn't find it at all funny.

Di could see that they were anxious. 'My son took a brown suitcase with him when he went over to Spain,' she said, trying to be helpful. 'He went to see John in prison on the Saturday morning, came home, packed a suitcase, and then went over to Jimmy's house. Jimmy thought they might have been followed, so he took him halfway to the airport and he caught a black cab the rest of the way.

'I've given him a letter to the bank so that he can open the safe-deposit box in Marbella. He's supposed to get someone to ring me, to let me know that he got there all right. He hasn't phoned and now I'm worried. He's supposed to be going to see a solicitor on Saturday to make his statement. He's going to say that every time he comes over to High Trees for a weekend he and John go jogging together in the mornings on the golf course. That should cover John for the Easter Bank Holiday.'

'Who was going to call you?' asked Alan. 'Cliff and Vera from the Fox?'

'No. Someone else,' Di replied, refusing to be drawn.

Di had a hefty insurance bill to pay and the Flying Squad had taken away all her cash. Alan still owed John £5,000, so the next time he saw her, he gave her a blank cheque.

£££

By the end of that week, Alan and Linda were both beside themselves with worry over the suitcases. They badly needed to hear it from the horse's mouth that everything was OK, that their suitcases had indeed been destroyed. The horse's mouth, as far as they were concerned, was John Knight.

On the Friday morning, Di turned up at Alan's house. They were going to see John in Wormwood Scrubs, but on the way they called into her mum's house in Bethnal Green to pick up his dinner.

Di was fraught. She had still not heard from her son. And she needed money. Desperately. Her mother produced the blank cheque that Alan had left earlier, and Alan filled it in for her.

Alan and Di went to the prison together but only Di was allowed in. By now Alan was desperate for some assurance about the suitcases. He couldn't get it out of his mind as he waited anxiously for Di to return.

'Wilton,' she said, as they drove back from the prison. 'Remember that name. "Wilton". John said I have to tell Jimmy to get hold of the copper that he knows and ask him to get hold of Wilton and straighten him out.'

'How was John?' asked Alan.

'Tense and annoyed,' Di replied. 'He's upset because I haven't gone through the house. He's also worried about our son going over to Spain. Don't worry about your suitcases,' she added. 'They weren't given to anybody else. They are all right.'

It was hardly reassuring.

£££

Following John's instructions, Di and Linda went to High Trees and together they started searching the house from top to bottom to make absolutely sure that there was nothing incriminating left.

'Look for anything with John's signature on it or anything to do with Spain,' Di said.

While they were searching, Jimmy telephoned and spoke briefly to Di.

'Come on,' she said to Linda. 'We've got to go over to Jimmy's house. My son's back from Spain.'

They arrived at the Limes to find Jimmy, his wife Maisey, and Di's son waiting patiently for them in the sitting room. Jimmy and Di immediately disappeared into another room, speaking in hushed voices. Later the two of them reappeared. Di pointed to the suitcase in the sitting room.

'Is that your missing Polish suitcase?' she asked.

Linda looked at it. 'No.'

Di and Jimmy retired to the other room again, to be joined by Di's son. Meanwhile, Maisey made Linda a drink.

While they were there, Di's son handed his mother a note from Ronnie and Sue, now safely ensconced in Spain. It read simply, 'Hope everything is all right. C is thinking of you. Hope J is all right.'

He told them that while he was in Spain he had stayed with Cliff and Vera, and had driven about in the new Mercedes John had just had delivered to the villa.

He hadn't been able to get into the safe-deposit box; the man had been away on holiday. But he had left a note with someone over there who would arrange it all for them. After a while Linda said it was time she went. Di's son drove, and Linda sat in the back, listening intently to the conversation.

'I've told the people in Spain that Billy Hickson is the squealer. He was the one that opened his trap,' he said. 'They're going to send someone over to shoot him and he'd better get on the phone tomorrow to tell them that it wasn't him.'

'No, no, you've got it wrong,' said Di. 'Hickson isn't the one.'

'Oh, I'd better get in touch with them and tell them.'

£££

Later on that evening, as Alan was travelling home with Linda, she filled him in on what had happened that afternoon. After leaving Jimmy Knight's place they had gone across to Jimmy's yard to burn the suitcase that Di's son had taken with him to Spain.

'It wasn't ours anyway,' Linda told Alan.

It was still a mystery to them where their Polish suitcase had got to, and it was to cause them sleepless nights for several weeks. They had nightmares as they imagined the suitcase turning up in all sorts of public places where it could be recovered by the police.

On Friday, 3 February, nearly two weeks after John Knight's arrest, Alan was supposed to go to the offices of John's solicitor, Lesser & Co., to make a statement, but he was so busy in the garage that he put it off. And then he was overtaken by a series of events that was to change his life for ever.

Alan Opiola had slipped up badly, and it had little to do with the Polish suitcase that had so preoccupied him and Linda.

12

THE WHITE VAN

Back at Arbour Square, the mood of the officers on the enquiry had swung from elation to gloom. The problems had started soon after Commander Frank Cater released John Horsley's name to the media. Cater was under serious pressure from above to pull something out of the hat, so Peter couldn't blame him for doing it, but the naming of John Horsley unleashed a chain of events that was to have a serious impact on the enquiry.

The newspapers naturally splashed on the story that January weekend. And then it all went pear-shaped. On the Sunday Horsley changed his mind about turning Queen's evidence. And that was that. They were almost back to square one.

Everyone on the enquiry was dumbfounded. The case had been more or less in the bag. Horsley had admitted meeting Terry Perkins and Billy Hickson, who, between them, had arranged for Horsley's private garage to be used for storing the proceeds from what Horsley had understood to be a robbery. He had admitted playing taxi service on the day of the robbery, running Hickson about in his car until late in the evening, at which stage Hickson started to put sacks full of money into Horsley's garage. There, he had been introduced to a man who he later found out was John Knight.

In short, Horsley would have made an excellent prosecution witness. He, as much as anyone else, was there while the logistics of the robbery were planned, and later, when the plans were put into effect. Most importantly, Horsley had seen faces. He could link names. Peter was absolutely sure that he would have been able to identify other members of the gang, which could have been vital in those first few days after the arrests. He was also certain that, with a few more clues, the enquiry could have identified the scruffy man with a beer belly Horsley had referred to in his interview.

Horsley was prepared to give all this and more as evidence for the Crown, right up to the day before he was due in the Magistrates' Court. And then suddenly, without warning, he chose never to speak to the Flying Squad again. He withdrew his statement, giving no reason. In fact, he pleaded guilty to robbery so that his earlier statement couldn't be used in open court.

Whatever it was that frightened him, or whatever reward he was offered to keep his mouth shut, he clearly thought spending eight years of his life rotting away in jail was well worth it.

Peter and his colleagues spent many an hour dissecting what might have gone wrong with the way they had handled Horsley. Leaving aside the force's tactical blunder, they concluded that allowing other people free access to Horsley's family while he was in jail probably hadn't helped.

His wife Gwen and her son had been released from custody on the Friday. Although Gwen had remained extremely helpful throughout Saturday, by Sunday the enquiry quickly got the message that she no longer wanted to know. It was clear from the phone calls that she was in quite a state. Someone had seemingly put the frighteners on the family. When Peter called to speak to her on the Monday, he was told that she was in bed and unavailable. She categorically refused to talk to him.

On the day of his arrest, Horsley hadn't wanted to say much at all, but the next day, after Hickson had been brought in, he was much more forthcoming, perhaps because he felt reassured. On Sunday he had really opened his heart. The enquiry had laid plans to get him onto a witness protection scheme.

Then, late on Sunday afternoon, it all fell apart. Somebody had got to Horsley's wife Gwen – Peter never did find out who. She, in turn, somehow convinced her husband to change his mind about giving evidence. He withdrew his statement, refusing to implicate Hickson any further, and asked to be represented by Ralph Haeems, who duly turned up at the station to see his new client. Before that moment, and throughout the entire weekend, Horsley had never once asked for a solicitor.

By contrast, from the moment of Hickson's arrest early on Saturday morning, it was evident that Haeems would be his solicitor. While the police were at his flat, Hickson had more or less told his wife, Maureen, that that was who she had to phone.

By now Peter was well aware of Haeems's skills and capabilities; he was a defence solicitor of some repute and a veteran of many great battles with the police. In this enquiry he had appeared on the scene almost from the moment of the first arrest, that of Rooston.

As the officers sat around morosely discussing the train of events, they couldn't help but ask themselves what would happen next? The answer was becoming all too clear. Now that Horsley had retracted his statement, Hickson was undoubtedly going to argue that the cash in the false cupboard was Horsley's and his alone. Hickson would also no doubt claim that Horsley had been cajoled by the Dirty Dozen into implicating him, to save his own skin. So where did that leave Horsley? Done up like a kipper.

Later Peter discovered that in 1975, when Hickson was in need of an alibi, his witness had been none other than John Henry Horsley.

Despite all the gloom and despondency, Peter and his fellow officers did manage to find one source of unlikely entertainment. Hickson used to smoke roll-ups in the van that took him to and from prison. As a dog-end from a roll-up was the only piece of forensic evidence found in the Security Express depot, they did their best to recover his roll-ups after he had finished with them so that they could do a blood-group saliva test. Hickson, in turn, did his best to keep his dog-ends from falling into their hands. Over the next few weeks it developed into quite a little game between them, which probably amused the officers far more than it did Hickson. They did it to get him going. It usually worked.

£££

While Peter pondered over what to do about Horsley and Hickson, Detective Sergeants Cam Burnell and Steve Farley continued interrogating John Knight at length. Knight was a cool customer, sitting in his cell, smoking his cigars. He was saying little of consequence. He put down his wealth to his business dealings, but they quickly worked out that he could not possibly have made the amount of money that he said he made from the garage, certainly not in the ten months or so since the robbery.

It was clear to the teams of officers that had taken part in the searches at High Trees that Knight had spent a lot of money on the large house. To the officers it looked as if the place had been neglected for years and had suddenly received a facelift.

Knight had been quite willing to be interviewed by the officers but had insisted that his solicitor, Tony Beaumont, be present when he gave details of his alibi. That move surprised Peter and made him suspect that John had prearranged an alibi, and now wanted his solicitor to hear it. Accordingly on his third interview, in the presence of his solicitor, Knight had put forward an alibi for the morning of the robbery. He told them that he had been running on the golf course with his son and said he could produce witnesses. No one was particularly convinced by this story at the time, and it was later proved to be a lie.

There were other matters about which Knight was not so forthcoming. Most importantly, he refused to tell them about the significance of the two small keys they had found on his person. To the officers, the keys looked like keys to a safe-deposit box of some kind. But where?

That Saturday, they had decided to delay Knight's arrest until after they had interviewed Hickson and Perkins. Peter was sure, however, that Knight knew of the other arrests before they had been officially released to the media, which would explain why virtually nothing incriminating had been found at either High Trees or M&M Bodyworks.

However, Knight had slipped up badly with the piece of paper that had been found in Diane Knight's purse. It was a list of amounts of money with the names of building societies written alongside them. On the other side was another list containing larger amounts. The total amounts on the list on the front came to around £100,000. The figures on the back came to a further £151,000. None of the building society books for the larger amounts were ever found.

Knight claimed it was money for his children, but Peter came to regard the list as something that had been overlooked in his attempt to cover up and remove all evidence. For the enquiry team, it was a very important find. Without the list, it would have been nigh impossible for them to have traced John's cash deposits. In 1984, banking systems weren't quite as sophisticated as they are today. Laundering cash was far easier, and banks and building societies were not obliged to report large or 'suspicious' transactions, as they are now.

£££

Although the enquiry couldn't use Horsley's statement as evidence, it did provide some valuable leads worthy of further investigation. That was some consolation. They had to find another way of convincing the jury who was behind the robbery, and that meant following up these leads as quickly as possible, before they ran out of time and were forced to release Hickson, Perkins, and Knight.

So it was back to basics. They traced people closely connected to Horsley and those who might have witnessed some of the goings on. It involved a lot of legwork, and to an extent it paid dividends.

House-to-house enquiries in the block of old people's flats where George Carter, Horsley's father-in-law, lived, threw up a curious witness, a pensioner named William Mackenzie.

Since his retirement in 1980 Mackenzie had been in the habit of keeping a record of the car registration numbers of all the visitors to the block of flats. He kept them all neatly in a reporter's notebook along with the dates and who they were visiting. He had noted Hickson's old Granada between 2 March and 12 April 1983. Then later on in the year, sometime after 13 October, he clocked Hickson's new Citroën.

Mackenzie recounted how, one day, Horsley had spotted him writing down number plates and had come round to have a strong word with him. Horsley was highly agitated: 'What are you taking numbers for? These are my business friends. You shouldn't be doing that. They're not doing anything wrong. I know these people.'

'A few more neighbours like Mackenzie around, and we'd all be out of a job,' thought Peter as he read the report.

The enquiry also revisited leads uncovered during the OP17 surveillance operation. Fred Halligan, who had been asked for help in identifying Terry Perkins, was called back in. Halligan told the officers that soon after he had helped them that summer, John Knight had come to see him, saying that he knew all about the police visit. Knight told Halligan that one of the 'faces' was on parole and the police were trying to fit him up. Knight then arranged what could best be described as an impromptu identification parade, starring Perkins and Billy Hickson, for Halligan's benefit. It was so that Knight could find out exactly who the police had identified. Halligan also confided to the officers that, soon after the robbery, Knight had asked him if he could build a concealed box into a pool table so that he could put a parcel inside and take it over to Spain. Halligan said he had refused.

Meanwhile, Malcolm Jeffery continued with the forensic examination of the haul of banknotes found in the secret compartment in the flat. He arranged for a team of police cadets to examine every single note, recording the serial numbers and denominations, and removing any with distinctive marks, scrawls, or scribbles. These were all photographed.

The notes that had been wrapped around the bundles were taken over to the forensic laboratories at New Scotland Yard where they were treated with special chemicals to reveal fingerprints. Malcolm would never forget the sight of the rows of the banknotes drying out on pegs dangling from wires strung across the lab. All in all, it was a laborious job that took several weeks. No fingerprints were found. Bank of England notes rarely yielded good fingerprints. However, some of the notes contained soil particles. That, together with their musty smell, told Peter that they had indeed been buried somewhere. But where?

£££

Despite all the legwork, the enquiry needed a shot in the arm. They were running out of leads. As Peter read again and again through Horsley's statement, it dawned on him that the key to the puzzle had to be the hired white van. It crossed his mind that, if only they could establish who had hired it, they might be able to prove the identity of the men behind the robbery via another route, thus circumventing the problems caused by Horsley retracting his statement.

Horsley had said that Hickson, Perkins, and Knight had returned after a few days to take the sacks stowed in his garage away in a white van. Horsley knew the van was hired because he had glimpsed the sign on the side of the van. However, now he refused to elaborate.

Peter got a couple of his officers to phone every single van-hire company in North London and ask for details of hirings between 4 and 8 April 1983. Tracking the van down was a disheartening task, a bit like looking for a needle in a haystack. White vans are ubiquitous, and on any given day there are hundreds for hire in London alone. The officers spent days on the telephone but, amazingly enough, their cold-calling routine paid dividends. They were able to turn up a hire agreement that was to give the enquiry the breakthrough it needed.

The name of the hire firm was Kenning Car Hire in Palmers Green. The manager, Alan Warwick, checked his files and phoned back to say that he had a van-hire agreement for a white Bedford van made out to a Mr Alan Opiola, of M&M Bodyworks. The van was hired for just one night, Wednesday, 6 April 1983, and was returned the next morning. It had travelled exactly twenty-seven miles.

The officers asked Kenning's whether Opiola had hired any other vehicles from them. It turned out that, after returning the van, Opiola had hired a yellow Vauxhall Cavalier, which was returned on 18 April. The car had travelled an intriguing 468 miles. Since the hiring, the Cavalier had been involved in a serious accident and had a new body shell. The officers traced the car to a salvage dealer in Banbury, though forensic examination of the car revealed nothing of note.

Through OP17, Peter already knew that Opiola was John Knight's business associate. They knew that M&M Bodyworks was part-owned by Knight. The garage had already been searched by the police soon after Knight's arrest. During OP17 Terry Perkins had also been observed visiting the garage.

It was time to bring Alan Opiola in for questioning. On the morning of Wednesday 8 February 1984, Rex Sargent and Reed McGeorge arrested him at his home in Southgate. Shortly afterwards, other Flying Squad officers went down to M&M Bodyworks and completely turned over the premises. They recovered counterfoil copies of the Kenning hire agreements for the white van and the Cavalier.

The interviews with Opiola that day were not easy. Peter felt that Opiola was covering up for something, or someone. First, Opiola spun a tale about his financial position, which later turned out to be a fabrication, for the benefit of John Knight. On the second interview he was questioned about the vehicles he had hired from Kenning's. He became extremely evasive. On his third interview he admitted to hiring the van and the car but was unable to explain why he had hired them.

And then the wall cracked. Just after 7 p.m. he was taken back down to the cells. He was just about to be locked up for the night by Reed when he suddenly burst into tears. 'I'm really scared,' he said, sobbing uncontrollably.

It was the kind of situation that Reed naturally handled very well. He consoled Opiola, alleviated some of his fears, and, best of all, got him talking. Opiola admitted hiring the white van and Cavalier for John Knight and Terry Perkins, but he said that he was frightened of them.

The next day, 9 February, Opiola started to spill the beans, and in the afternoon he agreed to give a statement. In it, he said he had known John Knight for more than ten years. After a few years working as a panel beater, John had offered him the chance to buy the garage for £28,000. John had wanted £14,000 up front, with the rest paid over seven years. During those seven years John would be paid £2,000 a year as a 'financial consultant'. In August 1975 Alan became the sole owner of the garage. Two years later, Alan and John started an MoT test station at the back of the garage, from which John was paid £75 a week.

The financial detail was crucial because it went a long way towards demolishing Knight's suggestion that he had gained his sudden wealth through undeclared cash jobs at the garage. Opiola agreed to give a statement under caution, part of which said, 'I can categorically state that John Knight has never received any other money [from the garage businesses] other than what I have already mentioned.' That sentence alone was music to Peter's ears.

Alan went on to describe how John would pop in most days to the garage to meet his friends and associates, particularly Terry Perkins, who, Alan said, had been a friend of David Knight's. 'I was not aware of what sort of man John Knight was until about four years ago when the police turned over my garage looking for firearms,' he added. He was referring to the police investigation into the murder of Zomparelli.

Opiola then admitted that Knight and Perkins had asked him to get them the white Bedford van for a day and had said that there was a 'drink' in it for him. They had asked him to buy suitcases for them and he had also agreed to launder cash for them. But that's as far as it went.

That day, Opiola also told them about John Knight's son's flying visit to Spain to arrange the recovery of the contents of a safe-deposit box. To Peter's way of thinking it amounted to attempted removal of evidence, and he considered the trip to be grounds enough for the son to be reeled in. He acted immediately. The fear that the son might attempt to remove evidence was one of the principal reasons why Peter insisted on treating the Knight family firmly and, some might say, harshly over the coming few months. John Knight's son was arrested, questioned, and later released pending further enquiries.

The next day, Friday, 10 February, Alan was remanded by his own consent into police custody. It was for his own safety. Peter immediately sent an armed protection unit up to his modest detached house in Enfield. His 32-year-old wife Linda, his mother-in-law, and his young daughter Jeni were all taken into safe custody. The protection unit was made up of Peter's most trusted men and included Charlie Collins and Reed McGeorge. Peter had learnt a big lesson from the Horsley episode. He wasn't going to let the same thing happen with Opiola.

The protection afforded to his family served to calm down Alan's nerves. On Saturday, 11 February, he made a second statement, under caution, in which he admitted that he had deliberately left 'certain matters' out of his earlier statement because he was worried about implicating his wife. In his new statement he admitted that the white van had been used by Knight and Perkins to move sacks of money about and that they had used his house to count the money and fill the suitcases. Opiola's statement was completed on Sunday morning. And then Opiola agreed to become a prosecution witness.

Bingo.

£££

By now, it was clear to everyone on the enquiry that Alan Opiola was John Knight's trusted man, just as Horsley had been Billy Hickson's trusted man. They both had had their errands to run, and at times were little more than gophers.

Peter couldn't help wondering whether Terry Perkins had someone similar, someone on whom they might be able to exert a little pressure. He thought that the one person who could fit the bill was Perkins's accountant, Robert Young. So, on 9 February, the day after Opiola's arrest, he sent a couple of men to pick up Young. The enquiry's timing was perfect. Phil Chapman, a detective sergeant from the Company Fraud Squad, which had been making its own detailed enquiries into Young's accounting practice, joined the officers for the arrest.

Young, aged forty-six, lived in Potters Bar, Hertfordshire, but had an office in Crouch Hill, North London. Jim Keeling and Detective Constable Bob Sayers interviewed him over two days, after which he was charged with handling stolen cash on behalf of Terry Perkins. He then gave a written statement under caution in which he said that he had known both Perkins and Hickson for more than twelve years, and had quickly formed the opinion that both were out-and-out crooks. He recalled that, way back in 1974, Perkins had come to see him carrying £4,000 in cash. Perkins was upfront. He told him that it was the proceeds of crime, which he now wanted to invest, so Young set him up with a furniture shop. It was the beginning of Perkins's career in legitimate business.

Young told the police that Perkins planned to speculate in property in Portugal, and had been over there twice. The first time he had gone with Hickson. The second time, in November 1983, he went with Young and a lady called Irene Easton, the 39-year-old wife of one of Young's clients. Although the trip was booked by Easton, it was all paid for by Perkins in cash.

About a month after they got back, Perkins had turned up at Young's office wearing an anorak, its bulging pockets stuffed with £50,000 in used notes. The two men took the £50,000 down to Crouch End, paid it into NatWest, and then transferred the money into an offshore deposit account in Guernsey. Young told the police that he knew the money was bent.

He also told the two officers that he had given Hickson an introduction to the Nationwide Building Society for a mortgage. That was to prove a key piece of evidence. It enabled the enquiry to track down a £4,000 cash deposit made by Hickson in October 1983.

Although Young was committed for trial, the case against him was pursued somewhat half-heartedly. He appeared to be a heavy drinker – in fact he had asked the interviewing officers if he could nip across the road for a 'quick pie and pint' – and may not have been fully aware of what he had got himself into. At the trial he was cleared of the charge of handling stolen cash. Nevertheless, his statement had helped the enquiry significantly.

With the arrests of Opiola and Young, it had been a truly great week for the enquiry. And to cap it all, at the beginning of the week, on 6 February, Peter learnt that he had passed the promotion board exams for detective superintendent. He was thrilled with his achievement and, of course, had celebrated in traditional style. However, in some respects, the celebration had felt hollow and empty. As with many other dedicated officers, the demands of 'the job' had taken a huge toll on his personal life. The hours spent away from his family had been devastating, and his marriage to childhood sweetheart Valerie was on the rocks. In a reaction typical of most men, the problems on the domestic front had made him put even more of his energy into the enquiry instead of into sorting out his failing marriage. The evenings spent at the office got longer and longer. The welcome at home colder and colder. His sole reward was, of course, promotion.

£££

The following Wednesday, 15 February, Peter made one final attempt to prise open the line of enquiry provided by John Horsley. He hauled in Horsley's garage partner Stan Atwell for further interrogation. But the impression Atwell gave was that Horsley had kept everything well out of his sight and hearing.

Detective Constable Simon Webber did the questioning. Atwell told him that Horsley had been his business partner for about ten years. They got on well in business but they had never been great social friends. Over the last couple of years the garage had become less and less viable and it had become harder and harder to cover all the bills.

He had first been introduced to Billy Hickson about seven years before. He knew that Hickson had something to do with a scaffolding firm in the old railway sidings at Ridley Road and that he had been to prison for armed robbery. Hickson became a frequent visitor to the garage, and infrequent customer. He had a Jensen car, which they sometimes worked on.

Around February 1983, Hickson started coming to the garage much more regularly. That was roughly when Atwell was first introduced to Terry Perkins, the property man.

More often than not, Hickson was to be found in the Albion. In the old days Atwell and Horsley would spend the odd lunchtime together in the Albion. But since Hickson and Perkins had arrived on the scene, Horsley had chosen to spend his time with them. Atwell had kept away.

Perkins used to turn up at the garage to meet Hickson, but if Hickson wasn't there he wouldn't hang about for long. Horsley would join them in the pub, leaving Atwell working alone in the garage.

Atwell said that at one time Horsley seemed to be running around after Hickson. He got the distinct impression that they were up to something, but he never found out what. At the time, he knew that Horsley had serious financial problems. He owed a lot of money to a bank, and he had received a County Court summons over a debt.

A few months later, in the summer of 1983, Atwell noticed that Horsley had come into money. He bought a car for himself and his wife, took a holiday, and had some work done on his house, all within the space of a few weeks. Horsley was flush with money. Atwell thought that Horsley's change in fortune might have had something to do with Hickson and Perkins, but didn't ask or, for that matter, care.

Simon Webber had heard that, sometime during the autumn, Atwell had received a hiding in the Albion one night because he knew too much about Hickson and Perkins's business. But Atwell disputed that. He told them that he had had a bit too much to drink and he had an argument with Hickson over the servicing of a car. He got a whack from either Hickson or Perkins or both. He ended up with two black eyes and left the pub.

Regardless, the incident didn't stop him from being invited to Hickson's lavish wedding reception in the Fox public house that November.

Atwell gave away another snippet that served to confirm what they suspected had happened with Horsley. One day he went over to see Gwen Horsley at a friend's flat. While he was there, Gwen implored him not to talk to the police. She knew that they had contacted him. 'Don't say anything,' she said.

'There's nothing I can say,' he told her.

As he was leaving, a woman by the name of Maureen phoned. Now there are plenty of people in the world called

Maureen, but Peter suspected that this particular one was hitched to one Billy Hickson.

£££

Meanwhile, Reed McGeorge had been tasked to prise every single detail he could out of Alan Opiola, and at the same time ensure that it was the truth. He was ideally suited, with his computer-like mind and keen eye for the smallest detail.

Over the next few weeks, Reed would look after Opiola's every need. First, playing the role of counsellor, he would talk to Opiola about his fears, his family's worries, and his future concerns. Turning 'Queen's' was not a decision to be taken lightly. Everyday care for Opiola included feeding him, making sure he had the right clothes, making sure he had plenty of things to do, and keeping his spirits up, for the psychological pressure on Opiola was immense. Then, Reed would gently tease out of him all aspects of his relationship with John Knight and Terry Perkins.

Based on Opiola's answers, on 21 February Reed began to take down a lengthy and detailed statement that, when it was completed, ran to some eighty pages. Most days he was assisted by Malcolm Jeffery. It took them a week to complete.

Although technically charged with robbery, the Director of Public Prosecutions had by now agreed that Opiola should become a 'resident informant'. For his own safety he was taken into witness protection and kept in police custody. Peter feared that he wouldn't have lasted five minutes in a normal remand prison. The Knights' extensive network of friends and associates would soon have 'nobbled' him. So, day after day, Reed would go to the police station in East London where they had secured Opiola. The station was one of the Met's best-kept secrets. Opiola's cell door looked just like any other cell door, but in fact it opened out into a whole suite of rooms. It was a self-contained flat, which had been specially designed and built to secure supergrasses. Looking at the station from the outside, you would never in a million years guess that it was there.

To the enquiry, Opiola's testimony was like gold dust, but

everything had to be checked and double-checked. That was a job that would take several weeks. Reed took Alan Opiola out on various trips to identify the places he mentioned and to check points that he had made in his statement. Although Alan was now a witness for the prosecution, Reed still had to follow the normal legal procedures as though he were an ordinary prisoner. Any time Reed went to interview him, Opiola had to be booked out by the custody officer.

At the same time, Reed had to be aware of what was happening at Opiola's family home. His family's security was paramount – without that assured, Opiola would have clammed up. So the Flying Squad moved the Opiola family into the safety of a specially rented house in Chigwell and then arranged twenty-four-hour protection. The location of the house was kept a tightly guarded secret. Reed was taking no chances. If he had just covered the house during the daytime, leaving the family alone at night, it wouldn't have taken too much for someone to pay them an unannounced – and unwelcome – visit. And then all the hard work would have been undone.

The men assigned to the close protection squad did nothing else. They had to go everywhere with the Opiola family, whether it was taking the daughter to school or shopping at the local supermarket. Life with the family had its ups and downs. The officers were living with them under the same roof, sleeping downstairs in the lounge. It was stressful, and tempers often got frayed.

WDC Julia Pearce, again assisted by Malcolm Jeffery, was tasked with obtaining a statement from Linda Opiola. Linda was quite savvy and knew a lot of what had gone on between Alan and John Knight. She, too, gave a detailed statement under caution. In some respects it was as good if not better than Alan's. Although Linda hadn't been a witness to everything, she had the more retentive memory and a clearer recollection of what had happened.

The official line maintained to the outside world was that Linda was free to come and go from her house as she pleased and had not been charged. She carried on working at the garage, keeping the business going, while Alan remained in custody. The fact that she also had turned 'Queen's' was kept a closely guarded secret.

During working hours Julia would frequently pose as a secretary at M&M Bodyworks. There she could monitor and tape the calls coming in to Linda in the office. Jimmy Knight was particularly persistent. 'What's going on?' he would ask Linda. 'Let me know if there's anything I can do.'

On one occasion Jimmy told Linda that he was arranging things for his brother John 'as a cover' and that he would get 'advice' for what Alan Opiola could say.

That conversation was later to prove to be Jimmy's undoing.

13

TELLING STORIES

The tale that, between them, Alan and Linda Opiola had to tell Detective Inspector Reed McGeorge was quite remarkable. It provided a deep and damning insight into John Knight's world.

Alan told Reed that he had first met Knight in January 1973. Knight had advertised for a panel beater. At the time, Alan worked for a nearby garage in Tottenham, and a garage rep told him about the vacancy. 'The money would be better at M&M,' he was told.

Something must have clicked because, barely a fortnight after Alan had started, John came into the garage and asked him if he wanted to become foreman. Alan's wages went up from £32 to £35 per week.

Alan wasn't entirely straight and John Knight had obviously warmed to that. Soon after Alan had started working at M&M Bodyworks, John asked him to make him up a set of number plates, as he didn't want them done in a shop. Alan got an extra fiver for his trouble.

Then Alan stole a Rover car, which had been left in a pub car park in Southgate. It was a fairly new car, just a few years old, and his own ten-year-old Rover was giving him a lot of grief. To make the theft harder to trace, he cut his own car up at M&M Bodyworks and put his plates, and engine and chassis numbers, on to the stolen car – a practice known as 'car ringing'. Alan was an expert at that – or so he thought.

One day his wife was driving the new Rover when a policeman stopped her. 'Does your husband collect old licence plates?' the policeman asked.

'What do you mean?'

'You see, ma'am, your licence plates are from 1963, but the model Rover you're driving is from 1970.'

The incident worried Alan enough to go out and buy a smashed-up grey 1970 model Rover car for £300. He had this one cut up at Jimmy Knight's scrap yard in Ridley Road. Then he transferred the engine, chassis, and registration numbers to the stolen Rover and sprayed it the same colour grey as the smashed-up one. He planned to sell the car a few years later.

Later that year, John came to him with another job. It had little to do with car maintenance. 'Do you want to earn a bit of extra money?' he asked.

'Yes.'

John showed him some bundles of dollars, marks and francs. He wanted them changed into pounds sterling. Alan was a bit jittery about it, but John talked him into it and told him how and where to go about it.

'Go to the airport,' he said. 'It won't be suspicious there.'

So Alan made a couple of trips to the airport on John's behalf. He took an Arab friend along – his name was Alex – who showed him what to do. The foreign currency came to around £5,000. It all went smoothly, and John gave them a drink out of it, but Alex was angry. He thought John should have given them a lot more.

Alan got on well with Alex. A year or so later he stood guarantor for Alex so that he could borrow some money from the bank to start a business. However, Alex disappeared and knocked both Alan and the bank for the money. Alan never saw him again.

In August 1975 John told Alan that he wanted to sell the garage and gave Alan first option to buy it, so Alan borrowed £12,000 from his relatives and £4,000 from the bank, giving him a little working capital on top of the purchase price. The deal was done using John's family solicitors, Lesser & Co.

Then, sometime during 1976, John came to the garage and asked Alan to change some more notes for him. These were new notes, mainly £10s and £20s. John told him he would give him 20 per cent. 'Don't go into the banks,' he warned. 'Go out and buy small things with the money, like a packet of cigarettes. You can keep what you've bought. Just give me the change.'

Soon Alan's flat in Turnpike Lane was rattling with loose change. Piles of it were dotted around the kitchen, bedroom, and front rooms, on the windowsills and in the ashtrays. 'What on earth is going on?' Linda asked.

Alan told her what he was doing for John. The deal was that he kept all the goods and that John wanted £8,000 back for the £10,000. Being paid to go shopping? It was a girl's dreams come true. So Both Alan and Linda ran around the shops for several weeks, buying things here and there. They kept the cash hidden in an imitation brick fireplace in the flat – in a space behind the gas fire.

A couple of years later, in 1978, Alan decided that he wanted to set up an MoT testing station at the back of the garage. He asked John if he would like to become a partner. John agreed, and put up £4,000 for the equipment, with the understanding that Alan would pay half of it back. They got a £3,000 bank loan, John putting up High Trees as security.

Business for the new MoT testing station was a bit rough to begin with, but by 1980 there was enough money coming in for them both to take £40 a week in wages. Alan's brother Dick started working there as an MOT tester.

That year John gave him another load of new notes to change, this time between £10,000 and £20,000. 'Don't use any banks,' he said, so Alan asked where the money had come from. 'From Heathrow,' John said.

John showed him a few tricks of the trade. He showed him how to dirty the money up and make it look well used. He would drop the notes on to the floor, rub his shoe on it, and then roll it up in his hand to make it look creased.

But Alan got fed up with changing money in shops all the time, so he started using banks and post offices, changing a couple of hundred pounds at a time, mixing the new notes with old. John paid him £4,000 for that job.

That same year John Knight was arrested for being drunk in charge of a vehicle. He was found drunk, asleep at the wheel. He asked Alan to cover him. 'Say to the court that I phoned you and asked you to come and pick me up,' he said. Alan did, and John escaped with a fine. The whole episode frightened Alan. Stealing cars and laundering cash was one thing, but lying to a magistrate was quite another.

Meanwhile, business at the garage was going well. Alan had paid off his loan to John and business at the MoT testing station was picking up. By early 1981, they were both taking £100 a week in wages out of the business. By the end of 1981, it was doing so well that they took out another £5,000 loan from the bank. John bought a new car with his share.

Socially, too, the Knights and the Opiolas were close. Quite often they would get together for an evening drink or dinner at one or other of their homes. One day in 1982 John was over at Alan's new house in Enfield. Alan was having a garden shed built and John was keenly examining the shed's concrete floor.

'When the shed's finished and the builders have gone, I'll get you to cut a hole in the middle of the floor,' he said.

'What for?' asked Alan, curious.

'So I can store some diamonds in it!'

John explained how it would have to be done. 'You put some chicken wire over the top, with a good thick layer of cement so that it doesn't crack. You dig a hole, brick it out, and seal it to stop water getting through. Then you put a manhole cover over the top and seal it with two or three inches of concrete.'

John told Alan that he would want to leave the diamonds there, buried under the garden shed, for two or three years. Alan thought John completely serious.

It was around this time, either January or June 1982, that John had another business proposition for Alan. His plan was to squirt some ammonia in the face of a man and snatch a bag he was carrying that contained wages for a local firm. John knew all about the man because Terry Perkins had a sweet shop opposite the bank where the man went to collect the money every week, regular as clockwork. John would watch him from an upstairs window. He asked Alan if he wanted to be in.

'All you have to do, Alan, is drive a car for me,' he said.

But Alan wasn't happy about it. He went home that evening

and talked it through with Linda. 'Don't get involved,' she said. He agreed with her that it was stupid, so the next day he told John that he wouldn't do it.

'It's all right. Don't worry about it,' John said. 'There's a much bigger job coming up soon.' He looked across at Alan. 'Would you be interested in driving then?'

'I'll see.'

That evening, Alan mentioned the prospect of a big job to his wife. She rolled her eyes. 'Don't get involved,' she told him. Again.

£££

By the beginning of 1983, Alan and John employed around ten people at the garage. There was a garage manager, three panel beaters, two paint sprayers, a mechanic, a part-time cleaner, and, last but not least, Ethel, the office manager, who was in her fifties. She had been there since 1972.

Most days John would pop into the garage, usually around mid-morning, to see if everything was all right. Then he would wait for Terry Perkins there, or sometimes he would go to the pub at the top of the road. The previous year Terry had sold up his local shops and gone into the property game. He had started to buy run-down houses, filling them with tenants. It was easy money.

One afternoon in February, John turned up at the garage with Terry. Ethel had already gone home and Alan was on his own in the office. They wanted a small favour done. 'Alan,' John said. 'Can you hire us a caravanette?'

'Where do I get one of those from?' said Alan.

'I think there's a place in Waltham Cross,' Terry said.

Alan flicked through the Yellow Pages and made a couple of phone calls. He found a firm in Cheshunt that hired them out, but they didn't start hiring them until late spring, the beginning of the holiday season. Alan put down the phone. 'No chance, John,' he said. 'Why don't you use an ordinary van?'

'No, it's got to be a caravanette,' said John. 'You see, we want to hide in it.'

'Hide?'

'Yeah, hide. You know. Look through the curtains at something.'

Alan raised his eyebrows. With that, John and Terry left the office, and Alan heard no more about it.

Four or five weeks later John mentioned to Alan that he had got a van. 'Could you put it in your lock-up garage for a few days?' he asked.

'Yes, sure. No problem.'

Alan had rented the lock-up, which was just around the corner, the previous year following a burglary at his house. He had inflated his insurance claim by some £5,000 by hiding a stereo, portable television and some jewellery in the lock-up. He also claimed for some chandeliers but nearly came unstuck. The insurance company wanted some proof of purchase. Luckily for Alan, Terry came to his rescue, agreeing to write a letter saying that one of his businesses had supplied the chandeliers. So Alan felt he owed them one.

He followed them out of the office and into the yard. Parked in Chelmsford Road there was a pillar-box-red Sherpa van. It looked to Alan as if it had been recently sprayed. What's more, the interior of the van had been sprayed with exactly the same colour red paint. The work was slipshod and looked like it been done very quickly. The paint had gone all over the wiring and the driver's seat belt.

'Must have been a cheap old spray job,' Alan jokingly remarked.

'It'll do for what we want it for,' John replied. 'It's cost a lot of money to set up, this one.' He handed Alan a pair of gloves. 'Now don't get any fingerprints on the van.'

Alan got into the van with Terry and drove it the short distance to his lock-up. John followed in his car. When they got there, Alan tried to drive the van in, but the roof scraped along the concrete beam above the door.

'Shit!' said Alan.

'Let the tyres down,' said John. 'That'll do it.' So they did. They just about managed to squeeze the van into the lock-up, but it was so tight they could hardly get out of the van doors. There the van stood, for about a month, just gathering dust.

Then, one day in March, John asked Alan to get the van out. 'Do us a favour. Check the plugs and battery, bung some petrol in it, and take it for a spin around the block and make sure it runs OK,' he told Alan. 'After that, leave it in Chelmsford Road.'

'Do you need it today?' Alan asked.

'No, not today. Over the weekend,' John replied. 'Something big's going to happen,' he added. 'Get three or four ignition keys cut for it. Put them behind the sun visor, and leave the van open.'

Alan went off to Halfords to buy a foot pump. It was quite a hassle getting the van going again. When he got to the lock-up it wouldn't start. The battery was flat. So he went off to get a new one. Then he had to replace the spark plugs. Finally, he got the van going, backed it out of the lock-up, and pumped up the tyres. Then he took it round to a local garage to put some more air in the tyres and some petrol in the tank. He drove it around for a while and then parked it in Chelmsford Road, outside M&M, just as John had told him to.

The van was still there when he left the garage that evening. When he got home he told his wife that John had said something was going to happen that weekend. 'It's going to be a big one,' he told her. That weekend they scoured the newspapers, but there was nothing.

On Monday morning Alan went into work as usual. The van wasn't there, but John and Terry turned up with it at around eleven o'clock. 'Alan, can you put the van back in the lock-up? We didn't need it this weekend, but we'll probably need it next weekend.' John never explained why the sudden change of plan.

Alan took the van back round to his lock-up, let the tyres down, and put it away, but a few days later John told him to get the van ready again. It was the day before Good Friday.

That Easter Bank Holiday, Alan closed the garage for the whole weekend. He had agreed to take part in a local charity bath race in Southgate on the Easter Monday, so, on Easter Sunday morning, he and couple of mates went to the garage to paint the bath.

He noticed that the red Sherpa van had disappeared again.

On Easter Monday, he collected the painted bath from the garage with the garage breakdown van and took it the few hundred yards up the road to the White Hart pub, on the big roundabout in Southgate. There was still no sign of the van.

He went to a friend's house, got himself made up, and then went round to the pub. His wife and daughter turned up mid-morning and followed the race in the car to the Queen's Head, Winchmore Hill. They stayed for a while, having a few drinks, before returning to the White Hart.

After the race he had a few drinks in the pub, and then went home to have a real bath. His wife and daughter came home a little later. He was knackered from the race and stayed in that evening.

On Tuesday morning over breakfast, he read all about the Security Express robbery. 'Bloody hell,' he said to his wife. 'Have a read of this.'

Linda pored over the paper with him.

'That must have been the job they were talking about,' he told her. 'They said it was going to be big but I didn't think it would be this big.' Alan went off to work at the garage as usual, and that evening he told his wife, 'John hasn't been around the garage today.'

The next time he saw John and Terry was on the Wednesday, two days after the robbery. They were glad to have caught him in and they looked extremely tense.

'Could you hire us a van?' John said.

'What for?'

'We've got some sacks to pick up,' said John. 'They've got money in them.'

'Can't you use Terry's Escort van?'

'No. We want to lay the sacks on the floor so they can't be seen as we drive along the main roads.'

Alan rang Kenning's in Palmers Green and told them he wanted to hire a van the size of a transit from them. They arranged to go and collect it immediately. But before they left the garage John had another favour to ask. 'Can we use your house overnight?'

'Er, well, yes. I suppose so.'

Alan rang his wife and suggested that she should go and visit her mother overnight. She was planning to go the following day anyway – she always went with her mother to visit her father's grave on his birthday.

At this point Linda and Alan's stories diverged. According to Linda's version of events, she asked Alan why he wanted her out of the house.

'John wants to bring some money round to count up,' Alan replied. 'Take my mum with you. John and Terry are coming round. If they get there before me, tell them I won't be long.'

But Alan put a slightly different spin on it. According to his version, he never told Linda why he wanted her to leave the house for the night. 'John had always told me not to say too much over the phone,' he explained to the two officers. 'You never know who's listening.'

It was a small discrepancy, but Reed quickly grasped its significance. It was clear that Alan was trying to protect Linda from any claim that she played an active role in handling the proceeds of the robbery.

Meanwhile, Alan continued with the story.

'Come on, Tel,' said John. 'We haven't got a lot of time. We're keeping the others waiting.'

The three of them got into John's blue Ford Granada, and drove to Kenning's. John and Terry hung back, while Alan signed the hire documents. Alan drove the van back to Chase Side and pulled up about 200 yards past Chelmsford Road, facing Southgate Station. Terry was sitting in the passenger seat. Alan got out of the van and Terry got into the driving seat. John had pulled up behind them in his car.

'See you later,' Alan said.

'I'll see you down there,' John said to Terry.

Alan remembered the white van passing him as he walked along the road back to the garage. After work, Alan went off to see his father, who was ill in hospital. Just before 7 p.m., John and Terry arrived at Alan's house. Linda was still there, getting ready to go, and made them a coffee. 'Have you seen the news?' she asked.

'No,' said John.

She put the television on for them. The two of them sat in the sitting room, drinking coffee, watching the Channel Four news reports about the robbery, while she went upstairs to finish packing with her daughter and Alan's mum.

Alan returned home at just after 7 p.m. The drive at his house was a U shape, and hidden from the road by overgrown bushes and trees.

He drove his car into the drive and parked his car behind his wife's. She was just on her way out through the front door, with her daughter and mother-in-law. 'John and Terry are inside,' she said.

'Yeah, I can see the van.'

John and Terry had backed the hired white van up to the six-foot-high wooden fence that separated the front drive from the back garden. A door in the fence opened out into a passageway which ran down the side of the house and into the back garden. From the passageway, a door in the house gave access to the utility room. This entrance to the house was discreet and well hidden from neighbours' prying eyes.

Alan went on into the house. He found Terry sitting at the kitchen table drinking his coffee. John was standing by the closed door of the utility room, his hand on the doorknob.

'Well, get the sacks in,' said Alan.

'No need to,' said John. 'We've already got them in.'

Alan poked his head around the door of the tiny utility room, which measured just six feet by ten feet. Most of the space was taken up by a freezer, washing machine, sink, and boiler. Piled shoulder-high in what little space remained were six plumped-up, dirty-brown hessian sacks, tied at the top with string. Each was about three feet high by about three feet in diameter. Through the cloth Alan could just about make out brown envelopes and bank notes. 'Bloody hell!' he exclaimed. 'You can't leave this lot here! I've got builders coming in, John.'

'Please, Al,' said John. 'It will only be overnight.'

From the way John spoke, and the way they had suddenly both appeared at the garage, it struck Alan that they had been let down badly by somebody.

'Well, OK,' he said, somewhat reluctantly.

He made himself a cup of coffee. Terry went outside to move the van, and while he was gone Alan got talking to John about the best place to put the sacks and count the money. 'What about our bedroom?' he said.

'Yeah, good idea,' said John.

When Terry returned, they each picked up a sack and heaved it up to the landing. John and Terry had no problems lifting their sacks, but Alan could hardly lift his because it was so heavy. They got them all upstairs and Alan showed them into the master bedroom. They shoved the double bed towards the window.

Once on the landing, John started to undo the sacks. 'Which one has the £50 notes in?' he asked Terry.

'One of the others must have it,' Terry replied.

They took one sack into the bedroom and spilled its contents out on to the deep-pile carpet. Alan looked at the floor. There were masses of brown envelopes and there were notes wrapped in paper – something like paying-in slips.

The three of them knelt on the floor and started ripping open the envelopes and wrappers. They threw the notes into a space between the white fitted wardrobe and the wall. The coins were piled in a corner to the left-hand side of the room. The empty sack was put on the dressing table alcove.

The first sack took about half an hour to sort out. The notes were of all denominations, but there seemed to be more tenners than anything else. After the first sack was finished, they brought the second one in, spewing its contents on to the carpet. It was much the same as the first. Halfway through this sack, Alan decided to put the rubbish into the first sack. The rubbish was no ordinary rubbish. It consisted of cheques, luncheon vouchers, brown envelopes, and the paying-in slips. Alan took this sack down to the patio at the back of the house. He found an old dustbin and started burning the sack and its contents in it. When it had finished burning, he tipped the ashes into a gully in the middle of the patio, and washed it down the drain with buckets of water from the kitchen.

By the time Alan got back up to the bedroom the haphazard heap of notes was some three feet high and had spread out two or three feet across the carpet. It took up so much space that they couldn't fit any more sacks into the bedroom. In fact, the three of them could scarcely move without upsetting the precarious pile. 'There's no more room,' Terry said to John. 'We'd better start sorting this lot out.'

Alan collected all of the remaining rubbish into the second sack and put it into the small box room opposite the bedroom. Then they started to sort the money out into separate piles of fivers, tenners, and £50 notes. At around 9.30 p.m. Terry stopped. 'Fancy a Chinese?' he said.

'That's a good idea,' said John. He rummaged around in one of the piles and gave Terry a £10 note.

Terry went off to get the order. John and Alan carried on sorting out the money for another quarter of an hour. Then they went downstairs and Alan made a cup of coffee while they waited for Terry to return.

The three men, by now exhausted, sat downstairs in the kitchen, eating their special fried rice in silence, surrounded by greasy foil cartons and cardboard lids. After the meal, Alan cleared up the mess in the kitchen, and John and Terry returned to the bedroom. Alan joined them shortly afterwards.

They carried on into the night, sorting out the sacks of money. The coins were put into a plastic carrier bag. The one-pound notes were put to one side. They started counting the £50 and £20 notes into bundles of £1,000. It was fiddly to count with gloves on, so John and Terry took their gloves off.

Some of the notes were packed together in bundles of £100. Some had rubber bands. Others had paper clips. Alan noticed the distinctive way John had of bundling them. One note would be folded in half and the others would be sandwiched between the two halves. He would secure the whole bundle with a paper clip.

It took them until the early hours of the morning to count the money from the first sack.

'Got any suitcases?'

'Suitcases? Yes, but they're my personal ones.' Alan clambered up into the loft and took down two cardboard, sky-blue cases. He tried in vain to scrape off the sticky labels.

'Don't worry. They won't go to anyone else,' said John, watching him. 'We'll replace them.'

Alan passed John the bundles of notes, John counted them, and then passed them to Terry, who stacked them neatly inside the suitcase. The £50, £20, and £10 notes were counted in bundles of £1,000. The £5 notes were in bundles of £250. Every now and then Terry would note down on a piece of paper how much was in the suitcase.

When the suitcase was full, they made a note on a second piece of paper, stating how much the suitcase contained. This was placed inside the suitcase with the money. The £50 and £20 notes all went into one suitcase. The tenners went into the other. Soon, both suitcases were full and there were still bundles of notes on the floor. Alan found another suitcase, a black expanding one, and they packed this one full of bundles of £5 notes.

'Got any more suitcases?'

Alan fetched a large brown suitcase belonging to his mother, which was made in Poland, but when this was full there were still many bundles of money left over. These were moved to one side, and the third sack brought in from the landing. The contents were tipped on the bedroom floor. Again, it contained brown envelopes, money wrapped in paying-in slips, and plastic see-through bank bags.

They started throwing the notes into the corner again. Foreign money, and Irish notes, were put in an alcove above the headboard of the bed.

Terry was getting tired, and lay down on the double bed and had a rest. Meanwhile, John and Alan carried on sorting through the sack. They counted in silence, saying little. For one thing, Alan didn't want to wake the neighbours. Alan came across a Scottish £10 note. He showed it to John.

'That's all right,' said John, 'that's legal currency.'

The empty sack was stuffed into the alcove under the dressing table. The fourth sack was brought in. Alan fetched the sack half full of rubbish from the box room and filled it with rubbish from the third sack.

After half an hour or so, Terry woke up. 'We should sort out all the sacks and send Alan out to get some more suitcases when the shops open,' he said.

By the time they started on the fourth sack it was first light of dawn. Alan made himself some more coffee, and then went back up to the bedroom.

'Can we stay here today?' asked John.

'You know there are builders coming in, John,' said Alan. 'You'll have to stay in the bedroom all day and keep the curtains drawn. And if you go to the loo, don't pull the chain. I'll tell the builders that I have a couple of cousins who arrived early in the morning after driving down from up north and that they were both sleeping upstairs and that they shouldn't make too much noise to disturb them.'

Alan got ready for work. He called Linda. 'You'd better come back in the evening rather than midday.'

'Why?'

'It's taking longer than they thought.'

Just before eight in the morning, the builders turned up. Alan told them about his 'cousins' sleeping upstairs. 'Don't make too much noise,' he said.

He made some more coffee for John and Terry and took it upstairs to them.

'Take the van back to Kenning's for us,' said John, 'and hire Terry a decent car for about two weeks.'

'A family saloon car,' chipped in Terry.

'And can you get us another four suitcases?' added John.

'Four?'

'Yeah. Make sure they have straps around them as well as locks.'

Alan left the house and drove the white van back to Kenning's. He hired a Vauxhall Cavalier for Terry and drove it to the Triangle in Palmers Green. There, he went into Woolworth's and bought four blue suitcases. Two were slightly smaller than the other two so that they fitted neatly inside each other.

Alan drove the Cavalier home, parked it in the drive, and

took the suitcases straight up to the bedroom. 'Bloody hell!' he exclaimed as he rounded the bedroom door.

The pile of neatly stacked notes was about four feet high and five feet wide.

John grinned at him. 'There's more money here, Alan, than you'll ever see in your house again. And that's only a third of it.'

'He should have seen the lot in there,' Terry said to John.

'Yeah.' John shrugged his shoulders. Alan surmised that they must have been talking about the Security Express vaults.

'Look at them suitcases, John,' said Terry. 'They've got little wheels on them! We can put more money in these because we can wheel them along the floor. We don't have to pick 'em up!'

'That's a good idea,' thought Alan, and made a mental note to buy some wheeled suitcases next time he went on holiday.

The rubbish had been cleared up.

'Can you take these two sacks and put them in the spare room for now?' asked John. Alan obliged.

He came back into the room and saw that there was still one sack to go. John was peering into the remaining sack. He was annoyed.

'That sack of £50 notes. I know we left it against the wall.'

'Well, don't worry John,' said Terry. 'The others must have it.'

Alan spied a pile of unopened brown envelopes on the floor.

He made them some coffee and sandwiches and then made some tea and sandwiches for the builders. He went off to the garage for a few hours, returning home to make the builders another cup of tea. Soon after, the builders left. Alan went back upstairs and looked into the bedroom with some trepidation. Amazingly, it had been cleared and tidied up.

The suitcases were sitting there, all in a row. Four spanking new ones, two old-fashioned cardboard ones, a black expanding case, and his mother's small brown Polish one. The two cardboard ones had been secured, one with a strap, the other with a piece of string.

Three brown hessian sacks were still full.

'That one contains brown envelopes with £500 written on

them,' said John. 'That'll save us a bit of time. We can count them some other time.' The sack had a label on it to show how much it contained. One of the other sacks contained money Alan wasn't sure had been counted. The third sack contained £1 notes, again, not counted. They were never very enthusiastic about the pound notes, or the coins for that matter.

'Here, Alan,' they said, handing him a heavy carrier bag, by now a third full of coins. 'That's for the baby.' It came to around £100.

All the foreign money was in another plastic bag by the suitcases. That bag was half full. Alan saw dollars, marks, francs, and foreign money that he had never seen before in his life. He thought it might have been 'Chinese yen' or something like that.

'Can we store the money here?' asked John.

'Christ, no!' said Alan. 'You can't store it here!'

'It's all right, John,' said Terry. 'I know where we can put the suitcases anyway.'

'All right,' said John. He turned back to Alan. 'Can you look after the sacks and the rubbish until tomorrow?'

'Yeah, that's all right. You'll have to put it in the loft.'

John went up into the loft while Terry stood on a chair. Alan gave Terry a hand to squeeze the cumbersome sacks through the narrow trapdoor into the loft. By the weight of the sacks, Alan could tell what was in them. The two sacks containing large denominations were very heavy. The sack containing £1 notes was not quite so heavy. The two sacks of rubbish were light by comparison.

'We can't give you much money now, Al,' said John, as they closed up the trapdoor to the loft. 'It's all got to be accounted for.'

The three of them went back into the bedroom. 'You're going away on holiday soon, aren't you?' asked John. He opened up one of the suitcases and handed Alan £5,000. Alan stowed the cash in the alcove above the bed, and then helped them lug all the suitcases downstairs to the utility room.

Alan went out to the drive and reversed the Cavalier up to the fence by the side of the house. John leaned over the fence from the other side. 'All right,' he said to Terry, looking up and down the road. Alan quickly opened the boot of the car and Terry put the two blue cardboard suitcases into the boot. Terry got into the car and drove off.

John and Alan went back into the kitchen. Alan made a coffee, but before too long Terry had returned. He reversed the Cavalier up to the fence again. John looked over the fence. The suitcases were heavy. This time he took a big one and a medium-sized one. He drove away again and John and Alan went back into the kitchen.

After another half an hour, Terry returned. This time he parked the car around the corner where the van had been parked. He came into the kitchen for a cup of coffee.

'Where did you put it, Terry?' asked John.

'It's in a garage,' he said. 'It doesn't look like a garage from the front. You have to park the car more or less outside and walk a little way with the cases.'

After the coffee, they asked Alan to bring the Cavalier round to the drive. Alan reversed it up to the fence as before, while Terry put two more suitcases into the boot and John kept lookout over the fence.

'Alan, can you go and pick up my Datsun around the corner?' John handed Alan a small black key.

Alan drove the Cavalier back to where the van had been, and brought the Datsun round, reversing it up to the fence. He opened the boot of the Datsun. John stood by the fence watching.

'It's all right,' said Alan. 'Nobody's about.'

Terry was standing by the gate with the two suitcases. He handed them to Alan, who then manhandled the heavy cases into the boot of the car. They were so heavy that he had to use his knee to lever them over the lip of the boot.

'See you tomorrow,' they said to Alan. Terry went off to fetch his car, while John hung around for a few minutes. When Terry appeared at the bottom of the drive, he pulled down the drive behind him and they both drove off.

Alan was alone. He went upstairs to the bedroom to push the bed back. As he entered the room, he noticed a peculiar smell. It was a smell of old, damp money. He opened the curtains and the window.

As he moved the bed, he found a few missed brown envelopes with 'Security Express' printed on them, together with a some paper clips and luncheon vouchers. The paper clips went into the kitchen bin. The rest was burnt in the dustbin on the patio, the ashes once again flushed down the gully with water.

Linda returned home that Thursday at around 8 p.m. with his mother and their daughter to find Alan alone. They all had a cup of tea together.

At this point, Alan and Linda's versions of events again diverge. According to Linda, she spotted the empty brown hessian sacks in the utility room soon after she returned. 'What's been going on?' she demanded. Alan told her all about the sacks of money John and Terry had unloaded from the van, how they had stowed them in the loft, and counted the contents on the bedroom floor. Alan told her that he had simply made coffee for John and Terry and bought them a Chinese meal. 'There are three sacks left in the loft,' he said. 'John asked if you would help count it.'

Linda put Jeni to bed, and then Alan got a sack down from the loft. The sack was three feet high and two feet across, the top tied up with string. Alan spilled the contents of the sack out on to the bedroom floor. It mainly contained £1 notes. Some were loose, others were in bundles with rubber bands around them. Alan and Linda counted them into £100 bundles and put them back into the sack. They made separate bundles for the Scottish notes, and put the sack back up in the loft. It was early morning by the time they had finished.

According to Alan's version, he had waited until Jeni had gone to bed before telling Linda what happened that day. 'They're coming back tomorrow,' he told her. She was not pleased, so he left it at that. He kept quiet about the sacks of money and rubbish in the loft until they had both gone up to bed.

Lying in bed together, they discussed what to do. It was a big worry having it all in the house. And then there were the builders and the rest of the family. They would have to be watched out for. 'You have to get the money out of the house as quickly as possible,' Linda told him. 'Get rid of it!'

According to Linda's version, the next morning, before Alan went to work, he got a second sack down from the loft and put it in the bedroom for her to count. As he left, Linda reminded him to get some more suitcases.

Looking inside the sack, Linda saw that the bundling of the notes was quite distinctive. Each person seemed to have a unique way of doing it. Some of the notes were still wrapped with the bank wrapper around them stating £500 in £5 notes. Others were fastened with rubber bands. Some of the £10 notes were in wads of £100 held together with a paper clip – five wads with a rubber band around them making bundles of £500. Other bundles consisted of wads of nine £10 notes wrapped in another £10 note.

According to Alan, the next morning – Friday – he went in to work as usual, picking up his secretary along the way. He stayed for a while sorting a few things out and then, mid-morning, went off to buy three more suitcases from Pearsons in Enfield. This time they were light brown, with straps as well as locks.

John and Terry had said they would be back that evening, so Alan went straight home with the cases. He was getting them out of his car when one of the builders spotted him. 'Going away on holiday?' he asked. Alan laughed.

Alan took the suitcases up to the bedroom, where Linda joined him. He had decided the best thing to do was to get the sacks out of the attic and count the money, so that they could get it out of the house as quickly as possible. The sacks were heavy. Linda had to help him get them down from the loft.

He got the sack containing the £1 notes down and emptied it on the floor.

'I've got to go back to the garage to do the wages,' he told her.

He left Linda to start counting the money. He told Linda how they did it. Linda started stacking the notes in the suitcase.

Alan returned at lunchtime to find Linda making some tea and sandwiches for the builders. Alan had something to eat and then joined her in the bedroom.

'What else is in the loft?' she asked.

'There's one more sack, but I don't think John wants it touched,' he said.

'I don't care,' she replied. 'It's in my house and I want it out.'

Alan got the last sack down to the bedroom. This one had a brown label on it, something like a luggage tag. The tag had the figure '£187,000' written on it.

For a while, he helped her count. Then he went back to the garage and stayed there until late in the afternoon, leaving Linda to it. Later that afternoon John and Terry turned up at the garage.

'I want the money out of the house,' Alan told them. 'Linda's at home counting it up for you.'

John looked annoyed. They all drove around to Alan's house. John and Terry parked up the road, and then the three of them went into the house.

Meanwhile, Linda had finished counting the second sack by mid-afternoon and put the bundles into another suitcase. Then she opened the last sack and tipped the contents out on the floor. It was full of large, brown, sealed envelopes. Each one had a blue stamp with a total on it.

She opened up the envelopes. Some of the amount was in the form of cheques, which she placed in an old cardboard box. While she was in the middle of sorting the sack, John and Terry came back.

Alan's mother and daughter were sitting in the front room watching television, oblivious to what was going on upstairs in the bedroom where Linda was counting thousands of pounds' worth of notes.

Linda showed them two suitcases, which she had already filled. One was full of pound notes.

'What's this one?' said John, pointing to the second.

'That's the contents of the sack you marked,' said Linda.

John peered inside the suitcase. It was full of higher-value notes. He glanced at the note, which recorded how much money was inside. John got annoyed.

'There was more in that sack than that,' he said.

'No there wasn't,' said Linda.

'Where's that bit of paper, the one I wrote on?' He looked around for the luggage label.

He was getting worked up. Linda got the piece of paper from the alcove above the bed and handed it to John.

'That's what should have been in there. Not what you wrote,' he said.

'Most of the envelopes had £500 in cash in them, John. But some only had £150 to £200 in,' she told him. But John wasn't convinced.

'John, if I was going to take any money I would have taken it from one of the other sacks, not from the one you marked.'

That seemed to cool John down. He went downstairs, leaving Terry and Linda to finish counting. 'Can I borrow Linda's Jaguar?' he said to Alan. He went off in the Jaguar, taking one of the suitcases with him. Terry stayed behind to give Linda a hand with the money. Alan went downstairs.

John returned after about half an hour, and seemed a changed man. He had forgotten all about his spat with Linda.

Upstairs, Terry and Linda had finished counting the money. John and Alan joined them in the bedroom. As a reward John offered Alan the suitcase full of £20,000 in £1 notes. 'Is £20,000 enough?' he asked.

'I can't take all those £1 notes, John,' Alan said. John swapped half of them and gave Alan £10,000 in £5 notes.

According to Alan, John then offered Linda £500 in £5 notes, but she refused to take it, so he gave it to Alan. 'Go on,' he said. 'Get her something nice for what she's done.'

John and Terry left with the last of the suitcases. They were both wearing gloves. As they were leaving, John turned to Alan. 'Once all the money has been accounted for, you'll get some more,' he said.

They also took with them the bag full of foreign currencies, torn £1 notes, and a number of £1 notes that had blood on them and thus could be traced.

But about five minutes later John returned. 'My car won't start,' he said. Alan took him round to his Datsun. Terry was in the Cavalier nearby. Alan tried to start the Datsun but couldn't. So they all pushed it out into the Grove. John got into the Cavalier. 'I'll contact the garage tomorrow,' he said. 'Can you burn all the rubbish for me, Al?'

Alan went back upstairs with Linda. She started cleaning up the bedroom, and Alan began burning the sacks in the back garden. Then they sat down in the front room and had a drink. It had been quite a week.

The counting of the cash had taken three days.

There was just one sack there, half full of rubbish, which he put up in the attic with the other two sacks of rubbish from the previous day. He put the £5,000 they had given him on the Thursday with the £20,000 in the suitcase, and took it to his office in the garage where he stowed it under his desk.

That Saturday he went to his office and sorted out about a thousand £1 notes. These, he put into a briefcase. He took the suitcase with the rest of the money around to his lock-up where the red van had been kept. The briefcase went home with him.

Back at the house he tried to burn another one of the sacks in the old dustbin, but by then the scorched metal was flaking apart with the heat of it all.

£££

The following Tuesday John and Terry turned up at the garage bright and early.

'We've not had a sort out yet, Al,' said John. 'When we have, you'll get some more money.'

'I don't want any more money,' said Alan.

'All right, Al. Anything we can do for you, just let me know.'

Alan told them about the problems he had had burning the rubbish. 'Get a garden incinerator,' said John. So he did. That evening he burnt the rest of the rubbish on his patio, swilling the ashes down the gully, just as before. Among the cheques, brown envelopes, and luncheon vouchers was a green canvas bag, something like a duffel bag. It had the words 'Security Express' written on the side. The bag had brass rings at the top for a drawstring to be threaded through. It posed some difficulty. The brass rings ended up in the kitchen bin with the paper clips.

On Monday of the following week, a fortnight after the robbery, Alan got one of the garage men to return the Cavalier he had hired for Terry. There was a query about a small dent in the car that the hire company said wasn't there before.

On the Wednesday of that week, John and Terry came into the garage. They were in good spirits. 'Today's the day, Al,' John said. 'We're going to the yard to have a little sort out.' When John talked about the 'yard' Alan took it to mean his brother Jimmy's scrap yard in Ridley Road.

They drove off in John's car, returning at around three o'clock in the afternoon, still in good spirits. 'We've just had the meeting,' John told Alan. 'We're £240,000 short of what should have been there. We had the old numbers in the lot. I drew the lowest number. Guess who got the foreign currency?' he added. 'I did.'

About a week later, Alan reminded them that they still owed him for the hire of the vehicles and the suitcases.

'Let us know how much, Al, and we'll square you up.'

'If you get caught, don't ever implicate me in this,' said Alan.

'Don't worry, Al,' said John. 'You've always been a straight guy and there's a lot of business people behind this.'

A couple of days later they handed Alan £700 in payment for the vehicle hires and the suitcases.

£££

Meanwhile, business at the garage continued as usual. Alan got back down to doing what he was good at – wheeling and dealing, twiddling and fiddling the motors. John would drop in most days just as he always did, and sometimes Terry would stop by too. It was as if the raid had never happened. But now, both John and Terry were flush with cash.

Sometime in May, John came into the garage yard with a proposition for Alan. He wanted to part-exchange his Granada and his son's Allegro for a metallic black Granada Mk IV, which Alan had up for sale for around £5,300.

John wanted £1,600 for his Granada and £1,000 for the Allegro, but when Alan checked out the suspension on the Allegro he found that it had been knocked back a couple of inches to one side. He told John what he had uncovered.

John confessed. 'Yeah,' he said. 'My son had a bit of an accident in it.' He told Alan that a firm in Jimmy's yard had carried out the repair work.

'It's a right bodge-up, whoever did it,' said Alan scornfully. 'Is it the same firm who sprayed that red Sherpa van?'

'No,' said John, laughing. But Alan wasn't convinced. It was a bad deal. 'I tell you what,' he said. 'I'll give you £500 for it.'

Reluctantly John agreed. He bought the new Granada, paying Alan the difference of around £3,200 all in £10 notes.

About a week later, Terry approached Alan for a favour. 'Can you get me a car like John's?' he said.

'I'll ask around for you, Terry.' Alan found one at a local garage in Edmonton and sold it to him for £5,400 cash.

Towards the end of May, Alan went on holiday with his family to Majorca. To pay for it he took £5,000 in cash from the suitcase stowed under his desk. By the beginning of June, Alan had managed to change the £10,000 in £1 notes given to him by John into fivers and tenners. He deposited the cash in his deed box at the Midland Bank, and talked to the manager about setting up an account in Jersey. It was duly opened on 20 June 1983.

£££

That summer was particularly glorious. Day after day the sun beat down relentlessly from a deep-blue sky, with not a cloud to be seen. Throughout the summer months, almost daily, John and Terry would meet at the garage.

One day in July, John stopped by the garage to see Alan. This time he was on his own. 'Can you do me a favour?'

'What?' said Alan.

'Change £10,000 into £50 notes.' John opened his bag. It was stuffed full of bundles of tenners. 'I'll give you a good drink,' he added.

Alan took the money to his bank in Cockfosters and asked them for £10,000 in £50 notes.

'We don't keep that amount in £50 notes,' said the cashier. 'It'll take a few days.' Alan paid in the money and a few days later withdrew £10,000 in £50 notes.

A few weeks later, in September, John asked Alan to do the same again with another £10,000. The garage was busy that week and Alan had no time to go to collect the cash. John turned up on the Wednesday. 'Where's the money, Alan?'

'I've had no time,' Alan said.

'Come on,' said John. 'Jump in the motor. Let's go get it.'

John drove him to the bank and waited outside while Alan collected the cash. He never told Alan why he wanted the cash at such short notice, and Alan knew better than to ask.

At the beginning of October, John came into Alan's office with a black attaché case. He opened it up. Inside there were two large brown envelopes containing cash, stacks of £500 with a rubber band around them. It came to £60,000 in tenners. He handed Alan the briefcase. 'Take your time changing it,' he said. 'Do it £500 or £1,000 at a time and different banks. £50 notes please.'

The notes were in bundles of £100 with the last note wrapped over the rest.

'Don't use the Midland Bank at Southgate,' he said. 'I've done a lot of changing there. You'd better not use the banks at Palmers Green and Wood Green either. I've got Terry to do some for me as well.'

Alan took the money home in the attaché case and put it under the bed. Depending on how busy he was, he would take a couple of grand with him a day to change at various banks in Ponders End, Barnet, Cockfosters, and Enfield Town.

Autumn half-term came and his daughter was on holiday,

so the family took a week's holiday in Spain, staying in John's apartment. They marvelled at how luxurious it was. When Alan came back, he asked John about the paintings there.

'I've spent a couple of grand on paintings for my new villa,' John told him.

Late in November, John stopped by. He was in a hurry. 'How much have you changed up?' he said.

'I thought there was no rush, John. I haven't done it all.'

'How much have you done, then?'

'About £25,000.'

'Can we go and pick it up straight away? I'm going off to Spain and I've got to pay some builders and my new car's been delivered as well.'

John followed Alan to his home and picked up the £25,000.

By December, Alan still had £35,000 to change, and he was getting fed up with it. It was taking up a lot of his time, running around the banks here, there, and everywhere. So he rang up the bank and ordered £30,000 in £50 notes.

He took money out of other accounts and paid them into his personal account at the Midland, arranged a £30,000 overdraft, and then repaid it at another branch with the money from the attaché case. He withdrew the £30,000 in new £50 notes and drove back to the garage with the money. As he was getting out of the car with the attaché case, Terry was pulling away. He leaned out of his window and pretended to make a grab for the case. 'I know what's in there,' he said, laughing as he drove off.

Alan went into the garage and saw John sitting there. 'We'd gone round the roundabout and saw you at the bank,' he said. Alan looked nervously around. 'Come up to the office,' Alan said. He handed over the money. John was wearing a hunting jacket. He took the money and stuffed it into his pockets and left.

Alan drove home and took out £30,000 in £10 notes. He drove all the way to a Midland Bank in Oxford, where he paid it in. He was just about to leave the bank when the cashier called him back.

'Hold on.'

Alan nearly jumped out of his skin. 'What?' he said.

'There's an Irish note here,' said the cashier. 'Oh. Sorry,' said Alan, breathing a sigh of relief. He fumbled in his wallet for a replacement tenner. When he saw John a few days later he mentioned the note. 'Here you are,' said John, handing him a British tenner.

Just before Christmas, John came into the office. 'John, you haven't paid me for changing all this money,' Alan said.

'I can't give you 20 per cent like last time,' he said.

'Why not?'

'What you was doing for me last time was new notes. These are old notes that can't be traced,' John explained. 'I'll square up with you soon,' he added.

A couple of days later, John came back to the office and gave Alan around £300. 'You've still got £5,000 of mine,' John reminded him.

'I know,' Alan replied. 'I can't do it before Christmas. It's gone into various deposit accounts.'

£££

A few days before Christmas, John's bank manager at the Midland Bank called the garage. Alan took the call. 'We have to speak to Mr Knight urgently,' said the manager.

John had always told Alan never to give out his home phone number, so Alan temporized. 'I'll get him to phone you,' he said, and then hurriedly called John, who was in Spain.

John, who had paid in £16,000 in cash just before leaving for Spain, was worried. Nevertheless, he phoned the bank.

'Ah, Mr Knight!' said the manager. 'So glad you called.'

'So what's up?' asked John.

'We just wanted to let you know that we found a forged £10 note in the money you recently paid in.'

John breathed a silent sigh of relief. 'Really?' he said. 'That's shocking.'

That Friday afternoon, the day before Christmas Eve, the lads from the garage all had a Christmas drink in a local pub. John was there too.

'Why did the bank want to see you?' Alan asked.

John took Alan to one side. 'The manager had found a forged note,' John said. He laughed. 'He's not a bad bloke. By rights he should have called the police, but instead he gave it back to me and I gave him another one.' John pulled out the forged note from his wallet for Alan to inspect. 'Has Terry been in?' he asked.

'Yeah. He's been in, had a few drinks with us, then gone to see his men over in Tottenham.'

£££

Alan had one other revelation to make. He told Reed that, in the summer of 1983, he had approached an off-duty police constable having a drink in the White Hart, in Southgate. Nearby was a Greek taverna, a favourite haunt for local off-duty policemen. Alan had got talking to the officer. He told him that he worked in a nearby garage.

'Now listen,' Alan said. 'How do I go about telling the police about a robbery?'

'Well, first of all, what type of robbery? Is it a large one or small one?' said the PC.

'It's the biggest one there's been.' said Alan.

'You'd have to see a lot of the guv'nors, then,' the policeman replied.

That put Alan off and he promptly dropped the subject. He knew how it worked. Just as the police had their informers, so did John's firm. He decided that too many people would get to know who was talking, and that was asking for trouble. So he just let it lie.

The enquiry eventually tracked the policeman down and found out that Alan's story was true. He had put the conversation down to drink and never thought to report it. It was a piece of the jigsaw that they had missed. If they had known it then, it would have saved them months of hard work.

14
THE SECOND WAVE

Peter read through the Opiolas' final statements with a great deal of satisfaction. Both were some eighty pages long and went into fantastic detail. However, there were still some things to consider before the statements could be used. For one thing, he had to assess whether Alan's various wrongdoings over the years were serious enough for the defence to use them to destroy his credibility as a witness.

The same was true of Linda. Like Alan, she was no angel. Some few years before, John Knight had asked her to take his wife Diane's driving test for her. Linda had booked the test in the name of 'Walters', Diane's maiden name. Posing as Diane, Linda borrowed Terry Perkins's old Audi to take the test. She failed. The second time around she used her own car, a Datsun automatic, and passed. John paid her £200 for the pass and £20 for the fail.

That, thought Peter, was clearly an offence of conspiracy involving Linda Opiola and John and Diane Knight, plus deception, forgery, and various offences under the Road Traffic Act.

But he wasn't really worried about any of these matters. They were hardly likely to be raised by the defence during the trial, because most of them would simply cause more embarrassment to John Knight, or, in the case of Alan's fraudulent domestic insurance claim, Terry Perkins.

Sometimes, to get convictions, you have to choose the lesser of two evils. Peter had been faced with that choice many times before in his long career in the CID.

The story that the Opiolas had to tell had not only given

the enquiry a deep insight into John Knight's business dealings, but had also thrown up new and surprising connections between the people then on remand.

One such connection involved one of Alan Opiola's suitcases. Alan had liked the suitcases he had bought from Woolworth's to store the cash in so much that he went out and bought identical ones for his family holiday at John's villa later that year. These suitcases had been found by officers searching his loft.

Exactly the same type of suitcase had been found in Horsley's father-in-law's flat. Horsley had claimed that Hickson had brought his money over in it. Therefore, it was likely that at least one of Opiola's new suitcases had passed through Hickson's hands on its way to the flat. In the end, Alan and Linda had worried about the wrong suitcase: the Polish one was never found.

The statement also illustrated how unlucky the Squad had been. The fact that the bank manager had not bothered to inform the police about the forged £10 note he had found irritated them immensely. One phone call from him might have given them a head start and saved them many months.

They also obtained their first clues about the involvement of Clifford Saxe, who managed the public house in Kingsland Road called the Fox for John Knight. Alan told the police that he thought that both Cliff and Vera, his wife, had helped John in some way, either before or after the robbery.

The gang could probably have gone to someone in the East End who would have provided them with a whole fleet of cars and vans to rush around in. But it would have cost them more. Also, they might not have known who they were connected to. Whoever it was could have muscled in and demanded a slice of the cake. So the robbers appeared to have gone for amateurs – tinpot garage owners unknown to anybody. Perhaps they could rely on them more because they wouldn't have known how to take advantage of the secret they had been let in on. Perhaps the robbers had learnt a lesson from the Great Train Robbers, some of whom had been sold down the river by their companions.

The robbers had chosen people that they had known for some while, thinking that they would be loyal to them. It was a high-risk thing to do. It was quite obvious to a few people that something was going on, and that it was going to happen that Easter Bank Holiday. The trouble with small-time people is that they lose their cool when confronted with the truth.

After the robbery, there had been a large reward put up by Security Express. It would have been better for Opiola to have gone down that line, rather than get mixed up with the robbers. In the end, it ruined his life.

The other thing that struck Peter was that it didn't sound at all well planned. There they were, two days after the robbery, hurriedly looking for a van to move sacks of money about. What a risk to take. Even moving the sacks into the house had been surprisingly risky. Someone coming around the corner could have put the kibosh on all of it. From 6 April to the early hours of the morning two days later, it must have been non-stop for them. Counting that vast amount of money would have exhausted anybody, thought Peter.

Then, to cap it all, Opiola was asked if he could store the suitcases. He didn't want to know, which was hardly surprising. Luckily for them, Terry decided that he had somewhere he could put them. In fact, Terry drove off with some suitcases but had come back within half an hour. He loaded up again, and again he was back within half an hour. Perhaps he had put them in his own house.

If they had been that professional, all of this would have been locked down tightly well before the raid. Peter concluded that either they weren't so clever after all, or perhaps, as Opiola had suggested, something had gone wrong with their well-laid plans at the last minute.

It was the breakthrough that the Dirty Dozen had almost had with Horsley, just a few weeks previously. Remarkable though the Opiolas' evidence was, however, there was much still to do. Now the focus of the enquiry had to shift, to corroborate as much of what the Opiolas had said as possible.

They had to give credence to Alan and Linda Opiola as witnesses. The parts they played in the crime were minor in comparison with the robbers, but their evidence was vital against the defendants then on remand.

He sent a forensic team to the Enfield lock-up garage where Opiola had said he had hidden the first van they had used. Sure enough, they found streaks of red paint scraped along the concrete beam supporting the roof, just as Alan had said.

He got two constables from the Traffic Division to measure the route the white van might have taken, from Kenning's in Palmers Green to Horsley's garage in Waltham Way, where the sacks of money would have been picked up, and then on to Opiola's house in Enfield, and then back to Kenning's. It came to just about twenty-seven miles, exactly as Kenning's had recorded it.

Peter was also worried that the staff at the garage might be 'leaned on' by John Knight and Terry Perkins, to keep their mouths shut. So one of the first things the Squad did was to get statements from all the employees at the garage, including Opiola's brother Richard, who also worked there. He explained how his brother and John Knight had built up the garage business. He also confirmed that regular meetings took place between John Knight and Terry Perkins, both at the garage and in nearby restaurants.

Ethel, the garage secretary, explained the ownership of the garage to them and told them all about the curious wage structure for John Knight and Alan Opiola. Referring to the garage records she also told them that John Knight and Terry Perkins had bought two cars for cash, apparently on the very same day, 3 May 1983. Knight had paid for his car in used fivers, and Perkins paid £5,400 for his in twenty and one pound notes. Perkins bought two other vehicles in September that year for cash as well. And later in the year Knight got his son's car repaired for cash.

The other garage workers' statements only added weight to the association between John Knight and Terry Perkins. Linda

Opiola, too, had said that from Christmas 1982 to Easter 1983 she saw John's or Terry's cars regularly parked at the garage. She knew they could usually be found together.

£££

Quite some days after the first arrests in late January, Peter had been forwarded an intelligence report from the Drugs Squad, which described the suspicious meeting that had taken place at Jimmy Knight's yard in Ridley Road in March 1983, almost exactly one month before the robbery. The report named John Knight, Billy Hickson, and Terry Perkins as present at the meeting, along with Jimmy Knight and two other men, Ronnie Everett and John Mason, about whom the enquiry knew precious little.

Reading the report had made Peter very angry indeed. He had stared in disbelief at the thin, beige file lying open on his desk. If only he had been given the names earlier, he could have moved much more quickly. The delay may have cost the enquiry days if not months – who knew how much time? Peter was sure that, with the other pieces of information coming in, and armed with the knowledge of the meeting, he could have acted much sooner against all of those on remand. He might even have been able to recover more of the looted cash.

Intelligence such as this was normally logged in the Criminal Intelligence Bureau at Scotland Yard and various departments were allowed to go in to extract the information if there were genuine enquiries on the subject. In this instance, however the system had failed. The Drugs Squad's report had only been released because Peter had by now arrested three of the six people who were present at the meeting. Peter had no idea why the information had been withheld from the Flying Squad in the early stages of the enquiry. All sorts of reasons sprang to his mind. Was it corruption? Incompetence? Or was it because the Drugs Squad had decided to put the information into its own system, and not into the overall system at the Intelligence Bureau? Perhaps they felt the information was too 'hot' to be allowed to go anywhere else.

Peter thought the latter was the most likely explanation. After all, police officers are only human, with the same needs and desires for success and reward as the rest of us. In 1983, there was no such thing as a police national computer. Each Metropolitan Police squad jealously guarded its intelligence files. It was a competitive thing. Good intelligence led to good arrests, which gave the squad officers added kudos. Added kudos meant fast-track promotion.

Officers progressed, particularly in the CID, on their ability to make arrests. They were reluctant to pass on information from their own particular branch in case other officers from other branches, armed with their information, pinched a yard on them. They were worried that someone else would make a capture because of the information that they had supplied, thus taking all the glory. There were six named criminals meeting on that day, which was probably why the information had been so slow in coming to light.

£££

Now, more than ever, Peter was convinced that the meeting at Jimmy's yard was somehow connected with the robbery. The Flying Squad's own investigations had already linked some of the names in the report together. He inferred that, as those who played a minor role in the robbery – Horsley and Opiola – had not been invited to the yard meeting, those present were likely to have been the major players.

During February, the Enquiry had been far too busy with the Opiolas to do much about the Drugs Squad's report. But by March 1984, with the Opiolas' statements more or less in the bag, Peter decided it was time to look at the other three names present at the meeting. Peter termed these people the 'second wave', but really it was 'catch-up time' for the Squad because, at that stage at least, they didn't have a lot of factual evidence against these men. They had to build it up as they went along.

Top of their list was Jimmy Knight. Before the January arrests, Peter, George, Reed, and the others had often discussed Jimmy's possible role in the robbery. They had already searched his yard once. But, without having the information on the meeting in the scrapyard, they had dismissed him as a man who was probably working on the periphery.

When they had gone out to make the first arrests in January 1984, Jimmy really wasn't in the frame. But during his interview Horsley had described an 'older man', and as the weeks went on they realized it might well have been Jimmy that Horsley had been talking about. After that, Opiola had suggested that John Knight and Terry Perkins had held meetings about the robbery over at Jimmy's yard. Now, Opiola's information seemed to be confirmed by the Drugs Squad's report.

There was an additional reason why Peter decided it was time to go for Jimmy. He was becoming increasingly alarmed at what he saw as a growing conspiracy among members of the Knight family to remove evidence and concoct cover stories for John Knight's wealth and his whereabouts on the day of the robbery.

Already, Alan and Linda Opiola had tipped off the enquiry about the attempt by one of John Knight's sons to recover the contents of a safe-deposit box in Spain. Peter had acted on that plot swiftly. The Opiolas had also told the enquiry about Diane Knight burning suitcases.

Jimmy Knight appeared to be central to both plots. He was the one who had arranged for Diane's son to go out to Spain and it was his yard where the suitcases were burnt. He had also taken Alan Opiola to the prison to see John Knight to help concoct a cover story about John's finances.

All this had been done with various explanations, some good, some not so good. It was what you might have expected a brother to do. Perhaps Jimmy was simply trying to protect his brother John's assets. But, as a result of the new information on the yard meeting, Peter was inclined to see a darker motive for Jimmy's actions. He concluded that Jimmy was acting this way because he didn't want people to explain his own involvement. Although Peter still considered Jimmy to be a handler and organizer rather than one of the robbers, it seemed that he was taking an active part in what the Squad termed 'perverting the course of justice'.

Jimmy's 'good deeds' had already prompted Peter to send his undercover men out to take a closer look at Jimmy Knight's scrap yard in Ridley Road. But in March things had taken a more serious turn.

Jimmy had been constantly phoning up Linda 'to see how Alan was getting on' and offering help and advice. The 'friendly' phone calls that Jimmy made to her had been secretly taped. And to Peter it seemed as though Jimmy was trying to make sure that Linda Opiola didn't talk out of order.

By now it was clear the Knight family knew full well that Opiola had turned 'Queen's'. Peter couldn't afford anything to go wrong and he was worried that the enquiry might find itself in the same position as it was with John Horsley.

Peter therefore decided to swoop on the whole family and pre-empt any trouble. Early in the morning of Tuesday, 13 March, he sent teams of officers to arrest Jimmy Knight, Diane Knight, her brother Albie, her son and his girlfriend, and bring them all in for questioning.

£££

The arrest of Diane Knight and her son sparked off another spat between the enquiry and the legal profession. With the benefit of hindsight Peter realized they had a job to do – and that job was always going to be in conflict with his. But at the time, the incident made him very angry.

Just before 9 o'clock that morning, soon after Diane was arrested, Eric Cheek turned up at Arbour Square demanding to see her. He was shown into the station's waiting room. Peter went down with Simon to see him.

'Hello. I'm Eric Cheek,' he said, stretching out his hand, but Peter was not in the mood for niceties.

'Are you from Lesser & Co?' he asked.

'Yes. I want to see Mrs Knight. What have you arrested her for?'

'For conspiracy to pervert the course of justice.'

'What is the allegation?'

'It's all within what I said.'

'Can I see her?'

'No. You can't,' said Peter firmly. There followed a heated exchange. They stood toe to toe while Peter argued his case. Cheek was close to boiling point but Peter held his ground. 'I may allow another firm to represent her,' he said.

'It's not up to you. It's her choice.'

'If she doesn't nominate someone at this stage, there won't be anyone. Look, you are representing John Knight, another Knight, and now Diane Knight. There is an enormous conflict and it would interfere with justice.'

'I can't believe I'm hearing this,' snorted Cheek, and with that, stormed out.

Later that morning another solicitor from Lesser & Co., a Mr Williams, came to the station, this time asking to see John's son. Once again, Peter refused.

That evening, first Beaumont and then Cheek called the control room demanding to speak to the Knights. In each instance they were refused.

There was little the solicitors could do but shout and stomp their feet. Peter was well within his rights and covered, at that time anyway, by the rules. He had double-checked: access to a solicitor was one of the five principles enshrined in the administrative rules by which the police operate:

> . . . every person at any stage of an investigation should be able to communicate and consult privately with a solicitor. This is so even if he is in custody . . .

But the principle carried an important proviso:

> . . . provided that in such a case no unreasonable delay or hindrance is caused to the processes of investigation or the administration of justice by his doing so.

Peter was worried that the firm might be used, unknowingly, to take messages between John Knight and other members of the family. This was not in any way illegal, but he felt it would hinder the investigation so he considered his actions to be covered by the rules.

There was another factor behind Peter's hard-nosed approach to Lesser & Co. The Flying Squad had already discovered that

Knight had used them when buying some property in Spain. Peter felt that the solicitors should have informed the police that they had dealt with large sums of money on John Knight's behalf when they were conveyancing for him.

In fact, Knight's solicitors were acting perfectly within the rules governing client–solicitor relations. It was their duty to keep their client's financial details confidential until such a time as the police formally requested the information. Moral rights and wrongs, at least as viewed from the police's perspective, didn't enter into it. Solicitors had a professional duty to their clients and that was that. Peter, like many policemen before him, found this hard to accept.

Diane and her son were both charged with conspiracy to pervert the course of justice. Her son was bailed on condition that he remained at High Trees. There would be no more trips over to Spain.

Later, the charges against both Diane and her son were dropped. Both were cleared of any wrongdoing. The Director of Public Prosecutions completely exonerated them. With hindsight, Peter thought that perhaps he may have over-reacted by charging them, but at the time he wanted to make sure that they behaved. A charge dangling over their heads was the best way of ensuring that. It was the oldest trick in the book. Peter was simply fighting fire with fire.

£££

That same day, Reed McGeorge and Jim Keeling led a team to arrest Jimmy Knight and search the Limes, his large house, restaurant, and nightclub in Wood Lane, Stanmore. Only his children were at home. Jimmy and his wife were away in Portugal. The officers searched the place and found two plastic carrier bags each containing £1,000 in cash, and a small key. Eventually, they discovered that the key fitted a safe in the bedroom, where they found another £18,350 in cash. Jimmy was quite an affluent man, however, and could easily explain the money away – his house alone was worth around £2.5 million.

Jimmy's scrapyard in Ridley Road was worth a fortune,

too. It may not have looked much to an outsider, but it was prime development land. Afterwards, when the team went on to search the yard, they found that it had all changed. It was all closed up.

A week later, on 19 March, Jimmy returned from Portugal and came voluntarily to the station with his solicitor, Peter Hughman. That day Reed McGeorge, George Moncrieff, and Simon Webber interviewed him at length.

Jimmy maintained his cool composure throughout. He was a tough old nut and well used to the ways of the police. Skilful interviewing by George revealed a picture of a man who had done his level best to help his brother out of trouble. He told them that he had gone to Portugal with £6,000 in cash because he wanted to buy a villa over there. The money found in the safe in his bedroom was, he said, his own personal money that he had saved over the years.

It still remained for the enquiry to counter John Knight's planned defence: that he had got his money from cash jobs at the garage. They already knew from Alan Opiola's statement that, on 28 January, Alan and Jimmy had gone to the prison to see John and that John had asked Alan to help him account for the money he had around him. Alan had told them all about the prison visit, down to every last detail. So Reed fired a few pertinent questions at Jimmy to see what he would say.

'Did Alan Opiola tell John Knight in your presence that he could not cover John for £400,000?' he asked.

'I can't recall that,' said Jimmy. 'But I do remember Alan telling me he could cover John for £200,000 that he'd given him in the past.'

'During that prison interview did you and John discuss keys?'

'No.'

'Did you discuss burning suitcases?'

'No.'

'What do you mean by the word "cover"?' asked George.

'Alan . . . was saying that he used to give John all the cash jobs. What John done with the money was his own business and he can cover him for that sort of money. Alan said this to me after the prison visit. He said that he had built the business up to £350,000 or so. I thought that Alan was in a position to account for John's possession of cash.'

'You do not recall Mr Opiola talking about this on the way to the prison or during the visit?'

'We were talking about things but what they were I can't remember. But it wasn't that.'

'What would make Mr Opiola talk about it after the visit?'

'Well, I don't know. He just said, "I can cover him for £200,000."'

'You said when you were with Mr Opiola in the car after the visit that all John had to worry about was the taxman.'

'That's what Alan said.'

'I'm saying that that is what you said.'

'I don't remember saying anything about that. I may have done.'

'How long has your brother John owned the garage?'

Jimmy shrugged. 'Couldn't tell you.'

'When Mr Opiola picked you up in the morning did he not tell you that he had checked the books and that John had only owned the garage for two and a half years.'

'No, he didn't.'

'Mr Opiola went on to say that there was no way he could cover John for £400,000. Is that correct?'

'No. He only said £200,000. I've not heard of £400,000.'

'Mr Opiola picked you up from your home address?'

'Yes.'

'This conversation about money was en route to the prison for the visit?'

'From the prison.'

'So you had no conversation about money on the way to the prison, or during the prison visit? Is that correct?'

'Yes.'

'Doesn't it seem strange that Mr Opiola should talk about the money after the visit?'

'No. He was more concerned about his business, buying and selling cars. He offered me a car on the journey there.'

'If I was to tell you, Mr Knight, that the first occasion

Mr Opiola saw your brother was on that prison visit with you, to your knowledge is that correct?'

'I don't know how many times he's seen Johnny.'

'I can tell you that from the time of Mr Knight's arrest until that visit on the twenty-sixth, Mr Opiola did not see your brother. If what you tell us is true, that no conversation took place on that visit regarding the money, why was it that, on the journey back from the prison visit, Mr Opiola has a conversation with you about "covering" money? How would Alan Opiola know that your brother wished him to do this?'

'I don't know. Unless he got the information from somewhere else.'

'Do you surmise from that, that your brother by whatever means made contact with Mr Opiola requesting that he do certain things?'

'I don't know.'

'Would you agree that, if Mr Opiola first saw your brother after the arrest on the prison visit and if, as you say, the only conversations were in general about how Mr Knight's family were, and whether his wife was receiving the income from the garage, then the only explanation for Mr Opiola's knowledge and reason for the conversation with you regarding covering monies is that someone made contact with him on behalf of John Knight?'

'I don't know.'

'Did you get in touch with Mr Opiola on behalf of your brother John?'

'No, I haven't seen him since all this business. Only on the day we went to the prison.'

'Did you know why John Knight wanted to see Opiola?'

'No. Only about Di's wages. Because you took all the money away from High Trees.'

'As far as you were concerned, that was the only reason John Knight wanted to see Opiola?'

'Yes.'

'In view of what you now know, Mr Knight, by which I mean the conversation you say took place in the car after the prison visit, aren't you surprised that Alan Opiola and your brother did not have a conversation regarding covering monies during the visit?'

'No.'

'Do you take my point?' asked George. 'It surprises me that Alan Opiola would speak to you about such matters and yet not say a word about them at the first opportunity he had to speak to John.'

'No, I'm not surprised,' Jimmy replied. 'Their business is their business. What they want to keep to themselves is their business.'

'But that isn't the case, is it?' said George. 'Mr Opiola told you about it. He didn't keep that business to himself. So your previous answer, to my mind, doesn't hold water.'

And so the questioning went on, all afternoon, round and round in circles, variations on the same theme. But, unfortunately for Jimmy, the circles were getting ever tighter and tighter.

After a break for a cup of tea, George moved on to other matters that the Squad felt had amounted to interference with their ongoing investigation. In particular, they asked Jimmy how and why he had arranged for his nephew, John's son, to go to Spain. According to Jimmy, it was because he was run down and needed a break. The officers already knew all the details of the trip from Opiola. They simply wanted to see what Jimmy would say.

'I put it to you that the reason for John's son's visit to Spain was to take a letter of authorization so that he could get into a safe-deposit box in Spain.'

'No. As far as I know, that was never what he went over there for. He just went over there for a rest.'

'Further, that the safe-deposit box in Spain was one belonging to his father.'

'As far as I know he never had a safe-deposit box. I knew nothing about it.'

'But you and John Knight discussed keys on the twenty-sixth in front of Alan Opiola.'

'I never mentioned nothing about keys.'

Jimmy also denied burning the suitcases in his yard – in

fact, he denied ever having a conversation about suitcases. And then the interview moved on to the subject of Jimmy wanting so desperately to meet up with Alan Opiola following his arrest.

'On the first occasion that you visited Linda, what was the reason?'

'To ask how Alan was. Johnny asked me to ask how they both were.'

'Did you ask what was happening to Alan?'

'Yes.'

'Why?'

'Because Johnny asked me to ask. We were all concerned about Johnny's business.'

'What about the business?'

'Because Johnny's not there. Who's going to look after the business? Linda said it was all right. I said, "What's the problem with Alan?" "Oh," she said, "he's not charged. They've taken all his books away and he can't cover for so much."'

'Was there anything else?'

'I asked if I could see him and she said he was away for a rest. She said when he comes back if I get in touch I could see him.'

'Was there any discussion about a solicitor?'

'Yes. I said, "Hasn't he got a solicitor?" He had Beaumont from Lesser & Co. at the garage. She said he's got his own solicitor, legal aid or something.'

'At any time, did you ask her what he had said to the police?'

'No, I don't think so.'

'Why did you want to speak to him?' asked George.

'To see if I could give him any help. To have a talk with him.'

'In what way would you help him?'

'In a financial way. I asked Linda if she was all right for money. She said, "The business is very good, Jimmy". I said if she did need money, just get in touch with me. Since then, I've seen her twice around her office and she said everything's all right. No problems. She's still supposed to ring me to meet Alan but she hasn't done so. So I've left it at that.'

'In effect, you are saying that you wanted to see Alan to see whether he was financially all right and that was the sole reason?'

'And her.'

'But you had already gathered from Mrs Opiola that there was no pressing financial problem.'

'Yes.'

'So, one might imagine, no reason to see Alan.'

'Not necessarily. They're nice people.' Jimmy paused. 'Or they were nice people.'

'Having assured yourself that there were no difficulties, you said that you visited her on two other occasions. Why was that?'

'To see how she was and Alan is.'

'But you could have done that by telephone.'

'It's a bit more personal if you go and see people.'

'So you travelled from Stanmore to Southgate on three occasions to make sure she was all right?'

'Yes.'

'How long after the first occasion did you go and see her the second time?'

'I couldn't say. I'd been in the yard a couple of times when she wasn't there.'

'Surely that's all the more reason for telephoning.'

'No.'

'What was discussed on the second occasion?'

'Only how Alan was and she was. She said he was still away. I said, "You should have gone away with him." She said she couldn't because of the kiddy, taking her to school.'

'Do you appreciate the significance if it were the case that John asked you to approach a potential witness to arrange a story about how he had acquired various capital? Do you know what that would mean?'

'No. Perhaps you could explain that to me?' said Jimmy.

£££

That evening, Jimmy was charged with conspiracy to pervert the course of justice and remanded in custody. With Jimmy behind bars, Peter decided that it was now time to move on the remaining two names on the report from the Drugs Squad – Ronnie Everett and John Mason.

Early the next morning, he sent teams of officers to Mason's house and Everett's pub, the Calthorpe Arms in Gray's Inn Road. Both men were arrested and brought in for questioning.

The information on the meeting in Jimmy's scrap yard had put both men in the frame. Now they were hoping that Jimmy Knight's answers would begin to paint them into the picture. So that afternoon, with Mason and Everett safely held at other police stations, Reed and George continued questioning Jimmy Knight, who was unaware of the arrests. This time, the questioning was in an altogether different vein. They started off by asking Jimmy what he was doing that Easter weekend. Jimmy told them he had been working in his disco at the Limes.

They established that Jimmy had known Terry Perkins and Billy Hickson for a very long time. Both had been friends of David Knight's.

He told them that he had never been to Spain in his life but had been over to Portugal three times that year. He had chosen Portugal because it was near and it was cheap. It was only £50 for the return airfare. 'I always stay in the Hotel Faro,' he told them.

'Why did you go to Portugal on three occasions?'

'Because we've been looking for villas.'

Jimmy said he didn't know Ronnie Everett and John Mason that well. Everett he had met the previous year, Mason he had known a couple of years and had met him through his brother Ronnie. Mason owned a launderette in Haggerston Road, just around the corner from his yard. One day both of them had come round to the yard and asked Jimmy whether they could rent it from him. They wanted to run a second-hand-car auction there. Jimmy told them no, because he had sold it.

He was asked whether he had met Ronnie Knight in Portugal to discuss buying property.

'I haven't seen Ronnie since kingdom come. Only Johnny,' he said.

'Were you and Johnny going to set up in business buying and selling property?'

'No, I'd never go partners with my brothers. No way,' he said.

Jimmy told them that, about six months before, he had closed the paper and rags side of his business. For a while he had run a car park on the site, but that had finished in November.

And as for the meeting at the yard, Jimmy said that it was sheer coincidence that they had all been gathered together there on the same day. The rest of the afternoon was spent exploring that meeting. But Jimmy was giving little away. He told them that John Knight had been on his way to see their mother, that Terry Perkins was usually with John and sometimes went with him to their mother's, and that Billy Hickson usually popped in to see his brother who had a waste-paper shed in the yard.

'Would John always call in and see you before going to see your mother?'

'Not always, no.'

'So it was a complete coincidence for him to be there at the same time as the other people?'

'Yes.'

'Can you recall whether or not they came in separate vehicles?'

'Yes, they did.'

'So presumably Terry would not be going with John to visit your mother.'

'Yes, I suppose you're right.'

£££

On the third day of questioning, the officers returned to the central issue – the meeting in the yard.

'I put it to you that this meeting was to discuss plans for the robbery at Security Express on the Easter Monday,' said Reed.

'Definitely not,' Jimmy replied.

'Why were Everett and Mason present?'

'I told you yesterday. They came down and they wanted to run a car auction on my site. I told them it wasn't available and I was negotiating with the Co-op to sell.'

'Why was Billy Hickson there?'

'No reason.'

'Why was Terence Perkins there?'

'Well, he generally goes about with Johnny.'

'Mr Knight. On how many occasions has John Knight, Terence Perkins, Billy Hickson, John Mason, and Ronnie Everett been at your yard, with you, at the same time?' asked George Moncrieff.

'Never.'

'Now, I can understand that John and perhaps Terry would have reason to call at your yard. You have given a reason for Everett and Mason being there. But you can give no indication why Billy Hickson was there, is that right?'

'I told you yesterday, didn't I? His brother has got a paper yard down there that he rents off me.'

'Now why would Billy Hickson give a false name?'

'I'm sure I heard him give the name "Hickson",' Jimmy replied. 'I'm sure he gave the name "Hickson" when the officer asked him.'

'Were any of the other men we've mentioned taken away by the police?'

'No.'

'Isn't it right that they were reluctant to discuss their reason for being on your premises?'

'No. I shouldn't think so, if they were asked.'

'There was a further meeting at your premises on 20 April 1983. Is that correct?'

'I don't know.'

'This is also a Wednesday. Were your aware of that?'

'I don't know.'

'That meeting was to sort out the money from the Security Express robbery.'

'Definitely not.'

'There was talk about being £250,000 short.'

'I know nothing about it. Definitely not.'

'They were obviously expecting more money than they actually got.'

'I don't know what you're talking about. Nothing like that happened on my premises.'

'Mr Knight. Going back to 2 March 1983. When the police attended your premises, when the men we mentioned were there, did the police seize any property?'

'Yes.'

'What was it?'

'Some glassware in a box.'

'The reason for this was that they believed that this was connected with drugs?'

'Yes.'

'As a result of that you were charged with an offence for which you were acquitted?'

'Yes.'

'Now, are you seriously telling us that the police officers who found these items of property, obviously believing they were found in suspicious circumstances, would not have enquired of the other men present what their business was at your yard at that time?'

'They didn't. They just searched.'

'An obvious question that would have been asked is, "What were they doing there?" Why is it that Mason and Everett did not put their proposed business venture forward as a reason?'

'Because they weren't asked.'

'In the meeting on 20 April there were a large number of suitcases all containing money. You divided out the suitcases. Is that correct?'

'Not correct. It's all lies.'

'Your brother John won the draw for the foreign currency. This was money stolen from Security Express.'

'I don't know what you're talking about.'

'When we asked you where you were on Easter Monday, you stated that you were at the Limes. Who else was present?'

'Just my wife, daughter, and two sons, I suppose.'

'Is there anyone else who can verify your movements on that day?'

'I don't think so.'

At 5.09 p.m. Reed McGeorge abruptly brought the interview to a close.

'Mr Knight, you have been remanded into police custody. I now propose to charge you with committing the robbery at Security Express, Curtain Road, on Monday 4 April 1983. You are not obliged to say anything unless you wish to do so, but anything that you say will be taken down in writing, and may be given in evidence. Do you understand?'

'Yes.'

£££

Truth to tell, the Dirty Dozen didn't have much on Jimmy Knight – just a hunch – but their case against him developed as the months went by. By the date of his trial, they could show that he had taken a lot of cash out to Portugal to buy a villa. In fact, he hadn't been exactly truthful over this. He kept saying it was just £6,000, but they found out it was a whole lot more than that. They also found out that he had carried the cash over to Portugal in a plastic shopping bag.

£££

Meanwhile, the interviews with John Mason and Ronnie Everett had not gone quite so well. At John Mason's house, Rex Sargent and Dave Walker had recovered nearly £3,000 in cash, together with airline tickets for Mason's wife Joan and Everett's wife. They also found a brochure for a travel company called Linglynne Property Services, which seemed to have a Spanish connection.

Mason was arrested and brought in for questioning. During the drive back to the station, Jim Keeling noticed that John Mason was trying to get rid of three small scraps of paper.

'I'll have those!' he said, snatching them out of Mason's hands.

One had a partial address written on it: '3614 Nicholson Road'. The other two had sets of unintelligible numbers on them. The pieces of paper were inexplicable, and the office puzzled over their meaning for many months. The address sounded North American, but North America is a big place. The numbers certainly didn't resemble the telephone numbers of any country the officers were familiar with. Nor did they seem to match any bank sort codes.

Mason, for his part, denied that he tried to get rid of the pieces of paper. He told them he had no idea what the address and numbers signified.

He was questioned at the station over two days and was asked about his presence at Jimmy Knight's scrap yard that day. He told the officers that he had wanted to rent part of the yard so that he could run American-style car auctions. He confirmed that he knew John Knight, Billy Hickson, and Terry Perkins well.

He said he ran a small launderette and struggled to make ends meet, but refused them access to his bank accounts to prove it. He gave them the name of his accountant in Ilford, who also refused them access to the books.

He was questioned about his whereabouts during the Easter Bank Holiday 1983. He said he had been at Ronnie Everett's pub, the Calthorpe Arms. A fight broke out, some youths were thrown out, and in revenge they had smashed in all the windows. The pub had to be closed for a week.

Mason told them that he had been injured in the fight and had broken a finger. He had left the pub before the police arrived and gone to the Whittington Hospital in Holloway, North London. He booked himself in but, sick of waiting, left before he could be treated.

The following day, with his solicitor present, Peter Hughman (who was also Jimmy Knight's solicitor), Mason spun an unlikely tale of how he and Everett were planning to go into the porcelain trade together. Everett, he said, was part of a crockery firm based in Florida. He told them that in pursuit of the business venture he had been to Spain and Switzerland to meet business contacts.

The contacts Mason named in Switzerland were later traced, and further investigations by the Swiss police led to two people being convicted of an attempted $7 million telex fraud against an American bank.

£££

At Ronnie Everett's pub, Charlie Collins and Detective Sergeant Phil Chapman, from the Company Fraud Squad, had found around £2,500 in cash and £1,500-worth of American Express cheques. Surprisingly, they found no passport.

Ronnie Everett, a giant of a man with huge hands, was taken down to Limehouse police station where he was also questioned, in the presence of his solicitor, over two days. He refused to discuss his financial affairs in detail. 'That's a matter between me, my accountant, and the Inland Revenue,' he told them. He put the cash down to the fact that he often bought used cars, which he would later do up for a profit.

'What about the American Express cheques?' he was asked.

'I like going to America to watch boxing contests.'

Everett, too, was asked about his presence at the meeting in the scrapyard.

'I didn't know any of the people there that day,' he replied. 'I just wanted to rent part of the yard for car auctions.' He did, however, know Ronnie Knight.

It seemed a trifle strange to the officers that someone like Everett should want to be locked into an upstairs office with complete strangers like that.

Everett had taken over the Calthorpe Arms in 1976, though his wife fronted the business because of his past form. He confirmed that his pub had been closed on the Bank Holiday Monday, the day of the raid, but he told them that its smashed-in windows meant that he could not leave it unattended.

The next day, Everett gave the police officers permission to examine his bank accounts, but the authorizations were withdrawn later and he never did produce his passport, as had been requested.

Everett denied any involvement with Mason's porcelain trade but said that he, too, had been to Switzerland.

£££

Somewhat reluctantly, Peter had to let Everett and Mason go – there was simply not enough evidence against them at the time to justify holding them any longer. The meeting at the yard was purely circumstantial. With Jimmy Knight, however, they were in a slightly better position. They had Horsley's reference to an 'older man', Opiola's talk of meetings at the scrap yard, and a behaviour that suggested that he was somehow involved.

Two weeks after Everett and Mason were released their property was returned, including the three mysterious slips of paper. The cash was kept, as were a series of photographs of what appeared to be a Spanish celebration party – in which all of the suspects were clearly visible.

Jim Keeling set to work getting together more background on the two men. He found that, back in 1968, Ronnie Everett had attacked a number of police officers and had fled to Australia, setting up in business with a man called Eric Flower, who was an associate of the Great Train Robber, Ronnie Biggs. The following year Everett had been arrested, extradited, and jailed. Keeling obtained Home Office prison records that showed that, while in jail, Everett had been visited by Ronnie Knight and Micky Regan, Ronnie's partner in the A&R Club.

They also tracked down Linglynne Property Services, whose brochure had been found at Mason's house. Linglynne managed properties in Spain and owned apartments in the Sköl Hotel in Marbella. In June 1983 John Mason had booked a holiday through the firm for himself, his wife, the Everetts, and a mysterious 'Mr and Mrs E. Jasper'. From records they discovered that 'Jasper' was an alias for Flower and that he was back in Australia.

Peter remained suspicious of Everett's story about why his pub was closed for a week, so he set about tracking down the youth who had broken the windows at the Calthorpe Arms. Eventually he was found. The youth told the Flying Squad that a group of youths had been playing pool upstairs when suddenly, at 10.30, they had been told to leave. They all objected. 'Come on! It's only half past ten! Closing time is eleven o'clock.'

'Drink up and get out!' they were firmly told. They refused, and were forcibly thrown out on to the street by the staff. A scuffle broke out and then, in revenge, the youth broke two of the pub's windows with his crash helmet. The police were called and the youth was arrested.

Peter thought that a couple of broken windows didn't justify the closure of the pub for a week. For one thing, Everett would have lost a fortune in takings. So why had the pub really been closed?

15

HOTELS AND SWIMMING POOLS

In early May 1984, the enquiry made its first foray abroad. The primary objective was to firm up the Flying Squad's case against Jimmy Knight, then going through committal proceedings, by proving that he was lying over his finances.

George Moncrieff and Jim Keeling were the lucky two chosen to go, but it was hardly a holiday. The enquiry knew by then that, like Terry Perkins, Jimmy's affections lay with Portugal. Jimmy was thought to have transferred large sums of money out to Portugal with which to buy a villa.

George had discovered that, the previous September, 1983, Jimmy, accompanied by his accountant, David Nunn, had visited a Barclays bank in Harrow with a suitcase containing £150,000, and that the money had been transferred to a bank in Portugal. Meanwhile Simon Webber had found out that David Nunn's son, Philip, lived on the Algarve where he ran a successful estate agency business.

Jimmy would stay in the plush five-star Hotel Faro, near the exclusive resort of Vale do Lobo, not far from Faro airport. With its golden sands, red sandstone cliffs, and luxury golf courses, the resort was a real eye-opener for the officers. This was what luxury was all about. All paid for in cash.

The enquiry had spent weeks going through the formalities needed to get a Commission Rogotoire, the legal document signed and sealed by the Home Office, which gave the officers the authority to operate overseas. The document was essential. Without it, they could not formally investigate. Even with it, they still had to work directly under the supervision of the local police.

The weighty document gave a detailed account of all the enquiries they wished to make while they were in the country, and it also summarized the evidence they had already obtained which justified those enquiries. As such it was highly sensitive and very closely guarded.

Within its pages, you had to be absolutely clear about what you wanted to do. You couldn't suddenly follow up a new avenue while you were out there, not officially anyway. If you wanted to do that, you had to go and get permission from the authorities all over again. That could take some weeks, by which time, of course the evidence you were after could well have been scattered to the four winds.

Luckily, the Portuguese were quite easy going and prepared to bend the rules. They were not averse to applying a little gentle pressure to get people to cooperate. One person was particularly reluctant to talk to George, so his Portuguese chaperone stepped in. Very slowly he put his hand on his holster. 'I'd like you to speak to him,' said the officer. Full cooperation was thus assured.

George and Jim discovered that in December 1983 Jimmy had £30,000 in another Portuguese bank account and had paid in a further £66,000 which he had carried over in cash in a paper bag. They spent some time talking to Philip Nunn, who had advised Jimmy about buying a villa. He told the officers that he never knew where Jimmy's money had come from, but thought that perhaps Jimmy had sold a club or something. He and his accountant father agreed to become prosecution witnesses.

£££

Towards the end of May, the enquiry made the first of several trips to Spain. The Spanish were stricter than their Portuguese colleagues, and everything had to be done very much by the book.

This time Bernie Butler and Steve Farley got to go, and the rest of the office was, once again, green with envy. Their trip was to last just a fortnight, although, again, they had spent many weeks obtaining the Commission Rogotoire which allowed them to go out and make their enquiries.

The objective was to gather further evidence against John Knight and Billy Hickson, but they were also keeping their eyes out for evidence on the two other suspects now in the frame – John Mason and Ronnie Everett.

Bernie and Steve's first task in Spain was to gain access to John Knight's deposit box at the Bank of Zaragonzana in Fuengirola. They had found keys to the box among his personal possessions, and they knew from Alan Opiola that John's son had been over to Spain to try to get the box opened. But they didn't know if he had succeeded.

With the Spanish police in tow, they questioned Luis Vazquez, the manager of the bank. He recounted how the son had told him that his father had had an accident and 'lost' the key to the safe-deposit box, and had given him a letter of authorization to get a replacement key. The son wanted the box opened there and then, but the bank's spare key couldn't be found. So they made plans to force the box open.

Vazquez told the officers that a new appointment had been made, but John's son couldn't stay so had authorized a man named Clifford Saxe and a local property dealer called Heinrich Lutzeller to be present when the box was opened. A few days later the box was opened and Saxe removed some envelopes containing around £14,000 in cash. The police already knew that Saxe was a long-term business associate of John Knight's, and had been the landlord of a pub in Dalston called the Fox.

Bernie already had the phone number of Lutzeller. He was a German national who ran a business in Fuengirola selling luxury apartments. They had found his business card among the personal possessions of John Knight, Terry Perkins, and Billy Hickson. He was to be their next port of call. He told them that he had officially retired but that he had arranged to buy some land on behalf of John Knight and Clifford Saxe to build two villas.

Among John Knight's possessions they had also found the phone number of another property developer. They traced the man's address and, with the Spanish police, turned up at his site office at the Alcazaba luxury apartment complex in Marbella. The manager in the office was Chilean.

'Do you know John Knight?'

'No.'

'Has he bought anything here?'

'No, no. I don't know John Knight.'

The officers thought that they had drawn a blank. It was hard to hide their disappointment. They had high hopes that the manager would be able to help them pin down exactly how and with what money John Knight had purchased his villa. Ruefully, they turned to leave.

Then the manager piped up, 'I know Ron.'

The officers turned back towards him. 'Who? Ronnie Knight?'

'Yes. And his big friend, Freddie.'

'Freddie who?'

'Freddie Foreman.'

'Oh, *that* Freddie!' they chorused.

It was then, for the first time, that they twigged that Freddie Foreman, a notorious underworld figure from south of the river, might also be involved with the robbery. His name had already surfaced obliquely in connection with Ronnie Everett. In 1975 both had been acquitted of murder.

The manager also put Ronnie Knight firmly into the deal. Foreman and Knight had bought four or five apartments in the complex and had rented some of them out. The manager went on to describe how Freddie and Ronnie had bought the apartments that day like there was no tomorrow. He had told them there was one apartment still left, and one of them said, 'Aww, I'll have that one as well, then.'

The officers had already taken a peek at Ronnie's villa, El Limonar, several times that week. They knew he wasn't there and had wondered where he might have been. In fact, Ronnie was in the apartment complex the very day they were in the site office. The Spanish police said, 'Let's go and ask him!'

'No. No, we can't do that.'

'Come on,' they said. 'Let's go and check his passport. Let's go and see him.'

'No, don't do that yet.'

A few days later, the most devastating thing happened. A local news magazine, *El Tempo*, had somehow obtained a photocopy of the Commission Rogatoire. Full details of the document were plastered over several pages of the glossy magazine, completely blowing their cover.

The British media at large picked up the story, and it gave Ronnie Knight the chance to counter some of the claims made. He told the press that he had made £90,000 from the sale of the house he had owned with Barbara Windsor. He had put this money into property and the income from that had funded his lifestyle. Peter took careful note of what he was saying and endeavoured to garner evidence to demolish it.

They also found out that, on 11 June, just about every single person they were interested in left Spain for the day on a boat trip from the playboy port of Puerto Banus, close to Marbella. It was a curious exodus, and they concluded that the group had heard about the Commission Rogatoire and had got together to formulate a battle plan.

Bernie and Steve had to return to London to explain to their bosses how such a sensitive document could have been leaked. They were more or less openly accused of selling the document to the press for money, a charge they strongly refuted. They never did find out exactly how it had happened, but they suspected that a Spanish court official or policeman had sold it to the magazine.

The officers brought back with them thick wads of documents, but for legal purposes they had to wait for the officially stamped copies, which came back through the lumbering diplomatic machinery. Pretty soon the paperwork in the office generated by their enquiries in Spain had reached avalanche proportions. They had to arrange for certified translations to be made of every Spanish document they planned to rely on in the trial before they could be served on those on remand.

The trip to Spain wasn't all work. The two officers did get

to spend some time relaxing. Steve earned the epithet 'Mr Lovely' because he appeared to spend more time doing his hair than anything else.

£££

In October 1984 the enquiry was ready to make its second trip to Spain. This time it was Peter and George Moncrieff's turn. Concerned about the 'accuracy' of the Spanish translators, they took with them their own translator, PC Roy Ives, also known as 'Pancho' because of his skills in translating and speaking Spanish.

An Argentinian by birth, Pancho worked magic for them. He was well known in Spain and knew all the angles – all the people to see and talk to, to get things done. What he lacked in stature, he made up for in sheer enthusiasm. He was as large as life and one of the funniest people Peter had ever met.

Peter, George, and Pancho were out in Spain for nearly a month. Part of the time they were in undercover, their cover story being that they were journalists. The Costa del Sol, with its growing collection of dodgy ex-pats, was a favourite stopping-off point for British journalists, so the story was quite believable.

The Hotel Cervantes where they stayed was full of the most beautiful women Peter had ever seen. And the women just loved these fit-looking Brits lounging by the pool, with their intriguing cover story.

Often when the police went abroad on assignment, their official allowance barely covered their daily needs, so because of that the officers were virtually confined to their hotel rooms in the evenings. But this time, they had enough spare cash from their meagre daily subsistence allowance to go out in the evenings and enjoy themselves. This was largely thanks to some string-pulling by the local Spanish police, who knew the manager of the hotel and had arranged a special discount for their British colleagues. It enabled Peter and his colleagues to live in some style.

For Peter, the trip was a spot of welcome relief. He had been going through a very difficult and painful divorce from his wife. The demands of the job had virtually destroyed the marriage, as it did the marriages of many of his colleagues. It was only in Spain that he first felt like dating again.

They spent days just waiting for permissions and this, of course, invariably meant spending days by the pool. It was there that Peter met a beautiful Austrian girl, Anna Marie, with long blonde hair. For the next week, the two of them became inseparable. After she left it was the turn of lovely, dark-haired Petra from Germany. She had a razor-sharp wit and didn't miss much. The next morning, she happened to be in Peter's hotel room when Anna Marie called to say that she was safely back home in Austria. Petra took it in wonderfully good spirit. 'I just called to say I love you,' she sang sweetly in Peter's ear.

Petra ended up going around with Peter on his undercover inquiries. At first the other officers didn't agree. It was not that they didn't like her – they just thought there was a time and place for everything. In their view, work was work and play was play. But Peter's argument – that a couple drinking in a bar looked much less suspicious than a single man – eventually won the day.

On 2 November they interviewed Clifford Saxe, the man John's son had stayed with earlier in the year and who had organized the clearing-out of John Knight's safe-deposit box. The episode at Malaga police station illustrated the kind of red tape the officers had to go through while working in Spain. Peter and George had to wait in another room while the Malaga police chief inspector put questions in Spanish to Pancho, who then translated them into English for Saxe, who couldn't speak Spanish.

Saxe told the Spanish chief inspector that he had come to Spain in April 1983, with the idea of buying a villa. He bought one from Lutzeller for £56,000 and, later in the year, another for £71,000. He said the money for buying the two villas had come from his life savings and the sale of his pub, the Fox, in Kingsland Road, Dalston.

He also confirmed that he had taken money out of John Knight's safe-deposit box to give to Lutzeller. He had forwarded the rest of the documents in the box to Jimmy Knight.

Saxe was then asked if he had any objections to being interviewed by the British police officers waiting in the station. He said not, and agreed to meet them.

He told Peter, George, and Pancho exactly the same story.

'But we've already checked this out, Cliff,' said Peter. 'You couldn't have possibly made £127,000 from the sale of that pub. Besides, we know that you didn't give up the tenancy until November.'

Saxe was a little lost for words. The two officers had done their homework. They continued to fire questions and facts back at him that, in the end, completely demolished his version of events. It was only after hearing his faltering answers that it struck the three officers that the robbery money could well have been hidden in the Fox. Saxe admitted that the Fox had been used to count money. But he denied any involvement. 'The press reports are lies,' he added. 'I never planned the robbery.'

Peter and George made copious notes, but Saxe refused to sign them. Nevertheless, the interview was a huge leap forward. The three officers left Malaga police station buzzing with excitement. Peter resolved to organize a search of the Fox from top to bottom as soon as they got back to England.

When they left the police station they took with them a copy of Saxe's passport, which showed that he had been a frequent visitor to Spain during 1983. It also revealed that Saxe had been among those who had left Spain for a day on 11 June, during the Flying Squad's last visit.

Peter and George also found a little time to concentrate on John Mason and Ronnie Everett. The investigation into Mason and Everett's financial affairs in the UK had proved frustrating, to say the least, but in Spain they had more luck. They had managed to identify Everett and Mason's Spanish bank, the Banco Industrial del Mediterraneo, in Marbella.

The manager of the bank confirmed that Mason and Everett both had deposit boxes in the vaults. However, he refused to open them up without a court order, so the next day they went to the local court to get a local warrant. It was issued at midday, but at around 9.20 in the morning someone had been into the vault and had emptied both the boxes of cash.

Someone, somewhere, in the chain of knowledge, had tipped off Everett and Mason. It was a bitter blow. It made them feel that they were working very much in enemy territory. However, there was one small consolation. While examining the documents left in the box, George noticed that one document referred to 'Bethlehem, Pennsylvania'. It seemed a small thing at the time but it was to prove to be the key to the puzzle of one of the three pieces of paper that Mason had tried to dispose of when he was arrested back in March. The piece of paper, with '3614 Nicholson Road' scrawled on it, had been almost forgotten. It turned out that there was a Nicholson Road in Bethlehem, Pennsylvania.

The address '3614 Nicholson Road, Bethlehem, Pennsylvania', also appeared on some of the title deeds to property that had been bought by Mason in Spain. Later, the American authorities were asked to check out this address, and they reported back that a Scotsman named Joseph McLean occupied the house. Further checks on McLean's background revealed that he had been in business with Freddie Foreman in the late 1970s.

Peter also took the chance to visit Dick Modiano, an American who had sold El Limonar to Ronnie and John Knight back in 1976. He had built for himself a beautiful villa right on top of a mountain, from which you could see across the bay. It was a marvellous view. He couldn't help them much, but confirmed the sale in August 1976 for £47,000.

While searching Hickson's house they had also found four Polaroid snaps of some newly built Spanish villas. They were believed to belong to John Knight, Billy Hickson, Terry Perkins, and Clifford Saxe. One of Peter's jobs was to identify the villas and arrange for them to be photographed by a man from C11. It was a time-consuming job, driving up and down the mountain roads looking for them. For court purposes, the identification photographs had to exactly match the Polaroid snaps found on the suspects.

Another task was to obtain a list of the passengers who had left Spain for the day on board the *Sherama* during the previous Flying Squad visit to Spain. It was an important task. The

British authorities stood a better chance of claiming retrospective extradition if they could prove that their targets had left the mainland and returned to British jurisdiction for a time.

The skipper of the *Sherama* had filed the passenger list with the port authorities in Puerto Banus, and they found that the passengers included Freddie Foreman and his wife, Ronnie Knight, Susan Haylock, John Mason and his wife, Ronnie Everett and his wife, John Trickett, and Vincent Schiavo. They located the skipper of the boat and established that the party had indeed gone to Gibraltar.

They had never come across the names Trickett and Schiavo before. So, when they got back to England, it started off a whole new avenue of enquiries with Greater Manchester Police, though the enquiries came to nothing in the end. Trickett turned out to be a boxing promoter based in Manchester, and Vincent Schiavo was his business associate.

£££

Meanwhile, Charlie Collins and Detective Sergeant Geoff Cameron had been over to Paris, where they had been tasked with finding out about Hickson's lavish spending spree there earlier in the year with Maureen, then his bride-to-be. They had obtained a photo that Hickson had had taken of himself in one of the Paris revue clubs, and now had to identify the club. Not an easy task.

They had turned up at the main office of the Préfecture de Police close to the Champs-Élysées, and were surprised to be greeted by a man wearing a pair of old jeans, open-necked shirt, and a brown leather jacket. To the smartly turned-out boys from the Met, their French equivalents looked decidedly scruffy. But that was the way the Paris equivalent of the CID worked. It was very different from the British way of doing things.

The Paris police were as helpful as they could be, but there was nothing in it for them apart from a willingness to be seen to cooperate internationally. Charlie and Geoff were assigned a detective who acted as their interpreter and quickly secured a statement from the George V Hotel that Hickson had stayed there, together with a list of his expenses.

The George V, a stone's throw from the Champs-Élysées, was one of the most expensive hotels in Paris. It was sumptuous. Charlie and Geoff marvelled at the art deco luxuriance of its décor. Eighteenth-century tapestries lined the walls. The private terraces on the upper floors of the hotel gave stunning views across Paris, that most romantic of cities. It was a traditional favourite of well-heeled British tourists. Hickson had lived like a king while he was there with his wife-to-be. Bottles of champagne, the best food the hotel could offer – and all paid for in cash.

By contrast, the two officers had to stay in a cheap but comfortable little hotel in Montmartre, near the red-light district of Pigalle. Both were shocked at how expensive Paris was. Halfway through their visit the two officers phoned Peter, pleading for more money. Peter, of course, told them flatly, 'No'.

'I've just paid fucking £5 for a half of lager,' moaned Charlie.

They ended up spending their off-duty evenings in the old American Services Club. There the beer was cheaper and more to British tastes. The club was full of black American war veterans who had fought in the Second World War and then decided to stay on. In Paris, with its rich pageant of African culture, they had found themselves accepted a little better than back home.

Having got a copy of Hickson's hotel bill, Charlie and Geoff's next task was to find the club where Hickson had had a photograph of himself taken. Their French interpreter, who was single, launched into the task with sudden enthusiasm. They toured a seemingly endless pageant of clubs, trying to track down the one shown in Hickson's photograph.

At one club there were lots of English girls, and the manageress turned out to be a woman from Lancashire. She helped them enormously. A uniquely eccentric and colourful figure, she would sit at the back of her club, watching her girls through a spyglass, to make sure that everything ran smoothly.

Nevertheless, Charlie told his wife afterwards, 'If I see another pair of tits and a G-string I'll go mad.'

£££

Towards the end of the year, somebody on the enquiry turned up various addresses in Switzerland for Jimmy Knight's bank accounts. Everyone was surprised and taken aback by this – it just didn't fit Jimmy's image to have bank accounts all over Switzerland. It was a sophisticated move, and suggested to them that perhaps he was more involved than they had first thought. Either that, or he had been persuaded by someone that Switzerland was a good place to stash some cash.

Reed McGeorge and Colin Burke were dispatched to Switzerland to obtain details of the accounts. What they found was a series of bank accounts that had been opened, but nothing had been put in them. It appeared that all he could do was sign his own name and that was it.

The Swiss trip became a bit of a joke in the Squad. Whereas everyone else had gone to a nice warm country, these two discovered that, in Switzerland, the weather was rather inclement. It was so cold and snowy in those mountains that they were forced to go out and buy anoraks and boots.

They were quite disgusted when, on their return, they tried – and failed – to get reimbursement for all the money they had laid out on warm clothes.

Another trip took Bernie Butler and Jim Keeling to Canberra and Perth in Australia, to trace Eric Flower, Ronnie Everett's associate. The trip turned out to be a wild and expensive goose chase, but at least Bernie and Jim had a well-earned break.

16

THE FOX

Kingsland Road is a busy thoroughfare leading out of the City of London. Slicing through a grim patchwork of run-down terraced houses, high-rise flats, flat-roofed industrial units, and sudden open spaces, it passes through some of the poorest, most deprived parts of London. Even today, these areas suffer from above-average unemployment and crime rates, and below-average life expectancy and literacy rates.

It has a large and lively ethnic community, with some of the finest Turkish restaurants in London tucked away in the back streets. Here, you are as likely to stumble upon a mosque as a church.

Travelling along Kingsland Road, it would be hard not to notice the Fox, a grand old traditional London pub. With its stark outline, distinctive glazed red tile and large painted sign, it has been a local landmark for more than a century.

It stands proudly on the corner of a crossroads, mocking a 1950s-style esplanade of a dozen or so shops and takeaways. Opposite, on the other side of the busy main road, stands a fine old Victorian hospital, in 1984 derelict, but now converted into a business centre.

To the east of the Fox is the area known as Dalston – the Knights' old manor. In the years since the Security Express robbery, gentrification and patronage have transformed neighbouring Islington, which has the advantage of better public transport, but it has yet to make a lasting impression on Dalston.

The side road towards Dalston curves slightly around the Fox, past some old workshops and offices. Then it forks in two, with both branches dipping under a disused railway line that once took commuters into the now-demolished Broad Street Station, which stood next to Liverpool Street.

Behind the pub, grimy, blackened arches underneath the railway viaduct are still occupied by small lock-up garages, warehouses, and workshops, just as they were back in 1983. Nearby there is a small, abandoned station, a relic of the Broad Street line.

Around the back of the pub, off the side road and slightly hidden from the main road, there is a small yard. Here, several times a week, clinking beer barrels are delivered by the brewery vans, unloaded, and rolled down into the cellar. Today, the Fox's tiles are speckled with dirt. Its faded sign could do with a lick of fresh paint. But in the days when Clifford Saxe ran it, the Fox stood spotless and proud. Inside the pub, a full-sized billiard table dominated the main room, with its grandiose lighting and bright-red decor. To the left of the table, an ornately panelled bar ran the length of the pub, along one side of the room, and then through into another room towards the back of the pub. To the right sat a small raised stage, edged by a wooden banister that looked like it might have come straight out of a Spaghetti Western. The pub had a private sound-proofed meeting room, discreet yet easily accessible from the bar, and upstairs, grand function rooms opening onto a balcony, all for hire.

The Fox and nearby shops were the focus of life for the locals, many of whom worked in the small workshops in the back streets. But it was not a place for outsiders. They would be quietly served their pint with courteous indifference that, at the wrong time, might have bordered on suspicion. Those asking too many questions might quickly get the message that they were not welcome here, not in this establishment. The staff reserved their friendly nature for those they knew well, and those they trusted.

Saxe had given up the Fox in November 1983, and soon afterwards he had moved permanently to Spain. A new landlady, Eunice Evans, had been brought in, appointed by the brewery. She knew nothing of what had gone on before, although she had heard some dark rumours. The regulars would sometimes tell her about the strange goings-on in the pub the previous year. There was much talk of the evenings when unidentified men with unknown allegiances would arrive unannounced. The men would huddle in a back room in heated debate, the pungent smoke from their cigars curling up towards the high ceiling. Sometimes, claimed the regulars, Saxe would close the Fox completely, throwing them all out into the street, well before time, while the mysterious meetings dragged on long into the night. The gossip was that both the Security Express and the Brinks-Mat jobs were schemed in the Fox, the plans laid out on the full-sized billiard table, with billiard balls representing the guards.

Despite the rumours and intrigue, Eunice must have thought they were all barking mad when, in early December 1984, a large contingent of officers from the enquiry turned up to examine her beer cellars. But they won her over with a mixture of charm, tact, and gentle persuasion.

'Of course you can look,' she told them, 'but I can assure you there's nowt but beer barrels and large spiders down there now.'

The officers trooped down the narrow stairs into the dimly lit cellar. She was right. There was nothing there but beer barrels . . . and large spiders. But there was something slightly puzzling about the cellar. It was smaller than it should have been. At one end, instead of brickwork, there was some hardboard that had been propped up against some beer crates. A false wall perhaps.

'That must be it,' said one of the officers.

It was the moment of truth. The landlady looked on with bemusement and some concern as the officers pulled the crates away and started to break through the makeshift partition. Behind it, they found an arched recess piled with old crates. The pungent smell was overwhelming. The more old crates the officers pulled away, the bigger the secret space got. It was a cellar within a cellar.

The landlady was astonished, as were the officers. They really hadn't expected to find anything. Most had simply looked upon the outing as a chance to sink a few light ales in good company.

Beyond the hardboard partition the brickwork was damp and blackened. It smelt of stale beer, damp rags, and mildew, quite distinctive and easily recognizable. In fact, Malcolm Jeffrey was sure he had smelt it before – on the notes found at Horsley's father-in-law's flat.

'Get some of that smell, Jim,' said Malcolm. 'That's evidence, that is.'

To the great amusement of everyone there, Jim played along with it. Dressed in his quirky white boiler suit, looking every bit like a mad scientist, he took out a sample bottle and started to waft it around the brickwork, quickly screwing on the lid to trap 'evidence', allegedly for 'continuity purposes'.

'How are you going to get that to the jury then, Jim?'

'I'll gather them all around me and whip the top off quick,' Jim replied.

They took a picture of him prancing around with the specimen bottle, but, sadly, it has been mislaid over the years. It probably wouldn't have been publishable anyway, because the lads had heavily doctored it in their own inimitable way. In the photograph, Jim grew a large pair of white rabbit's ears, and, owing to the unfortunate position in which he was holding the bottle . . . well, you can imagine what that was turned into.

But Jim had the last laugh. The real irony was that he wasn't so far off the mark. Some months later, the smell in the secret cellar at the Fox did indeed become evidence, of a kind.

Back at the office, Peter was studying a large-scale map of East London. The Fox was just about a mile from the Security Express depot. Straight up Curtain Road, turn right into Old Street, and then left into Kingsland Road, an old Roman road that ran due north, straight as an arrow, past the Fox and out into the open countryside of Essex and Hertfordshire.

On a good day, with no traffic, it could have taken the robbers less then ten minutes to get to the Fox. They could have dropped the sacks of cash straight down into the cellar, and then been on their way. Nearby, underneath the railway arches, there were lock-ups and garages where the getaway vehicles could easily have been hidden.

So, Peter thought, the Fox could well have served as 'first

base' for the robbers. It was ideally placed. Within twenty minutes of leaving Curtain Road, the haul could have been safely stowed underground, the van hidden away, ready to be re-sprayed.

The guards had been told by the robbers not to move for thirty minutes. That would have been ample time to get to the Fox.

But there were other local connections. Half a mile to the south-east of the Fox, at 88 Haggerston Road, was John Mason's launderette and dry-cleaning business. Around half a mile or so to the north of the Fox, at Ridley Road, lay Jimmy Knight's huge and sprawling scrap yard. Less than half a mile to the east, along Middleton Road, across Queensbridge Road, and then south along Malvern Road, was John Horsley's garage workshop. Just around the corner from Horsley's garage was the Albion pub, where, in June 1984, OP17 had linked Billy Hickson, Terry Perkins, and Horsley together for the first time.

All four locations were within a half-mile radius of the Fox, and could be discreetly reached through the back streets of Dalston within minutes.

The Barclays Bank branch that Saxe had used to telex cash to Spain was just along the road. The Leeds Building Society branch where Hickson paid in cash was close by, too.

To the west of the Fox lay De Beauvoir Town, with its derelict warehouses and disused canal basin. South of that was Hoxton, the Knights' old stamping ground. It was their manor. They must have known the area like the back of their hand, thought Peter, as he folded up the map.

If nothing else, the Fox was the perfectly situated meeting place for Mason, Hickson, Perkins, Horsley, and the Knights. Perhaps Saxe was little more than the master of ceremonies. Or perhaps he played a more important role. Peter really didn't know.

He recalled the musty smell of the notes found at Horsley's father-in-law's flat. He surmised that, within a few hours of the robbery, the notes had probably been moved from Horsley's garage to the Fox public house. Or vice versa. Either way, they must have stayed for a while in that damp cellar. After that, they must have been taken to Opiola's house, where they were counted and divided up. From Opiola's house, some must have gone to Hickson who then gave them to Horsley to store at his father-in-law's. Saxe may have kept his share in the pub's cellar. The Knights and Everett and Mason must have taken their share somewhere else. But where?

For the moment, at least, it was all just a working hypothesis.

Down at the station, Eunice, an experienced publican, had been asked how much revenue the Fox brought in. She painted a picture of a business that would be struggling to break even on takings of less than £2,000 a week. Since she had taken it over, takings had risen from £1,200 to £1,800 a week. She told the officers that Saxe had once told her that he had been 'subsidized', although he had never told her how.

Charlie Collins had been tasked with the job of obtaining records of Saxe's bank accounts and drawing up schedules. From those, they could clearly see that Saxe's financial fortunes had swayed from being in debt to just about being able to make ends meet. And then, in April 1983, he was suddenly flush. Shortly afterwards, he repaid his bank loan and transferred £25,000 to his bank account in Fuengirola.

Terry Mills and Malcolm Jeffery had also discovered that when Saxe gave up the Fox, he had presented his daughter and son-in-law with an £8,000 gift for a deposit on a new house.

So where had all of Saxe's money come from? Just as important, where was it now?

To Peter it was patently obvious. Pieces of the jigsaw were beginning to fall into place. Peter was certain that he could now link Saxe to the robbery. But there was one thing that still troubled him. He turned to the notes he had made of an anonymous tip-off the enquiry had received nearly eighteen months earlier, while it had been based in City Road.

'So it wasn't the "Axe" pub after all,' he thought. 'The operator must have heard it all wrong.' The informant could have been saying 'Fox' or, for that matter, 'Saxe'. Either way, he could have got to John Knight a good deal quicker. Perhaps if the Dirty Dozen had got the name right early enough they might even have found the money, which had probably been hidden in the Fox during those first few days after the robbery. It was wishful thinking, perhaps. The misinterpretation of the name was such a simple mistake, so easily done. 'Perception', they called it.

£££

By Christmas 1984 everyone was in ebullient mood, but with the trial date set for February 1985 and rapidly approaching, there were many loose ends to be tied up. Much of it consisted of painstaking analysis of bank accounts. Quite early on, Peter had realized that in order to secure convictions he had to make the financial case. That was why Phil Chapman from the Company Fraud Squad had been brought in to assist the team. It was the finances that were going to crack it.

The case against Terry Perkins, in particular, involved a lot of careful digging. He, of all of them, had the best cover story for his ill-gotten gains.

Perkins had been arrested at his house in Enfield at the same time as Billy Hickson. The £5,000 in used notes found at his house was sent off for forensic examination. They had hoped to be able to prove that it had been hidden in the same place as Hickson's cash, but the results were inconclusive, even though the notes had been folded in exactly the same way as Hickson's – a distinctive signature.

Perkins had put his wealth down to property dealings, which meant that a complete schedule of all his property interests had to be assembled to prove that the money could not have come from property. That was done, and the enquiry worked out that he had made at least £250,000 since the robbery. His wife had also benefited from the robbery: she had paid some £12,500 into her account, but said that she was deeply suspicious of where the money had come from.

But the biggest surprise of all was Mrs Perkins senior. The enquiry had obtained photocopies of her cheques and cash paying-in slips, and had put together a detailed schedule of the cash that had been paid into her personal bank account at Barclays Bank in Tottenham.

The list of credits to the account was quite extraordinary. It started on 6 May 1983 with £4,500 in used notes. Four days later another £3,000 had been paid in, and by the end of May a further £6,600.

Then, for some unknown reason, there was a gap of around six months. And then the credits started rolling in again. First £4,000, then £1,600, then £8,200, all in used notes. By the end of the year, Mrs Perkins's bank account had benefited by more than £35,000.

'Not bad for a lavatory cleaner,' Peter thought, as he examined the schedule.

Just as interesting were her cash withdrawals, because they went some way towards showing that, as Peter suspected, someone, somewhere, had been talking.

On the very day that Horsley was arrested, a Friday, Mrs Perkins withdrew £15,000 in cash. On the following Monday she withdrew a further £2,000 in cash. No one was supposed to have known about Horsley's arrest. So how did she know? The police never got to the bottom of that one.

John Knight's payments were not so hard to fathom because of the list of building society and bank accounts that had been found in Diane Knight's purse. The accounts were all traced and statements and balances obtained. They discovered that, within a five-day period in October 1983, Knight had paid in nearly £44,000 in cash into various building society and bank accounts. He had bought a new Mercedes worth £4,500 as well, which was delivered directly to his apartment in Spain.

Once again a schedule was prepared, ready for the trial. They were astounded at how crudely and simply Knight had dealt with the cash. He hadn't exactly covered his tracks. Most of the payments in were made at bank and building society branches in or near Southgate.

Peter also spent some time finding evidence to counter John Knight's alibi that he was running on the golf course on the morning of the robbery. He sent Jim Keeling over to Germany to track down a witness who had been put up by John Knight as someone else who could verify that he had been running round the golf course that Easter Monday morning. The man, a young British Army sapper, was a friend of John Knight's son. As usual, Jim fell headfirst into adventure. He stayed in a baking hot hotel room, so before he went to bed he opened all of the windows. The next morning he woke up to find a great big pile of snow in the room. 'I scraped it all together and phoned the reception to say there'd been a leak in the radiator,' Jim said. It could only happen to Jim.

Peter by now strongly suspected that the Fox had been used by Hickson to store cash, so he got an officer to go and talk to the staff at the Leeds Building Society in Mare Street, where they had discovered that Hickson had paid in £30,000 in cash. Three members of staff were taken down to the Fox's damp cellars and asked whether the whiff was the same as that on the notes Hickson had paid in. They said that it was. It was very similar indeed.

By now, the number of officers on the enquiry had dwindled down to the Dirty Dozen. Many officers had gone back to their squads, and some had gone on to the Brinks-Mat investigation. Others had been reassigned to the Harrods bombing case.

The smaller numbers proved to be more effective. It was more controlled. They knew where they were going. Friday-night debriefings usually took the shape of a formal meeting, when they would discuss what they had done and what was planned for the next week. After that, they would all have a drink. It was a tight-knit circle of officers, all dedicated to the job in hand.

The seemingly crude way in which the Knights and Billy Hickson had dealt with their money led to a lot of discussions in the bar after work between Simon, Peter, Reed, George, and the others.

'If you have £300,000 plus, do you put it in a loft where the Old Bill can find it? Do you bury it in the garden?' Here, they had John Knight wandering up and down the high street looking into building societies, and Jimmy putting it into the Barclays over at Harrow. Meanwhile, Hickson clearly expected to get turned over at any moment. At the time, he was living at Peabody Buildings, and there were so many thieves around that area that they would have screwed him for the money in no time, so he had to get away from there. But the real fox was Horsley. He had a dip on the night, and then, when Billy said, 'How much have I got?' he helped himself to more.

'I don't think Billy was best pleased,' observed Simon.

17
REMAND

John Knight met his main adversary face to face for the first time in February 1984, at his hearing for bail. He had managed to get his bail set at £2 million. A businessman he had met through the lodge had been prepared to chip in with the money, but John had found his application blocked by the Flying Squad. They claimed that John would abscond from justice, so now it was up to the judge to decide.

John was sitting on the wooden bench in the court waiting room on his own when suddenly a short, thick-set police officer came in, carrying a thick folder full of papers under his arm. John had never seen him before.

'All right, John?' asked the officer.

John looked up with surprise. 'Hello. Who are you, then?'

'I'm the guv'nor. My name's Wilton. Flying Squad.' He stood there for a moment, papers in hand. He tutted. 'I don't know,' he said, looking John up and down. 'You should've swum to shore, John.'

'What don't you know?' said John. 'I ain't done nothing wrong.'

Peter nodded his head. 'We'll be going in in a minute.' He turned quickly on his heels and disappeared into the courtroom. A few moments later, John was called in. The hearing lasted barely fifteen minutes. John asked for bail and, of course, Peter vehemently opposed it, citing the fact that John's brother Ronnie had already skipped the country. The judge concurred and John's application was refused.

John was immediately taken out by two burly officers, put into a holding cell, and taken back to Brixton Prison by van.

He had really hoped to get bail. It was a huge disappointment, not only to him but to his brother-in-law Albie, who was sitting in the court, waiting to give John a lift home to High Trees.

£££

With so much money still missing, Peter had been worried that the robbers on remand might be tempted to pay for their escape from jail. He had therefore sent Jim Keeling along to New Scotland Yard to persuade the top brass that John Knight and the others had to be given the highest prison security category possible.

Jim turned up clutching a bacon roll, not really knowing what to expect.

He was ushered into a meeting room dominated by a long, black, polished table. Photographs and plaques lined the walls. There sat the cream of the Met, their silver buttons and badges shining in the dim light.

'Come in and sit down, detective constable,' said the bespectacled commander.

'Now, let me get this straight.' He looked down at his file. 'You are requesting that this man, John Knight, and the other Security Express men should all be categorized as double-A prisoners?'

Jim nervously placed his half-eaten bacon roll neatly on the table in front of him.

'Yes, sir.'

'Why is that? Surely he's just a robber, not a terrorist? He's not an IRA bomber, is he?'

'Because he's highly dangerous, sir. He's got accomplices still on the run. They could easily blow him out of jail.'

The men looked at him in silence. You could have heard a pin drop. 'Go on,' said the commander.

'There's a lot of robbery proceeds out there still,' said Jim. 'Millions of pounds, in fact.'

He suddenly remembered a newspaper story he'd seen the previous week, all about how easy it was to obtain Exocet missiles, which the Argentinians had used to sink two British ships in the South Atlantic. The British had little or no defence against these highly accurate French-built weapons. 'They could even afford to buy an Exocet missile,' Jim piped.

The senior officers looked at each other in horror. 'Goodness! Well, we can't have that,' one of them said. 'We can't have people wandering around buying up Exocet missiles to blow people out of jail.'

They talked among themselves for a few minutes before turning to Jim. 'Very well. We had better heed your advice, then. Thank you for coming in to see us.'

With that, Jim left, still clutching his bacon roll.

John Knight was given category AA status, the highest possible, because the Law had been convinced that he had access to the outside resources – money and men – needed to mount a daring escape.

£££

The human consequences of Peter's decision are difficult to imagine, unless you have been through it yourself. Category AA is the highest security category a prisoner can have, and is normally reserved for terrorists. Everywhere you go, you have to have two guards with you. You are never alone. No human contact is allowed. All visits are conducted behind a wall of glass, with guards looking on. It's hard going for everyone involved.

John Knight will never forget that first visit from his wife Di while he was on remand in Wandsworth Prison. It was one of the saddest moments of his life to see her sitting there, tears streaming down her face. A thick pane of meshed glass divided them. She was sitting just two feet away from him but it might as well have been the other end of the universe.

It was very cold outside. There was snow on the ground, and she had arrived wrapped up in a thick brown fur coat. She'd done her best to look nice for him, but the stress showed in her face.

'I don't know which way to turn,' she told him, tears in her eyes. 'What do you think is going to happen?'

'I don't think there's much chance,' he replied. 'I think they will send me away for a long time. You will have to adjust to this. They told me when I was arrested I was going to get twenty years.'

She burst into tears again. 'Don't you think you can get out of this?'

'I can't tell you.'

He was frequently moved about between prisons for no apparent reason. The wardens would never tell him where he was going, nor was he given much notice. They would simply bang on the cell door and shout, 'You're on your way.'

'Where am I going?' he would shout.

'You'll find out when you get there,' they would say, the sound of their echoing footsteps receding along the landing.

From Brixton to Wandsworth and then back again. He remembered the screaming sirens and the sudden lurch of the prison van as it took the corners at breakneck speed. It was all very disorienting.

The conditions at Brixton were abysmal, even by prison standards. The food was none too clever. On top of that the wardens were pigs. 'Whatever happened to "innocent until proven guilty",' he used to say to them as they did their rounds. 'Yeah, right,' they would sneer at him. 'You're going down, Knight.'

Nevertheless, he did his best to keep his spirits up. On remand you could have a visitor every day. You could even have your dinner sent in. John would have pie and mash brought in on a Saturday.

He kept his mind active, and got chatting to others on remand. While in Brixton he met two Americans, Joseph Scalise and Arthur Rachel, accused of stealing the 45-carat Marlborough diamond from a Knightsbridge jewellers. One of them told John that he had an uncle who was killed by Al Capone with a baseball bat. No witness at their trial could identify either of the men as the men they had seen in the jewellers. They were nevertheless convicted and got thirteen years apiece – the diamond was never found. John was impressed. It reminded him of Opiola's hidey-hole under the garden shed.

£££

John's solicitor, Eric Cheek, was a family friend. With greying hair and a kindly nature, he had handled many things for John over the years. He would do the groundwork on John's case during the week, and on Sundays he would go to see John in Brixton and tell him about any developments.

One Sunday, Eric was particularly excited. 'I've found someone who was on that golf course who saw you running,' he said.

'Really?' said John, with surprise.

'Yes!'

It turned out that Eric had been playing detective. He had been up to the golf club beside High Trees and had asked to see the records of everyone who had played golf that Easter Bank Holiday Monday. He was given the names of a businessman and his sons.

Eric called the businessman up and he told Eric that he remembered that morning well because it was so cold and icy. He happened to know John and was adamant that, around eleven o'clock, he had seen him jogging around the golf course with his son, though he never got to see their faces as both were obscured by woolly hats and scarves. However, Eric didn't see that as too much of a problem. It was easily explained away by the exceptionally cold weather.

'This is great news!' said Cheek. 'It means you couldn't possibly have been on that robbery.'

John couldn't believe his luck. It was a case of pure and simple mistaken identity. In fact, John's son *had* been out running that morning – but with an army friend of his called Mark. Eric proceeded to obtain statements from the businessman and sons, and John decided to go with this defence and plead 'Not guilty'.

The businessman was unwavering. 'He always runs on the golf course at that time,' the businessman told Eric. Best of all for John, the man really believed what he was saying.

£££

Some months later, John was moved again, this time to Wormwood Scrubs, which was a big improvement on Brixton. He worked during the day in the laundry. While he was there, the Brinks-Mat people came in. Although most were held in Brixton, Kenny Noye was put in the Scrubs. John remembered seeing him come in with a black eye. Noye would sit quietly in his cell working on his case.

'They're going to stick me away for life because of that copper,' he told John.

'Why?' said John. 'It was a stranger trespassing on your property. Anyone would have done what you done.'

That was what Noye eventually pleaded, and Noye's argument won the day. John got on well with him. 'He seems to be a very clever guy,' John thought. There was an additional, deeper bond between them. They were both Freemasons.

When Billy Adams turned up on remand for attempted robbery, John realized just how much homework the Flying Squad had done. Adams told John all about Peter Wilton's surveillance operation on the Commercial Road. 'I only got nicked because of the Security Express investigation,' he said.

Some of the inmates in the Scrubs told John that he shouldn't have a family solicitor specializing in property. They recommended that he had someone else, and John took their advice. Cheek was annoyed and upset when John told him the news. 'Why, John?' he asked. 'After all I've done on this case.'

'I've got my own reasons,' John replied. As events unfolded, he regretted the decision. He knew deep down that he should never have changed solicitors.

The new solicitor got John legal aid as, by that stage, all of John's assets had been frozen. He wasn't very encouraging. 'What is against you is not what you have had before the robbery, but what you have now. There's a lot of money around you, and you have to prove where it's from,' he said. 'They're going to try to persuade the jury that it's all stolen money.'

There was no forensic evidence against him, but he thought that the money alone was enough to turn the jury. 'Haven't you ever thought about pleading guilty to handling?' he said. 'They might accept that and give you a reduced sentence. You would also save High Trees. They can't make you criminally bankrupt for that.'

'Why should I?' he said. 'I didn't do the robbery. There's evidence that I wasn't there.'

Even his barrister suggested that he change his plea to one of handling, although he added that he would still have to persuade the prosecutor to stand for it. John told the barrister that he was a Mason. 'Oh. Are you one of us?' he asked.

'Yes, but I don't want to bring any of that up,' John replied.

One day, while they were at a pre-trial hearing at the Old Bailey, in a private room and locked in, his barrister laid it out on the table for John. 'You see, you've got too much around you, John. Have you ever thought about changing your plea? Even your business partner has said that you can't have earned that amount of money.'

John said, 'No.' He decided to plead 'Not guilty' to robbery. He wanted it to go to trial, and that was that.

At the time, John didn't know that Opiola had gone the other way on him.

It was a gamble that he was going to live to regret. By late summer, John realized that it wasn't going to be easy to convince a jury that he was innocent, particularly once he realized how much the Flying Squad had on him. He could see that he really was going to go down for this one. His only concern was for his wife and children.

He'd been told about some of the goings-on at High Trees, with the police turning up out of the blue and taking away money from the house. He made a mental note to challenge them to produce a receipt for it. Likewise his lovely paintings which were taken as 'evidence' and never seen by John again.

He would never forgive them for what they did to his family. In particular, he felt they had treated his wife Di, his son, and his brother Jimmy terribly. All his son had done was what any son would have done. He stuck up for his family, helping Di meet the bills, and defending his father.

Di, too, didn't deserve the harsh treatment ladled on her.

£££

That wasn't the end of Di's troubles, though. Later, sometime in March 1984, she had gone to the garage to pick up the MoT wages. She went up the stairs and saw a girl in her twenties sitting in the corner, with Linda behind the desk. She spoke to Alan Opiola's brother Dick.

'Who's the new secretary?' she asked.

Dick shrugged his shoulders. 'I don't know her,' he said.

'Ethel has gone,' said Linda.

'Why's that?'

'Because I'm taking over.'

Di walked out in a storm, saying she was going to see John about that. Then Linda came running after her. 'Where are you going, Di?' The questioning was odd, cold, and furtive. Linda kept asking how things were, and whether Di had any more money from Jimmy. 'She was trying to pump Di for information,' concluded John.

Di was no fool. Later, she called Jimmy and told him that the garage had a policewoman up there. Shortly afterwards, Wilton and a female officer called Julia really put Di through the mincer. They went up to High Trees and searched it again.

At first, the female officer had been sympathetic: 'I understand,' she would say to Di, 'you shouldn't be in this position.' It was all lovey-dovey. But Julia kept pushing and pushing. John heard that Di had snapped and flown off the handle, throwing a tampon at the officer. 'See what you've done to me,' she screeched. John didn't blame her for doing it. They were pushing her out on to the street and into bankruptcy. Most women with four children to worry about would be upset with that.

Di was arrested again, taken down to the station, and locked in a cell. This time they used every dirty trick in the book. They tried to tell her that John had been messing around with other women. 'She made light of it at the time but it must have hurt,' thought John.

'Do you love your son?' one officer asked her.

'Of course I love my son,' Di replied.

'I love my kids more than I love my wife. I'd do anything for them, you know,' the officer replied. Then he dropped the bombshell. 'We've got your son in prison,' he said.

Di went ashen. 'You're bloody joking,' she said.

'You tell us what we want to know and he can go right now.'

'I've got nothing to tell you,' she said.

The officer shouted at her in exasperation.

After that they tried the nice-and-cuddly approach, telling her not to worry and comforting her tears. 'I must say, Di,' said one of the officers, 'if ever I was in trouble I hope my old woman would be like you. In those circumstances me and you could be good mates.' He leered at her.

'Yeah, really?' said Di.

She, along with her son, was charged with conspiracy to pervert the course of justice. Cheek had been brilliant at getting her son's bail down from £10,000 to £5,000, on the understanding that he would remain with Di at High Trees.

Eventually, Di had a nervous breakdown over it all. She woke up one day in intensive care. To John, Wilton's mob really was the Dirty Dozen. They had acted way outside their remit. 'With Wilton, there are no survivors,' he thought.

It was all the more painful because there was nothing John could do. There was no one really to help Di except her own family and the children. His family couldn't help: Ronnie was over in Spain; Jimmy was inside; and John's sister didn't want to know, and anyway he hadn't seen her for years. She was living in the south of France and was happily married to a wealthy Indian entrepreneur. His mother was in no position to help – she was beginning to suffer terribly from Parkinson's disease.

What had happened to Jimmy was worse. His place was searched at the same time as High Trees. 'Jimmy had come back voluntarily from Portugal, where he was looking at buying a villa, and agreed to answer Wilton's questions of his own free will. He could prove where his money had come from. He was a wealthy man, what with his club. But they wanted him out of the way because he kept going to ask Linda Opiola for me. That's where he got involved too much. They wanted Jimmy out of the way so they could save Opiola.'

£££

Over the next few months, John would awake to the sound of keys jangling as his cell door was unlocked. For an instant the neon lights of the hallway would flood into the dim cell. The warder would stand, framed in the doorway, holding a large bundle of bound papers in his hands.

'John Knight?'

John would get up from his bed. 'Yes.'

'These are from the High Court.'

The warder would wait for John to take the papers out of his hands. And then he was gone and the cell door would be slammed shut.

John had been on remand for some months now, and the court papers were coming thick and fast. Every day he seemed to be getting new witness statements, all of which were bad news. He was left alone in his cell, with the piles of police statements and documents to go through by himself.

It was upsetting reading.

Lots of pieces of evidence mystified him, not least a Marks & Spencer wrapper the police said they had found at Alan Opiola's house. John could never understand that. He knew how careful they had been when they were sorting out the money in the bedroom. Maybe the police had planted the wrapper there to put the frighteners on Opiola. Or, more likely, Alan had helped himself to it. With hindsight, Alan had never seemed happy with just £25,000 in payment, and John started wondering whether he had taken some more money on the sly. He often pondered on that while sitting in his cell. He remembered hearing one of the sacks fall over while he and Terry were counting, and wondered whether Alan had tip-toed up the stairs in his socks, nicked a £5,000 bundle, taken it back downstairs, and stuck it behind the washing machine in the utilty room.

However, there were things he knew for certain that he hadn't said. Things that, he was convinced, had been twisted by the Flying Squad to make him appear the archetypal guilty man. According to one statement on his arrest at High Trees, an officer had said, 'I'm arresting you for the robbery of Security Express.'

'After so long? That robbery was a year ago,' he was supposed to have replied.

'I never said that,' he thought. 'Why would I say such a stupid thing?'

Neither did the guards' statements make any sense to him. Greg Counsell had said that the robbers in the yard had caught him on his second trip to the gate control room. That's not how John remembered it. They caught him the first time he poked his head out of the door. Counsell had gone to collect the milk from the hatch in the yard.

Then there was the business of the petrol, which Jamie Alcock said the robbers had threatened to pour over his leg. John's firm had taken everything into the depot they might have needed. But no petrol. They never took any petrol in with them.

Either someone had found it on the premises and threatened to use it without John knowing, or Alcock was trying to find a reason for handing the keys over. John didn't know. After all, he had been up with Counsell most of the time, waiting for the guards to come through the cage one by one. He had no idea what the others had got up to, to get the guards to say where things were. But he did remember that things had got a little fraught towards the end. They were running out of time. Tempers were getting frayed. Things happen when tempers get frayed. That's the way it is.

All these points were minor irritants compared with the shock John got when Alan's thick statement landed with a thump on his threadbare mattress. John knew the statement was coming and was dreading its arrival. Eric Cheek had warned him during one of his Sunday visits that Opiola had 'turned Queen's'.

It read like acid. John found it hard to believe that someone so close to him had shopped him – someone who he had looked after so well in the past.

The week after the robbery, John had been faced with a dilemma. He had got his half of the robbery proceeds out of the barn and into Horsley's garage, but he knew it was only a temporary fix. There were far too many people around Horsley's garage to count the money there. It was just an ordinary lock-up garage on a housing estate. If anyone had broken in there, they would have had a lovely find. So John had to wait until it was quiet in order to move it again to the place where he had planned to count it.

Then, just the week before the robbery, the woman had changed her mind. It was only then that he decided to go and see Alan. After all, he couldn't exactly drive about the Hertfordshire countryside looking for new hidey-holes. John hadn't wanted Alan to know anything about the robbery. He was a partner in many other crimes with him – fiddling motors and the like – but not that.

Sitting in his cell, the conversation he had had with him that day repeatedly ran through his mind.

Alan had been all for it. 'Do you want me there?' he had asked.

'You can stay there if you want,' John had said. 'Just make us tea or maybe get us something to eat.'

Opiola's breach of trust affected John deeply. If there was one thing he really couldn't tolerate, it was disloyalty. Now, he had plenty of time to dwell on it. Too much time.

John thought back over all the evenings they had spent together. All those dinners at High Trees, all those glasses of wine. It made him feel physically sick. He remembered the diamond hiding-place incident well, which the police had made such big a fuss over in Alan's statement. At the time, it had seemed such a trivial thing – just a laugh between friends.

He had chosen Opiola because he was low-profile and therefore less suspicious. All his life John had owed his success in crime to keeping a low profile. Experience had taught him that the higher the profile, the more trouble you attract, whether it be from the police or other criminals. John was the sort who would far rather carry his money in a carrier bag than a shiny black leather attaché case.

Hindsight is a cruel thing. Now he could see that the decision to ask Alan if he could use his house that week was probably one of the worst decisions he had made in his life. 'If only I hadn't been let down at the last minute. Maybe none of this would have happened and I would now be safely in Spain, enjoying the sunshine, just like my brother Ronnie,' he thought.

John was hurt. Terribly hurt. Alan was not only his business partner. He was supposed to be a mate. It was torture, sitting in the same cell as all those papers. You can't do anything in the cell. There's no one to help you. You are on your own – until you get a visit.

Linda's behaviour, too, had upset John greatly. When Di came to visit him at Brixton, he had warned her that Linda was only after information.

'I ain't got a chance now, Di,' he had said. 'You'd better give me my wedding ring back. Expect that I'm going to go away twenty to twenty-five years.'

'Don't be silly,' she had replied. 'We've been together too long.'

After some months, Di thought about what John had said. They decided to get divorced before the trial, partly because they thought that by doing that they could at least protect some of their assets from the looming threat of criminal bankruptcy. It made Christmas 1984 a particularly miserable time for John. Christmas is, after all, for families.

He had heard through the prison grapevine all about the Flying Squad's raid on the Fox. The secret compartment in the cellars mystified him. He never gone down there, but he was certain that the only money hidden in the Fox would have been Saxe's own takings from the pub. He knew that Saxe would often stay open for 'afters' and had probably made a small fortune on the side.

'No one on the robbery would have been stupid enough to have hidden their money in the Fox,' he thought to himself. And if Saxe had done anyone a favour, it had been done without John's knowledge. If he had known, he would have been horrified. The place was far too obvious.

John had thought very carefully about where to take the haul from the robbery. Using the Fox as a staging post had certainly crossed his mind. But he knew it had no pull-in, where they could have discreetly unloaded the bags. The yard at the back didn't belong to the pub.

'You could hardly have carried green bags across the road. Unloading them and carrying them across the pavement, you'd have soon got nicked,' he thought.

'Besides, there was too much money. There was tons of it.' There's no way he could have taken it in through the back door or the side entrance. 'You couldn't have carried those green bags round the back of the Fox for half an hour. You'd have been seen. The police would have been all over the place by that time. If the police hadn't spotted you, someone else would have done.'

If the Fox had had its own pull-in, it was very likely that John would have used it. But not for long. He would have been quick in and out. Villains used that pub. Faces. Word would soon have got out.

It was a thieving area.

18
THE TRIAL

The trial of John Knight, Terry Perkins, Jacqueline Perkins, Billy Hickson, James Knight, John Horsley, and Robert Young took place at the Old Bailey between 18 February and 7 June 1985. At the time, it was one of the longest criminal trials ever. All except John Horsley pleaded not guilty. Peter was the officer in charge.

It got off to a somewhat faltering start. The police rejected some of the people chosen at random to serve on the jury. When the jury was finally sworn in, after three days, the judge, Richard Lowry QC, promptly dismissed them all because of a legal hitch. The new jury was immediately told that 'special arrangements' had been made for their safety.

The Crown's case was simple enough. Sudden inexplicable wealth, coupled with evidence of plans being made and put into effect. A 'robber's share' of the proceeds came to some £400,000. That was the mantra that the prosecution stuck to throughout the trial.

The lead prosecution barrister, Michael Worsley QC, an extremely capable and thorough man, described the viciousness of the raid that Easter Monday. He told the jury all about the defendants' lavish expenditure after the robbery date, and he compared it with their financial circumstances prior to the robbery. Then he took the jurors on a fascinating journey through the heart of the Flying Squad investigation.

He told the story of Alan Opiola and the four-foot-high mountain of cash in his bedroom. He related how money had been stored in old suitcases ready for laundering in banks up and down the high street. He described the secret compartment full of cash at Horsley's father-in-law's flat, its scrawled tote, and its less-than-honest banker. He described the musty smell of the notes. Rosemary Rees, a credit checker from Security Express – one of the ladies who made up the wage packets – testified that a squiggle on one of the £20 notes found at the flat was in her handwriting.

He took the judge and jury into the Fox, so that they could compare the smell of the notes with that of its boarded-up secret cellar. He told them that the forensic lab had tried in vain to compare particles of dust and dirt from Hickson's money with samples from the cellar but had come to no firm conclusions. However, three members of staff at the Mare Street branch of the Leeds Building Society had testified that the smell on some notes paid in by Hickson was very similar to that of the cellar.

He told them about the meeting in Jimmy's yard, a month before the robbery, at which he claimed the robbery had been planned. He said that the surprise visit by the police had unnerved the gang so much that they had considered abandoning their daring plan.

Finally, he related how they had lost the race for much of the loot stowed in Spain. The name that constantly came up in the prosecution's case was that of the exiled Ronnie Knight – so much so that the judge asked why the name was being mentioned so often when the man was clearly not on trial. He ordered the prosecution to stop referring to him.

A parade of witnesses was brought on to illustrate parts of the prosecution's case. Two Security Express guards gave evidence in person: Jamie Alcock, the guard who had been threatened with petrol, and Pat Lynch. The rest of the guards' statements, including Greg Counsell's, were read out to the court.

Every day the Crown took their star witness, Alan Opiola, into the court through elaborate security procedures to prevent him from coming into contact with anyone who might harm him. He waited downstairs under armed guard in a special room before being called up to give his evidence, which, even to the cynical, was pretty damning against the men on trial.

Worsley was sharp. There was nothing that could get past him and he had most of them tied up in knots. Despite that, however, he was fair. If something didn't go his way he would concede graciously. Peter thought he was a good, old-fashioned barrister. Every day they had sessions with him, just before court, so that they could discuss what they were going to do and the problems they were likely to face.

The defence claimed that the men had become wealthy simply through their businesses or through tax evasion.

Against the advice of his silk, John Knight took the witness box. He stated that he had been jogging on the morning of the robbery and therefore could not have done it. He pointed to two witnesses who had seen him running that morning. But on cross-examination his alibi – that he had been running on the golf course with his son – began to fall apart.

He admitted being Clifford Saxe's financial backer, even though the prosecution had already claimed that the robbery had been planned in the Fox and that the robbery money had been counted there.

Despite the seriousness of the proceedings, there were lighter moments. Under cross-examination, John Knight was asked about whether he had made a 'trust deed' for his villa in Spain. 'Yeah, we did trust each other,' he replied, to the amusement of everyone in court.

The case against Jimmy Knight was touch and go. It rested on evidence obtained from the visit to Portugal the previous year when George Moncrieff had been dispatched with Jim Keeling to bolster the case against the elder Knight brother. They found proof that Jimmy had two bank accounts in his name there and that he had lied to the officers. Jimmy had told them that he had only paid in £6,000 while he was in Portugal, but the enquiry could show that he had in fact transferred the £6,000 from his main account to open a new account. Jimmy's main account had contained £66,000 and they found that he had paid out £72,000 for a villa.

While they were there, George, as was his wont, had gone off on his own, leaving Jim behind in the hotel. George's disappearance so worried Jim that after a couple of days he called Bernie back at the office. 'Has anyone seen George?' he asked.

'Well, no. But then we wouldn't have, Jim, because he's with you.'

'Oh. I haven't seen him since we booked in.'

When George surfaced, he had obtained a list of the calls made by Jimmy Knight to England from the Hotel Faro, where he had stayed. The Portuguese authorities had been quite cooperative and were certainly more relaxed than the Spanish about allowing British officers to go off and investigate on their own. However, in order that the evidence obtained could be later used in court, the enquiry had to go through the usual diplomatic formalities. This, as with Spain, took months to process. In fact the witness statements from Portugal arrived only just in time for the trial. Back in England, armed with George's list of telephone numbers, they had traced the numbers and found that while in Portugal Jimmy had regularly called a telephone box that was right outside his front door at the Limes. The question was, why would you do that when you had a telephone in perfect working order in your house? They didn't really know the answer, but it did point to skulduggery of some sort.

'Well, I'm going against all the rules of the bar,' said Worsley. 'You are supposed to just ask the questions you know the answer to.'

Nevertheless, he put the question to Jimmy's son, who admitted that he had been told to leave the house and go to the phone box to take the calls from his father. The information about the call box had come in right at the last minute, and almost certainly secured the conviction against Jimmy Knight. It was enough to convince the jury that Jimmy was up to no good, handling stolen cash. But it wasn't quite enough to convince them that he was a robber.

The jury also heard about a little anecdote involving Jimmy's son and his nephew. The Limes kept getting burgled, and Jimmy sat there for days on the sofa with a fully loaded shotgun. One day his son and nephew had found the shotgun behind the sofa and were playing with it in an outhouse. Jimmy was furious when he saw them. 'If you're ever going to point a gun at anyone you've got to bloody fire it,' he bellowed.

The case against Hickson was the trickiest one of them all. To counter the fact that Horsley had pleaded guilty to robbery, effectively taking the money found at the flat away from Hickson, the prosecution tried to argue that Horsley had made only £38,000 from the robbery. This could be proved by his bank and building society accounts, and the enquiry had found a witness who had backed up Horsley's story. Worsley pointed out that in Hickson's interviews with the police, he had indicated that he knew about the old man's flat, and that tears had welled up in his eyes when he realized his nest egg had gone. At the end of the interview Hickson had asked to 'do a deal' with some names. As well as that, he had given a graphic description of his spending spree in Paris with his newly-wed.

Hickson refused to take the stand, but Charlie Collins had given a detailed precis of Hickson's movements during 1983. 'Come on, then,' Hickson's barrister had chided. 'If you know so much about my client, why can't you tell us what he was doing between *these* dates? Why do you have gaps in your records?'

The truth was, Hickson had been in jail, but the police couldn't say that because it would have influenced the jury and given grounds for a retrial as past convictions cannot be mentioned. Still the barrister tried to get Charlie to say something. Finally, the judge intervened. 'I should be careful what you say if I were you,' he warned the barrister. Peter and the others puzzled over the incident for some time, but they never did work out whether the barrister had deliberately tried to trick the police into mentioning Hickson's past convictions, or whether he simply didn't know what he was getting into.

Terry Perkins was defended by Ronald Thwaites QC. Perkins's defence remained that he had made his money out of property transactions, which at first was mildly convincing. The prosecution countered by dissecting the transactions, proving that his wealth could not possibly have come from the deals because of their timing.

The trial was almost too much for Terry Perkins. He

suffered a little from heart trouble and while in custody he had to have a doctor called.

Media interest in the case reached its zenith at the end of April, when Barbara Windsor appeared to give evidence on behalf of John Knight. Some cash had been found at High Trees and John's defence had claimed that this had been given to him by his brother Ronnie in 1982 as payment for his half of their villa in Spain.

Barbara backed up the story. She told the court that she and Ronnie Knight had sold their house in London in September 1981 and she had given Ronnie his share of the proceeds, which had amounted to some £50,000. She had paid Ronnie in cash over six or seven months during 1982. Ronnie had collected and signed for the money at the office of her accountant, Albert Fox, in Camden Town.

She told the court, 'Ronnie had given John £65,000 for his share of the villa towards the end of 1982.'

'So where did the extra £15,000 come from?'

'I think Ronnie sold a club, the A&R Club,' she replied.

'And when did he sell this club?'

'I don't remember when.'

'And for how much?'

'I'm not sure.'

She later gave permission for her accountant to produce details of her payments to Ronnie. Police got a court order and Fox produced a schedule for the first five months showing that she had handed over around £47,000 to Ronnie.

During the trial, Peter fractured his jaw while playing rugby. The consultant gave him the choice of eating soup for five weeks or having the jaw wired up. That would have stopped him giving evidence, so he chose to eat soup. With hindsight, he thought he should have had it wired up. He would have had longer to reason out and write down his answers.

£££

The jury of seven men and five women deliberated for sixteen hours. Then the men were called back into the dock, together with John Horsley, who had pleaded guilty to the robbery back in February 1984.

The jury found John Knight, then aged 50, and Terry Perkins, 37, both guilty of robbery. Judge Lowry sentenced them to twenty-two years each, and described them as 'two evil, ruthless men'. He made both of them criminally bankrupt.

There was evidence that they had stowed away large sums in Spain and Guernsey. So far police had traced only £2 million.

'The powers I have to extract the ill-gotten gains are most limited,' he said. He told the jury that with fines or orders for criminal compensation the penalty for non-payment was only an extra twelve months in jail. 'That is derisory when one examines the large sums concerned,' he said.

'Although no one was injured in the coolly planned and ruthlessly executed robbery, those who had invaded the security firm's premises had made sure that they did not meet any resistance. They put other human beings in terror.'

John Horsley, 43, whose initial confession helped the Dirty Dozen put the others away, got eight years for robbery. The judge described him as the gang's banker.

Jimmy Knight, 59, got eight years for handling £200,000, largely because of the last-minute detective-work by George Moncrieff, which had been deftly put to use by Worsley.

Robert Young, 47, Perkins's accountant, who had been charged with assisting in the disposal of stolen cash, was cleared. He had admitted to handling stolen cash during his police interviews. At the trial he didn't dispute his statement but said that he had agreed to it because he wanted to get out of the police station quickly.

Hickson, 42, was found not guilty of robbery but was given six years for handling £30,000. That was the amount Hickson had paid in at the branch of the Leeds Building Society in Hackney. The jury was partly influenced by the 'smell' factor, witnessed by the cashiers of the branch, so Jim Keeling had the last laugh after all.

The prosecution more or less abandoned its case against Jacqueline Perkins, 36, during the course of the trial. She was cleared by the jury, and as she left the dock she kissed her husband Terry on the lips. 'Good luck,' she whispered.

The judge directed that the jury should not be asked to serve on another jury for twenty-five years, because of their ordeal – all had been under twenty-four-hour close protection to guard against attempts to 'nobble' them.

In spite of the jury's decisions, Peter remained convinced that Billy Hickson and, for that matter, Jimmy Knight had been part of the team that went through the door of Security Express that April bank holiday.

He had watched Hickson's behaviour in the witness box and noticed the constant eye contact with one of the female jurors. Hickson had played her like a fiddle, and Peter was sure that she influenced the whole jury to clear him of robbery. After he was sentenced and the jury were told that Hickson had a history of armed robbery the lady almost wept.

The trial had cost £1 million. The Flying Squad's investigation had cost a further £1 million.

£££

'Sixty-six years for the gang who grabbed £6 million', the headline screamed. 'The ruthless raiders who pulled off Britain's biggest cash robbery were jailed for a total of 66 years yesterday.'

Wilton was dead chuffed with the outcome. It was a great success for the Flying Squad and did something to repair its tarnished image following a wave of high-profile corruption scandals. Back at the office, the Dirty Dozen celebrated in some style. Admittedly, they hadn't got everyone convicted but it was still a successful conclusion to a lot of hard work by everybody. They owed much to Worsley, who in Peter's mind had acted like a true CID officer.

The gang may have been good at planning the robbery, but when they had come to disposing of the money they had really slipped up. They just weren't geared up to putting the money to rest and waiting for things to happen before they started moving it about. It was the same with the Great Train Robbers – they, too, just didn't know how to handle spending money.

There were some curious things about the trial result, though. Peter was amazed at the way that Hickson got off so lightly, and also wondered what it was that had made Horsley agree to take the hit for Hickson's money by pleading guilty to robbery. Was it fear? Or reward? Either way, Hickson was clever to do that. By moving £280,000 found in his father-in-law's flat on to Horsley's shoulders, it enabled Hickson to get away with pleading to handling just £30,000.

Someone in the office – nobody remembers quite who – penned a rather cynical verse to mark the end of the trial. Part of it went something like this:

Oh, Opi, what a bad man,
He had his little ways,
Inspector Wilton talked with him,
For days and days and days.

Said he: 'If I do help you
You will protect my life?
You will keep us safely hidden
Both me, my son, and wife?'

'I'm a resident Informer,
And every bean I'll spill.
I'll plead my part quite fully.
My hands were in the till.'

'My wife is almost blameless,
Just helped to count the take,
And if you don't accept that,
You can go and jump in the lake!'

£££

Each defendant was lost in his own thoughts. No one said a word. Judge Lowry's words echoed in John's mind as he waited with the others on the cold wooden bench for the prison van to come. He had been the first one to be sentenced. 'John Knight . . . I have no alternative but to sentence you to twenty-two years . . .' He remembered the pallid, drawn faces of his wife and son sitting up in the public gallery, the stillness of the court, and the agonizing walk down the stone stairs leading out of the dock, through the dungeon-like corridors to the waiting area. There was no time to say goodbyes. No time for words. It was all so sudden. 'You'll probably only do ten years,' his counsel told him as he snapped shut his black leather attaché case and prepared to leave the room.

Some consolation.

They sat there for what seemed an eternity. The vans turned up at five o'clock.

£££

Far away in sunny Spain, Ronnie heard about his brothers' convictions on the radio. Within hours he was besieged by reporters, peering over the fence on the mountainside, looking down on the steps leading up to the villa. 'Have you heard the news?' they shouted down to him in glee.

'Why don't you all fuck off and leave me alone?' Ronnie shouted back. He shut the door on them. He knew they just wanted him to say something – anything – so that they could make a front page out of it.

19

'BEYOND JUSTICE'

Although the investigation into the Security Express robbery was far from over, after the trial of Knight, Hickson, Perkins, and Horsley, Peter was to play a much smaller role in it. In February 1985, just before the start of the trial, he had been assigned away from the day-to-day running of the enquiry – officially, at least. Shortly after the trial, and largely because of the success of it, he was transferred firstly to the Intelligence and Surveillance Unit based in Caledonian Road then to the Area Major Investigation Pool.

AMIP had four or five detective superintendents, with a detective chief superintendent in charge. Staffed by highly experienced officers, the unit dealt with murders and other major crimes that appeared to cross the normal divisional boundaries, or that were considered too demanding to be handled by the divisional CID.

The Flying Squad had by no means given up on the case – in fact, quite the reverse. The end of the trial was the start of a new lease of life for the enquiry. The targets were now Clifford Saxe, John Mason, Ronnie Everett, Freddie Foreman, Ronnie Knight, and, to a lesser extent, Susan Haylock, Ronnie's girlfriend. The Flying Squad had no evidence to place any of these people at the scene of the robbery. However, they did have evidence to suggest that all had suddenly become very wealthy indeed soon after the robbery.

Reed McGeorge took over from Peter and would continue to lead the enquiry for the next thirteen years. In all, Reed spent sixteen years on the one investigation, which must be a record. With George Moncrieff as his deputy, his aim was simple enough – to get enough evidence against all these suspects to bring them home from Spain.

By this stage, the number of men on the enquiry had shrunk to a handful, but that was amply compensated for by great enthusiasm among all concerned to finish the job. For that reason Peter, too, kept himself closely acquainted with the investigation.

Before Peter handed over the reins to Reed he had written up a report on Clifford Saxe's involvement with the case. It covered in great detail the evidence of Saxe's wealth in Spain, and the secret compartment they had found in the Fox.

On the basis of Peter's report, in March 1985, the Flying Squad obtained a warrant for Saxe's arrest for 'handling stolen goods'. But in practice it didn't mean a thing. The Spanish extradition laws would keep Saxe and the others well out of their reach. All were now resident in Spain, 'beyond justice'.

In November 1985, all of the suspects were called to account when the Spanish authorities commenced expulsion proceedings against Saxe, Mason, Everett, Foreman, and Knight. The proceedings failed. But the way each of them responded, and the answers each of them gave, allowed the enquiry an early opportunity to see what kind of defence they would be likely to put up if ever they were put on trial in the UK. The Spanish authorities' main concern was whether the men were working illegally and with what income they were supporting themselves.

Saxe simply refused to attend the local police station to answer the allegations.

Mason sent a formal response to the proceedings. He said that he had come to Spain after a brain operation in 1971. He owned a £90,000 house and businesses in London. He received his regular income from those.

Everett turned up at Malaga police station with his solicitor. He, too, said that he had had a brain operation. As a result of that he had sold his pub and decided to retire to Spain. He told the authorities that he supported himself from the £300,000 proceeds of the sale of his pub. He also told them that he had been completely cooperative with the Flying Squad. He had, he said, even allowed them access to his safe-deposit box! The

Flying Squad had to laugh at the cheek of that. They had got there and the box had been cleared.

Knight told the Spanish police that he had no outstanding matters in Britain and that he got his money from two bars in London.

Foreman prepared a declaration that he was getting an income from two British businesses and an American drinks-machine distribution company, which he had set up in 1978. He also said that he had set up a property company with American partners, which was investing in property on the Costa del Sol, and that he had put money into a clothing boutique in Puerto Banus for his daughter. He also wanted to promote boxing matches in Marbella.

Just after seven in the evening on 27 November 1985, Foreman turned up at Marbella police station with his solicitor, Peter Hughman, and handed in the documents and a sworn statement from his solicitor. He refused to make any other statements, but at eight in the evening he agreed to be questioned. He told them he managed a Panamanian company called Ultramarine Ventures Inc., and owned 25 per cent of its shares. Unknown American investors owned the rest.

Foreman's story now was very different from the pleading-poverty story he had spun the British police when he had been arrested in 1982 for conspiracy to supply drugs.

£££

Hard on the heels of the Spanish extradition attempt, George Moncrieff and Reed McGeorge planned another trip to Spain, the Flying Squad's third. They would stay there a month, visiting banks and collecting statements from witnesses. By now the investigation was turning into an exercise in accounting. George and Reed were ideally suited to that. Both were meticulous and thorough, with a keen eye for detail.

On 22 January 1986, they arrived in Barcelona at the start of what was to one of their most taxing trips. After much red tape and waiting around, the two officers were eventually allowed to proceed to the Costa del Sol.

On 10 February, they visited Ronnie Knight's bank, the

Bank of London and South America. They were astounded to discover that the manager had not sent the official notification from the local judicial authorities to enable them to interview the staff, so no one could make a statement about Knight's bank account. The manager suggested that it had closed shortly after the police had visited on their second trip, in November 1984. Much of Ronnie Knight's finances were now being handled by Susan Haylock.

A week later, they visited the Banco Industrial del Mediterraneo in Marbella – Everett and Mason's bank. Reed was shocked to be told by the manager that Mason and Everett had visited the bank on 23 January – the day after the officers had arrived in Spain – and both had closed their accounts.

It then became obvious that there was an insider, leaking information about their enquiries to the suspects.

Mason's safe-deposit box at the bank had to be forced open because he could not be located. Everybody gathered in the strongroom for the occasion – the manager, his assistant manager, an officer from the Spanish court, plus several Spanish police officers. The British officers present thought it was going to be an oxyacetylene blowtorch job, but then a man ambled in with a small tool kit containing what looked like an ordinary screwdriver. With a deft flick of his wrist, the box sprang open. It was as simple as that.

Inside the box they found a wad of documents on Mason's tax affairs and his properties, together with photostats of one of his passports. Back in London, the letters to the taxman led to a call on the Inland Revenue. The Inspector of Taxes would not discuss Mason's financial affairs with the police, but he did give the Flying Squad a fascinating piece of gossip. Mason had told him that in the mid-1960s he had been involved in a number of robberies for which he had never been caught.

£££

The investigation into John Mason and Ronnie Everett's financial affairs had proved frustrating, to say the least. The enquiry had already been thwarted in its attempts to recover cash from

Mason's safe-deposit box at the Banco Industrial del Mediterraneo in Marbella.

At the end of the trial, two underworld sources had told the police that a high-ranking official in a Spanish bank had been paid to 'lose' a bank account containing robbery proceeds.

At the time, the tip-off hadn't been taken seriously, but when the Banco Industrial del Mediterraneo was visited it was obvious that Mason and Everett's accounts had been tampered with. Documents were missing and, despite court orders, only accounts covering the period July 1983 to October 1984 were ever produced.

The same two underworld sources later confirmed that, in November 1984, Freddie Foreman had been tipped off about the impending Flying Squad search at the bank. Foreman had then told Mason and Everett. They had then turned up the next day and cleared their boxes before the police had arrived. The incident had concerned Peter greatly. He often wondered who tipped Foreman off. Surely it wasn't anyone in the Flying Squad? He had always assumed it was someone in the bank or in the local Spanish police.

While at the bank, Reed was shown the records of the safe-deposit box and found that Everett had given an address in Florida: 638 Gordonia Road, Naples, Florida. He recalled the fanciful story told by Mason and Everett about investing in a porcelain business based in Florida.

They immediately asked the American authorities to look into the address, which turned out to be the address of a man named Norman Head, president of the English China Company, which had an office in the nearby Pavilion Shopping Center. This turned out to be Mason's brother-in-law.

They found out that Everett had agreed the sale of the Calthorpe Arms in June 1984 for £222,000, around the same time as the Flying Squad's first visit to Spain. The sale was completed in September, at which time Everett paid off loans to the brewery.

It was becoming obvious to everyone that Everett and Mason liked doing things together. They opened their bank accounts at the Banco Industrial del Mediterraneo on the same day. They had bought apartments virtually next door to each other. Both appeared to have invested money in the Channel Islands, thought to have been as much as £100,000 each. Both entered Malaga on the same day in May 1983. Both had obtained false passports on the same day in June 1983. Both had been on the *Sherama* trip during June 1984, but with one important difference – Mason and his wife had left on their new passports, but returned on their old ones. And both had had brain operations.

In June 1986, the remaining officers on the enquiry embarked on their fourth trip to Spain. Once again the trip lasted a month and this time it was more successful. They concentrated on Clifford Saxe.

An appraisal of Clifford Saxe's British bank accounts had shown that on 1 April 1983 he was overdrawn by £133. His change in fortunes was remarkable. By November that year the British accounts were more than £13,000 in credit.

Saxe was paying large sums of cash into his Spanish banks during June and July 1983. He had deposited more than £40,000 in one Spanish bank account and had withdrawn £25,000 in cash. In October alone he had banked nearly £25,000, most of which was in used fivers. They were soon able to show that Saxe had had access to approximately £287,000 in cash.

On their return, the officers also tracked down Clifford Saxe's accountant, Kenneth Waller. He told them that the Fox public house made around £5,000 in its first year of trading, in 1979–80. That was the first and last set of accounts Waller ever produced for the Fox. However, he did represent Saxe at a meeting with the Inland Revenue, which was trying to find out how Saxe had got the money together to start trading. At the meeting, Saxe told the Inland Revenue that he had no savings of his own.

Two months later, they got word that all the suspects had been expelled from Spain. However, the celebrations in the office turned out to be a little premature. All of the men appealed against the order.

Reed saw that there was a chance that if he pushed the

Director of Public Prosecutions to issue warrants against the remaining suspects he might be able to influence the Spanish extradition proceedings and get the appeals dismissed. So in September he wrote up the results of their investigation, and this was sent in to the DPP. They had stuck to the view first suggested by Worsley during the trial – that a 'robber's share' came to around £400,000.

The Flying Squad sought arrest warrants for Ronnie Knight, Sue Haylock, and Freddie Foreman for handling, and warrants for Ronnie Everett and John Mason for robbery. In December, the evidence gathered from their trips to Spain in January and June proved to be sufficient grounds to obtain these warrants.

Later, the officers had a clearer picture of Foreman's finances. Reed had also seen Foreman's passport at Malaga police station and had noticed that on the day that John Horsley had been arrested, Foreman had flown into Malaga. So they asked for his warrant to be 'upgraded' to that of robbery.

The warrants were a huge leap forward. They enabled Reed to gain access to numerous bank accounts, including accounts in the Channel Islands. The enquiry obtained court orders to examine bank accounts going all the way back to January 1982, with the intention of showing that the men had suddenly become wealthy soon after the date of the robbery.

They were hampered because the banks were only obliged to keep credit notes and cheques for three years. Nevertheless, the schedule they put together clearly showed that the suspects had suddenly become very rich indeed.

£££

The following year, some painstaking work on Mason's accounts revealed some startling facts. The team discovered that, between May and December 1983, Mason had paid in some £397,000 into accounts at the Allied Irish Bank in Croydon and Lloyds Bank, St Brelades, Jersey.

Within five days of his release from police custody in 1984 Mason had transferred more than £177,000 from his British bank account at the Allied Irish Bank in Croydon to an Allied Irish account in Jersey, presumably because he thought it more likely to be beyond the Flying Squad's reach. They found that between May 1983 and March 1984 Mason had paid nearly £373,000 into this account.

The bank accounts also provided the key to the puzzle of Mason mysterious scraps of paper. The numbers written on two of the pieces of paper led to a separate Lloyds Bank account in Jersey. Between September and November 1983, Mason had credited £85,000 to the account.

The manager of the branch, John Jones, told officers that he had personally never met Mason. If he ever needed to get hold of him he would contact him through an ex-boxer living on the island called William Walker. Everett's daughter had married Walker's nephew. Walker would often meet Mason when he came to London on business, and visited Everett's Calthorpe Arms.

On 30 March 1984, Mason transferred some £75,000 to another bank account in Florida, the home of the English China Company. Reed surmised that he had obviously forgotten that he actually had £85,000 in the account. Solicitors acting for Security Express froze the remaining £10,000.

Although the strange numbers on Mason's scraps of paper had been solved, it was soon replaced by another, more intriguing mystery.

The team discovered that in November 1984, while the Flying Squad were on their second visit to Spain, £164,000 was transferred from Mason's Channel Islands Allied Irish account to a Mr Richard Martin. In February 1985, Mason organized the transfer of a further £8,000 to an account in Martin's name at the National Bank of Nigeria. And then, in February 1986, while Reed was attempting to get details of Mason's bank accounts at the Banco Industrial del Mediterraneo, Mason closed his Allied Irish Channel Islands account altogether, transferring the rest of it to the account in the name of Martin.

The whereabouts and identity of Richard Martin has remained a mystery to this day. The officers went to the Bank of Nigeria in London and were shown his banking records. His old address was barely half a mile from Curtain Road. In November 1984, he gave a Spanish address, which turned out to be an accommodation address.

Peter followed Reed's investigation into Mason and Everett with more than a passing interest. In a way, the information had come too late. Both Mason and Everett had been arrested, questioned, and reluctantly released soon after Jimmy Knight's arrest in March 1984. However, if Peter had been aware of some of the things that George and Reed later found out, both would almost certainly have been charged with robbery and put on remand at the same time as the others.

20

'RUNAWAY RONNIE'

During the 1970s, 'French Lou' was a well-known figure in London's Soho. A dapper, thick-set man, he always had a suit and a tie on, and a trilby hat. Whatever colour his suit, his hat would always match.

Lou had come over as a refugee during the war and made his business supplying wine to the clubs in and around Soho. In the early 1950s he had got in with Jack 'Spot' Comer and Billy Hill, the men who, in those days, controlled Soho and its clubs. Lou had a dingy office at the back of a wine bar in Old Compton Street. Years later, Ronnie Knight found out to his surprise that Lou never owned the wine bar, but the owners liked him so much that they let him take it over and use it as his base.

Lou was always off at the wine auctions buying cases of the best and most expensive wines there were. 'I've got something special for you boys,' he would say to Ronnie and Micky Regan, who were then running the A&R Club in Charing Cross Road. 'Come around and see me.' They would trip around the corner to his office, and were rarely disappointed. Lou's wines were indeed the best.

Ronnie, Micky, and Lou became close friends. They would often go out for meals together. One evening, years after they had first met, Lou had a proposition for Ronnie. 'How would you like to go into the "dirty" business?' he asked.

'Dirty?'

'You know. Girls. But we won't tell you where it is.'

Ronnie looked at Lou as if he was barking mad. 'How do you mean, you won't tell me where it is?'

'Of course, it's round here, Ron. It's in Soho, but if you're seen anywhere near this place, the police will shut it. In fact, if they see you walking anywhere near that club, you'll be in trouble. We'll all be in trouble.'

Lou was quite serious. He went on to tell Ronnie that there was someone else involved who he wouldn't – and couldn't – name. 'We'd like you to come in it with us,' he said.

'How much?'

'£30,000.'

It was the unlikeliest story Ronnie had ever heard. A club that couldn't be seen and a partner who wouldn't be named. But he trusted Lou.

'OK, count me in,' said Ronnie, 'but don't let Barbara know.'

In fact, the investment worked out very well. Lou would give Ronnie brown envelopes every Friday night. If he couldn't get to Lou's office that week there would be two envelopes waiting for him the following Friday. It was good money.

The 'dirty' was a stage 'bed show' and a 'money' peep show, where for a few shillings you could see five minutes of the girls in action. There were cameras for the punters, so, for a fiver, they could take snaps of the girls posing. Or whatever. Ronnie himself never saw the place, but he did try to find it. 'Don't go near it, Ronnie. You'll ruin it,' Lou warned him.

Ronnie had other irons in the fire. He bought another club around the corner from the A&R called the Tin Pan Alley. In the early hours of the morning he would close up the A&R and invite the regulars around to the Tin Pan, which would then stay open until dawn. It worked a storm.

Above the Tin Pan, Ronnie ran an escort agency. Poorly paid nurses from the local hospitals would do the night jobs there to make ends meet. They would come up and hand in a photo, which would go in a big book. Clients would come up from the club and have a look and book them for the night. It was strictly escort, but what the girls did later with the clients was their own private business.

By now Ronnie was getting bundles of cash, money coming in from everywhere. He had something like £3,000 coming in every week. John used to go mad at his spending sprees. 'What do you keep spending money like that for, Ronnie?' he would moan.

'It's all right,' said Ronnie. He knew it was all coming back in again the following week.

But by the late seventies the clubs were getting too much for Ronnie. The police were always raiding them, especially after the nasty business with Zomperelli. Soho was changing. Ronnie decided he wanted to sell the clubs and he also told French Lou that he wanted out.

'That's OK,' said Lou. 'There's a lot of people that want to get into this.'

A couple of weeks later Ronnie went around to pick up his share of the investment.

'There's the money you put in,' said Lou, 'plus your weekly take, and there's a nice surprise for you.' He handed Ronnie a brown-paper package. 'Are you going to count it now?' he asked.

'No. I trust you,' said Ronnie, and stuffed the package into his pocket.

'I can tell you now who the other partner was,' said Lou. 'Drury's his name. Commander Drury.'

Drury had been the head of the Flying Squad. When, in 1977, the full story emerged of his links with the underworld it became a national scandal. Drury and his henchmen in the Obscene Publications Squad, known as the 'Dirty Squad', had organized the collection of tens of thousands of pounds in bribes from all the leading Soho pornographers. The web of corruption was like nothing ever seen before. Extortion and blackmail were rife. One of Drury's officers had even charged honest officers a £100 'transfer fee' to leave their corrupt squad.

An anti-corruption unit set up by Sir Robert Mark, then commissioner of the Metropolitan Police, had investigated some seventy-four officers. Around forty left the force – some were dismissed, others were jailed, and the rest resigned or retired early. Drury himself was sentenced to eight years in prison and the Flying Squad of the day was disbanded. The Central Robbery Squad took its place until that was renamed the Flying

Squad. It took the Met years to overcome its tarnished reputation.

The whole of the West End had been protected by these senior policemen. If there were any smash-ups, Drury would tell his people and they would sort them out. The West End had never been so peaceful. Afterwards, Ronnie thought Drury must have been the one who said, 'Don't have that man in here because it'll go up in the air.' He must have known that such a high-profile figure would have led to a few awkward questions from his fellow officers.

Ronnie's farewell package from Lou contained £80,000 cash. He had been into the 'dirty' for about three years. Not a bad return on £30,000. Lou quickly found someone else to take Ronnie's place.

Ronnie took the cash to Barbara's accountant, Albert Fox. Fox's plush Camden office sprawled over a couple of floors, one for the girls in reception, the one above for him and his brother. Fox was more than just an accountant. He was a shrewd money manager, one of the best. He looked after a lot of football players' investments.

'Where you get this?' he asked, gazing at the pile of grubby banknotes on his desk.

'Dirties.'

'Cor, I wouldn't mind getting into one of them,' Fox joked, leafing through the notes. 'I'd like to be in that business.'

Ronnie laughed. 'So would everybody else. It's not that easy, you know.'

Fox didn't know it was cash from John as well, which was why he thought it was such a good business. Ronnie had walked in with about £200,000 altogether.

Sometimes he had asked Barbara to take money to Fox for him, though to her there was nothing strange in that – Ronnie always had money lying around the place. But favours aside, his relationship with Barbara was by now in tatters.

Any job going, Barbara took it. Although Ronnie had been married to her for twenty-two years, he felt that, if he cut that in half, that was the time he had actually spent with her. Barbara had always wanted him to be her manager, but that just wasn't Ronnie's scene. It wasn't his game to watch her work and pick her up afterwards. He had his own businesses to run, which in itself was a full day's work. Still, he used to go with her on opening nights and last nights.

After he sold the clubs, Ronnie had nothing in Soho at all. With no office to go to, he was always travelling around in his car or on foot. So Ronnie thought it was time for him to go for good. By then, he already had a couple of businesses going in Spain, Wyn's Bar and Supermarket, and a minicab firm. He also had plans to open an Indian restaurant, complete with clay ovens, one of the first ever along the Costa. And, of course, he had the villa – El Limonar – that he shared with John.

Ronnie never forgot the first time he ever clapped eyes on El Limonar, or more accurately, the barren piece of Spanish mountainside that was to become El Limonar. It was 1975. He and Babs were staying with his sister and her husband at their villa. They had a place on the top of a mountain and it was lovely. Ronnie and Babs enthused over it.

'I want to introduce you to the American who owns all the property around here,' his brother-in-law said.

'That'll be nice. Has he got property that we'd like?'

'Well, he's coming round to see me. You can talk to him and he'll show you round a few places.'

A couple of days later Dick Modiano took them on a guided tour of his villas. They were beautiful. Every last one of them.

'Like this villa, Ronnie? I built this,' Dick would proudly say, leaning out of his car.

'Yeah, I do like it,' said Ronnie. 'My brother-in-law says you've got some more like this.'

'Come on,' said Dick, 'I'll show you a spot that'll do you the world of good.'

He took Ronnie and Babs up to a spot in a cul-de-sac that was just bare rocks. They scrambled up and all they could see was the sky above and the sea far below speckled with boats.

'This is unbelievable,' said Ronnie. 'How on earth do you build up here?'

'Oh, no,' said Dick laughing. 'This has all got to be flattened. But this is your property.'

Ronnie immediately fell in love with it. 'I can't say nothing for sure because I'm sure my brother Johnny would like to be in it with me,' he said.

'OK,' said Dick. He showed Ronnie a few more spots but there was nowhere in comparison. Ronnie spoke to John when he got home and three or four weeks later they both went over to have a look. As it happened, John loved it too. Dick built the place in six months. It came to about £50,000.

Ronnie had tripped back and forth to Spain to make the villa more liveable in, to turn it from a holiday home into a real home. While he was over there he built up his businesses in Spain. He knew you couldn't live out in Spain unless you had something constructive to do. Otherwise you'd end up going on the piss night and day. He'd seen it happen. There was little else to do out there unless you happened to be a sportsman, particularly a golfer.

£££

Ronnie's best-laid plans had to be rapidly brought forward after John's sudden arrest in January 1984. After fleeing to Spain, Ronnie began a new life with Sue Haylock. Together they expanded Wyn's Bar and moved its supermarket over the road. Sue brought a lot of style to the place. Before Ronnie employed her at the A&R, she had had a job delivering Rolls-Royce cars to their new owners. Wyn's Bar thrived in her capable hands.

But although Ronnie was gone from Britain, he was not forgotten. The press interest in him never let up. In fact, it got worse. Here was a larger-than-life figure, once married to Barbara Windsor, now on the run, living it up in Spain. Meanwhile, his two brothers were rotting in jail for their part in a £6 million heist. It was something of a feeding frenzy for the tabloid press, who dubbed him 'Runaway Ronnie'. The nickname was catchy and it stuck in the public's imagination.

To Ronnie's mind, 'runaway story' would perhaps have

been more appropriate. He remembered a time when a couple of reporters came a-knocking on the villa gates. He had pretended to be out, but little did the reporters know that he could hear their every word through the intercom.

'What shall we do now?' one said to another.

'Well, we'll just have to make something up.'

Ronnie became a symbol for a whole community of ex-pats living on the profits of crime, fugitives from justice every last one. It was an image that the Flying Squad was happy to encourage, albeit discreetly, through off-the-record briefings and 'chats' with the newspapermen. Ronnie felt badly for his two brothers and would send them whatever they needed in the way of clothing or money. But he knew that he didn't want to go to jail. Not again.

Ronnie and Sue did their best to escape from the watchful eyes of the press and the police. Security at El Limonar was tight, and the circle of people they associated with were fiercely protective of each other. They rarely broke ranks. In June 1984, having been tipped off that the Flying Squad was in town and making its endless and highly irritating inquiries, Ronnie and Sue took a trip over to Algiers to escape the tension. But so much for a relaxing holiday. Ronnie hated it. The locals were all wearing what he called 'Tommy Cooper' hats, and they hassled the ladies all the time. The men would leer at anything white and female. The hotel had bits of string dangling down for the light switches. The place was frightening. If anything happened to them over there, Ronnie was sure that no one would ever find them. He and Sue came home early, vowing never to go there again.

A few days later, one of Ronnie's friends from Manchester stuck a notice up on one of the boards in the La Alcazaba apartment complex saying that he was organizing a boat trip to Gibraltar. Quite a few of them went, though it was mainly a trip for the ladies to replenish supplies. They bought everything they needed, all the peculiarly English things that they couldn't get in Spain, like Oxo cubes, Marmite, Bovril, PG Tips, British cured beef, and the like. Personally, Ronnie wasn't that impressed with Gibraltar. 'Why does everyone go mad for

Gib?' he thought. There were washing lines all over the place, stretching across the street from one window to the other – sheets, pants, and everything on display. He couldn't understand why anyone would want to spend a holiday there. Sure enough, there were English pints and English bobbies, but that was about it. Ronnie couldn't see any sense in it. In future, he asked other people to get what he and Sue needed.

The disclosure of the Flying Squad's Commission Rogatoire in one of the local magazines unnerved Ronnie enough to go to see his Spanish lawyer, Fernando.

Over the next few months, Ronnie Knight lost count of the number of stories that appeared in the tabloid press about him and every aspect of his life, both past and present. During the trial of his brothers John and Jimmy, it reached fever pitch. One incursion particularly annoyed him. In April 1985, Sue's parents were in town. They were all having a nice barbecue, a family affair. Ronnie was cooking sausages. He was unaware of it at the time, but an ITN television journalist, Brent Saddler, was filming them all. The footage was later shown on prime-time television. Saddler had quietly crawled through the mountain scrub above the villa to film them sitting on the terrace.

£££

By the time of Ronnie's wedding to Sue in 1987, he had got used to his status as Britain's most wanted man. The wedding, on Thursday, 4 June was a small, private affair, the civil ceremony taking place in Fuengirola Town Hall with just a handful of friends present. The best man was Ron Popely, an old mucker of Ronnie's who used to run a pub in Bethnal Green. The reception was held at El Océano, a restaurant and sports centre right on the beach, the following Saturday. Ronnie and Sue were originally going to arrive on a motor launch, but the press was, of course, out in force.

The local Anglican priest, the Revd Ronald Matheson, blessed their marriage, and came in for a lot of criticism for it. But his reply was simple: 'If someone asks for God's blessing, who am I to refuse?'

Sue wore a £3,000 ivory-coloured silk and satin wedding dress, carried a bouquet of orchids and salmon-coloured roses, and sported a large, diamond-encrusted wedding ring. Ronnie's wedding present to her was a very sexy top-of-the-range black BMW 325i sports car.

The celebration was capped by a midnight firework display with the words 'Ron' and 'Sue', surrounded by sparkling pink Catherine-wheel hearts. The reception was an extravaganza, and cost him around £10,000. Everyone who was anyone on the Costa del Sol was there that night, and among the guests were Freddie Foreman and family, Ronnie Everett, John Mason, and Clifford Saxe.

Nearby, in unmarked cars, were men from the Flying Squad, discreetly watching and photographing the guests come and go. Reed McGeorge was still on the trail. The newspapers, too, were out in force, some spying with telephoto lenses from motor launches. One news organization even hired a helicopter, which constantly circled overhead as the guests arrived, but on the ground hired heavies kept the hacks well away from the club.

Don't let the facts get in the way of a good story, as they say, so what the press couldn't get for real, they made up. Some of it was quite poisonous, mostly variations on the 'Runaway Ronnie' theme. Ronnie's wedding cake was said to be in the shape of Wandsworth Prison. The guests were supposed to have all joined in the chorus of 'Jailhouse Rock', and Ronnie was quoted in one newspaper as saying, 'It's a fair cop . . . this is one sentence I don't mind serving.'

It was all small beer, but the petty jibes and catty remarks irritated Ronnie. 'Why can't they just leave us alone?' he asked his friends. 'With all the killing and tragedy in the big wide world, why spend so much money on a couple of people getting hitched?'

Weddings, not wars, sell newspapers, and the media circus continued unabated. Ronnie's ostentatious wedding reception appeared to anger Barbara Windsor so much that she agreed to give a succession of interviews to the gleeful *Sun*. She told the paper that she was amazed that Ronnie, who had always kept himself in the shadows, had suddenly made such a public spectacle of himself. It wasn't like the Ronnie she knew. She assumed that Sue had somehow put him up to it.

But the truth was that Ronnie secretly loved every minute of it. He felt as free as a bird. And he was in love. For once, he – not Barbara – was the celebrity, and it wasn't such a bad feeling after all.

£££

After the wedding, life for Ronnie and Sue settled down much as it was before. But back in England, things were stirring.

A month after Ronnie's wedding, Reed contacted Barbara Windsor and asked her to come in to Leman Street police station for questioning. It was clear to him that Barbara still had feelings for Ronnie Knight – after all, she had been married to him for some twenty years – but he suspected that the way Ronnie had treated her over the previous four years had probably done him few favours. He was sure that that, combined with the disclosures he was about to make concerning Ronnie's life in Spain, would encourage her to be a prosecution witness, and warned her that they would have to tell her a lot of hurtful things about Ronnie's private life.

It was a reasonable gamble and not a bad tactic. Hell hath no fury like a woman scorned, as the saying goes.

In case any feelings still remained, Reed tried to put Barbara's mind at ease by telling her that they already had the evidence they needed against Ronnie, and that her evidence was really not that important. Barbara told them that she had left her financial affairs completely in the hands of Fox Associates, and that she knew nothing of the payments Ronnie Knight had made to Albert Fox that, the Flying Squad was now convinced, were the proceeds from the Security Express robbery. She only remembered two payments, and recalled that in February 1983 Knight was short of cash, and had asked for £5,000 in cash from Fox Associates.

Reed was keen to see her appointment diaries for 1983, but she had no entries for the Easter Bank Holiday weekend. She told Reed that, by then, she and Ronnie were leading separate lives. She couldn't remember what she did that Easter weekend, but she did recall Knight calling her up. 'Remember I was with you,' he had said. That, if true, was pretty damning.

In June 1983, Windsor travelled out to Spain with Ronnie. He showed her some luxury apartments in the La Alcazaba complex in Marbella and told her that he was planning to buy them. She told Fox Associates to telex £20,000 to Knight's bank in Spain, this being the proceeds from the sale of their flat. She assumed that the rest of the money for the apartments would come from the sale of his villa, El Limonar.

Between July and September 1983, she had appeared on stage in the seaside town of Scarborough, in the north of England. She lived there during the week, returning to London only at weekends. But there was one weekend she particularly recalled, because she felt that Ronnie hadn't wanted her around. It was the weekend of the 23–25 July.

To Reed, those dates were more significant than Barbara might have realized. He knew that, between the 19th and the 21st July, Knight had deposited some £102,000 in cash with Fox Associates. After the weekend, on 27 July, he deposited a further £80,000. It may have been just coincidence; perhaps Ronnie had personal reasons for not wanting her around, but Reed was sure that the main reason was because of the cash.

Towards the end of 1983, Barbara bought a house in Hampstead. Ronnie came to see her and she noticed that he was driving a different car. The last time she saw him in England was Saturday, 21 January, just before his brother's arrest. At that time, Ronnie had made no mention whatever of going over to Spain, but the following evening, at around 10 p.m., he called her and to her surprise told her that he was now in Spain.

'Why?' she asked.

'The Old Bill's after me. They've nicked Johnny.'

Over the subsequent months Ronnie would occasionally call Barbara from Spain and would specifically mention the Easter weekend of 1983. 'Remember I was with you?' he kept saying.

Barbara was sure that she was at their home in Hendon that weekend, but she told Reed that she couldn't remember if Ronnie was with her or not.

She knew about his clubs in the West End and remembered him talking about a 'peep show', but she never saw any documents relating to them. Ronnie never had a bank account or credit cards. His businesses were strictly cash only.

Barbara told the police that she knew all the other people they were interested in except Ronnie Everett. She had met them all through Ronnie.

All in all, Barbara was interviewed six times by Reed. On the final occasion he produced some photographs that he had deliberately kept back until the very end. One in particular upset Barbara greatly, but not for the reason that Reed expected. The photograph showed Ronnie, Sue Haylock, John Knight, and his wife Di, sitting around a Spanish pool and lapping up the sun.

Sue and Ronnie were very much an item in the photograph, but that wasn't what upset Barbara. Rather, it was the fact that Di had lied to her. Di had told Barbara that she had only met Sue once and, in her words, couldn't stand her. That certainly wasn't what the photograph suggested. Barbara thought that was two-faced, and unforgivable.

She told Reed that she knew all about Ronnie's affair with Sue, even before the robbery. Back in 1981, deeply suspicious of him, she had hired a private detective to do the works on him. The detective spotted him regularly turning up at Sue's flat in Edgware. The following Easter, when Ronnie left the house with a rather lame excuse, Barbara had turned up in a taxi at Sue's flat and confronted them both. It was quite a scene, something that Barbara could not forget easily. After that she had stayed with Ronnie because he promised that things would change. He said he would stop seeing Sue. He didn't, of course.

By showing Barbara the photographs, Reed had secured Barbara's full cooperation. It was perhaps more valuable than she had realized. At the time, the only other people who knew anything of Ronnie's financial affairs was Albert Fox himself, although he had no idea of the real source of Ronnie's money, and Sue Haylock, who was out of reach in Spain.

£££

Meanwhile, over in Spain, Ronnie heard through one of his contacts that Barbara was talking to the police. Hurt, he called her up one day. 'I hear you've become a grass,' he said.

'Of course not,' she replied. She told him that she had had no choice but to talk to the police. It was a cold, frosty phone call, and it signalled the end of what little love remained between them.

£££

In 1987 the 'Costa del Crime' runaways captured the imagination of Roger Cook, the veteran investigative television journalist. For his investigation, he hooked up with an English journalist based on the Costa del Sol who had unusually good contacts with the Flying Squad.

Cook was famous for his unique confrontational style. He would research his targets thoroughly before moving in for a killer interview with whoever it was he was targeting. The confrontation between Cook and his hapless victim was usually the climax of the programme. Sometimes it ended in blows, but more usually the victim would walk out of the room, or close the front door, or run away down the road, or drive off. Whatever they decided to do, it was usually highly entertaining, because Cook just kept on coming at them. Ronnie could see how it made great telly, seeing these big underworld figures chased by the tenacious Cook, closely followed by his cameraman.

Cook got away with it because he was a big man and he could run bloody fast. He also came across as highly belligerent. He had the benefit of an unrivalled network of informers and contacts, built up over many years. Some were policemen or former policemen. Others were themselves crooks, acting in their own self-interest, squealing on their rivals, and by doing so protecting their own empires.

One night Ronnie was in Wyn's Bar having a drink with a

few friends. One of them came up to him. 'Hey, Ronnie. Did you know Roger Cook's in town?'

'No.'

'He's been asking questions about Clifford Saxe.'

Ronnie laughed. 'He's wasting his time. He won't get anywhere with Saxey.' Secretly, however, he was worried. Cook was no lightweight. He had the resources of a major television station behind him, and shouldn't be underestimated. If Cook was interested in Saxe, then the chances were he would try to pay Ronnie a visit too.

Sure enough, a couple of days later, just before midday, an unannounced visitor turned up at Ronnie's villa. The gate to the villa was equipped with a security camera and a microphone, and Ronnie instantly recognized Cook's rotund, larger-than-life figure.

Cook rang the bell and Ronnie got Sue to go down to the gate and talk to him. 'Is Ronnie Knight in?' he asked. 'No. He's not in,' she replied, and without further ado shut the gate in his face. Ronnie remained inside the villa, watching and listening.

Ronnie and Sue thought no more of it, but over the next few days they got regular updates through their friends and neighbours about what Cook and his television crew were up to. They knew who he was visiting, when, and where, sometimes even before it had happened.

They heard that Cook had been up to Wyn's Bar, which was also one of Saxe's favourite haunts, to have a word with him, and that Saxe had thumped him, giving him a black eye. They also heard that Cook had tried to interview Mason and Everett with little success. But they assumed that Cook had probably given up on trying to get to Ronnie.

So imagine their surprise when, a couple of days later, while sunbathing on the patio, they heard a helicopter flying in from over the mountains behind the villa.

It was unusual. Helicopters quite often flew over the villa, but they nearly always approached from the direction of the sea. Ronnie was suspicious. 'Let's go inside,' he said.

They went into the villa, closed the windows and pulled the

net curtains tight. Through the netting Ronnie watched as the helicopter hovered over the top of the villa. He could make out someone perched on a rail on the outside of the helicopter; he couldn't see who it was, but it looked as if they were filming.

The helicopter flew over three times and appeared to be trying to land on the rough hillside behind the villa. Ronnie smiled at that – the hillside was so rough and rocky the pilot would have a hell of a job. Just to be on the safe side, however, Ronnie and Sue got changed, got into the car and drove down the mountain into the town. They were very much on their guard now, but Cook wasn't going to give up quite so easily.

A few days later five or six men visited them. They came to the bottom gate of the villa and started banging it, and that set the dogs off. Ronnie, however, wasn't going to fall for that one. He knew that they wanted him to come out so that they could get him on film, so he stayed put in the villa and after some minutes they left.

Some of the local residents complained about Cook's helicopter flying in from over the mountain. The wind from the blades had blown their patio furniture about, which was one of the reasons why helicopters never flew that route.

Following the complaints from the neighbours, a Spanish policeman came up to see Ronnie. He was polite, and seemed genuinely concerned about the nuisance helicopter flight. Ironically, Ronnie always got on well with the local Spanish police. They thought highly of him because he was a businessman with clubs and restaurants. He also employed Spaniards.

'Was it you they were after?' the policeman said.

'You know that,' said Ronnie. 'You've seen the press around here. I've chucked them away from my front door enough times.'

'Mr Knight, you should have told us. You should have phoned us up,' he said. 'We would have put Cook away for a few days. He'd have been in prison.' He gestured up towards the mountain behind the villa. 'Even we can't come across there.'

Ronnie and Sue heard no more from Cook, but some weeks later he was showered with phone calls from his friends in

England. 'You've been on TV again,' they said. Ronnie had starred in the Roger Cook programme. It looked as if he had been filmed from a helicopter. It was the first he knew of it. 'Do us a favour,' he said, 'send us a video.'

A week or so later, when he sat down to watch the video, he was amazed by what he saw. The film showed Roger Cook standing outside his villa talking to Sue. Then it showed Cook talking to the camera. 'He's in there all right, I just caught a glimpse of him at one of the windows, but perhaps there's only one real way of getting close,' Cook said.

The film then showed a helicopter flying towards Ronnie's villa. Helicopter noise played in the background. Then it showed him and Sue on the patio.

Ronnie thought that he and Sue had managed to avoid being filmed by the helicopter and wondered whether the footage of them on the patio was the same footage as had been shot some two years previously, while Sue's parents were there. Either way, watching the programme got Ronnie riled again. There he was free in Spain, clearly having a ball, while the British police were tearing their hair out with frustration. It made good telly but that was not the way Ronnie saw it. He had been highly irritated by the unwelcome intrusion.

21
PRISON

John had spent the first week of his twenty-two-year sentence in Wormwood Scrubs. He remained in his cell, far too upset about his sentence to want to see anyone. To cap it all, because of a chronic shortage of space, John had been put in a small wing full of prisoners with short sentences. Sometimes the officers would point John out to the youngsters. 'You should be lucky that you've only got only six months,' they would say. 'He's doing twenty-two years.' The word soon went around John's landing, and every time John slopped out, the lads would be standing there gawping at him. It upset him greatly. He wanted to be with people who could understand. After a week he'd had enough. He complained to an officer and was moved to a cell in the long termers' wing.

Over the next few months, John settled down. Prison life had come a long way since his time in the Sixties. Back then, the cells had been painted a dingy yellow, the food was rough, and you could only bath once a week. Now, the cells had been brightened up, with curtains at the windows. There were showers, and the food was entirely different – as much sliced bread as you could eat. But you still had to slop out and wash in the mornings with a jug of cold water. There were still no phones for the prisoners, but at least he was close to Di.

But that was about to change. One day a prison officer told him that someone had put a note in the prison 'grass box' claiming that he was earning £500 a week in the prison from selling baccy. 'You'll very likely be moved on,' the officer told him. Someone had done the dirty on him. It was as if someone wanted him out of the way.

Within a week or so, John had been 'ghosted' to Brixton and then was on his way to Albany Prison on the Isle of Wight. Those first few years on category AA at Albany were the worst. He wasn't allowed many visits and it was a struggle for Diane to visit him, although he had plenty of letters and Ronnie would send him the occasional parcel from Spain. The security measures at the prison were, to John's mind, absurd, especially as everyone knew that if you wanted something bad enough you just had to ask the right person. One time when Di came to visit with her three-week-old grandson, the authorities insisted on searching the pram and baby – nappies and all. They even examined his water bottle.

In Albany, John had plenty of time to muse on what had gone wrong at the trial. With hindsight he never really stood a chance, with all the evidence Wilton had amassed against him. The only thing he could have done was to plead guilty to handling. Maybe then he would have got a shorter sentence. The thing he had done wrong was to invest the proceeds. If he had gone and buried it, there wouldn't have been much of a case. He would still have had the supergrass around him, but it would have been much harder for them. It would have been purely his word against Alan's. In fact, Alan would have had more money around him than John. He would have had £25,000. That would have posed a few problems for the Crown's case.

The most unlikely result was Hickson's and Horsley's. John had often been told by his brief to watch out for Hickson. When he was on remand they were letting Hickson out regularly, saying he was seeing his solicitors, but John's brief told him Hickson was really seeing the Old Bill.

He remembered that someone had scratched 'Billy Hickson is a grass' on one of the seats in the meeting room at Wormwood Scrubs. Someone else had scrawled next to it, 'Whoever wrote this is a grass too.' John didn't know what to believe, but he did wonder whether a secret deal had been done after Hickson had been interrogated at the station following his arrest. After all, Hickson had said in his statement that he wanted to do a deal, and John's own arrest had been much later that day.

Towards the end of the trial and before he got 'weighed off', John remembered seeing all sorts of notes being passed backwards and forwards between the judge and the prosecution. He often wondered what the notes had said. He guessed that they were plea bargains of some sort for the two – or possibly three – people who had stitched him up.

Now, with an unimaginably long stretch in front of him, John had to adapt to survive. He knew he had to keep himself busy, to go to work, to keep his mind occupied. Most of all he knew he had to get off 'high risk' so that he could have open visits with his family. He longed to get hold of his children and sit down with them for an hour and have tea and biscuits together, as if they were in a hotel.

John used to work in the prison laundry. He did a good job there, and it gave him a little bit of status. In the laundry, the routine was reassuringly monotonous. Monday was No. 1 landing, Tuesday was No. 2, Wednesday No. 3, Thursday No. 4, and Friday was 'all trousers' day. Saturday morning was when you could have your special things done – jeans and the like. Those were the orders from the prison authorities.

There were two sorts of smells in the prison cells. One was Old Holborn tobacco and the other was cannabis. A lot of people couldn't do their sentence without cannabis, and the drug was routinely smuggled in. The authorities knew about it but it kept the inmates cool, so they appeared to turn a blind eye. Without their drugs, half of the inmates would have been on the hospital ward. John was offered a smoke many times but he always refused. He was never a drugs man.

There was no bullying with John. He was well respected, as were all the big robbers, from the Great Train Robbers to the Brinks-Mat people. The established faces inside the prison knew him, so he had no problems there. Many of the youngsters looked up to him. But, as in the outside world, he kept as low a profile as he could. Nevertheless, he had a couple of rows with people inside, mostly over their laundry. It was hard to avoid, even if you kept yourself to yourself.

One day, in March 1986, John got a letter from Barbara

Windsor, who was doing a pantomime season. She wrote, 'I know how unselfish you are with your feelings and you only care if Diane and the kids are OK. I wish I could be of more help to you . . . but I want you to know that if there's anything you need or want doing, just let me know. If I can I will.

'I never hear from Ronnie, which suits me. I gather the female in his life has put barbed wire round him and she is the guv'nor, which I think is the reason for his lack of concern for you and yours, although that is no excuse, but I have friends over there who say he has changed considerably.'

Barbara kept in touch with John throughout his time in prison. Despite what had happened with Ronnie, she remained close to him and especially Diane Knight. Barbara had started running a restaurant with her boyfriend Stephen Hollings, and from prison, John, with his business mind, gave them much-appreciated advice. It kept his mind alert and relieved some of the tedium of prison life.

On the advice of his solicitors, John appealed against his sentence on the grounds of its severity. While on appeal, he was moved to Wandsworth Prison, which at least made it easier for Di to visit him. John was hoping to at least get a few years off his sentence to bring it down to eighteen but his appeal was refused. In truth, he had no chance, as the appeal judge made quite clear in his judgment. 'If there was such a thing as a Mafia in this country, then the Knights were it,' he thundered. Terry Perkins, who also appealed, didn't even bother to turn up to the hearing. It was as if he knew deep down that it was a hopeless cause.

John's criminal bankruptcy order meant that High Trees and his Spanish apartment and villa all had to be sold. As is so often the case with bankruptcies, they went for much less than they were really worth. A curious accident with a crane smashing into the balcony, followed by an inexplicable reluctance by his insurers to pay out, meant that the apartment was sold for next to nothing.

He felt especially bitter about the sale of High Trees. After all, he had bought the house long before the robbery. There was no robbery money involved. Luckily, his paper divorce from Di had given her a share of the proceeds from the sale – enough for her to buy a small mobile home to live in!

£££

While at Albany, John felt like he was getting short of breath. 'I'm going to do all this bird, and then go out and die,' he thought to himself. So he gave up smoking, and embarked on a rigorous keep-fit regime, running and jogging four miles a day. He used to run with Harry Roberts because he had the same pace. John always thought that Harry didn't look the type to shoot three policemen. But who does look like anything?

John remained in Albany for three years. After that, he asked the Governor if he could be moved. To be fair, there was lots of outside help, especially from Di, who said she'd like her husband nearer for visits. The suggested prison was Gartree, in Leicestershire, still high security, but closer to home.

He was sitting in his cell on the third landing, soon after he had arrived at Gartree, when an officer poked his head around the door. 'There's someone at the gate downstairs to see you,' he said.

It was Reggie Kray. He shook his hand. 'Need anything John?'

'No, I'm fine Reggie. I'm OK for sugar and I'm OK for tea.'

'I go out and exercise at 10 a.m. in the small exercise yard,' said Reggie. 'Perhaps you'll come out in the morning and join me?'

The next morning, while pacing themselves around the yard, they caught up on all the family gossip. 'How's your mum?' Reggie asked.

'None too clever,' John replied. 'She's got a tremor.'

Reggie was sorry to hear that. He was always very fond of John's mum.

John remained in Gartree for the next three years. Once again, he got work in the laundry, which had been newly built.

In the back room John set up a little stove and a frying pan, where he would make himself breakfast in the mornings. Sometimes Reggie would drop by. 'Want a fry-up?' John would say.

'Yeah.'

They would go into the back room and John would cook Reggie some fried eggs and maybe a bit of bacon. Perched on a rickety chair, Reggie never said much to John – but then, John never asked much. That was the rule. Just a bit of gossip about prison goings-on. Maybe a few past reminiscences. They went back a long time, the Knights and the Krays.

Over breakfast they used to have some good chats about people and loyalty. 'I'm only here because of grasses,' John would say to Reggie, 'and I know you are, too. I bet you can count the people you trust on one hand.'

Reggie sat in silence eating his egg, and raised three fingers in the air.

Once, Reggie was clearly upset with his brother Charlie over something or other. It was just a family upset, and John didn't enquire too much what it was about. That's what Reggie appreciated about John. 'You always were a quiet person,' he said. 'Hear nothing, see nothing, and say nothing – just like the three wise monkeys.' John laughed. That was indeed the way the Knight family was.

John would always do Reggie's laundry separately.

£££

It took a lot of skilful lobbying by Diane to get John taken off high-risk category A. She pulled strings. She had a cousin who was a councillor, who knew Chris Smith, then a Labour Party Opposition MP. Smith had a keen interest in the Prison Service. He took up John's cause and wrote to Angela Rumbold, who was Conservative Minister of State responsible for prisoners at the Home Office from 1990–92.

Shortly after, John was taken off category A and transferred to lower-security category B. He was now in the eighth year of his sentence, and for the first time he was allowed unsupervised visits.

One morning in 1995, Ann Widdecombe, then Minister of State at the Home Office, came to visit John, who had by this time been transferred to the Mount, near Hemel Hempstead. He met her downstairs in the communal mess area where they ate their meals. 'It's OK to come to my room – it's clean,' he told her.

She briskly climbed the metal stairs on to the landing and walked with him to his cell. She sat down on a chair. Her eyes darted around the small, cluttered cell, and settled on his collection of photographs, prominently displayed on a bedside table. 'Who are the photos of?' she asked.

'That's my wife,' said John. 'There's my kids,' he said proudly, pointing towards another photograph.

'You must have been a very home-loving man,' she said. 'How do you feel now?'

'I'm looking forward to going home. My family is waiting for me to be a father to them,' he told her. 'There's no way you can be a father while you're inside.'

'Are you still with your wife?' she asked.

'Yes.'

She looked surprised. Few marriages last through such a long sentence.

'And your children. Are they well?'

'Yes.'

And then she fixed her gaze on him. 'Do you feel remorse? Do you feel sorry for what you did?'

'I feel very remorseful,' he said. 'I do, because of my family.'

She nodded and stood up. 'I have to go and write a report,' she said. 'I can't tell you what it will say but it could be in your favour.' She smiled at him. 'It's nice to meet you, Mr Knight.'

And then she left.

Over the years, John had had lots of knock-backs from the prison high command, but they realized that they had to let him go eventually. They couldn't really fault him. He had stayed clean all the way through his sentence. After ten years in prison, it was time to prepare him for going home. His visits had become more frequent, and he was moved to a hostel in Hemel Hempstead, ready for parole.

Jimmy, by then out, came in his car one day and picked John up from prison to see their mother, who was then in an old people's home. She was discreet about everything, and overjoyed to see them both, but John could see that the whole thing had affected her badly. She had tragically lost two of her sons, one to a brain tumour, the other in a stupid fight. And her three remaining sons had been branded criminals. It must have hurt.

John felt he had let her down badly. They all had.

He got a job with a local plumber and, always a keen handyman, learned the trade quickly. One time, they went to do the plumbing in an officers' mess on an airbase. John had to laugh. There he was, a notorious criminal, fixing their plumbing. If only they knew. When Ronnie was arrested they stopped him working outside for a few weeks, worried that he might try to escape, but after a while, John was allowed to go home for weekends.

Terry Perkins was allowed the same privileges at around the same time as John, but the first weekend he was let out he did a runner. John couldn't believe it when he heard the news. 'Why would he do a runner when he was virtually a free man?' he thought. It didn't make any sense to him, or to any one else for that matter.

Then one day a prison officer came up to him. 'There's a note in your cell,' he said.

'What's it say?'

'Go and look. You'll enjoy reading it.'

John went up to his cell, opened the little brown envelope, and unfolded the thin paper. It said that he had been accepted for parole and had been assigned a probation officer, who wanted to come and see him.

The greatest feeling was ringing Di. 'I've got a letter,' he said. 'I'm coming home.' A few days later she came to pick him up. Since his arrest Diane had waited twelve years for him.

They went out for a celebratory meal at a swish restaurant, paid for by their son. John ordered a sirloin steak. A few months later John and Di remarried. Di had somehow managed to keep the family together. She had visited him as much as she was able. She had stayed with him. But everyone was now twelve years older. No one was little – or young – any more.

22
GETTING FOREMAN HOME

A constant cause of frustration for the ongoing enquiry into the Security Express robbery was the lack of intelligence cooperation between the British and the Spanish police. It was lamentable, though it had little to do with nationality. At home it was much the same story between the Metropolitan Police and HM Customs, between different police forces, and even, as Peter had discovered, between different divisions of the same police force.

But in 1988 that was to change, and the man who was set to change it was a man after their own heart. Cliff Craig had been on the enquiry in its very early days, when it was still based at City Road, but shortly afterwards he had been promoted and assigned to another division.

In 1987 he had been promoted again, and was appointed the official liaison officer between the Met and the Spanish police, working out of the British Embassy in Madrid. Cliff's new job was to build up confidence and trust between the British and Spanish police forces. It was a difficult job to do, as both sides were naturally suspicious of each other and loath to share information, but gradually he succeeded.

For the officers remaining on the enquiry it was a stroke of luck to have someone they knew personally, working directly with the Spanish on their behalf.

In July 1988, a meeting was organized in Madrid with the aim of trying to improve the sharing of information. The meeting was designed to encourage everyone to get his or her act together. There were thousands of messages about various individuals flying backwards and forwards through Interpol, but nothing was getting done about them.

There were perhaps half a dozen detectives present at the meeting and, for once, no political agenda. It was simply policemen talking about bad men and how they could be arrested and brought to justice. Everything they had on these people – speculations and rumours included – was put, quite literally, on the table. Naturally, the topic of conversation edged around to the subject of the Security Express robbery and the British suspects who were still living in exile.

At the end of the meeting, just as Cliff was getting ready to leave, he was taken aside by the senior Spanish police officer. 'Tell me, Cliff. Out of all the British criminals on the Costa del Sol, which one would you like back the most?'

Cliff thought for a moment and made a quick assessment. 'Freddie Foreman,' he said.

After the meeting, in typical Spanish style, the detectives went out for a sumptuous lunch, with plenty of wine. Work conversation ended.

£££

There were many reasons why Cliff had singled out Foreman. For one thing, he knew what Foreman was up to on the Costa del Sol – there was a widely held suspicion that he was involved in drugs trafficking. Secondly, Foreman had been involved in a drugs-smuggling operation that had led to the killing of a customs officer. And then there was his suspected involvement with Security Express, of course. In short, out of all of the renegades on the Costa, Freddie Foreman was considered by the British police to be the nastiest of the lot.

The customs officer was called Peter Bennett. He was thirty-two years old, married, with a year-old son. He was the first customs officer to be killed on duty in mainland Britain. In October 1979, Bennett was working on a huge undercover operation called 'Operation Wrecker'. It had been going on for some eighteen months and also involved Hampshire Police and the Regional Crime Squad. The investigation was nearing its conclusion.

Bennett was part of a four-man undercover team that was trailing a suspect lorry through the streets of East London. As it stopped in Commercial Road, Stepney, a man got out of the cab. As he did so, the officers challenged him. He pulled out an automatic pistol and shot Bennett, running off as shoppers scattered for cover. When other customs officers closed in on him, the man tried to turn the gun on himself. He fell to the ground, wounded, but not fatally.

Customs spent more than five hours dismantling the lorry, eventually turning up a secret compartment containing one and a half tons of cannabis resin, then worth more than £2 million. They raided the offices of the freight-forwarding firm in Rotherhithe, and, over the next few hours, detained more than thirty people. The lorry had delivered shoes from Pakistan to a Tesco supermarket in Essex.

Foreman was one of those sighted in the area at the time of the shooting, loitering near a telephone box. Soon afterwards he fled the country to Spain, returning some months later. In February 1980, he obtained a false passport in the name of George Newbury. Two weeks later, he flew to New York and moved to Allentown, Pennsylvania, buying a house in the name of his new identity.

In January 1982, Foreman returned home to England, and soon afterwards he was arrested outside Ronnie Knight's A&R Club in Soho. At the time of his arrest he was with Micky Regan, Knight's partner in the club.

Hampshire Police questioned Foreman at length. He told them that he had lost his business in the UK because of his involvement in the drugs-smuggling operation. He said he was now penniless, of no fixed abode, and had had to sell his house in the UK to pay for his family's keep in America.

He pleaded guilty to 'conspiracy to supply controlled drugs' and got a two-year suspended sentence. After that he moved with his wife Maureen to a Bermondsey council estate.

For HM Customs and, for that matter, the police, it was an unsatisfactory end to the matter. Cliff had himself been involved with some major drugs investigations. He had a lot of respect for the often dangerous work customs did undercover.

As gangsters went, Freddie Foreman had an impressive

pedigree. At eighteen he joined a gang of shoplifters, which called itself the 'Forty Thieves'. For that he got his first prison sentence, nine months for robbery.

Once out of prison he formed his own firm and attempted a robbery in Southampton. It didn't go according to plan and Foreman went into hiding, aided by the Krays, who were destined to be guiding lights in Freddie's career.

During the early 1960s he became involved with a string of high-profile robberies. He turned down an offer to be part of the team that pulled off the Great Train Robbery but, in 1966, agreed to act as a go-between for one of the robbers, Buster Edwards. Some £50,000 of Great Train Robbery proceeds turned up in a public telephone box, and in return the police agreed to reduce Edwards's sentence.

A few months later, Foreman allegedly shot dead Frank Mitchell, known as the 'Mad Axeman', as a personal favour to Ronnie Kray. The Krays had helped Frank escape from Dartmoor Prison and had hidden him in a house for months, but it hadn't worked out. Mitchell had become a liability, so according to the police Foreman had stepped in to sort it out for them. He was brought to trial two years after the event but acquitted.

The following year Foreman helped dispose of the body of Jack 'The Hat' McVitie, murdered by Reggie Kray in a house not far from David Knight's old yard. Foreman was found guilty of being an accessory to the murder and was sentenced to ten years' imprisonment.

Shortly before his release in 1975 Foreman, along with Ronnie Everett and Alfie Gerard, was charged with the murder of Thomas 'Ginger' Marks. Marks had been involved in the shooting of Foreman's brother and the police suspected his killing was an act of revenge. All three men were acquitted.

£££

The question from the senior Spanish police officer at the end of the meeting had come straight out of the blue. Cliff had no idea why he had been asked, and he had left the lunch without giving it much further thought. But the very next day, to his amazement, he learned that Foreman was on a plane bound for London.

He heard through his contacts in Marbella that it hadn't been easy to get Foreman on to the plane. He had been tricked and taken by surprise. The Marbella police picked him up from his house on a pretext and Foreman went voluntarily to the police station, wearing nothing but shorts and a T-shirt. He asked for his lawyer and the police willingly obliged, but they sent the lawyer to a different police station.

It had taken Foreman a while to realize that he had been set up, but when he found out that his lawyer wasn't coming, and that he was on his way home, he put up quite a fight. When he grasped they were going to take him to the airport he didn't want to leave the room – he knew that was it, the game was up, and there would be no return. Legend has it that there are still teeth marks in a wooden doorframe that he bit into to stop himself being dragged away.

Under the procedure used by the Spanish, they didn't have to take Foreman to court, but if his solicitor had got to the station they would probably have had to. The whole operation would have foundered in the Spanish legal process.

At the airport, to the bemusement of other travellers, Foreman was bundled unceremoniously on to the plane, but he had to be well and truly sedated before it could take off. One passenger shouted at him, 'Go back to England, do your time, and leave us in peace.'

For the duration of the flight, Foreman sat in a drug-induced stupor, flanked by two rather hard-looking Spanish police officers. He was met on the tarmac by members of the Flying Squad, among them Simon Webber. The Spanish officers remained on the plane and went straight back home. Foreman was taken by high-speed squad car to Leman Street, put into custody, charged with the Security Express robbery, and committed for trial.

The surprise move by the Spanish was interpreted by the Flying Squad as a sign of the Spanish authorities' own frustration with their extradition treaty with Britain. It was a gesture of international goodwill. Besides, the Spanish were sick of being derided for harbouring every kind of drug-dealing lowlife going. The 'Costa del Crime', with its British enclave of crooks and conmen, was becoming the standing joke of Europe.

The Spanish could do little within the strict terms of the extradition treaty, but there was something they could do within their own legal system, and so that's what they did. When his British passport was found to be false, Freddie Foreman was made officially *persona non grata* – an undesirable alien.

Trying to get the men on the Costa del Sol extradited through legal channels had always met with a huge amount of frustration. The 'gift' of Foreman was a reward for the mutual trust and confidence that Cliff Craig had built up with the Spanish over the years.

£££

As far as Reed McGeorge was concerned, the case against Freddie Foreman was straightforward enough. It relied on a tried and trusted formula: a sudden increase in wealth after the robbery, together with a provable association with those already convicted or those under suspicion.

The sudden increase in Foreman's wealth was startling. On 1 April 1983, he had just £72.69 in his bank account and was living in a grim council flat, but within four months he had deposited more than £358,000 in a new bank account.

They also had evidence that he had bought three luxury apartments, in the name of a Panamanian company called Ultramarine Ventures Inc., in the La Alcazaba complex in Marbella.

His association with other suspects – particularly Ronnie Everett and John Mason – was easy enough to prove. The enquiry had established that, on 27 May 1983, Foreman had travelled to Spain to meet John Knight, Ronnie Knight, Everett, Mason, and their respective wives. Terry Perkins had met them all two days before. And then, on 5 August, both Foreman (through Ultramarine Ventures) and Ronnie Knight bought luxury apartments in the same block of flats in Marbella.

Foreman could also be connected to John Mason through the scrap of paper taken from Mason when he was arrested. Although the scrap had revealed only part of an address, George Moncrieff had spotted another reference to it when he examined Mason's Spanish deposit box. The enquiry had found that the house was the home of one of Foreman's associates, Joseph McLean. Foreman/Newbury's house in Allentown, Pennsylvania, was not a million miles from 3614 Nicholson Road, Bethlehem.

A month after the robbery, Foreman, Mason, and Everett had all opened accounts with the Allied Irish Bank. The three men had all told the same story to the manager – that the large cash deposits they subsequently made had come from the sale of their vending-machine businesses.

Reed tracked down the details of Foreman's bank accounts at Barclays in Borough and at the Allied Irish Bank in Lewisham. Foreman's accounts at Barclays seemed to paint a picture of a relatively unsuccessful businessman struggling to keep his family. Indeed, around the time of the robbery, several of Foreman's cheques had bounced.

However, the account at the Allied Irish Bank in Lewisham, which Foreman had opened a month after the robbery, told a different tale. John McCann, a manager there, remembered that Foreman had told him that he was flogging off his vending-machine business. Foreman would call him just before his arrival at the bank. He would stride in carrying a suitcase and would be ushered into a small side office. There, he would open up the case, revealing neat rows of cash.

McCann said that on 12 July 1983 Freddie's son Jamie had also come to the bank, with £50,000 in cash. He had asked the manager to forward the money to his father's account in Marbella.

The following June, while the Flying Squad was poking around in Spain, Jamie had authorized the transfer of another £25,000 to his father's account in Marbella and £50,000 to another account in Alicante. The next month, a man by the name of Peter Arrowsmith turned up at the branch, along with

Danielle Foreman, and produced a letter from Freddie asking the bank to open a new account in the name of Claystar Ltd. Freddie asked the bank to transfer £15,000 to this new bank account. The bank soon discovered that their favoured customer, Freddie Foreman, was not to be a director of Claystar, so they declined to handle the account. In any event, by that stage Freddie's name had already been linked to the Security Express robbery by the media.

Armed with this information from the bank manager, the Flying Squad made a few inquiries at Companies House and found out that Claystar had been set up in May 1984, and in July that year had begun trading as Benetton (Romford) Ltd. In August 1986, Jamie Foreman had officially become a director of Claystar, along with his girlfriend, Linda McConnikie, the manageress of the Romford fashion boutique.

It was all very intriguing. Reed had cast a wide net and some surprising names had become caught up in it – people who might later prove to be useful witnesses. However, he was reluctant to gather more information by interviewing the people directly involved with Claystar. Such interviews could well have given the police new leads, but the flipside was that Reed would have shown too much of his hand. He would have been forced to reveal his evidence against Freddie Foreman in connection with the robbery charge, which might have enabled Foreman and the other suspects still at large to fabricate evidence in relation to the outstanding warrants. The Flying Squad therefore decided not to act on the Claystar information – at least not until Freddie Foreman was safely locked away behind bars.

According to the officers looking after him, while he was on remand in Brixton, Foreman complained that he wasn't getting any respect from other prisoners because they were all young blaggers. 'Who the hell are you?' they would say. He felt he should be treated as a respected senior member of the criminal classes. He also complained that he couldn't get any sleep 'because all these lunatics were screaming all night'.

He regularly whinged at the Flying Squad officers when he

appeared at Lambeth Court for his pre-trial hearings. 'It's not a five-star hotel, Freddie,' Simon would tell him. 'It's a prison.'

£££

The trial took place in March 1990 and Foreman pleaded not guilty to robbery and handling stolen goods. The lead prosecutor was Michael Worsley, who had performed so well at the earlier trial. It was revealed that Foreman had just £72.69 in his bank account before the raid. On the day of the robbery, the local council had cut his rent from £32.96 to £7.75 a week, because of his 'financial difficulties'.

Two Spanish officers were flown over specially for the trial. One told the court that, while in Spain, Foreman had confessed to the Security Express robbery and had told him that Ronnie Knight had also taken part 'along with some other people'.

The Spanish officers were put up at a hotel for the duration of their visit. When it came to settling their bills the Flying Squad discovered to its horror that one of the Spanish officers had spent the lonely nights watching hours of pay-to-view erotic films on cable TV.

In April 1990, Freddie was cleared of robbery but was convicted of handling stolen cash, and was sentenced to nine years' imprisonment. It was another notch for the Flying Squad. But four robbery suspects still remained in Spain, living the high life, seemingly beyond the reach of the Flying Squad. Ronnie Knight particularly irritated them. For one thing, he was constantly in the news. For another, he openly taunted them. But now, after what had happened to Foreman, Ronnie's days in Spain were surely numbered.

23
ENOUGH SUN

Ronnie Knight had followed Freddie Foreman's kidnapping and trial with mounting unease. Freddie had been a pal of Ronnie's for years. They had had lots of business ventures together and had known each other since the latter days of the Krays when Freddie had his own firm south of the river.

Freddie was a good friend of Micky Regan, Ronnie's old partner in the A&R Club. Ronnie and Micky had got some pool tables going in pubs around the Angel and were making a killing with them and, when Freddie came out of prison after the business over the Jack 'The Hat' McVitie killing, they suggested that he put tables into his sites in South London. The three men met at the A&R to sort out the details. 'Give me a couple of days,' Freddie said. He had six sites straight away. He started moving the tables into them and they got some more. In all he got about twenty sites for Ronnie and Micky, mostly in minicab firms. That was where you made the money. The cab drivers had hours to kill waiting for their next job.

Ronnie would go around in his car to collect up the cash from the tables, and once he was pulled over by the police, who found a policeman's truncheon in the back of the car. Ronnie told them that he kept it to protect himself and his money. They didn't believe him, of course, and he was charged with possession of an offensive weapon.

The proceeds from the tables were split between the three of them, which is how Ronnie and Freddie's friendship developed. If there were boxing matches on, they would all get together, wives and all. It was through Ronnie and Barbara that Freddie's son Jamie had first got into acting.

One day, Ronnie was telling Jamie all about Barbara's many exploits in film and on the stage. 'I'd love to get into that,' Jamie remarked, so Ronnie promised to introduce him to Barbara.

'It's hard work, you know,' Barbara told Jamie when they met. 'But if you want to come in one day and watch us all rehearse, then you can.'

'Yeah, I'd love that.'

Jamie went along to the rehearsal, and couple of days later, Ronnie asked Barbara how it had gone. 'I bet he walked out, didn't he?' he said.

'No, he never!' she said. 'Everyone was saying, "Sodding hell, he really wants to be in the business!". He never moved. He was there all the time.' After that, there was no stopping Jamie.

Freddie and his family had been travelling backwards and forwards to Spain for years, and he knew everything and everyone in the place. Great fuss was made in Foreman's trial over the fact that both he and Ronnie owned flats in the same apartment block. Ronnie kicked himself over that. The connection between them had been a little bit too close for comfort. The flats were a new development right near the port, and Ronnie saw them as sure bets. 'Wouldn't it be nice to spend a few days of the week in Marbella?' he thought. 'For one thing, it would save having to drive home after a night on the town.' He had already bought the two apartments when he mentioned them to Freddie. The next thing Ronnie knew, Freddie had bought some too.

Ronnie thought that the way Freddie had been picked up was sheer vindictiveness on the part of the Flying Squad. The whole episode had sent shock waves through the tight ex-pat community, but soon life settled down once more to the usual round of parties, parties, and yet more parties.

Nonetheless, there was an air of paranoia about the place. Everywhere Ronnie looked he was sure he saw Flying Squad detectives in disguise, sitting in restaurants, in cars, on the beach. And if it wasn't the Flying Squad, it was the press. Freddie's kidnapping worried Ronnie enough for him to go and see his Spanish lawyer, Fernando, to make sure that he really was safe in Spain. 'It can't be done,' Fernando told him for the umpteenth time. 'You've been here for years. You've got property here and you were here well before the signing of the treaty.' That satisfied Ronnie. He knew Fernando's brother was a big-shot lawyer in Madrid, so Ronnie had faith in him.

The local Spanish police had also reassured him. 'If the Flying Squad ever come to you, just remember that they cannot come to you without us being there,' they said. 'If you want to see them then you let us know and we'll be with them, and if they are in your way then you phone us up and we'll get rid of them for you. The same goes for the press.'

By then, Ronnie and Sue had developed their own highly effective way of getting rid of the press. Sue would turn the garden hose on them and give them a thorough drenching.

£££

One day, in October 1990, Ronnie had a surprising call from his lawyer in London.

'Someone wants to see you,' he said. 'A policeman named Peter Wilton. He say's he's retired now.'

Ronnie didn't have a problem with meeting Peter, but his lawyer urged caution. 'Watch what you say,' he said. 'I'm sure he's working for the *News of the World*.'

They arranged to meet in a few days' time by the bus station in Fuengirola.

£££

For Peter, the meeting was the chance to draw a line under some unfinished business. Although he had officially moved on from the Security Express enquiry in 1985, he had never ever lost his interest, or his influence for that matter, in the case. How could he? How could anyone?

In May 1988, he had sent Knight an invitation to his wedding to Paula, who he had met through a friend at the rugby club. Peter scrawled on the back of it, 'My boys came to your wedding – can you come to mine?' He told the newspapers that he had reserved a pew for Ronnie and Sue at the ceremony, held in the aptly named Church of the Holy Innocents in Loughton, Essex. The rowdy reception was held at the

Metropolitan Police Sports Club in Chigwell and Ronnie was invited to that too. The newspapers lapped up the tale. Ronnie was quoted as saying, 'It's very nice of him, but Sue and I are fully booked for the day.'

Peter made a more serious attempt to persuade Ronnie to come home the following year, in February 1989. He had been in touch with a freelance journalist called David Bromfield who worked for the *News of the World.* and who had had several meetings with Ronnie. He told Peter that Ronnie wanted to meet the officers in charge of the case to discuss whether they had a case against him and also to seek assurances that he would not be 'stitched up', as he put it.

Peter had sent a memo to his chief superintendent recommending that the case against the Security Express suspects, particularly Knight, who was by now regarded as a folk hero by the media, should be concluded as quickly as possible. He was worried that over time the case would be weakened through a loss of witnesses. He urged his bosses to send officers to Spain to get Ronnie home. 'I feel as time progresses, the case could cause some embarrassment to the Metropolitan Police,' he stated. He went on to say that Bromfield had offered to help the police persuade Ronnie to come home, and assured his superiors that it would not be a 'newspaper trial'.

Despite all the good words, nothing came of it. Ronnie stayed resolutely in Spain and the great scoop of the day – Ronnie's return – remained a tabloid wet dream.

A few months later, in June 1989, Peter received a tip-off that Ronnie had sneaked into the country and was going to be at Royal Ascot, so he and half a dozen other officers all dressed up in top hats and tails to go to the races. Backs to the course, they relentlessly searched the crowds through powerful binoculars. Suddenly, one of the officers shouted and pointed towards the hospitality box.

'There's Ronnie!' he said. The rest of them followed his line of sight.

It was the diminutive comedian Ronnie Corbett.

£££

The bus station in Fuengirola stood in the centre of a small, bustling square, paved with pink and white flagstones. The chequerboard square was surrounded on three sides by open-air cafés, bars, and restaurants. Ever cautious, Ronnie and Sue arrived in the square well before Peter and Paula were due to meet them. Ronnie had a good look around to make sure there was no set-up.

'I won't recognize him. Will he recognize me?' he said to Sue, as he searched the café tables for signs of photographers.

'Not much he won't!' she replied. 'He's been after you for bloody years.'

He looked across the road and saw Peter and Paula standing by the bus station. 'Ronnie!' Peter waved him over.

Ronnie grinned and waved back. 'No, you come over here!'

Peter and Paula walked over to join them. 'Let's go and have a coffee over there,' Peter said, pointing to a nearby bar. But Ronnie was having none of that. He was still suspicious of Peter's motives for coming to see him. 'No. Get in the car and we'll go to a quiet little place I know.'

He drove to a small café, run by two brothers, which overlooked the beach. There, he could spot any members of the press instantly. 'Jerry, I want a nice table on the front there.'

They sat there drinking tea, looking out across the road towards the sea, Ronnie squinting in the sun, constantly scouring the beach for signs of photographers and the flash of camera lenses. The four of them stayed in the café talking for over an hour. It was mostly polite conversation. Both were careful to avoid anything too contentious, picking their way through subjects carefully.

The conversation wound its way around to the recent court ruling in Madrid, which had prevented the extradition proceedings from continuing against Ronnie.

They joked about some of the many things Peter had done during his seven years in hot pursuit of Ronnie. They talked about the time when Flying Squad men had mingled unobtrusively with the guests arriving at Ronnie's wedding to Sue. 'Did you know?' Peter asked.

'Of course we did!' said Ronnie. 'You all stuck out like sore thumbs.'

But amid the mostly harmless banter, Peter had to ask that one burning question. 'So, Ronnie. Haven't you had enough of being here? When are you coming home?'

'Soon,' Ronnie said. 'Soon.' He gave Peter a wan smile which said nothing and everything.

'You know, the law won't always be in your favour,' added Peter. 'It will change after 1992, when the Schengen agreement between all the European Union countries comes into play. Cooperation will be better. Extradition will be a lot easier then.'

'My lawyer says there's no danger,' Ronnie replied nonchalantly.

Just before leaving Peter asked him for one small favour. 'Can I have a picture of you and my young lady?'

'No,' said Ronnie. 'When I come over you can have one.'

Ronnie knew the value the press would place on that picture. For one thing, it would prove the meeting and validate any story Peter cared to sell.

It was a poignant meeting. After all those years of hard graft Peter had finally got to meet his adversary face to face. In a way it was a personal signing-off. It was an acknowledgement of defeat, and, in one sense, respect, because the man sitting here in front of him had thus far eluded the Dirty Dozen.

For Ronnie, seeing Peter sitting there sparked a newfound sense of reality. Sooner or later he knew he would have to go back home to face the music. But not yet.

The sun beat down. They clinked their glasses together for the last time, and watched the relentless lapping of the waves on the sandy beach.

As he drove back up the hill towards the villa, Ronnie pondered over the bizarre meeting. Here was the man who had helped to jail two of his brothers and who had spent the best part of seven years trying to snare him. Yet there they had been, sitting in the sunshine, chatting away as if it had all been just a big game. It's a strange thing, human nature.

He knew that the meeting would, one way or another, end

up in the British papers. Sure enough, it did. 'Costa Ronnie's Cuppa with Top Yard Tec' was the headline.

£££

When Peter got back home from his holiday, he found the time for a little bedtime reading in the shape of Ronnie Knight's autobiography, *Black Knight*, which had just been published. The book had been written with the help of Barrie Tracey, who, Peter knew, had been the source of many of the stories about Ronnie that had appeared in the tabloid press. Of all people, Tracey would be in a position to know what was going through Ronnie's mind, thought Peter.

He went through all 217 pages of the book, searching for clues and hints that might help the Squad with its enquiries.

Much of the book was about Ronnie's life with Barbara Windsor, but there were a few chapters that especially caught Peter's eye, because in them, Ronnie had more or less set out the defences he might use to any accusation that he had been involved in the Security Express robbery. He explained not only his connections with other suspects but also how he had come to have made so much cash.

In Chapter 11, for example, Ronnie revealed his involvement with French Lou and the 'dirties', and one paragraph in particular caught Peter's eye:

> So we sold everything. It all added up to a tidy sum, I don't mind admitting. Not the millions some people might think, but enough for me not to worry about paying the mortgage for the rest of my life. And my little nest egg was not the ill-gotten gains of bank robberies and other villainies, either.

Ronnie went on to relate how he had given the £80,000 cash proceeds from the sale of his one-third stake in the game to his accountant to look after:

> When I deposited the sizeable cash on my moneyman's desk he nearly had a fit. His embarrassment was that he had to pay the notes into the bank. 'I'll have to think up some explanation for having so many readies,' he mused.

'After all, I can hardly put it down as "profits from the porn business".'

'So,' thought Peter, 'that was how Ronnie would very likely try to explain away his cash pile.' Peter already knew who the 'moneyman' was. Albert Fox's name had already surfaced in John Knight's trial because John's defence had claimed that cash passing through Fox had come from Ronnie's purchase of John's share of their villa, El Limonar, and not the Security Express robbery.

In Chapter 15, Ronnie explained his close relationship with Clifford Saxe and Freddie Foreman by saying that he had known them from his youth. He told how he had been getting between £1,500 and £2,000 a week from his pool-table business with Foreman.

> I am the first to admit that for Ronnie Knight the picture looks rather black. The circumstantial evidence, on the face of it, is pretty damning . . .
>
> I do not deny it all seems very suspicious indeed, veering far beyond the realms of coincidence, even though I first discovered the Costa long before anybody had heard of multimillion-pound security raids. I do not deny that I did a bit of business with one or two of them. But never business of your criminal kind.

In Chapter 20, Ronnie threw down the gauntlet. He stated:

> The question has been thrust at me a thousand times. 'If you are innocent why the hell don't you go back home and clear your name?' Let me say this loud and clear so there is absolutely no doubt. I know I am innocent. I had nothing to do with that Security Express robbery.
>
> My firm belief is that the police do not have enough evidence to bring a charge against me. But for some perverse reason they seem to get a kick out of the cat-and-mouse game they play with me. I concede that you can never be sure of anything in this life. Maybe the Old Bill do feel that they have a case. Perchance they have been wound up by some aspiring Supergrass telling a pack of porky pies . . .

Then, towards the end of the book, he set out his own terms for coming back to England:

> This is what I am prepared to do once and for all to end the highly publicized conviction that I am guilty. I will return to Britain if I am given an absolute guarantee that I will be allowed bail pending any hearing or trial. I want a written understanding that I will not be locked away and left to stew for months while the police 'continue with their enquiries'. They have already had seven years to prepare any prosecution against me. If that is not time enough to sort things out at their end, then what do you think?

'Fat chance,' thought Peter as he closed the book. There was no way Ronnie would be given bail. A few weeks later he had one of his regular meetings with some of the officers still on the enquiry. They discussed the book.

In setting out his defence, Ronnie had given away a lot, perhaps more than he had realized. The Flying Squad now knew what they had to do to demolish his defence. All they had to do was to prove that the money could not have all come from the 'dirties'. That, in essence, was what Reed McGeorge set out to do.

The Spanish government had not made Reed's task easy, but the real source of frustration was the Spanish police. Pleasant though they were to the British officers still on the enquiry, they appeared slow, dogmatic, and ill equipped to deal with this kind of investigation. Because of this, relations with the Spanish police were somewhat strained at times.

One day Simon Webber and Detective Sergeant Neil Wraith had to go from Marbella, where they were based, to Malaga, to take a five-line statement from a Spanish police officer. It was maybe a thirty-minute drive eastwards along the coast, followed by a ten-minute chat with the policeman, and then five minutes to take the statement. They went for a beer with the Spanish and drove back to Marbella.

Simon then wanted to take a five-minute drive to the marina at Puerto Banus, just to the west of Marbella. He wanted to get a copy of the harbour master's log detailing the movement of the yacht *Sherama* in June 1984. But the Spanish police told him, 'We've done enough today.'

They dropped Neil off, who was feeling unwell, and then Simon gave the Spanish officers a bit of a hard time about their short working day. The following day, one of the Spanish officers went sick, and Simon interpreted it as a kind of protest statement. It was like saying, 'You've overworked us.'

The new police station in Marbella was unfinished and about five years behind schedule. To Simon, the old police station at the back of the old town was like something you would see in spaghetti westerns. It was a ramshackle building and he half expected to see chickens flying out of its first-floor windows.

The boss used to come into the station at about 10 o'clock in the morning. It was a struggle for him to get up the stairs. He used to sit at his desk, light a 'la-di-da', and examine the solitary piece of paper in his in tray for a while. Then he would walk back down the stairs, go into the café next door and get a large brandy and a coffee, and stand there playing the fruit machines. After that he would go home for his siesta. Sometimes he would reappear at teatime and do another two minutes' work.

The equipment the Spanish had to work with was abysmal, as were the wages they were on. The two British officers always got the impression that the Spanish were resentful because they were aware of the kind of money their British counterparts got. They tried to be as friendly as possible. They would say to the Spanish, 'Bring your wife, we'll buy you a meal,' but they just didn't want to know.

Simon and Neil were initially given ten working days to complete their enquiries in Spain, but they ended up doing over five weeks out there. After about two and a half weeks, the officers started getting a bit of stick from their bosses on the fourth floor back in London. 'Come on guys, it's not a holiday. Haven't you had enough sun?' the bosses would say.

Personally, too, Simon was exasperated with the speed at which the Spanish worked. One night they finally managed to persuade a couple of the Spanish officers to come out for a drink with them. Simon took the chance to explain to them that they were getting hassle from above, and that they had to crack on faster.

The conversation came to a head. 'Why can't you pull your finger out?' he said to one of the officers, jabbing his finger towards him. He made the mistake of touching the officer, a big no-no.

The Spanish officer didn't say a word. He moved his jacket back to reveal a standard-issue police revolver stuck in his belt. He gave Simon a steely look.

'Ah,' said Simon, looking at the gun. 'OK. Let's do it your way. Another beer?'

The next day, the Spanish police complained to their boss at the station, who then rang Cliff Craig in Madrid. 'If your blokes can't behave, we can stick them on a plane home,' Cliff was told. Cliff then rang the fourth floor. 'What the hell's going on?' he asked. 'Are you putting the guys under pressure? Because if you are, this is the result. If they're not careful the police down there will just get the Spanish government to stick them on a plane back home.'

Shortly after, the British officers got a frantic call from the fourth floor telling them to take their time. Simon rang them back. 'Fine,' he said. 'Send us more money.'

They soon discovered that the more they agitated, the slower the Spanish police got. After all, there was little in it for them. The Spanish felt they were just doing the Flying Squad's work. From their point of view, these people that the British authorities so desperately wanted were bringing money into the region and that meant jobs for the locals. They saw themselves as simply doing the British a favour. So in the end the British police officers had little choice but to resign themselves to days sunbathing by the hotel pool, waiting. And waiting.

Simon came away from there with the firm belief that they needed an English-manned police station on the Costa. Simple things like checking out a British-registered vehicle were an administrative nightmare for the Spanish. A simple enquiry like that could take them three or four weeks. The Spanish officers would often come to the Flying Squad and they would make a phone call and get the answer for them in minutes.

£££

By the end of 1993, Ronnie Knight had had enough of living on the Costa del Sol. He was fifty-eight years old and things were not quite as fun as they used to be. There were writs from lawyers acting for Security Express's insurance companies flying all over the place, and it had got to the point where he wouldn't answer the villa door. The agents would simply leave the crisp parchment envelopes lying on the step.

The constant media attention never let up, and he was sick of the sight of unmarked cars with smirking Flying Squad detectives in them waiting at the bottom of the hill. Reporters turned up at the house posing as Flying Squad officers – and vice versa.

He had had a few problems at Wyn's Bar, too. One fight at the bar had particularly caught the tabloid imagination. Ronnie said that he had intervened to break up a fight between two men over a woman, but, for his trouble, had a glass ashtray slung in his face. He had to go and have some stitches put in.

The British red tops turned that into 'gangster wars'. They claimed that Ronnie had been 'bashed senseless' and that he had 'needed blood transfusions and a brain scan', no less. They claimed that the man who attacked Ronnie had a serious grudge, and a Spanish detective was quoted as saying, 'We'd like to talk to this man before Ronnie Knight's friends get their hands on him.'

It was fairly typical of the wild and woolly write-ups Ronnie had had over the years. Every little incident in his everyday life had been squeezed and moulded to fit the stereotype of a gangster on the run. He was growing tired of it.

There were repeated press claims that he and Sue had secretly flown into the UK to get fertility treatment at Harley Street, allegedly flying by private plane to a small aerodrome near London.

Then there were the madcap threats of kidnappings. One

scheme particularly amused him. A team of Welsh rugby players had driven down to Spain in a van, staying in an apartment in town. They hatched a plan to abseil down the mountain behind his villa, bundle him into the van, drive to the beach, and put him in a waiting dinghy. The next port of call would be Gibraltar where, they thought, they could claim a £60,000 reward put up by Security Express. Unfortunately, the lads got a little rowdy in the town one night and had their van towed away by the local police. That put paid to that. Apparently a Welsh member of the Flying Squad had orchestrated the plot and the rugby team were going to get a backhander for their troubles.

Joking aside, Freddie Foreman's kidnapping and trial had shown Ronnie that he really wasn't as invulnerable as he liked to think. They had bent all the rules to get Freddie home.

The previous year, Ronnie himself had had a close shave. He and Sue had both been arrested by the Spanish police and thrown in jail for the night, and the next day they were in court to be deported as 'illegal aliens'. However, without any real explanation, the hearing was abandoned in the afternoon. The police chief put it down to a misunderstanding. They were released and returned to the villa to find the rat pack waiting for them. 'Been let out to pack for the home trip then, Ronnie?' one of the reporters shouted. Ronnie sent him flying.

That year, in July, Ronnie's British passport expired. He sent it to the British consulate to get it renewed, but the consulate wouldn't send it back to him, so he had to go with his solicitor to the town hall in Fuengirola where even the Spanish officials thought he had been given a raw deal. 'We don't agree with this,' they said. 'Everyone should have a passport. We wouldn't do it to our citizens.' They gave Ronnie a slip of paper. 'If you do get stopped by the Spanish police just show them this and you'll be all right,' they said. Nevertheless, Ronnie felt trapped.

Above all else, things were not like they were between him and his wife Sue. They hadn't been for a couple of years. It was always a tempestuous relationship, but they were arguing more and more. She loved all the parties, the drinking, and the social scene, but Ronnie was getting tired of it. He wanted a nice, quiet, peaceful life, with just him and Sue.

He had set her up with a nightclub that stayed open until five in the morning. It was called, naturally enough, Knights. Now and then Ronnie had to put in an appearance, as it was him that the punters wanted to see. When the club closed Sue would often go out partying with her friends, many of whom also worked in the club. She was seventeen years his junior. That was the lifestyle she enjoyed, but Ronnie, of course, had been there, done that, many years before. So there came a time when she didn't mind if he wasn't there. And he didn't mind if she stayed out.

In addition, his dear old mother was ill in a nursing home, and showing no signs of getting better. He badly wanted to see her before it was too late.

In short, he wasn't happy.

The suggestion first came from Barbara. They were back on speaking terms and she had tried to make amends for some of the things she had said to the newspapers about him. He, for one, appreciated having someone he was able to talk to, a confidante.

One day in February 1994 she called him up and told him that a journalist friend of hers wanted to come over to see him. 'He has a very interesting proposition,' she said. 'He's all right. Talk to him.' She knew that Ronnie had tried to sell his story to the *Sunday Times* for £80,000 and the deal had fallen through. She had mentioned it to a journalist by the name of Robin McGibbon who worked for the *News of the World*. McGibbon thought he could get a better deal for Ronnie, and called Ronnie up within a few minutes of Barbara putting the phone down. Ronnie was up for it. So the next morning McGibbon went in to News International's bunker in Wapping to speak to his editor Piers Morgan and his deputy Phil Hall. They agreed £150,000 for the exclusive story and packed McGibbon off to Spain.

McGibbon turned up at Ronnie's villa with his wife. The deal that he wanted to broker astounded Ronnie. If he was prepared to fly back home, give himself up to the police, with the *News of the World* exclusively in tow, they would pay him £150,000. McGibbon had the contract with him in his briefcase, ready to be signed.

Ronnie wanted another £30,000 for Sue's side of the story. McGibbon called the *News of the World*, which agreed, and rewrote the contract. The next day, McGibbon turned up at the villa, this time fully expecting Ronnie to sign on the dotted line.

'What about expenses?' said Ronnie.

'Expenses?'

'You know. My legal costs.'

'No newspaper will pay those, Ron,' said McGibbon.

'Well, you can forget it then.'

And with that, the deal lapsed.

What McGibbon didn't know at the time was that Ronnie had turned to Barrie Tracey, the journalist who had helped him write his book *Black Knight*, for advice. Barrie had told him that he would handle the negotiations directly with the *News of the World*, so Ronnie had deliberately stalled McGibbon for time.

A few days later Barrie came back and told Ronnie that another, alternative deal was on the table. He had checked out the legal position. After a few weeks, Barrie said that the *News of the World* was having second thoughts. In fact, the *News of the World* had got cold feet after it learned from police sources that its plan to take Ronnie around London to be photographed, before handing him over to police, might have resulted in its reporters being charged with conspiracy to pervert the course of justice. But by that time Barrie had firmed up the alternative offer. The money wasn't as good, but he told Ronnie that there might be a film in it.

'OK, I'll do it,' Ronnie said.

Ronnie did the deal. £45,000 was the price for the exclusive, and it went to the *Sun* and Sky TV. The precise timing of when he was to go home was all down to Ronnie. For Barry, it was the climax of a string of scoops on Knight over the years.

Ronnie remained in two minds for some weeks about going home. Some days he would look out across the azure-blue sea sparkling in the sun and say to himself that he couldn't possible leave it. But other days, he felt he had had enough of it all. Then one day, it suddenly became clear to him. His mind was made up. He called Barrie Tracey. 'I want to go now,' he said.

'Are you sure? You're not going to change your mind this time?'

'Yes. I'm sure this time.'

'OK. We'll get the plane organized.'

Ronnie put the phone down and started packing his bags. He went out to dinner with Sue.

'Sue, I'm going back.'

She was expecting it.

At 7.30 a.m. the next day Ronnie was woken up by a phone call from Barrie. 'Ronnie. You'd better get ready.'

'What do you mean?'

'The press have got to hear about you coming home,' he said. 'Get ready. We've got to go. We're coming to pick you up.'

Sue had already gone out shopping, so Ronnie left her a note. It said: 'Sorry. Had to go. Couldn't wait.'

Barrie arrived soon after eight and he drove Ronnie to the *Sun*'s hideaway hotel. Sue joined them there later that day. The journalists had told the hotel management to tell all callers that no journalists were there from the *Sun*.

He spent three days with the *Sun*'s people, who intended to make the most of their scoop. Pictures were taken of Ronnie holding bags, staring wistfully out to sea, and of him and Sue dangling their feet in the hotel's swimming pool.

The journalists were jumpy and worried that Ronnie would change his mind at the last minute. He was constantly watched. At one point he and Sue hopped over a fence into a field to have a talk by themselves. Suddenly, a dozen figures jumped out of the bushes at them. 'Where do you think you're going?' they said.

On the third day Ronnie was taken to a small, secluded airfield, where a Lear Jet stood waiting to take him to Luton. There, on the tarmac, surrounded by the men from the *Sun*, he said his goodbyes to Sue. There were a few tears but he wasn't too worried. He thought he would be back before too long. But as he looked out of the window of the plane at the tiny figures of Sue and Barrie's wife Pat, standing together, waving up at him, he felt the butterflies go in his stomach. He wondered if he was really doing the right thing. Still, it was too late now. He'd done it. He was on his way home after ten years in exile.

On the plane they passed him a bottle of champagne, 'Like some champagne, Ron?' they said. He fell for the oldest ruse in the book, and put the bottle up to his lips. The snappers went crazy. It was an image that was going to stick in the minds of the general public. There was Ronnie Knight, living the high life, even on the plane home, glugging champagne straight from the bottle.

During the flight, he thought about what he was going to say. It had all been worked out beforehand with the *Sun*. It was to be maximum publicity. He was going to be driven by the newspapermen from Luton to Holborn police station. Once there, he would walk in and casually say, 'I believe you have been looking for me?' A great line for the newspaper. He smiled to himself at that. Possibly a night in the cells . . . a quick hearing . . . arrangement of bail . . . and then on to see his mother. 'It will all work out fine,' he told himself as he looked out over the English Channel, sparkling in the sun. He couldn't have been more wrong.

24
RONNIE'S RETURN

'Goodbye to this' ran the *Sun*'s headline. A large picture of Ronnie and Sue together, sitting on the edge of a swimming pool, their toes dangling in the water, dominated the splash in the centre of the paper. 'Ronnie talks it over with Sue,' read the caption. Inset was another picture of Ronnie, posing in front of a scrub-covered valley leading down to the azure sea. He was holding his packed bags in his hands. 'Saying a last goodbye.'

'Cockney Ronnie Knight took a lingering look at the spectacular view from his Costa villa – then headed eagerly for a plate of pie and mash back in Britain.'

Peter carefully scrutinized the story. The splash had given Ronnie the chance to air his defence, something that did not go unnoticed back at the Flying Squad. He had told the *Sun* that the villa had been bought in 1976 when he was still married to Barbara Windsor, and insisted that it had been used as a holiday home before he was linked to the Security Express robbery.

Ronnie continued: 'I was in London for months after the Security Express robbery. I was never once questioned by the police. The way I see it, the police have had plenty of time to work things out. Over the past few years, there have been several cases of them fitting people up. But they have had ten years to bring any charges against me and I'm confident they have nothing.'

'Fitted up.' Peter shook his head in disbelief as he folded up the paper.

Although he had by now been retired for some five years, Peter couldn't get the Security Express case out of his mind. In part, it remained unsolved. He regarded it as a mission still to be completed. He kept in regular contact with Reed McGeorge, who was now in charge of the case. Reed had warned Peter that Ronnie was coming home soon, but he had kept the exact date close to his chest.

He called Reed at the station. 'How did it go?'

£££

Ronnie's plane had touched down at Luton airport a little after 4 p.m. but, instead of being spirited away to Holborn police station in the *Sun* newspaper's waiting limousine, he had been met by Reed McGeorge and Julia Pearce. They boarded the jet as soon as it had come to rest on the tarmac, and slowly made their way up the cramped aisle. They nearly arrested the wrong man.

'Ronnie Knight, we're arresting you on suspicion of—'

'No, he's over there,' said the newspaperman, gesturing towards the back of the plane.

Ronnie, clutching his bag, was led out along the aisle and down the steps of the plane. He was escorted through Customs and Excise in handcuffs.

'Anything to declare?' said the customs officer.

'Only my innocence,' said Ronnie, grinning from ear to ear. 'And twelve pairs of shoes.'

The two police officers looked on with bemusement as Ronnie opened his travel bag to reveal the pairs of shoes. That was all he had brought with him.

He was unceremoniously bundled into a waiting squad car and taken to Leman Street station for questioning. It didn't take long before it dawned on Ronnie that it wasn't going to be the song and dance that he had expected. It was all going horribly wrong.

'That's your lot, Ronnie,' taunted the officers. 'You're here. We've gotcha now.'

£££

Meanwhile, the *Sun* intended to eke out its exclusive for as long as its readers could stomach it. That could be for some time.

Ronnie was after all, Britain's most wanted man. He had become larger than life, a scapegoat for all that was wrong with the extradition laws. To be sure, there were much nastier crooks on the Costa del Sol, but Ronnie was the most newsworthy. He was the one that had once had the show-biz wife. The public could relate to that. And they lapped it up.

The day after the *Sun* trumpeted Ronnie's arrival home, it was Barbara's turn to join in the melee. As soon as the paper knew that Ronnie was safely on his way home, it had sent a reporter round to Barbara's to whisk her away to a hotel, out of the way of the rest of the pack. Safely ensconced in the hotel, Barbara opened her heart – and her photo album – to the *Sun*'s compassionate and understanding hacks. The resultant spread formed part of the second instalment of the continuing Ronnie Knight saga.

£££

Within days of arriving back in the UK, things began to go seriously wrong for Ronnie. His plan was awry. On 3 May, at Bow Street Magistrates' Court, he was refused bail. His friends had already warned him that, even if it was granted that day, they wouldn't be able to stand bail for him because they would be deemed to be financially involved with him.

After a few days' searching, he had managed to find someone else who could stand bail. Four days later they turned up with a cheque, but each time he applied for bail the police opposed it. They claimed that a key witness, who was married with two young children, had received threatening phone calls. The family was afraid, and if Ronnie was released they would all have to be put into protective custody at great taxpayers' expense. The police also claimed that Ronnie had no idea how much evidence they had against him, and that if he did he would surely skip the country again, just as he did all those years before.

The arguments convinced the judge. Ronnie was refused bail. He appealed; twice at Bow Street, twice to the High Court, and then, once more, to the Old Bailey, but with no luck.

£££

While Ronnie was in Brixton Prison on remand, Security Express's insurers made another attempt to serve a writ on him for the robbery. One day he had a call from one of the warders to say that he had a visit.

'But I'm not expecting any visitors,' he said. 'Who is it?'

'It's an insurance man from Lloyd's.'

'Tell him I don't want to see him.'

'You've got to see him, Ron. It's the new law. You go and see him and if he says something to you, you turn around and walk away. You must go and face the man, otherwise we'll have to take you.'

'OK. But if I turn round I don't want you to tell me that I've got to sit down because I'm not going to have it.'

'OK, but you must go.'

Ronnie walked into the visitor's room. The sharply suited man got up from his chair. 'Yes, I'm from Lloyd's . . . I'd like to talk to you about—'

'No thank you!' interrupted Ronnie, and abruptly turned around and marched right out of the room.

'Come on, take me back to my cell,' he said to the warder.

Later on, the insurance man claimed that he had tried to give Ronnie the papers and Ronnie had dropped them on the floor, which would have counted as 'service' of the writ, but Ronnie got the screws to stick up for him. In the end, it went all the way up to the prison governor, who agreed with the warder that there had been no service of the writ.

Eventually, however, Ronnie had to accept the writ. Lloyd's offered him a settlement figure, and he sold his villa for £100,000 to friends to stop himself going bankrupt. It was a snip at the price.

£££

All the while, Reed McGeorge was hard at work tying up the loose ends in the Flying Squad's case against Ronnie.

To Reed's mind, Knight was the linchpin because of his association with everyone involved. He had already obtained records that suggested that Ronnie Knight was a close associate of Everett, Mason, and Foreman. In 1977, Knight had been arrested for possession of an offensive weapon, and his diary at the time contained telephone numbers for Freddie Foreman and a John O'Donnell. Reed knew that Mason had obtained a false passport in that name in June 1983. Knight had also been spotted frequenting Everett's pub.

In August 1983, Knight had bought two apartments at La Alcazaba in Marbella at the same time as Freddie Foreman and they also bought another flat in the Jardín Miraflores complex. He had also tracked down their venture into the Indian restaurant business in Fuengirola.

Reed called both Barbara Windsor and Albert Fox back into Leman Street to give more detailed statements.

Barbara's was some forty pages long. She claimed that, when £50,000 worth of jewellery was stolen from her flat in Hendon, Ronnie had tried to stop the Yard from taking fingerprints. Her suggestion was that Ronnie had done it himself, just before leaving for Spain.

Albert Fox, Barbara's accountant, also gave a statement and opened up his books. His evidence was mainly records of transactions made by Ronnie.

The Crown planned to say that within ten months of the Security Express robbery Ronnie had deposited nearly £300,000 in cash. They claimed that no legitimate source for these funds had ever been found and, according to their tried and tested formula, £300,000 was likely to be a robber's share.

Ronnie's alibi for the night of the robbery was that he was at Barbara's flat in Hendon. It was something she should have remembered but was unable to in the statements she had made to the police.

Nevertheless, Ronnie planned to produce a witness, the caretaker of the flats. Ronnie told his lawyers how he was always promising to give the caretaker clothing that he never wore. He recounted how that evening, the day of the robbery, shortly before midnight, he had walked in and taken the coat off his back and handed it to the caretaker who, according to Ronnie, was well pleased.

His legal team couldn't find the caretaker. His other witness, a former housekeeper and chauffeur, was too frail to give evidence in court.

Ronnie's legal team had also banked on the fact that it would be very difficult to get a jury sworn in, because of the amount of publicity Ronnie had received over the years, and pointed to the well-publicized witch-hunt embarked upon by the police over the previous few years. It was a compelling argument for any judge. How could a man who had been in and out of the news so much expect to receive a fair trial?

One day in October Ronnie was sitting in his cell reading the *Sun* when he suddenly found himself staring at a picture of himself, sitting in his cell. From the picture it looked like Ronnie had just had his shower. It had to have been taken by a warder. It was all supposed to be *sub judice*, but he didn't give it much thought at the time. An hour or so later he was called in to see the prison governor, who fully understood the legal significance. He asked Ronnie how it had happened.

'How the fucking hell do I know?' Ronnie said. 'Hundreds of people come to talk to me in that cell. I never saw no flashguns.'

'Listen, Ronnie, they can be in a buttonhole. They are little, weeny things now, these cameras.'

His legal brief, Richard Ferguson, came up to see him later that day. 'There's no way that the judge will let this go, Ron,' said Ferguson. 'He'll want three days to consider his judgment and he'll say he can't allow this. It could have grave implications, Ron. It's the first time ever that a prisoner has been photographed in his cell and the picture sold to a national newspaper.' Ferguson fixed a questioning gaze on Ron. 'Did you?'

'No!'

'Well, I'll write a formal letter to the governor asking for an investigation. We'll just have to wait and see what it turns up,' he said.

About a week later, Ron was visited by a friend who told him the good news that they had found out who had taken the picture. A prison warder had smuggled a camera in, taken the picture, and then sold it through an intermediary to the *Sun*. That sounded reasonable to Ron. The bad news was that the warder was prepared to go on oath and say that Ron had paid him to do it.

It remained a mystery who took the picture or how it had got in the hands of the *Sun*, but one thing was for sure: it didn't do Ronnie any favours. Ronnie's lawyers had planned to argue that he could never get a fair trial as a result of all the articles over the years, most of which assumed a degree of guilt.

'There's not a judge in the land that would try you,' Ronnie had been assured by his legal team, which had gone to great lengths collecting all the newspaper cuttings and television footage of Ronnie over the years. From Ronnie's point of view the more publicity the better, but he couldn't get any more than he was already getting anyway.

That argument might have worked – until, that is, the jail photograph turned up, which allowed the prosecution to argue that Ronnie had actively courted publicity, even, so it seemed, while on remand awaiting trial. That would have been enough to convince the judge to ignore any argument about 'unfair' publicity, and allow the trial to go ahead. It was a major blow for Ronnie, who had been certain that he would not have to stand trial.

That photo had destroyed his legal argument. 'They knew that,' he told his friends. 'They fucking knew that and that's why they done it. They were going to say, "You planned that photo to be taken, so its your own publicity, and now you're fighting against it." How did they know it was going to be my defence?' Ronnie claimed it was a 'fit-up' but the police response was, 'Well, he would say that, wouldn't he?'

Ronnie had been told by his friend that the warder had a job on the side at the Hammersmith Palais, and Ronnie also found out later that the man had been caught red-handed by the Drugs Squad selling Ecstasy tablets. 'Well, that's it then, he's done a deal with the police,' he had exclaimed.

Regardless of what really happened, the practical result was that it looked as though Ronnie had deliberately broken the rule of no publicity before trial in order to stop a jury being sworn in. That was perverting the course of justice and carried a hefty sentence.

It got worse. His lawyers had talked to the prosecution and they had said that if Ronnie pleaded guilty to handling the Crown would accept this, although the robbery charge would still stand, but they would drop the charge of perverting the course of justice. It was a tough call, but Ronnie decided to plead guilty to handling. For that, his legal team thought he would probably get a five. He had, by that time, done ten months on remand, so he thought he may as well just do the time. In January 1995 Judge Gerald Gordon gave him seven years, which really shocked Ronnie – he had no idea why the judge had given him so long.

The police had told the court that they had not recovered a single penny of Ronnie's estimated £314,813 share, which he used to buy properties and finance his lifestyle in Spain. Ronnie, who appeared on legal aid, said that he had spent it all.

Judge Gerald Gordon said, 'Clearly, I don't know what your precise role was but I do know that professional robbers are not going to hand over the sort of money you got – a similar sum to the actual robbers – unless that person is very deeply involved. You benefited by an enormous amount and not one penny has been recovered.' He gave him some credit for returning voluntarily and for entering a guilty plea, and declined to make a compensation order as he said that there was not enough evidence to show that Ronnie had the means to pay one. 'Security Express is free to take civil action,' he added.

The prison authorities never investigated the taking of the jail photograph, which was illegal, and to this day Ronnie will claim that the police had something to do with taking it, though that, of course, is vehemently denied. His return to England had been a disastrous error of judgement all round.

As for the money he was paid by the *Sun*, a quarter went on lawyers' and accountants' fees, and the rest was paid to Sue. The newspaper's lawyers blocked the separate deal with Sue, because, they argued, she had 'volunteered' the story. They claimed it was therefore no longer exclusive.

£££

Ronnie started his sentence at Parkhurst, where he ran into many of his old mates that he hadn't seen for many years. Then he was sent to Littlehey in Cambridgeshire, which he wouldn't recommend a dog going to. He hadn't realized that the place was full of paedophiles. 'One of these people could be walking around the grounds with you chattering away and you'd never know it,' he told John afterwards. On top of that Ronnie and the governor didn't rub along together too well. Ronnie never said a word to her but he thought she seemed to have it in for him. Ronnie wanted an easy job in the prison garden but the governor insisted that he work in the shop for three months. He tried to get another nice job with a hotplate – catering – so she put him in with the bricklayers. Things came to a head after he got nicked for having too many telephone cards in his cell. The prison rules said you were only allowed ten. Ronnie had twenty. He was up before the governor but the warder who claimed to have found the cards never showed up. Ronnie had a row with her about it, so she confined him to his cell and he was moved on soon afterwards.

From Littlehey he went to Bedford, then on to Blundeston, and then to Send Open Prison, and it was while he was in Send he found that he needed a hip operation. He had the operation in a hospital in Surrey, staying there for twelve days. The nurses there treated him like royalty. It was wonderful.

Shortly after, Send Open Prison was turned into a women's lifers' prison and everyone had to move. Because he was still recovering from the hip operation, Ronnie had to go to a prison with a hospital wing, and the only one they could offer was a category A prison called Highdown. The hospital wing was a real shock to him – it housed mental patients, and he couldn't wait to get out of it. He wasn't able to sit in normal chairs and had to bring a special chair from the hospital into his cell. Because of that he couldn't go to the visitors' hall. He spoke to the governor, who, for the first time ever, allowed visitors into a hospital-wing cell. Eventually, Ronnie was moved out to Springhill in Hertfordshire, close to his family and there he would get the occasional Saturday home.

£££

Ronnie didn't have much trouble in prison, although he did get into a bit of hot water in the television room sometimes. The younger inmates would fart and not bother about it, and the older cons found that disgusting when they were all sitting there, ready to watch a good film.

'Why don't you go outside and do it, pal?' said Ronnie to one particularly unpleasant youngster. 'No one's laughing at you, you filthy bastard.'

And then there was the time when he was queuing to use the phone. He'd been there for ages, waiting to make a call, and finally he was about to pick up the receiver when someone came out of the television room and snatched it out of his hands.

'It's my turn.'

'But you've just come out of the TV room, mate.'

'Didn't the man in front of you tell you that I was next?'

'No, he never, and you ain't fucking next,' said Ronnie, and carried on dialling.

The man tried to grab the phone, but he was yelling and screaming and getting so worked up that eventually he was hit across the forehead with it. He scampered off and shouted for the screws.

'What have you done, Knight?' they said.

'I've been waiting here for the phone, that's what I've done.'

The screw quickly saw what had been going on. 'Just ignore them, Ronnie,' he said. 'It's always happening here. They're bullies.'

£££

While inside, Ronnie had time enough to think about what had happened over the years. The suspicions of insiders and informers worked both ways. Just as the police were certain that there was an 'insider' at Security Express, so Ronnie became more and more convinced that the police had an informer within, or close to, the firm.

One day, back in 1983, some time before Ronnie hopped off to Spain, he had driven up with Sue to see her relatives in Cambridgeshire. While they were there they called in to see Alec East, who had retired from the police and was running a pub called 'Six Mile Bottom' in Newmarket. All the jockeys drank there and it was supposed to be the best place to pick up racing tips.

In his day, Alec was a legendary detective. If a job broke, within a couple of hours he would know someone who knew something about it. Some thought that he sailed mighty close to the wind: perhaps he was a bit too friendly with the villains, and sometimes he would even play one villain against the other. But nevertheless he got results, and that's all that counted then.

He was forced out of the Met over an affair with a younger woman. In those days, married officers could be disciplined for having extramarital affairs. At his disciplinary hearing, he dryly asked his senior officers for a further 252 instances to be taken into consideration.

After that, Alec retired to Cambridgeshire, running his pub with the new love of his life. But he kept in touch with the likes of Ronnie, and he was still tapped for information by the Met.

The two of them soon got reminiscing about some of the old East End characters they knew, and the topic moved on to police informers.

'They've got someone close to your lot, you know,' Alec said.

'Who?'

Alec laughed. 'Ronnie! You know I can't tell you.'

'Come on, Alec,' said Ronnie. 'We won't hurt him. I promise. Just give us the name.'

'No, I can't.'

Ronnie was prepared to offer him money, but Alec wouldn't budge. He had driven home wondering who it could possibly be. A criminal. Someone *close* to him? He was puzzled by that. It remained a nagging thought in the back of his mind for years to come.

Information. That's what they relied on. They couldn't have worked out the Security Express robbery if they hadn't had the tip-offs. It was impossible to find out any other way.

Where does an informer stop being an informer and start being a criminal? Where do you draw the line? Is it just a case of the lesser of two evils? Should some be given immunity from a life of crime, in order to bring others to book?

Something to think about, that is.

EPILOGUE

It is the year 2000. A sunny September day. John Knight has a certain melancholy in his eye as he turns down the gravel drive towards High Trees, the house he once owned. We bump along the gravel track and stop just short of the entrance to the drive. John gets out and walks over to the closed, black cast-iron gates and studies the immaculately kept gardens. The house is now worth an estimated £4 million. To one side of the house a patch of scrub leads to a ploughed field, and we scramble through thorns to get a better view of the house. 'I see you're not a thief,' says John as he effortlessly slips through the brambles without a scratch, leaving me trailing behind.

Since his release from prison on licence in 1995, John has got back together with Diane, who waited for him all those years. They live together in a compact bungalow, just two bedrooms, a kitchen, bathroom, and lounge. Space is tight and, as you would expect, everything about it is neat, ordered, and in place. Outside, the patio, measuring just a few square yards, is without weeds, its hedged borders neatly trimmed.

John has worked hard to make the place look good. Naturally gifted with his hands, he has done a fine job. He proudly shows off his latest DIY handiwork, and talks about future projects: this week, new bathroom tiling; next week, new kitchen cupboards. John, as always, has grand plans.

The small lounge is filled almost to overflowing with relics and reminders of High Trees. A picture here, a chair there, the vase on the table. On the walls are photographic portraits of John and Di, elegantly posed, professionally framed in gold leaf. In the photographs they lean against antique English chairs, and behind them you can just make out the white marble fireplace, ornately carved, which the Flying Squad once threatened to break open with a hammer.

John points out the photographs with some pride. He can't hide his bitterness as he looks up at them, yet he's realistic. He accepts that he was found out, caught, and jailed for what he did. 'I paid for it dearly in every way. My whole family suffered.'

John is an anachronism. The years of prison have added lines of sadness to his face. But he still looks dapper, impeccably turned out in a dark suit and tie. His darting eyes didn't miss much then and they don't miss much now. He's from a bygone age, when gangsters played by a set of rules and kept their code of honour, however callous it may have seemed to the outsider. The rise of drugs-related crime has changed all that. That has rules of engagement that John doesn't understand.

John's code of honour still runs deep. Thus, many aspects of the Security Express robbery remain a mystery, the most enduring, perhaps, the identity of the 'mole' who provided the inside information needed to successfully carry out the raid. Sitting on his couch, John recalls the private meeting with some glee. But he won't mention any names. The meeting took place some months before the raid, in a local pub.

'I'm here to ask you a few questions about your work,' said John

'Oh. Is there something wrong, then?' said the employee.

'There's nothing wrong. But there's going to be something wrong pretty soon,' John replied.

According to John, the employee was happy to tell him all about the internal layout of the depot, the control rooms with their myriad buttons, and the cameras in the yard. Most important of all, he told John where the depot's weak spot was.

He recounted how, when the guards washed their cars, they would have to prop open the back door to stop themselves being locked out. He told John all about the daily routine to collect the milk from the hatch in the mornings. 'Once you are in that back door, the building is yours,' he told John. 'All you have got to do is be patient, and do what you've got to do.'

The man also mentioned one other Achilles heel. He told John that the guards were under strict instructions never to resist if their lives were threatened. John would later use that information to great advantage.

The one thing that the man could not tell John was where the keys to the vault were. But he could get John into the building, After that it was just a waiting game, catching the guards one by one, as they trooped in for duty. He gave John personal information on the guards, where they lived, their relationships, their emotional vulnerabilities. He told him which ones would put up a fight, and which ones would just put up their hands.

'When I leave you after our conversation I'll forget about you and everything we've discussed,' the retired employee said.

'You won't forget about me, because I'll put something in your hand,' John replied.

'I'll leave that up to you.'

John had got all the information he needed, and he triumphantly broke the news to the rest of the firm. They didn't believe him at first. They thought he was setting them up for a fall.

'Are you sure? Are you sure?' they kept asking him.

'Listen. I'm not going to tell you who's told me what, but you've got to believe me. I'm not sending you in those premises on your own. Don't worry,' he reassured them. 'I'll be coming in with you.'

'You'd fucking better be,' they chorused.

To be doubly sure, they tested out some of the information John had been given, particularly the cameras, to see if it was true.

John never did tell the rest of the firm where he'd got his information from. The mole was paid handsomely for his information for, some months after the robbery, a fat brown envelope containing £10,000 in cash was stuffed through his letterbox. To John, crime was no different from business and he believed in fair recompense for services rendered. And he prided himself on prompt payment.

£££

For Peter Wilton, the mole in Security Express always represented the final mystery. Discussion about who he or she might have been became something of a pastime for the Squad, and many theories were bandied about. Peter firmly believes that there was an insider, possibly even two. Peter remains sceptical about John's assertions that the information came from a former employee – he thinks that one of them must have been quite senior in Security Express to have known the detail.

Since his retirement, Peter has led a comfortable yet busy life, playing golf, spending time at the Metropolitan Police Sports Club, and running the bar at his local rugby club. After leaving the force he ran a restaurant for a while in Loughton, close to the police station, and many serving officers and former colleagues would drop in to say hello. One of his sons also joined the Met. All of these things have enabled Peter to keep in close contact with his former colleagues, both retired and still serving, thus allowing him to keep his fingers on the pulse of the Met.

From this, Peter knows that over the past decade the morale of the Met has been driven lower and lower. One of his great hopes is that this book will show the people of London that they had a very good police force – and that they still have a very good police force – if the officers are allowed to do their job. Today, he says, the hierarchy and prevalent political correctness don't allow the officers to be their natural selves. 'The characteristics that made you enjoy going to work, working late, get results and combat crime are now being suppressed.

'The CID in particular is completely demoralized. There was nothing wrong with the system we had in our day, breeding young detectives and putting them in that line, getting them trained up with the detective training school that we had. It was horses for courses. If you wanted to be a beat bobby, you could be a beat bobby. If you wanted to be a detective, you could be a detective.

'Nowadays, the police are stymied by the rules and regulations of what they should and shouldn't do. They are becoming zombies, frightened to use their own intuition and do what they feel they should do. The public should realize that we are human beings. Every officer in the Met is asked to put their lives on the line. Anything can happen and every day they face people with guns, knives, and bombs, all sorts of things. Yet here we are saying to them that you can't do this and you can't do that. You can't follow your instinct.'

Peter also laments the decline of sports and the lack of encouragement to play sports. 'That was where you got the camaraderie.' Peter himself played in the No. 3 District Metropolitan Police rugby team. 'Lots of the players were detectives and they looked after each other and they were boisterous. We went on rugby tours and did lots of things that other rugby teams do. But we knew where to draw the line. And that's the way we were. We looked after each other, we helped each other, we enjoyed each other's company, we worked hard and we played hard as well. You couldn't do those sort of things nowadays.' The rugby team is no more. The cricket team doesn't function at the district level. Nobody seems to care these days whether they play sport or not.

But the positive side is that over the last few years Peter has seen a number of high-profile criminals come unstuck. 'It's a lesson to all those youngsters of today. Crime doesn't pay. It may feel good to have a few shillings in your pocket for a short while, but it's never worth it. At the end of the day you end up with nothing.'

£££

In January 1999, Ronnie finally worked free of prison, but contrary to popular belief he came out virtually penniless. It is true that while inside he collaborated in the writing of a book of his memoirs with crime writer Peter Gerrard, but the project ended very much in tears.

It had all started with a seemingly innocent phone call from an old school friend called Jim Lumley while Ronnie was over in Spain. Ronnie didn't really remember Jim that well but nevertheless invited Jim and his wife out to the villa. Naturally gregarious, he was happy to reminisce about old times and they all got on very well.

Jim idolized Ronnie. He suggested that he could get wall-to-wall publicity for him and a book deal too, and he and his wife trooped over to see Ronnie in Spain several times to discuss the deal. Although Jim gave Ronnie the impression that they were well-to-do this was far from the truth as Ronnie was later to find out. Jim had gambled on cashing in on Ronnie's name.

Things began to go seriously wrong after Ronnie came back to the UK. The rules on prisoners profiting from crime are quite strict, but tabloid newspapers have traditionally edged their way around them by arranging to pay 'expenses' or by paying a friend of the prisoner who then passes the money on. Ronnie had agreed to let Jim act as his nominee, receiving payments on his behalf. Jim repeatedly told Ronnie that he had 'put it away for him'. In fact, no money was ever put away; the one thing Jim feared most was Ronnie coming out of prison, because he would then have had to explain to him where all his money had gone – not an easy task. When it came to Ronnie's release date, details of a book-signing session were leaked to the prison authorities so that his release was deferred.

Things came to a head when Jim's daughter Diane was invited along to Ronnie's birthday party. He was by then on day release from prison and, naturally enough, was happy to spend time in the company of an attractive young woman. However, Diane's father was so jealous that he turned on her and did his best to drive a wedge between Ronnie and Diane.

When Ronnie was finally released, he had to fight for his share of the proceeds from his own book, which was by then a best-seller.

The one good thing to come out of the whole unpleasant episode was Diane. They now live happily together in a North London semi with her three children from a previous marriage, Jessica, Hannah, and William.

Soon after coming out of prison in January 1999, Ronnie was approached by researchers from the Roger Cook programme. They wanted him to talk about the extradition proceedings. Ronnie agreed, but on condition that the interview would not mention the Security Express robbery. That would be strictly off-limits.

Several researchers from the programme came to visit him at his home, and as they pushed and prodded him for information he soon realized that he was going to be interviewed by the great man himself.

He was looking forward to that. It was a chance to tackle Cook about that intrusive programme from a few years earlier.

The meeting between Ronnie and Roger Cook was to take place in a wine bar and to Ronnie's glee the moment was to be captured on film. Cook would be filmed walking regally into the wine bar, shaking hands with Ronnie, and then sitting down at the table. It would all look very congenial: Cook, the magnanimous headmaster, the champion of justice; Ronnie, the naughty schoolboy, his lesson duly learned.

Just as Cook made himself comfortable at the table, Ronnie pounced. 'Hello, Roger. So we meet at last.' Ronnie put a special emphasis on the 'at last'. 'Do you remember that time you came after me in a helicopter?'

For a moment Cook looked embarrassed and pretended not to hear. Then he ignored the question, deftly changing the subject. Ronnie's comment was cut from the transmitted film.

The media always get their way.

£££

One cold Sunday morning, some months after we first met, John Knight took me along to Curtain Road to demonstrate at first hand how he had organized and carried out the Security Express raid. Today, the road is barely recognizable to him. Sure enough, the vans of the market traders still jostle for space on market days, but many of the buildings that John knew have long disappeared. The brick warehouses and sweatshops have largely been replaced by a nondescript glass-and-granite overspill from the City financial district. The better-looking warehouses have been saved and turned into 'character' loft-style apartments. The Security Express depot itself has gone, to be replaced by a hulking brick office building presently occupied by the NSPCC.

The narrow, cobbled alley that ran down the side of the depot just about clings on to existence. At its far end, mottled Victorian cobblestones have been shattered and broken up, and the alley now leads directly into a wired-off building site.

Remarkably, the seventies-style office building from which John cased the depot is still standing, for the time being anyway. The low, flat roof that he scaled to gain entrance to it has been taken down. John's eyes light up as he demonstrates with his hands how he replaced the lock in the door of the building, peering around its recessed entrance to make sure that no one was looking.

We walk down to a café, past the pub whose landlord gave John so many headaches as he walked his dog up and down the alley late at night. On the way, John points out the red telephone box, still on the corner, where the fake Security Express van waited for the signal to go into the yard and load up with cash.

In the warmth of the café, a fried-egg sandwich in one hand and in between mouthfuls of hot, sweet tea, John describes the excitement of that Easter Bank Holiday Monday. Listening to him, one can't help feeling that, despite the remorse for his family and all those years in prison, John remains secretly proud of his achievement. Nearly twenty years later, the Security Express raid remains the largest cash robbery ever and, with the rise of electronic payment systems, is likely to remain so for all time. Three suspects are still at large, despite the thousands of police man-hours and millions of pounds in public funds that had been spent in attempting to bring them to justice.

It begs the question, does crime pay? In this case, for some of the Security Express firm at least, the answer has to be 'yes', but for how long remains to be seen. The stakes were always high for armed robbers, and that made them the elite of the criminal world. It was a risk John and his accomplices were prepared to take. It brought them the kudos and respect from their fellows they secretly yearned for. This raid was intended to be 'one for the road' before they all disappeared into gangland legend and folklore. But how much is twelve years of your life worth? Four million pounds? Forty million? For that matter, how much is a day worth?

Annexe: Where Are They Now?

THE FIRM

Billy Hickson was released from prison in 1990 and afterwards went to ground in East London. However, in January 1996, Hickson and an accomplice, Bill 'Chainsaw Woody' Woodruff, were caught in a Flying Squad 'sting' operation, apparently attempting to steal £32,000 in an armed raid on a Post Office in Manor Park. They were accused of stealing more than £300,000 through a string of seventeen armed post office raids. In April the following year, Hickson and Woodruff were jailed for fifteen years for conspiracy to rob, robbery, and possession of firearms. Woodruff had earned his nickname by sawing a Security Express van in half in a £1 million raid in 1979, for which he was jailed for eighteen years.

Hickson and Woodruff were dubbed 'the Wrinklies' by the press because they deliberately accentuated their age to lull their victims into a false sense of security. They put talcum powder in their hair and emphasized the lines on their faces with make-up. Woodruff completed his disguise with an old hat, a stained raincoat, and a neck brace. He had hobbled into the post office with a limp.

Both had been reduced to living on state benefits. They purportedly told police, 'We wanted the good life in our old age.'

After the conviction it emerged that some of the Flying Squad officers involved in the 'Wrinklies' operation had become caught up in an anti-corruption probe surrounding an unrelated case.

An investigation by the BBC also found evidence that suggested that the police video film of the post office raid was unreliable. Hickson won his appeal. The prosecution maintained that there had been no foul play involved and the case was sent for retrial, but that hearing collapsed. The judge threw it out after hearing that the prosecution wanted to proceed without calling the officers under investigation but simply relying on a statement about their investigation. Hickson was freed in March 2000.

Terry Perkins hasn't been sighted since he skipped Springhill Prison in 1995. Average height, well built, with greying hair, blue eyes, and sporting several distinctive tattoos, he remains 'unlawfully at large' and on the police's 'wanted' list.

Jimmy Knight sold the lease on his scrap-yard site in Ridley Road for a small fortune to Sainsbury's for development into a superstore. After completing his prison sentence in 1989, he and his wife went to live in their villa in southern Portugal. He was rarely in touch with his brothers. In February 2002, John and Ronnie were saddened to learn that their brother had died of a stroke. They would like him to be remembered in this book.

Soon after the trial of John Knight, **Alan Opiola** and his immediate family were given new identities and relocated under the police 'witness protection' programme. **John Horsley**, who the Flying Squad believe took the rap for Hickson's money, was released in 1989 and now lives in the Home Counties.

Freddie Foreman was released in March 1995. He is now a successful crime writer and recently won a contract to model for a Saville Row gentlemen's outfitters.

Clifford Saxe spent his remaining days drinking in the Spanish sunshine. At the end of 2000 he was interviewed by British police officers planning to commence extradition proceedings against him, but it was later decided that he was too frail and in too poor health to be extradited. He died in March 2002, virtually penniless, according to his friends.

Ronnie Everett has been extradited from Spain for various drugs-related offences and is currently awaiting trial. The Spanish authorities refused to allow him to be extradited for the Security Express robbery, arguing that the events occurred too long ago. Meanwhile, his close friend, **John Mason**, continues to live in some style on the Costa Del Sol. Because of the Spanish decision over Everett, the Crown Prosecution Service has withdrawn its request to extradite Mason, but he could still be arrested under an international warrant if he were to travel to another country. **Sue Haylock** was long wanted for questioning in connection with the Security Express robbery. Police claimed that she handled £36,320 in cash for Ronnie, but now accept that she has no case to answer.

THE POLICE

Reed McGeorge, who took over the running of the enquiry from Peter, retired in 1999. He handed in his papers soon after the Security Express enquiry closed and now works as a private security consultant. Aside from a two-year stint back in uniform towards the end of the enquiry, he spent most of his CID career on Security Express.

Julia Pearce, who looked after Linda Opiola and Diane Knight, remained with the enquiry until the arrest and conviction of Ronnie Knight. After that, she specialized in murder investigations. For a while she worked as a lab technician in the forensic science laboratory. Now she is back in the Area Major Investigation Pool, which was based at Arbour Square until the station was closed in 2002 – leaving the Peacock pub high and dry. **George Moncrieff**, latterly Reed's right-hand man, retired in November 2001. **Malcolm Jeffery**, the enquiry's exhibits officer, and **Steve Farley**, are still serving police officers. **Rex Sargent** was always famed for leaving more tobacco on the floor of the squad car than in his roll-ups. After the Security Express enquiry, he was transferred to Stoke Newington police station and later took early retirement.

Bernie Butler, the enquiry's officer manager, and his assistant, **Jim Keeling**, one of the nicest, funniest men you are ever likely to meet, both work as private investigators for an insurance company. **Terry Mills**, involved with OP17, also works as a private investigator. In January 2001 he relocated to Cyprus. **Charlie Collins**, his partner in OP17, sustained a serious back injury some years ago during a Robbery Squad operation and retired soon afterwards. The injury has not prevented him from slipping in the occasional game of rugby – strictly against doctor's orders.

Geoff Cameron, who went over with Charlie to Paris, is now retired and lives in Malaga. **Simon Webber** has also retired and now runs a pub and banqueting suite deep in the heart of the Sussex countryside. **Ron Chapman**, Peter's friend since cadet days, and the supervising officer on the Robbery Squad the day of the raid, left the Met to pursue a successful career as a self-employed artist and picture framer. **Cliff Craig**, who played a key part in getting Foreman back home, now has a high-powered job advising the United Nations on drugs-related crime.

Apart from **John Fordham** and **Roy Chivers**, two other police officers involved in the investigation have since died. **Cam Burnell**, a great tower of a man and keen rugby player, died a few years ago while keeping fit in the gym. **Roy 'Pancho' Ives**, the Squad's interpreter in Spain, died of cancer. Pancho was extraordinarily well regarded throughout the Met. He is one of only a handful of police constables to have had no less than the Metropolitan Police Commissioner himself (then Sir Peter Imbert) turn up to his farewell party.

SECURITY EXPRESS/THE GUARDS

Twenty years on, **Greg Counsell** still remembers the events of that Easter Monday, as if they happened only yesterday. He can recall every last detail.

As the control room radio operator Counsell had had to calmly talk his colleagues through a whole swathe of armed robberies, including Chainsaw Woody's raid on a Security Express van which he sliced open, a terrified guard still trapped inside. But the raid on Curtain Road tested his nerves to their limits. In truth, he was in fear for his life; at one point he remembers asking his captors if he could leave a note for his family.

Counsell knew there were security flaws in the way that the Curtain Road depot was run, and in its design. He says his concerns were shared by others. A few years before the robbery, senior management had decided to move a control room, which had a panoramic view overlooking the yard, so that the nearby wages-counting department could have more space. John Bates, Security Express's London regional manager, tried unsuccessfully to get them to reconsider, but his objections were overruled. So a new control room was built down by the gates thus creating the main security weakness that John Knight's men had homed in on: that the guards were vulnerable as they walked across the yard from one control room to the other. Bates went on to propose other security measures, such as double 'airlock' gates to prevent vehicles driving straight in, additional cameras in blind spots, and steel drop-down shutters on doors leading to the vaults. He spent many hours wrangling with senior management, and eventually detailed plans were drawn up to make the depot less vulnerable. But the blueprints remained tacked to a notice board in the London branch manager's office and were never implemented.

Counsell remains bitter about his experiences at the hands of the Flying Squad, not least because of the stress it placed on his wife, pregnant at the time. The Flying Squad's insistence that he destroy his antique British army revolver particularly irked him, as it had been left to him by his grandfather. But he recognizes that they had a job to do.

He left Security Express a couple of years after the raid, to become a security manager for a luxury goods department store. He stayed there for ten years, before setting up his own business. Occasionally he hears from **Jimmy Alcock**, testy as ever, but long since retired. Alcock's fellow vault custodian, **Alan Grimes**, left Security Express a couple of years after the robbery, and now works in the construction industry. He too believes that security at the depot left much to be desired. The other guards have scattered to the four winds, but without doubt, all of them had their perspectives on life radically altered by their experiences at the hands of John Knight and his men. Security Express itself, once the flagship of the British cash-in-transit business, never quite recovered from the raid. A few years after the robbery, the business was sold by its owners, De La Rue. Since then it has been broken up, sold on again, reorganized, and rebranded; the familiar name and logo have all but disappeared from Britain's High Streets.

£££

More information on the Security Express robbery, Ronnie and John Knight, Peter Wilton and the Flying Squad can be found at http://www.gotcha.cc

Source Notes

Prologue Interviews with John Knight and Peter Wilton.

Chapter 1 London historical records, Companies' House records and interviews with Peter Wilton and John Knight.

Chapter 2 Based almost entirely on police witness statements taken from Security Express guards David Howsam, Greg Counsell, Keith Jordan, Pat Lynch, John Atkinson, David Sawyer, Steve Hayes, Alan Grimes and Jamie Alcock. Additional corroboration came from John Knight, who was the man standing in the control-room doorway as the guards trooped in.

Chapter 3 Interviews with Peter Wilton and Simon Webber, plus witness statements from Jamie Alcock, David Howsam, and printer Noel McCabe. The section in the barn is based entirely on an interview with John Knight.

Chapter 4 Interview with Peter Wilton, plus witness statements from Jamie Alcock, John Atkinson, Alan Grimes and Vic Vincent.

Chapter 5 Interviews with John Knight and Ronnie Knight.

Chapter 6 Interviews with Peter Wilton, Jim Keeling, Bernie Butler and Simon Webber.

Chapter 7 Interviews with John Knight and Ronnie Knight.

Chapter 8 Interviews with Peter Wilton, Charlie Collins, Terry Mills, Simon Webber, Jim Keeling and Bernie Butler.

Chapter 9 Interviews with Peter Wilton and Simon Webber, and police records of interviews with John Horsley and William Hickson.

Chapter 10 Interviews with John Knight and Ronnie Knight, and Alan Opiola's witness statement.

Chapter 11 Alan and Linda Opiola's witness statements.

Chapter 12 Interviews with Peter Wilton and Malcolm Jeffery, and witness statements from Alan Opiola and Stan Atwell.

Chapter 13 Alan and Linda Opiola's witness statements.

Chapter 14 Interviews with Peter Wilton, witness statements from Alan Opiola and Ethel Williams, records of the police interviews with Jimmy Knight, John Mason and Ronnie Everett.

Chapter 15 Interviews with Peter Wilton, Bernie Butler, George Moncrieff and Charlie Mills.

Chapter 16 Interviews with Peter Wilton, Simon Webber, Malcolm Jeffery, Jim Keeling and Bernie Butler.

Chapter 17 Interviews with John Knight, Peter Wilton, Bernie Butler, Jim Keeling and Diane Knight.

Chapter 18 Interviews with Peter Wilton, John Knight, George Moncrieff and Ronnie Knight.

Chapter 19 Interviews with Peter Wilton, Simon Webber and George Moncrieff.

Chapter 20 Interviews with Ronnie Knight and Peter Wilton.

Chapter 21 Interviews with John Knight and Diane Knight.

Chapter 22 Interviews with Peter Wilton, Cliff Craig, Simon Webber.

Chapters 23/24 Interviews with Ronnie Knight and Peter Wilton.

Epilogue Interviews with John Knight, Peter Wilton and Ronnie Knight.

Index